MY LIFE BEGAN AT FORTY

Michael Irwin

L.R. Price Publications Ltd

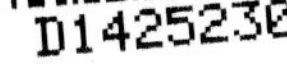

My Life Began at Forty

Published in Great Britain by

L.R. Price Publications Ltd 2017
27 Old Gloucester Street,
London, WC1N 3AX
www.lrpricepublications.com

ISBN13 : 9780992903763

ISBN10 : 0992903769

For My Father, Sam Irwin

MY LIFE BEGAN AT FORTY

Michael Irwin

PART ONE:

On Remand

SUNDAY

The news is back on; it must be 11.30 – a break in the…

No, spoke too soon - buzzer back on again.

Only twelve hours until I fall asleep - or will I? No medication.

Will there be a canteen now this has happened? Monthly lockup today anyway. Shouldn't be too bad, methinks.

Where will I get a fag? Smoked the last one at 8.00am. Headache getting worse. Don't want to get in trouble. Be cool, be cool.

Oh, here we go - bloody chest pains starting again. Know I'm going to the hospital soon, but that's for my stomach; I keep telling them - nobody listens. Fear I've a bigger problem with my plumbing: blood in the toilet.

Hear Chris (servery orderly) talking outside (*bang, crash, growl, "shit, help, why", anger, frustration…*). Maybe we're getting fed!

To hell with it - swallow my last two paracetamol. Heart racing, head thumping, hard to breathe.

Hear an officer and another convict talking – ain't a conversation, more like barking; get the drift? I presume they are informing us convicts that 'That what's occurring!' (*'It Ain't Half Hot, Mum'*). There are twenty-eight cells to a landing - four landings. How long will this take?

Happy days - can use my new calculator, which took me four weeks to get through reception!

(*bang, crash, growl, 'shit, help, why', anger, frustration…*)

Bollocks! Can't concentrate - the buzzer is literally driving me crazy! All I hear is *bang, bang, buzzer* - guys screaming like little girls! Fuck, I need a fag!

More screaming, banging, shouting. What's happening? Cell feels as if it's vibrating, the noise unbearable.

(*bang, crash, growl-)* Shit, the whole wing has kicked off!

Frightening.

Glad I'm in the cell. A bit silly, but what do I know.

There'll be a few sore hands and knuckles come morning. Previous experience dictates that steel doors and concrete walls normally win in the battle against flesh and bone.

Oh God, why did I do that stupid thing?

Is this what is meant by 'doing your time'? Is this what is meant by 'rehabilitation'?

Ah, well, if I'm guilty I deserve it.

Do they dangle stuff like education, rehabilitation and sense of achievement in front of you, only for it to be taken away if you complain?

Hear more voices and the sound of vans reversing outside my penthouse window, which is permanently open (no glass). What's happening?

Feeling pretty shit, I think I'll have a wee lie down and watch the athletics. Jesus, I could murder a Chinese - the athletics is being held in Osaka (I've had to explain this for those of you who aren't Irish and don't get the word 'association'. Please try to keep up in future, thank you).

Now I can smell food. Shall I get dressed? Don't want to hang about - the officers will be seriously edgy, so will the convicts.

Will it be the whole landing let out as usual?

Could scrounge some tobacco (he thinks, as he rubs his hands together, a bit like *Scrooge*).

Will the more serious convicts start giving orders?

Will I rip some poor bastard's head off (*bang, crash, growl, 'shit, help'...*)?

Who knows?

The smell of today's delicacy has now been wafting under my door for what seems like an eternity.

Bollocks - just missed the women's 220m writing this! Mind you, it was only 22secs and enough titillation for one man in one day *(nudge-nudge, wink-wink, say no mowah)*.

At this stage of the proceedings I think I should explain the situation with the buzzer. The buzzer is an electronic alarm, and there is a button in each cell which activates said buzzer - this is for use in 'extreme emergencies only' (i.e. heart attacks, drowning, fire, accidental murder of cell–mate, etc.). It may also be used if you have been overlooked during unlock, not let out when you should have been, or to make an enquiry of a very serious nature *(could you get us some sugar, guv?)*.

Them's the rules, honest.

There are two speakers for the buzzer on the landing - one of them just happens to be outside my fuckin' cell door. I suffer from a hint of tinnitus, so every time the buzzer goes off I will type (*'why', anger, frustration, etc...*) and I hope it will give you an inkling of the mental hell I'm going through.

Need a fag - more banging and jangling of keys.

Better get dressed.

Is anyone dead yet? This place is a mad house.

I want to smash that fuckin' buzzer off the wall! May become a hero on the wing or have the shit beaten out of me and be taken down the block.

Court next week - don't get into trouble.

I think I'll name the buzzer to humanize it - make it an imaginary friend. Think I'll call it *'Wilson'* - the same name Tom Hanks gave the football in *'Castaway'*.

More banging. My temper flares. Some say 'life begins at forty'; well, if it's true mine has well and truly started with a bang.

Feel angry, remorseful, fed up, pissed off. Know that deep down inside I've got to be strong all over again, day by day, moment by every dragging moment. After all, it's 'good to be alive' (the juke-box in my head kicks in; I tend to do that a lot if I say or hear a line or lyric from a song - I start to sing the song in my head. *Ha-ha, ho-ho, he-he!* Please try to keep up - *I* am.

Sid from *'Eastenders'* is back on the telly. Used to see Sid knocking round Knightsbridge back in the day.

Wilson again! *(bang, fuck, bollocks, aagghh!).*

Will I write this as a book? Will I send it to anyone? Can anyone understand the madness that goes on in these places, will it help, and who will listen? Getting tired again, Wilson - need a fag, need milk, need help!

Robbie Williams is singing *'Angels'* on the TV now; the song reminds me of Katie.

Boy, was I ever in love there?

Wrong time, wrong place, yet again.

Wonder how she's doing. She was one of the most beautiful, kind and loving girls I've ever had the pleasure of being with in my life. Never mind all of the silly bollocks that happened.

Wonder if she ever became a lawyer (fuck me - I could bloody well use her now, Wilson).

Must be quiet; don't ask them for nothing - don't give them the satisfaction of saying no. Keep your cool.

Jesus, I'd like to beat seven bells of crap out of that prick that keeps setting the buzzer off.

Mind you, it could just be the officers winding us up.

The buzzer is going on and off every one or two minutes now. Please tell me this torture isn't going to happen all day.

Hear lots of voices on the landing - that's how you know when people are being let out. Looks like our landing is last again.

I'm on the fours (the upper floor, normally reserved for the privileged few). The food isn't too bad here; won't bother to elaborate for the time being - I don't want to put a jinx on it.

It's been a really crazy morning; surely it won't be long now until we get fed.

Hear Scousers complaining, the usual suspects - nothing strange there! Not that I have anything against Scousers, but they don't half know how to yap *(eh, soft lad!?)*

It's just been announced on the TV news that the prison officers' strike is unlawful. At least they're in the right place, he-he.

Can't help but worry about my family, worrying about me. I suppose the prison officers' story is like any other – you don't get given all the facts, and this can create a wrongly one–sided picture.

Lots of screaming, shouting and arguing on the landing outside – convicts going nuts. Can't understand the mentality of some of these pricks - today is the last Wednesday of the month: monthly lock–down day - we're meant to be banged up today *anyway*; no movement, no Association. So what's the fuckin' problem?

As an ex–union rep I can understand where the prison officers are coming from, but, as public servants, they're not allowed to strike. I'm pondering the rights, the wrongs and the general injustices of life when an article about Nelson Mandela comes on the TV.

Mickey wanna be in Cape Town!

Been to Robben Island a few times, and I try to make the make comparisons between here and there. Prisoners over here whinge about the injustice of getting caught for a crime they *have* committed, and prison officers (P.O.s) want to be treated the same way as doctors and nurses; the ones I've met (with a few exceptions) are just happy to send someone to casualty via the end of their boots. Convicts and P.O.s whinge about government, money, and being hard done by, yet take a look at this eighty year-old man on the TV: a unique individual and statesman who made the world sit up and pay attention, from a chalk pit on Robben Island, in a country developing from conflict - struggling, but trying to put one foot in front of the other; a country full of kind, proud and resourceful people, whose poverty is still hard to believe (unless you have seen it), scrapes together an existence.

You make the comparisons.

Still no food. Did they forget? Did I shout too loud earlier on?

I've just had a strange notion: if the prison officers' actions are illegal and they get arrested, maybe I could share a cell with *Miss Chewing-Gum*, due to the overcrowding, eh? I hope (*Wilson, aagghh!!*) she's okay - she has a big roar, but an even bigger heart. Mind you, I wouldn't like to turn up with twenty quid short on payday!

Am I getting fuckin' fed or what? These fuckers are starting to get on my tits!

I'm looking forward to having a walk, stretching the legs.

These fuckers don't know how lucky they are: I recently spoke with an Afrikaans guy about being locked up in South Africa – it doesn't bear thinking about, trust me; I lived close to Pollsmoor prison in Cape Town - my friend's father is a top guard there, and he tells me they carry out four or five bodies a week.

Keys jangling by my door - am I getting fed?

Bloody hell! My door was opened by a beautiful woman in a suit - must be a prison governor, or maybe a secretary; they'll give anyone a set of keys these days! She was very helpful and informative, with a stunning smile.

This is the first time I've spoken to someone in a suit since the magistrates' court. Although, when I think about it, she was trying to look calm and confident, but not quite getting there. Shame!

Us convicts have a knack of telling if someone's out of their depth. Still, it was good to know what was happening, with a rough idea of how the day would unfold.

Simultaneously collected my meds, breakfast and lunch, then straight back to cell.

The nurse (God love her) wanted some of my paracetamol - the poor medical staff had to deal with over three-hundred pissed off convicts, only being let out six at a time - a 'controlled unlock'.

Back in my cell, I hear some of my fellow assholes shouting for a DVD to be played. The suits won't even know where the DVD player is, never mind how it works - one knows how childish these disputes can get. Subtle points could be made here - if I was a P.O. I'd grasp every opportunity to make a point; the suits will get as much abuse as the officers, and, hopefully, get a feel of how their policies affect everyone. Should I kick–off - help the proceedings?

No, don't get involved - it's not your problem. Don't want to be *obtuse* (*'The Shawshank Redemption'* comes to mind).

Need my prayer: *God grant me the serenity to accept the things I cannot change, courage to change the things I can and the wisdom to know the difference.*

This little prayer helps me focus... calm down.

Back to earlier; I had a choice to get my meds first or get food - easy choice if you're hooked on crack or heroin. Gone for the grub, fat bastard that I am. Got some extras - maybe it'll have to last a day or two. Here's what I got: two jacket spuds, with ham and mushroom pasta, consisting of three pieces of fatty bacon, five slices of mushroom and twelve pasta shells! Fuckin' marvellous!

Was lucky: received two spoonfuls of rice, the last plum tomato and four slices of bread. But no butter; remember the scandal about 'butter mountains' in the '80s? Bloody scandalous now for the lack of! Mashed up my lunch and made two sandwiches - bloody marvellous! All in all, well chuffed.

Scrounged some tobacco from the new neighbour; eight people asked him the same, after me. I've now got one roll-up to last until I get my canteen.

News just coming in: a 'fire has broken out at a prison in Birmingham'. Shit, there's plenty of arsonists in here - I hope we survive! Hear an officer on the radio just outside my cell - he sounds quite worried; I hear him say, with a woeful sigh: 'Oh, God, no - not today, of all days!'

Now, this is just the sort of thing we paranoid schizophrenics need to be overhearing when we are 'banged up' and 'riots' are breaking out across the country!

Wish I'd one of the many illegal cell phones, which are readily available for two- or three-hundred quid - would text what's occurring to the media, giving the world a minute by minute account of what it feels like being in here at this particularly frightening time. Wonder how much they would pay.

The main gate constantly beeps, opening and closing. Is it S.W.A.T. teams? Maybe it's the fire brigade. More banging, shouting, muffled voices. Oh God, my imagination is running riot.

Fuck's sake - don't mention 'riot'!

With my powers of premonition, it could well happen!

Madiba (Nelson Mandela) is still on the telly, and my thoughts again drift to Africa - it could be a lot worse. Suppose it's easy to get caught up in 'the moment', as any ex-con will tell you. I try to sit back and relax, but hear lots of taps being turned on and off. Here at H.M.P. Lewes one often hears the old Victorian plumbing rattling. Maybe, like me, the other cons have started to plan ahead, filling every conceivable container with water for the inevitable outbreak of fire! I've filled drawers, empty yoghurt cartons, overflowing slippers and soaked socks. Bring it on! Maybe they'll send me to Greece to put out their forest!

I'd planned to catch up on some work today - no chance now!

Can feel the painkillers kicking in. There's now a chorus of inmates shouting to get a DVD played – fuckin' idiots! Some of these guys are not well-blessed with the art of decorum. The movie's an oldie based in south Africa, of all places; I drift off into a comfortable snooze and dream of Africa, a country I've grown to love; although, in retrospect, it nearly killed me.

Hard to breathe in these penthouse suites. I presume for 'Health and Safety' reasons, my window will only open about six inches. There is a big metal block attached to the frame, with metal bars, a wire mesh cage and a sheet of perspex surrounding the window. No doubt, a succession of great ideas used by the powers that be, in their never-ending war on drugs, and to hinder prisoners' associates from shooting crossbow bolts with dope attached, from the forest on the other side of the wall. If my mates were doing it they'd be using an RPG7 rocket launcher, with cans of Strongbow attached. Some people, believe it or not, use fishing rods to cast a line into people's cells, then send the gear across.

Mental note: check the library for *'Fly Fishing' by J.R. Hartley*.

I'll be out by the time I get my 'fly fishing' back up to speed.

Pondering the lack of oxygen, when I realize that there's a six inch gap at the window and a good three inches under the door - this should create a nice, cool breeze in the winter! I'll keep you informed of the suite situation - that is, if I haven't died from carbon monoxide poison from my own breath and farts.

Wilson!!!

More sounds of taps running. Does someone know something I don't? Is there a fire?

Panic sets in. Shit, I can hear sirens!

Oh yes I can!

Oh, it's coming from the TV.

Tried to get a single cell.

Followed medical route, by being truthful - was told to go forth and multiply. The officers put me on *'High Risk'*, for the safety of others.

Wanted to complain about the carbon monoxide poisoning in my cell, but felt that the amount of paper already being wasted on Apps (an abbreviation for *Application/Request Form*) was contributing to global warming.

The shouting has started up outside the windows again. Why can't these guys just fuckin' relax?

I've flashes about making this story into a movie (Peter Sellers and *'The Pink Panther'* in mind) - wonder how I'd go about it.

Feel as if I'm losing the plot, when it suddenly occurs to me that 'most comedy stems from madness' - think of Spike Milligan's gravestone: *'I told you I was ill'*.

My head feels a bit like a washing machine at times. Have you ever sat in a launderette and stared aimlessly at the blur of the washing, tumbling around in the machine? Every now and then you clearly see a sock, a sleeve or the bottom half of a leg of a pair of trousers pressed against the glass. Well, that's how my thoughts are at the minute: I've got scenes, songs and statements from *'The Wee Man from Killy–Burn–Brae'* and *'The Quiet Man'* competing for pole position.

Lying face down on my bed, staring at the telly - muffled footsteps outside, then a single sheet of A4 slipped under the door. Want to see what the note says, but don't want to be seen as *too* eager - start to argue with myself.

Get up, read it...

..don't bother - don't let this place get to you, that's what they want: they want you jump at their every whim.

Cannot stress how important the quest for information becomes in these places - it ambushes you; before you know it, you're a gossip, every meaningless conversation suddenly meaningful. Is this not what prison - your punishment - is about: one's loss of liberty? Of rights?

What rights? You're on remand, yet as guilty as the armed robbery doing ten in the next cell! I lie there, forcing myself not to get up. Then the questions start in my head:

Who's it from?

What if it's bad news?

Maybe I've been granted a pardon by God-knows who – ha-ha, ho-ho, he-he?

I hang it out for as long as I can, but it's like trying not to chew a Fruit Pastel.

Voices outside my cell; *is there anybody out there?* (*Pink Floyd*!). Voices outside, vans reversing, people shouting, doors banging. Losing the plot again.

Engrossed in my writing, I feel as if I'm in enveloped in a warm cocoon, wrapped in words on the page - safety and sanctuary between the lines of text and diction; if only I could stay there, safe and warm, and didn't have to face the reality of the events that surround me.

I've never written so much and at such speed in my life, my arms killing me. *'Inffoorrmmattion* (the voice of Homer Simpson in my head) - *muuuussst reeaddd iiinnnfffoorrmmattioon!'*

Bet the sheet's a statement from the governor telling us what's just been announced on the news: that the system's actions are illegal.

The pressure becomes too much - I give in.

Don't believe it - I'm definitely psychic!

H.M.P. LEWES

LOCAL NOTICE TO PRISONER NO: ---------

RE: Industrial action by the Prison Officers' Association

The Home Secretary has successfully gained a High Court injunction against the Prison Officers' Association, which means their industrial action should cease.

The P.O.A. National Committee will be contacting branches to inform them of the outcome of the court case.

Later on this afternoon I would expect staff who are on strike to return to duty. As soon as this happens we will return to a normal routine.

I know this has been a frustrating time for you and I would like to thank you for your co-operation.

Signed by the Governor.

Typical bloody prison service: reaction instead of action.

Can they read my thoughts? Can they read my writing? Is *Big Brother* (MI5) watching? Is there a hidden camera in my cell?

Relax, be cool, take another tablet, don't get into trouble.

Should try to get this published. I know - I'll try and smuggle it out whilst the officers are on strike, ha-ha, ho-ho, he-he.

I figure my Mum will understand this - how close I am to losing the plot, and how ridiculous and funny all of this is, all at the same time. If she does eventually read this and 'gets it', it will all have been worthwhile.

As my prediction was correct, I think I'll treat myself to another Mars bar. Maybe not - I've *Homer*'s voice in my head, and not so far behind in the stomach department. Be strong, be cool.

Maybe the message from the governor will self-destruct in five seconds, my cell will catch fire, people will die and it'll all be my fault. Oh my God - how did I get into such a mess? I'll survive the fire anyway, as there is limited oxygen in my cell. I'm safe, as long as I spend the rest of my days 'in' the page. *Never stop writing, never stop writing, never get out of the boat, never get out of the fuckin' boat ('Apocalypse Now')!*

The taps have stopped!

Sanctuary (a vision of Peter Sellers as *Quasimodo* appears in my head)! *Aarggh, the bells, the bells!*

Why can't logical thoughts appear as fast as mad ones?

This document needed to be written with subtlety, scoring points, achieving some sort of moral victory for the Home Office over its employees, the P.O.A. (Prison Officers Association). The wing responds with a collective roar. Perhaps the governors are escorting a few prison officers down the blocks – oh, the irony! The government will obviously be blameless, as the strike is unlawful, thus creating a smoke-screen of deniability, seeking public empathy or sympathy - whichever way one decides to look at it. More shouting, banging, screaming - convicts generally going mad on the wing.

Many convicts will take great delight in taunting the officers on the wing about their 'unlawful action'. Mind you, the same convicts who involve themselves in such intolerable behaviour are not blessed with a substantial amount of the old grey matter, are not that high up on the food chain, and will be eaten alive by pissed off officers.

10.30pm

I'm watching *'As Good as it Gets'* and *'The Queen'* at the same time. Thanks for the remote control, Steve - worth all the tobacco in the world.

I've watched *'As Good as it Gets'*, starring Jack Nicholson, in three different countries, at different stages of my life and of feeling sorry for myself. Trying to make a comparison, but, for the life of me, I can't. Imagine if I was in

Belsen or the likes. What have I to whinge about?

Wilson has been the centre of attention all day - stealing my thunder, the bastard. Still, he's very persistent!

Had my one and only constructive conversation with 'Mr. Angry' (throughout this book I will refer to officers and fellow inmates using aliases). Shock, horror! Now there's a candidate for MI5 membership if ever there was one - he'd be right at the top of the list (oh, I nearly forgot - you're not allowed to make *lists* in prison; *Health and Safety*, I presume. 'Health and Safety' covers a multitude of obscure and ridiculous prison rules). Mr. Angry said he'd love to take the very serious issue of *Wilson* to his MI5 controllers, but, alas, he feared he may be scoffed at! Hard to believe that even spook officers are working in fear. This worries me somewhat – if, in here, Mr. Angry is afraid to approach the bosses, then what chance have we?

What a breakthrough though, with Mr. Angry - fair play to the bloke for being honest. He's gone up on my shit-list. Never judge a book by its cover, eh?

MONDAY

6.48am

My e-motions are all over the place - I've just had my first proper motion in six months!

Mind you, was watching the news through slanted eyes *(asshole glasshoppa)*, which is full P.O.A. officials giving pointed views and puffed up statements about yesterday's day of action. They have to wait until tomorrow to find out if they have broken the law.

Last night's Association was a hoot - was surprised to see a full quota of regular staff on duty. Myself and Mick were leaning on the landing railing, watching events unfold below us.

Must explain about Mick: he's got the same surname as the current

Northern Ireland MP/IRA in charge of Education; four doors down from me, the name on the card outside his door says 'Martin McGuinness'. My card reads 'David Ervine' (David Ervine is UVF, and another political figure in the Norn Iron arena). Mick and I've had a laugh about this since my arrival - somebody somewhere obviously has a sense of humour.

Or have they actually made so much progress that they can put two of the top players in Northern Irish politics on the same landing of the same prison?

Hooray, the system works - my God! In an English jail in East Sussex, Martin McGuinness and Davy Ervine are getting along like a house on fire!

If only life could be so simple.

I have to ask myself if MFI (Northern Irish slang for MI5!) was involved in this trickery. Fuck me, they ain't half clever! Though, I can't help but wonder why they didn't do it sooner. Just think of the countless lives that could have been saved, and atrocities that wouldn't have been committed in my beautiful country at the hands of those murderous bastards, now sharing tobacco, sweets, showers and jokes.

My paranoia about MFI - the never ending quest for information - has no bounds.

Myself, Mick and a couple of officers watched as a procession of cons got nicked or 'red-entried' (a 'red-entry' is an official warning) for slabbering. A few fights broke out - nothing serious, just some junkies freaking out 'cos they can't get their shit.

A door utters an unfamiliar creak in the darkness of the still night - this means it's a different door! Where's it coming from? The paranoia begins again.

No sign of any humanity yet.

Way too quiet for my liking.

Must have a wee chat with Martin later - he's the boy to speak to; been in and out of prison for most of his life. Just come from the block after hospitalizing four officers.

He's not doing me any favours though. He told me officers are changed after any major incident, I quote: 'in order to confuse individuals who may be organizing *things* or trying to stir *things* up'.

The word 'things' covers a multitude of sins in prison. Oh, the joy.

Must get more innffooo (*'Snagglepuss'* is now talking in my head - fuck off, 'Puss). MFI are definitely at work - after all, I'm *believing* things that Martin's telling me. It must be true: he's the 'education minister', and he wouldn't lie to children, now, would he? So there!

Shit, I must see a doctor soon!

Actually, I really have gotta see the doctor later, anyway – I forgot to ask him for a note allowing me to attend the gym. I'll miss a morning of Education - prison regimes seldom allow two activities or appointments during the same session. A doctor's appointment normally takes five minutes, then back to cell and 'bang up'.

Different characters to the voices in my head: *'Snagglepuss'* has some sarcasm and a slight hint of irony... *Homer*'s not an ideal model; they're constantly bouncing around in there.

I must be careful - I don't want this literary masterpiece turned into a comedy, especially when it's about a topic of such serious magnitude. Feel this tale needs to reach the outside world; the more I think about what is happening 'in here', the more I think about what *isn't* being done 'out there'. My sobriety and my situation are forming some rather strong opinions in me, and I think I'll have to pay a bit more attention to my thoughts and feelings during this mental road trip.

Mumblings outside; hard to make out - must be one of the Scousers.

It is - it's Levi, getting out today, lucky bastard. He said that he'd hold up a banner with 'H.M.P.' on it at this weekend's Liverpool derby- must remember to watch the highlights on Saturday evening. Are we allowed messages from the outside world? Shit! We'll only get the highlights of the game - MFI will receive the message first, and use it against us.

Disinformation. Paranoia back again. Must tell Mick, must relax, must be cool, take a tablet, chill.

4TH SEPTEMBER 2007

7.05pm

I've just woken up to a lot of activity on the landing, jangling of keys and banging of cell doors.

Yesterday was a bit weird - my solicitor 'Danny Crane' (a fictional Boston lawyer played by William Shatner - hilarious), was forty-five minutes late - a common complaint in nick - and he told me he'd been waiting outside for ages. To overcome this problem, he had booked a double visit. Yet again.

The officer in charge had made a snide comment about solicitors always being late and telling pork-pies – I pretended to be annoyed and agreed with him, just to shut the prick up. Danny was innocent - I'd grilled him for ten minutes when he came in, even checked his breath to see if he'd been to the pub; this was when I made a general observation: there ain't half a lot of fat fuckers running around the prison system - must be due to the pork-pies.

Sitting here, feeling fraught. Footsteps, jangling of keys - must be Association.

Got a lot going on at the minute - who said 'life in prison is boring'? I haven't friggin' stopped! Feeling rather drained - it's very difficult to keep on top of the ever–changing daily events. Enjoyed the 'Listeners' interview yesterday morning – 'Mr. C' promised he'd inform all candidates in the afternoon if they were successful, and that he'd work through his lunch-break - sacrificing his pork-pie - to make sure this would happen. Still waiting - fat bastard!

All I want to do is help people help themselves - prison is all about getting a break, especially from the constant change and bullshit the management throw at you. Sometimes - only sometimes - I feel sorry for the officers, as they have to dish out the crap and deal with as much shit as we do.

Still, I shouldn't harp on; I've accomplished nearly everything I set out to do when I first came to prison (what was that exactly?). All I really want is to get my trial over and done with. Danny and I have deliberated my case: I'll plead 'not guilty' on Thursday, and my trial should follow in six to eight weeks. Levi told me to plead 'guilty' immediately, and I'd get seven or eight years - out in three or four.

It's been eleven weeks and twelve hours since I had to phone my Dad from Brighton nick and tell him I'd been arrested at Gatwick with a bag containing cocaine.

Jesus!

That was fuckin' hard.

Just realized, this is the first time I've counted the time I've spent behind bars - I'm sure it won't be the last.

Still, tomorrow's another day and I'll be back up, ready to continue with my battle against paranoia and MFI.

For now, my battles are with detox, cramps, pain and stress.

Put the feet up, relax, take a tablet and watch the telly.

3.30am

I wake up dazed and confused (*Led Zeppelin*), eventually get out of my pit and roll a fag.

Been at Lewes for three months now. Pondering about what type of disease or super–bug I've picked up in't nick. Feel as if I've been hit by a bus; been detoxing for three months now - all painkilling, mind numbing effects of cannabis, cocaine and alcohol should have left my body for greener pastures. I'll have to see the quack again, 'cos this ain't right: how I'm feelin'.

Bollocks to that! I've discovered that the doctors work for MI5.

I'm up for a kangaroo court (adjudication) this week and my actual trial should start any day. Fuck me, I have a busy week ahead.

What do you think, Wilson? Wilson?

No reply. Suit yourself then, grumpy bastard. Maybe he's sleeping - shame. If only I had one of those hand held fog-horns.

'Oi, wake up, you son of a bitch!' I scream, a bit too loud, a bit too venomous, my volcano venting. Don't need to get into any more trouble this week. I'm the only fucker here with a Belfast accent.

On my travels the women loved it - not so good in here though: a lot of the officers are ex–army and have served in Northern Ireland. Put yourselves in my size nines - am I fucked, or what? My stay here is already a monumental battle of cunning and wit - don't be surprised if I slip into moments of sanity (not a spelling mistake). Wilson's now become my constant companion and we 'talk' regularly. Was just mentioning the other day 'how great it would be to walk out of these places and still have all of your marbles intact'!

Bring it on you bastards. I blow a raspberry to no–one in particular.

Think I'll have a wee lie down, toss and turn for another wee while.

After all, I'm in the biggest ever fight of my life.

4.49am

Just had an amazing dream - extremely vivid pictures and images flashing in my head about having wild sex with the librarian (Miss M). She's lovely - can't help but wish that I'd met her at different time of my life, not in here. Aren't dreams meant to be about what's at the forefront of your thoughts during the day? Always look forward to chatting with Miss M, as she's the only person, thus far, who talks to me like a human being, and someone that I can have a laugh and a joke with.

Okay, okay, so I fancy the pants off her.

Watched *'The Bourne Identity'* earlier - had one of those spooky moments as Matt Damon says: 'I don't know who I am'! How true - I've just been thinking the same thing, me ol' son.

'Road to Nowhere', by *Talking Heads*, starts to play in the juke-box in my head; *'Baby it's all right, baby it's all right'*. Aagghh!! The Volcano spews - losing the plot.

Have a fag, relax, take another tablet - too tired to work it out. My mouth is so dry - hard to breathe. So much for my great battle plan! Time for another nap - thinking about stealing some ideas from *'The Bourne Identity'*.

8.05am

Wake up in the middle of a dream about trying to roll a fag.

There's a kids' programme on the telly – *'The Slammer'* - where all the children are in 'toy prison'; needing to perform certain tasks to get out of jail. Is this what TV has come to in the UK?

Oh, and by the by, it's a bit too close to what actually does happen, for my liking.

Feel sick again, going back to sleep.

5TH SEPTEMBER 2007

1.49am

Starting to enjoy these wee hours of the morning. It's deathly quiet; sometimes the ghostly, soft rubber squeak of the night–guards' shoes, or a muffled cough, invades my space. It's such a contrast to the daytime, when all hell is breaking loose from unlock to bang–up.

Got a cold-sore on the boil on my lip, my mouth permanently dry; the whites of my eyes have gone red again - itchy as hell. I'm in the process of having a full M.O.T. done by the cool nursing staff. Thankfully, most of the tests are coming back negative. Unfortunately, my stomach is a real problem, and I've been told that I'll have to attend outside hospital. I'm thinking about the hospital visit outside, whilst watching *'Prison Break'*. If only, eh!

Made a new friend today: Johnny - seems like a good guy.

Watched him walking around in his Jesus boots (sandals) for the past few days, and thought: 'I bet he's in for drug trafficking'.

This outstanding deduction was formed by the fact he'd been wearing shorts and sandals, and had no other property when he landed on the wing; one tends to arrive in prison with just what you were wearing when nicked. Assumed that he'd been travelling from a hot climate, then straight here, via Her Majesty's Customs and Excise.

Made me smile when he said: 'Most convicts just want to get sentenced, move on and get on with being convicts'. Think we'll get along fine; a partner in crime (tried to avoid the pun), as he's also doing a bit of writing. We're taking a light-hearted view of life in general; both on the same page - good therapy.

Wish I'd paid more attention to *'Prison Break'*, as it's just occurred to me that if I do have some sort of incurable disease, I'm over the wall, spending the rest of my days on the run (or should I say the *crawl*?).

I've something to say: it's better to burn out than to fade away (The Kurgan in *'Highlander'*).

Would like to be able to repeat the *'Serenity Prayer'* each morning, but, alas, the days are starting to blur into one another. Shouldn't be watching *'Prison Break'* in my present state of mind.

Relax, be cool, have a fag, take a tablet. I fall asleep almost immediately.

6TH SEPTEMBER 2007

3.48pm

Not going to mention my health again. Let's just say it's not the best - getting on my tits. Take a deep breath, and my paracetamol, sigh, relax and I'm cool again.

Get on with the daily ritual of pretending to be positive - to be positive, to be positive! On the out, feeling like this, I'd be on the phone getting some chemical assistance; not for pain relief - I'd just settle for getting the numbness back. Still, I'm in here, and a fag and a cup of tea is as good as it gets!

'Smallville' is on the TV; young Superman is a great source of inspiration - feeling better already.

Wilson!

Where the fuck have you been, my old pal - I thought you were dead?

Maybe Wilson possesses the very same Kryptonite that saps Superman's strength, 'cos he's sure having a fuckin' good go at sapping mine, *every–single–fuckin'–day!*

Although, when I'm in my head, I escape to the beach at Muizenberg, in False Bay, South Africa. Wilson's never been, and can't fathom the solitude I used to feel, in contrast to the false highs, whilst being surrounded by some of the most beautiful scenery this Earth can provide. Like one of the billions of grains of sand, I was but a mere speck in the vastness of the universe - used to look at the stars when I'd had a puff and a few grams, and it literally 'blew my mind'. The constellations in Africa aren't like London or Belfast; in its own way Africa made me feel small, and helped me to realize that the world didn't revolve around me.

I'm better off in here for now - need to save myself from myself, need to heal; most of all, need time. Now there's progress for you: three months inside and thinking of staying permanently.

My socks are dry! Most people won't understand how important these minor details become for a person behind bars.

Can't help but imagine how carbon emissions and greenhouse gases created by my constant farting and coughing are affecting me, in my penthouse suite.

Mental note: put in an App for a Geiger counter. God, I'm good - making myself laugh again.

Just figured out why officers don't stick their head round the door in the mornings - it's too fuckin' dangerous; not from the fear of being attacked by the psycho killer (*Talking Heads*) lurking behind the door, but from the blast of toxins that would envelop them.

Think I'll go and have a wee kip, and see if I can't wake up in a better frame of mind.

Think I'll push for a different cell to see if it makes any difference to my health, which I'm not going to mention anymore.

I know, I know - blame Wilson; after all, it has to be someone else's fault that I'm here (*'Nobody's Fault But Mine'*, by *Led Zeppelin*, plays in my head, my mind running amok; wish the voices in my head would go away).

Need a challenge, a goal of some sorts - something to achieve. Think I'll get this published.

My goals? To get my trial out of the way, get back to Norn Iron , start a degree and get this book into the public domain. If one person picks it up then I'll have achieved what I set out to do now; if 'you' are reading it then I've done a lot better than I've hoped for at this particular stage of my life. Feel as if there's something stirring in me - not sure, yet, what that is.

MFI is constantly at work, breaking me down. The paranoia starts to creep back – starting to feel *better* as adrenalin pumps through my body, my brain finally building up to warp speed again, for all the wrong reasons! No bloody wonder I sought sanctuary in dope and booze. Going for a lie down - truly frightening myself.

Why does nobody fuckin' listen to me? Fuck the lot of ya - fuck off and leave me alone! Aagghh!!

7.45am

This is the worst part of the day for me.

You're primed, on the starting block - had a sink-shower, shave and several shits; ready and waiting to use the next thirty minutes as efficiently and speedily as possible. Thirty minutes to fill in your Apps (if they have any), queue up and collect your meds (if they have them), queue up to check the 'PAMs' (Prisoner Appointment and Movement) list, informing you of your day's activities (normally fucked up), queue up to tell landing staff about fuck-up with PAMs list, wondering all along how much time you have left - you find this out when the officers shout: 'Five minutes to lock up'.

Don't want to complain about the admin' department, as I'm worried about the repercussions of giving them bad press: *'Goodfellas'* springs to mind - the bit where the gangsters have a quiet word with the postman; i.e. the family didn't receive any mail, at all, after that.

Sometimes I've time to have a proper shower or phone my Dad, if I've phone credit (phone credit is normally fucked up as well). Dad normally wins, if I've enough money.

As much as I love my father, like most fathers and sons, we tend to have the odd disagreement. No need to explain myself.

The phones get cut off at 8.30am sharp, leaving one in mid-heated discussion and fuming for the rest of the morning.

There are one-hundred and fifty convicts with seven phones on this wing; can't imagine the amount of bacteria being passed from mouthpiece to mouth! Fuckin' mingin'! Did I mention that we get checked for Hepatitis-B? Wonder when we get checked for Legionnaires, malaria, tape-worm or the dreaded lurgy. Human rights? Fuck 'em - they're cons.

Think I'll ask one of the more helpful officers about my ever-increasing, Howard Hughes-like symptoms – panic, anxiety; I well-up and scream: 'Let me out!'

At last, 'Crazy Horse' (officer) bellows: 'Twos, threes, fours unlock.'

Thank fuck for that – freedom.

Officers say you've plenty of time to get your bits and pieces sorted out in the morning - if the well-oiled machine worked *properly* you would. However, human error dictates *not* - come Friday, you have more problems than you started with on the Monday, resulting in an ever-increasing feeling of frustration; sore hands and heads from punching and butting walls.

'Dreamer', by *Supertramp*, is echoing around my head.

5.16am

Mornin' all.

Got no fags, but I'm in good form.

Got no milk, but I'm in good form.

Ain't got much of anything now - just me, the mirror and my demons.

Ordered a limited canteen for tonight - Croydon Crown Court tomorrow, and a sneaky suspicion I'll not be coming back to Lewes; the system's full, and convicts seldom return from whence they came.

I'll do some scrounging during the course of my dull and boring day. Managed to scrape one together from the dog-ends in the ash-tray (left there purposely, just for this very sort of emergency). A truly fuckin' disgusting task, but…

..it's just as bad as crawling on all fours, looking for bits of white powder that may have fallen during the previous evening's festivities, reheating bits of silver foil, using used needles, drinking half a tin of stale, flat beer that's been in the fridge for over a week. Oooohhh, the joys of dope and booze. Not very glamorous, is it?

You'll find that most people, in this position, say they are in control. Fact.

Complete bollocks!

They know they've no choice, and will still sniff, swallow, inject or drink it. Nevertheless, the denial continues until something snaps and you end up doing the hard part: admitting, to yourself, that you have a problem.

Hope I get a chance to share what I've gone through and maybe, just maybe, get to help others. Still haven't heard from Mr. 'Genesis' about the 'Listeners' course.

Stop. Hold the fort!

I don't believe it - Martin's on the telly, making a statement about the Northern Ireland Assembly.

Could write a book about Northern Ireland and the bollocks that goes on there; unfortunately, I gave up trying to work it out years ago - like so many of my generation, who tried to make a difference growing up with the 'Troubles', I left.

THE DAY BEFORE MY FIRST CROWN COURT APPEARANCE.

I'm meant to be going to the dentist this morning - broke my tooth in Trinidad three months ago. Also need to get the lump on my bollock looked at. Then, back to cell – bang up. Won't be able to go to any other activity - they simply don't have the foresight or infrastructure in place, and I'll lose three hours of Education and essential intelligence gathering; torn between looking after my health, or my brain. Although, the thought of standing before a judge, slobbering and scratching my crotch, sways me towards Education.

These are some of the on-the-spot decisions you have to make in jail: will I stay in pain, unable to eat properly, continuing to stress out because of lumps on my lip and my bollock, or do I do nothing, and look sensible in front of a judge?

I've a bigger hill to climb than health: eight weeks to convince myself I'm 'Guilty'!

Need to make myself believe that I'm going down for at least ten years, so anything less than the max will be a bonus. Easy enough to say this at the time -

doing it is a completely different ball game, trust me. Watch this space.

Having a real battle at the minute over whether I should go to court or not - just found out that the Listeners' meeting with The Samaritans is tomorrow morning, and they're bringing a full ploughman's lunch!

The thought of real cheese and pickles makes it a close call.

As I let rip and pollute my already toxic room, I'm filled with a sense of dread. How can I sit through a training session, never mind a trial, with my loud and embarrassing stomach problems? My back pain will also be a major factor.

Had the same problems for nearly ten years now - put it down to lifestyle. Lost many a job, because I was always laughing and looked healthy - nobody believed me when I told them I was in pain, especially employers.

8.35am

Court's been put back a week.

Pretend to be unaffected, but deep down I'm seething. One gets used to pretending in jail; it's *all* a big act - everyone pretending to be something they're not. No time to think - keep moving.

No PAMs list this morning. Three of the phones are broken, and I cancelled my health appointments.

The officers were walking around in groups of four and five last night – not normal. Managed to scrounge some tobacco from 'G', who's gay. He's still stressing about some of the YPs (Young Prisoners) who've been giving him a bad time; doesn't know I've had a quiet word with Martin – his problems will soon be over! I like being helpful and giving encouragement to new arrivals. These little boys will be getting some unfriendly advice before the end of the day - they'll soon figure they're living by a whole new set of rules, and they are the weak ones. Bet you Jeffrey Archer wasn't privy to this sort of information when he was writing *his* book.

I'm relishing being busy, but can't deal with all the attention.

Wonder if we've been made Listeners yet.

Wilson is still on top form.

Hopefully I'll get over to Education this morning - can't wait to get the librarian's opinion on my writing. She's gets me thinking about my freedom, though. If I was on the out I'd definitely ask her out, for a pint. I'd stay off the booze, though; this place and the past three months has taught me I don't need drink or drugs - I'm mad enough without them! Doesn't help the pain though.

My mind drifts to Table Mountain, South Africa, red wine and beautiful women; *'Always Look on the Bright Side of Life'* by Eric Idle kicks in.

Flamin' hell! Chelsea Steve just opened my door with a set of keys! I know he gets around a bit, but this is taking the proverbial... Where the fuck did he get the keys!? He's looking for the *Argos* catalogue.

Crazy Horse then sticks his head around the door, and we all have a good laugh - he'd given Steve the keys to open my door; they said the look on my face was priceless. Little moments like this are precious in prison.

Much later a letter is slipped under my door, stating that I've been accepted for the Listeners, but warning that any further adjudications or adverse reports will result in my immediate dismissal. Well chuffed, elated even (*Snagglepuss* is back), though, at the same time, I'm fuckin' fuming that my alleged wrongdoing has even been mentioned.

Oh yeah, nearly forgot: went for a piss test - part of the vetting procedure to become a Listener - and it came back positive! Benzo's in my urine! Couldn't explain it properly.

Wrote a letter to the governor instead, after being informed of alleged wrongdoing:

'<u>Adjudication</u>

Dear Sir/Madam,

Yet again I find myself in a state of emotional turmoil, thinking of what to do for the best now that my initial shock, anger and bewilderment have subsided.

I returned to the wing after a frustrating session at Education. I was happy enough that a certain amount of progress had been made with certain course applications; we are all well aware how infuriatingly slow things can be in the prison service - e.g. I've been waiting patiently for three months to attend PICTA course, and I had just been informed that my application had never been received. Nothing strange there.

As is my nature I had assisted another inmate with his application – he is now doing the course.

So, you can understand if I was a bit miffed.'

I was looking forward to having some dinner and putting the feet up.

As I walked past the landing office, I'm having a laugh and a joke with the usual suspects, when someone says: 'What you been up to, naughty boy? What have you done Mick?'

I thought to myself: *What the hell is going on – everyone is staring at me?*

At the same time, Mr. T says: 'I'm very disappointed with you, Michael - I thought you were better than that.'

Then I see my mate Steve's face – he looks me right in the eyes and says: 'He's not joking, mate; you're on a report - you have to go see the governor.'

I told them all to 'Piss off' and 'Stop fuckin' about'.

Then I jokingly said: 'I look forward to meeting him (the governor) - I believe he's a nice chap.'

Steve told me not to worry - if I hadn't taken anything I'd be okay.

I now realize this is serious. I see the report on the desk with my name on it.

I ask Mr. T: 'What the hell is going on?'

He replies: 'You have been taking illegal drugs. Your VDT (voluntary drugs test) has come back positive for benzodiazepines. I didn't expect that, especially from you.'

I can't believe it! I'm totally fucked off; Steve drags me away before I get into some serious trouble.

Can't take it in. I'm on remand, accused of drug-trafficking! Obviously, I don't want five inmates and three officers standing on the landing discussing my personal business. After a few more heated words I head back to my cell; haven't lost my temper, but I can assure you, I'm very close.

I've toed the line so far, and I've done everything that has been asked of me. I'm angry and confused.

I've asked a fellow inmate to come to the adjudication with me as a 'Mackenzie friend'. I'm not too sure of the procedure, but it looks as if it's similar to the judicial one – i.e. *guilty until proven innocent.*

I've a lot to lose from *any* allegation of wrongdoing, never mind one which involves drugs. Asked for legal representation – refused; asked to speak to my friend or a Listener – refused. Was in a bad state of mind and was told to pack it in, everything will be sorted out in the morning - I was then left to stew all night.

During the course of the evening I heard another inmate ask to speak to a Listener - he seemed to be in a bad way (crying and moaning). He was told to 'Shut the fuck up - no Listeners are available' - the usual attitude from certain officers on this landing.

I'm sitting in my cell trying to figure out what has happened, when I spot a bottle of cough medicine, purchased from the prison canteen. I look at the ingredients on the label - it has an ingredient called Sodium Benzoate (E211). I ring the buzzer and inform Mr. T.

He laughs and says: 'I'm happy now - you have nothing to worry about.'

First thing in the morning I was strip-searched, told I wasn't allowed to bring anything, marched along the landing as far as G's cell. We're then marched down to the bowels of the jail, which holds 'The Block'.

Fuck me! What a frightening and intimidating place.

We're put in a cell with nothing in it - just a concrete slab, about eight-by-four, raised about six inches from the ground. No windows, toilet… nothing. Four others are marched in five minutes later. What a fuckin' stink! We're all packed together in the dungeon - the cocktail of heat, sweat and claustrophobia is overwhelming. I glance at G - he's shitting himself!

I laugh - tell him not to worry.

We're there for about an hour, luckily the first to be called, and escorted into a room; told to stand at the end of the desk.

The governor looks up and says: 'Anything to say?'

Start to try and explain that I shouldn't have to defend myself– 'Shut up,' was the reply.

G tried to speak–

'Shut up.'

Then back to me: 'Mr. Irwin, there seems to be a problem with your urine. Case adjourned for a week – no action at this stage. Take back to the cells.'

In the dungeon-esque corridor we double up laughing. Incredulous! What did just happen in there?

Back on the landing everyone's out, hanging over the railings, shouting and cheering. Some of the officers shake their heads.

This isn't a joke, many people have been falsely accused and punished during this kangaroo procedure. And some have even self-harmed and committed suicide because of such treatment?

5.30am

Wilson wakes me, or was it the torch being shone in my eyes? Some of the officers in here really are bastards! Starting to feel dehumanized.

Had a restless night, due to my alleged drug-taking and the treatment thereafter.

Looking over the pictures, taken by Her Majesty's Customs and Excise, of the cocaine hidden in the lining of my bag.

I still can't believe it! What a nightmare! I'd previously searched the bag from top to bottom, squeezing all around the sides to try to find anything foreign - was convinced there was nothing there. The customs boys seemed to know exactly what they were looking for - as I later found out, they'd been waiting for my arrival.

Trying to stay positive every day. Don't think the average man or woman on the street can ever fully grasp what a body goes through when it's unceremoniously dumped into the 'Legal System'. There's a long process called 'rotting on remand'- you also have to wade through a pile of bureaucratic bullshit, day after day. You wouldn't believe how draining a day in prison can be – the strength, willpower and determination a person requires in order to get through the next twenty-four hours.

Fuck me! If it's like this now, how on Earth do you get through a lengthy sentence?

I consider myself lucky; I'm daft enough and stupid enough to get through this. My heart goes out to the poor bastards who can't.

Wilson! *(Bollocks, aagghh!)*

I'll cherish these experiences - these hardships - and I'll use the ones I've already gone through as positives for future reference.

At the start of this mental road-trip I found myself wondering how people coped. If you are in the unfortunate position of having *already* lost the plot, then the courage and the strength you need to even ask someone for help *must* overcome the will to give up.

How many people are there, in this place alone, that have some sort of mental problem or learning difficulty? They should be getting treatment, not thrown into a lions' den full of predators! I've watched as others prey on the vulnerable, fueling their addictions and lining their pockets, while the staff turns a blind eye. Didn't ever believe how easy it is to get some gear in prison.

Got a million things to do today, and, as usual, all I want is to go to Education, switch off, attend my first I.T. class, have a chat with the librarian and dream about getting out.

No chance.

Instead, I've to deal with a cacophony of emotions, and phone my poor Dad; who I love more now than I ever have since I was a kid. Only now do I see the man for his strengths and not his weaknesses. Feel a sense of pride knowing that he is my Dad - a bit like when I was a kid; he'd turn up, out of the blue, to watch me play football. Filling up with tears thinking about the shit I've caused him.

Have to block it out - block out the kangaroo court I attended, block out the trip I made, block out my emotions. Can't feel… can't feel!

Be cool, be cool-

'Wilson!' Fuck me, that fuckin' bastard of a buzzer is driving me fuckin' nuts!

For the greater good and mental well-being of the other inmates I should get a table leg and smash the fuck out of the buzzer.

Be cool, keep taking the tablets.

I think it would be in my best interests to stop taking all medication - I'd then know that nothing illegal has entered my system. Maybe I should go on bread and water – nil by mouth. Maybe MI5 are slipping 'stuff' into my food – trying to make me crack.

My quest for information is reaching fever pitch again, my ears ringing like crazy. Had to turn the TV down - every noise seems to be magnified:

Aagghh, smash, bang, kill, buzz, buzz, anger, madness, taps, washing machine..!

Relax. Be cool.

Why don't they understand? This is all in my head. Don't you fuckin' get it?

Outside I look cool, calm and calculated, but inside I'm going fuckin' bananas and want to unleash hell, a bit like the scene in *'Mean Machine'* with 'The Monk': Monk catches the ball, while Bob and Bob comment on his mental state - everything goes into slow motion, and in the Monk's head he beats seven bells of shit out of the officers; then, his thirst not yet quenched, he turns on his team-mates and does the same to them. Everything speeds up and the Monk appraises the carnage he's created with a devilish grin. Then Bob and Bob say:

'The Monk: no better hands in the game; cool, calm and calculated. Un-be-fuckin'-lievable.'

Well, let me tell you something: I feel like that several times a day, every day of the week! I want to rip and tear and smash and maim - create carnage - and I have done ever since I was old enough, and able to feel bone crunching under my fist.

Why've I got a table leg in my hand? Where's the buzzer gone?

Big sigh; *'The Sound of Silence'* by *Simon and Garfunkel* is playing in my head: *'Parsley, sage, rosemary and thyme, you've always been a good friend of mine... la la la la la...'*

Why are all those officers running towards me? Ha-ha, ho-ho, he-he.

Need to slow down! Buzzer, taps, MI5, Wilson… *Unbe-fuckin'-lievable, Bob.* Feel the walls closing in - can't take much more of this; take a beta–blocker and four paracetamol.

I've got to defend myself in *real* court and a prison kangaroo court! Can't do it!

It'll be okay… need help; now tell me if I'm weak and emotional, you bastards.

BANG… BANG… BANG. Fuck it! Fuck it all! Started screaming and shouting at nothing in particular, like a barking, rabid dog; my nerves are fried.

Come on, son, pull yourself together - you'll be okay. Think I'll have a wee lie down for five minutes; going to explode - want to lash out at anyone or anything. Can't - got too much to lose!

Fuck! Am I going mad? Can someone help me?

No, only *I* can help me - there *is* nobody else. You're in your own mind… *you're on your own, kid.*

The warmth of the tablets envelopes me, and I slip into a gentle slumber.

2.40am

Can't sleep - woke up and threw up. It's that peaceful time of morning - no buzzer; maybe that's what woke me up. *'Things Can Only Get Better'* by *D–Ream* plays continuously in my head. If only.

I've just had a look at the contents of my toilet - the usual pile, with some blood and a few whole chips. Someone complained about the chips being 'too dry' at lunch-time; had lunch at twelve o'clock yesterday and there are now whole chips in the bog! Now, correct me if I'm wrong, but this can't be normal. My digestive system is fucked!

Passed out around ten - so, I've had a good three hours kip.

'Prison Break' is on the telly - the title of this episode is *'End of the Tunnel'*; how apt. Not that I'm digging a tunnel, although things are moving

forward - yesterday was fuckin' mad.

Must watch my language; got told off by my Dad again - he'd read some of my writing. As per usual he doesn't get it - ended up having to write another letter explaining my intentions. Why do I always have to explain myself to him?

Fathers and sons, eh? Who'd 'ave 'em?

This only proves to me how badly he's coping with all of this, how every day I'm behind bars causes him more and more pain.

Can't afford to take his feelings into account; he's always in my thoughts, but I don't want my love and concern for him to screw up my chameleon-esque coping strategies. After all, this is about me and all the other poor fuckers who may have had or are going through the same shit as I am now.

Ouch! Got a searing pain in my left eye; look in the mirror – the temple vein is throbbing away nicely.

Oh yeah - did I mention I'm in crown court today?

The '*Ali G'* film is on The Movie Channel. This should be fun - it's bad enough having Homer and Snagglepuss in my head, all I need is for Ali G to make an appearance!

Even with the voices, I feel mentally strong and just want this day to be over, allowing me to knuckle down and get on with things. Ten years, probably! Ali is talking to a straight-laced professor about drugs – class-A and ecstasy – and taking the piss as only he can.

Think I should turn it off. Got to start packing.

Imagine standing in the dock with Ali–G, Homer, Snagglepuss and Pete Sellers buzzing around in your head; if I burst out laughing they'll throw the fuckin' key away.

I think Sasha Baron Cohen is a bloody good comedian; like Billy Connolly, he has the knack to make people laugh at regular, everyday thoughts they are too frightened to mention.

The pleasure I've just had from that last fag was unbelievable - I feel quite stoned; similar to my first puff at thirteen, shortly before I threw up in my mate's toilet.

Had a right laugh last night - one of the servery guys came round with the new menu sheet. When I slipped it back under the door, he said: 'Thanks, David.' He'd obviously read the card outside my door.

'I've been in this prison three months mate, and my fuckin' name ain't David.'

'Aw-white - keep your fuckin' 'air on,' he says.

I told him to: 'Fuck off!' No time for fools.

My wee brain is a circus at the minute. Have always managed to see the funnier side of life, and with all of these voices in my head, I may go a bit cuckoo every now and then; kill Clouseau… kill Clouseau… kill Ali G.

Need to get packed.

4.00am

That's me packed.

I've had many different experiences of packing over the years, and I think I've finally got it down to a fine art - tucked everything into a black bag, ready for the bin, and kept a toothbrush. I've found that when you pack you end up reliving the previous chapter in your life, the last place you packed - it may have been a paradise in the Pacific or a black hole near Calcutta. You physically have to tear yourself away from previous memories; I defy anyone to say different.

I have to pack, in case the well-oiled machine doesn't work, and I don't come back to Lewes – I have a fifty-fifty chance of sitting back here this afternoon, discussing the day's events.

Feel rather excited. Oops, just threw up! The endless chain-smoking and cups of coffee are taking their toll. Need a shower - think I'll have a sink shower.

Don't know what time I'm leaving at; have a rough idea - probably around seven-thirty. I've lain awake so many mornings in the past three months, listening to other people leaving – not knowing if they were going to court or going home – never to be seen again. That's what it's like in here: people come, people go - never the same faces. You make friends... they come, they go - just like that. After a while you tend not to get too close - it's easier.

I'll probably go just before unlock. Want someone from the machine to tell me.

Not everyone is as clued up as I am. Not trying to sound arrogant or big-headed - just want people to stop, consider and think about others who are less fortunate than me. If I hadn't whined, bitched, moaned and generally made a nuisance of myself, I'd be none the wiser - no officer will volunteer you information, simply because they don't fuckin' know!

They think I'm in front of a kangaroo court again this morning about my unfounded charge of illegal drug-taking. Not, I repeat: *not* in front of a real judge, answering 'not guilty' to a real charge which will affect the rest of my fuckin' life.

The volcano inside has a minor event and I end up with chest pains; need to take my beta-blockers, but I want to save them for later. Maybe I'll swallow the whole fuckin' lot in front of the judge, only to make a fuckin' point! Aagghh! Fuck this!

Ali-G is over and there's a wildlife programme on about South Africa; my thoughts drift to a place I love and miss - feel compelled to keep writing to help you understand a turmoil within.

Someone has just kicked off in their cell; the screams - the horror of another man's nightmares - caress me into the reality of prison. The world in here slowly crawls back to one's psyche.

Think I'll keep watching the rhinos and elephants - they block out the pain, allow me to ignore the madness of others. *Fuckit-fuckit-fuckit!* I'll have my sink shower now, if you please.

Must tell you about my first ever sink shower:

Picture this: a forty-year old, pregnant man, standing bollock-naked, with one foot in the sink, washing his arse (who, by the way, feels a great sense of achievement at his agility and suppleness at still being able to stand up with one foot in said sink!), generally laughing at life and some of the situations he gets himself into, when suddenly, with no warning, the door flap opens, and the female officer on duty peers in. My heart goes out to the poor woman and her family! I'm sure she's seen some weird and wonderful sights in prison, and might be able to forgo counselling - or maybe she'll end up in the female equivalent of here. At least I was able to clean the rest of the floor with my other foot.

Shit, must talk to someone - a Listener, perhaps.

Had a bad thought: I'm meant to *be* one soon - these poor bastards don't stand a chance if *I'm* the one who comes to see them in the wee, small hours.

It's a beautiful balmy morning and there's a lovely, calm, soothing draught blowing under the door, circulating around the room.

'The Jeremy Kyle Show' is on the telly - why the fuck am I watching this shite!? He's talking to some poor bloke about going through the day-to-day traumas of rehab and detox.

Popped my first beta-blocker of the day. Only meant to take one in the morning and one at night - think I might cheat a little today; after all, it is a special occasion.

Had a chat with my Dad last night, and was telling him about the great sense of relief I felt about being in control of my faculties - if I was in a similarly stressful type of situation on the outside, I'd be straight down the pub for a pint or six. I'd then turn up the next morning, rough as fuck and try to bluff my way through what I was easily able to face after several pints the night before (*'Comfortably Numb'*, by *Pink Floyd*, strikes a chorus). I'm telling him how relieved I am not to be thinking like that anymore, and yet I'm sitting here now, popping pills in rehab/detox at five in the morning. What a hypocrite. The problem is, I meant it.

Think I will have to stay in here a bit longer – need more time to work it out. Nothing changes, eh?

On a serious note, though, I do feel a lot better in myself. At least I'm confronting these situations head-on, and not making any more feeble excuses, or trying to blame something or someone else. Isn't this some sort of progress?

Switch over and listen to the music on *Ceefax*: elevator music – very calming; think I'll have a wee lie down. Got a million things going on upstairs - the washing-machine working its magic again; must lie down and let the wash finish its cycle.

Ha-ha, ho-ho, he-he.

FIRST CROWN COURT APPEARANCE
THURSDAY 6TH SEPTEMBER 2007
6.00am

Sorry about last night - lost the plot a bit. Was taken down the block for smashing my cell up, slashing my wrists and trying to hang myself. Just my luck: the fuckin' shoelaces broke!

Have I got your attention?

That's how quick and easy it is to lose it in here.

Of course, I didn't do any of the above, but I thought about it and wanted to and I did lose the plot a bit. Well, when I say 'a bit', I mean *completely* - all of my fear, anger, frustration and hopelessness tumbling around in my mind, my soul, tearing and battering my senses; stubbed my toe on the table leg, and that wee bit of pain was enough - the catalyst… the trigger - to vent my fury; had the good sense to roll my mattress up and pounce on it.

Biting, screaming, clawing, punching, laughing, crying, tearing, crying..!

Wasn't worried about all the sweaty arseholes who'd lay on it before me. When I was spent, I lay there, face buried in the soft material - blood, sweat and tears mingling with the unsavoury, stale odour of a broken man.

Glad I was able to hold back and 'do' the mattress. Unfortunately, there are many who haven't held back. There are many who don't understand what's happening to them; a little shove in the dinner queue - just like at school ..a dirty look, enough to set them or you off, unleash the fury.

Getting ready for court - feeling fine, although I know I'm not quite right in the head. Take solace in the fact that I know I'm a strong person with a certain degree of intelligence, and I've the backing of my father and those closest to him. Wish I could mention more people, but, alas, at this moment in time, the list is small - I've known, befriended and looked out for hundreds of people over the years, and, at this particular moment in time, I can count six people who have got my back. This makes me very sad, but I can't dwell, mustn't stop, can't stop - got to keep going.

I wonder how many put their thoughts into action and self-harm or commit suicide at this time of the morning. Nobody gives a fuck.

Think I'll have another fag – chain smoking now. My thoughts turn again to Health and Safety in prison - looking around my cell I take stock of the potential health hazards: five empty glass coffee jars, four empty Branston pickle jars, a bottle of Worcestershire sauce, cans of tuna, and of sweetcorn, a ceramic plate, razor blades… (a highly flammable cocktail can be made from milk whitener, sugar, washing powder, contact-lens fluid and baby oil!) ..pens, pencils and pencil sharpeners… It's then that my eyes fall on the biggest potential killers of all: mayonnaise and salad cream!

It never ceases to amaze me how 'security' can ban one item in one prison and allow it in another - they once banned eggs because they could be boiled and used to throw at officers, despite the fact that prisoners are given boiled eggs three times a week for breakfast. I mean *really* - this is not made up or *scrambled.* Pepper is another one they won't allow. A lot of these perceived potential threats are ludicrous and have been passed down through the generations, from movies like *'Cool Hand Luke'*. Pepper is used to put the dogs off, but there are no dogs inside a prison (well, that's another loose statement, open for interpretation). *Fuckin' unbelievable Bob.* What to do?

About an hour ago, a news article came on about two men who stole a hearse, while on a drinking spree in South Africa. They eventually got caught when they ran out of petrol and, yes, there was a body in the back. I'm on the, floor laughing my head off, when my observation hatch is opened again by the same female officer - she whispers: 'Hello, my lovely'.

Picture this: I'm wearing prison-issue, blue boxer-shorts, that are too tight round the waist, but not in the groin area, and one bollock is hanging out, got a pair of brown slippers on, and I'm suffering from 'death by salad cream' (18-stone). I'm caught in the headlights again, slightly startled by having to have a conversation with an 'eye' - a *female* eye.

Eye says: 'Up early, aren't ya?' Blink-blink.

I can't think of anything useful to say, so I splutter: 'Yeah, couldn't sleep.'

Eye replies: 'Ah, well – sure, you'll be out soon.' The flap closes as suddenly as it was opened. Is Eye referring to my imminent release, or just my getting out for the day?

Can you imagine how the scene may have looked to the female officer, who subsequently had to fill in a report of her patrol?

> 5.35am. On my normal patrol on 'F'-wing I did a random check on cell 42 and opened the cell door observation flap of David Ervine, number VP4677. To my immediate distress I observed Ervine rolling on the floor, exposing his genitals and in obvious pain (or ecstasy), with tears running down his face. In my professional opinion as an experienced officer, I can only assume that Ervine was having some sort of fit, mental breakdown or playing with himself. Out of

genuine concern I asked him if he was OK. All he could do was splutter 'can't sleep.' If I didn't know any better I would say that he was laughing at me, innit. I told him that he shouldn't worry - he'd be out soon. I hope I didn't say anything wrong because I could have sworn I heard him mumbling incoherently: something about the system, someone called 'Wilson' and MFI.

Who said they didn't care, eh? Think I'll try and have a wee lie down.

Dozed off and woke with the TV still on. That kid's programme *'The Slammer'* is on again (kids getting banged up in the name of entertainment) – a bit too real for my liking. Turn over to the news and they are talking about ASBOs. No friggin' wonder kids are on the rampage: they've been banged up on the other channel. No fuckin' wonder kids grow up thinking life in prison is a game, a joke, something to be sneezed at or wear as a badge of honour. Does anyone really think these programmes through?

Hear Crazy Horse barking out instructions. He's also half mad - that's probably the reason why we get along so well. Suppose you need a sense of humour to work in these places; wonder if it's a job requirement, or does it build up in one over the years?

Pink Floyd kicks in: *'Is there anybody out there?'*

Just spilled my cod-liver oil tablets all over the floor - they have a weird, psychedelic sheen as the sun bounces off them; *wow, man.* Oh, for a joint now.

Figured out how I got my cold sores: it's the constant dipping of fingers in the ashtray, causing my fingertips to get dirty, and by smoking small roll-ups.

Must get ready now.

Julio Iglesias is singing on the telly - reminds me of Amanda, in Cape Town. Wow, what a beauty! Couldn't believe it when I found out she fancied me! She unknowingly turned my world upside down - still get a wobbly stomach and goose-bumps when I think about her.

Snap out of it, son - you've got bigger fish to fry today. Can't afford to wonder - today is about facts.

The librarian makes me wonder though; still, different time, different place…

The same female officer opens the flap - she says: 'They're coming to pick you up around seven', and asks me if I'm going back to bed.

Is that an order or an invite?

I tell her: 'I've been awake since two.'

'As if I didn't already know. Make sure you're packed,' she says. Then, cheerfully: 'Least I won't have to wake you up, then.'

She walks away, giggling. My previous concern for her welfare was unfounded: the horrific visions of earlier seem to have had no effect - obviously made of tougher stuff.

Think I'll have a wee lie down and do some breathing exercises.

Can't stop worrying about how I look - it feels as if a forest is growing on the mountain of herpes protruding from my bottom lip. Why is it always the bottom lip?

Never mind. Try and relax – wait for the drugs to kick in. Feeling tired, nervous and excited.

Crazy Horse opens my door; 'Well, that's you, Michael - got everything? Hope everything works out for you. If you don't come back let us know how you got on. Be lucky.' He shakes my hand and claps me on the back. I'll never forget him for that. Cheers, Mr. H.

CROYDON CROWN COURT – HOLDING CELL

1.09pm

What a fuckin' palaver!

Pleaded 'Not Guilty' and have been remanded into custody until trial date: 5th November 2007 - trial expected to last for two days. This means I can't talk about or discuss my case with anybody - phone calls are recorded, interviews are bugged, they have people who can lip-read, and, of course, there are the grasses. Everything I do or say from now on can and will be used in a court of law to fuck me up.

Two more months of limbo!

What a day… big sigh.

Have all of my stuff with me, so I'm not bothered about where I end up. One part of me (*Wilson! Aagghh!* – yes, he came along as well, though not as loud) wants to go back to Lewes, another part to some other resort, and the last part couldn't give a flying fuck! That's just the sort of mood I'm in - I'll deal with each scenario as it arises, but for now all I want is to get the fuck out of here and get my head down, as I'm mentally and emotionally drained.

Had lunch - one of those cheap microwave jobs. What a pleasant change.

It's a bit awkward trying to write in here (borrowed four bits of A4 paper and a red pen from one of the gaolers) - the light's bad and there's nothing to lean on, unless you kneel on the floor and write on the bench. Glad I'm on my own (High Risk). This is going to be a horrible day.

A young officer just came and gave me lasagne and some more paper - doesn't cost much to be nice in this world, eh? For now I'll just try to relax.

No more questions, no more enquiries and no more 'what if?'. Quite pleased that my case is going to be heard in front of a judge and jury - this is all I wanted. After all, I'm in no fit state to be making decisions about the rest of my life, best let someone else do it for me - if I screw up, I can't blame me, simples; it's a win-win situation, exactly what the doctor ordered. Might have to see a doctor after that lasagne. Still, it filled a dent. Can't wait until dinner, though.

'Someone's crying, Lord, kum-ba-ya…'

No, seriously, some young lad is crying! Poor soul.

Oh, he's just started screaming - fuck 'im! Completely lost the sympathy vote; dry your fuckin' eyes, dickhead. Got a funny feeling he's just had the lasagne too.

Hear Pavarotti on the news in the reception area; I'd forgotten: his death was announced earlier - I'd turned up the TV in my cell at Lewes when *'Nessun Dorma'* played. The hair on the back of my neck stood up as the song reached its crescendo, and I let a roar of pure emotion out of me and burst out crying. Got up on the table and stood looking out of the window, trying to get some breath back… hypnotized - frozen in time - staring at a big seagull perched on top of the obligatory prison flagpole; the Union Jack fluttered on the warm gentle breeze.

'Where were you when Pavarotti died?' Will I tell the truth? It's a moment that's ingrained on one's memory for the rest of one's life.

The journey from Lewes was a bit different. Managed to fill one of the piss bags – no mean feat. The piss bag is a fantastic and wonderful invention, and using one is a unique and fascinating experience. Knew I'd be pissing for Ireland due to the amount of coffee I'd drank during the night. It's a small bag, about the size of a bag of crisps, filled with some sort of absorbent gel - as you pee into it, the pee gets soaked up by the gel, and the bag starts to swell; by the time it's finished it's about the size of a bag of sugar. Pretty fuckin' cool. Got a bit of a shock when we pulled up at the traffic lights beside a bus: was standing with yours-truly hanging out, and a little old lady is looking straight at my bits. Must remember to check and see if the windows on the 'sweat-box' are tinted - some aren't.

The fuckin' 'sweat-box' is aptly named; I'd forgotten about my trip to Brighton nick after my arrest at Gatwick - was passing out, falling on the floor, throwing up, hallucinating, the full works; would recommend it to anyone. It certainly made me sit up and pay attention - back to earth with a bump. It seems like such a long time ago - a bit of a blur - although, when I think about it, every memory is as clear as day. Won't be travelling down that road again.

It's weird sitting here, alone, in this green holding cell, where thousands have been before me, listening to telephones ringing, people chatting and the day-to-day noises you would normally associate with a busy office. After three months with Wilson it's a strangely pleasant change; the 'Wilson' at Croydon is totally different, in a quirky sort of way.

Someone's figured out that their shoes squeak on the highly polished concrete floor - how fuckin' exciting; let's all have a go, shall we? Fuckin' pricks - shut the fuck up! A bit like running your nails down a blackboard. Still, mustn't grumble - I find sanctuary with pen stuck to paper, blocking out the chaos, keeping the madness at bay. When I'm in the page nobody can get to me.

My arse and back are killing me - I'm gagging for a fag!

Don't get the wrong idea - I'm on my own and mean I require a cigarette!

Did have some tobacco and a lighter in my pocket, although they confiscated them earlier - must remember to figure something out for the next time. Seven hours now without a cigarette! No problem - I can take it; trying to keep occupied - get up and do a few laps around the eight-by-twelve, green room.

Anyone who's ever been in a police or court cell will tell you how impossible it is to achieve this. It's the same as being in the seg (Segregation Unit / *'The Pokey'*), only in the court you don't have a hard rubber mattress to lie on, just a thin wooden bench. It's much worse at court, as there are no windows or natural light, and a poxy, wee ventilation vent that doesn't work - makes you stir crazy.

Want to lie down, but I can't - spilled some of the lasagne on the bench, and nothing to clean it up with; refuse to ring the buzzer. Starting to lose the plot again: the room's too small, the bench is made of wood, and I'm wearing a new shirt. At Hayward's Heath Magistrates the lady with the keys gave me a couple of cardboard boxes to lie on - felt and looked like a piece of shit, going through 'cold turkey' and the 'DTs'; didn't give a fuck - when I got my head down it felt like heaven. Starting to feel the same way now. Having an out of body experience, honest.

Current events cause me to get agitated and the fatigue isn't helping. The colour scheme and paint fumes are starting to play havoc with my co–ordination; keys constantly jangling up and down the corridor outside, but they never unlock my door. *'Give me Crucifixion Any Day' – 'Monty Python's Life of Brian' (Bwian and Wodewick).* Feel an anxiety/panic attack coming on, but I'm too knackered to do anything about it. Some prick's banging and shouting; it's too confined a space to be making so much fuckin' noise (know who I'd like to bang - my sexual desire returns the bookkeeper at Lewes).

WW (William Wallace), my barrister – not his real name – whom I met for the first time, said: 'I can see you're a bit of a character'. What did he mean by that, exactly? Must be the fuckin' shirt. It's not the first time that has been said to me over the years - they obviously know something I don't; for me, I'm still the same loveable dickhead I've always been.

Lots of growling going on now - place is full of fuckin' animals. Imagine- No, don't, for that matter - it's a horrible thought! Take a bit of time to consider if *you* had just been sentenced to ten to fifteen years (or two weeks, even) and you had to sit in this madness, wondering what the fuck was going to happen next - where or what hell you are going to.

Sometimes, I find the cockney accent on women extremely hard to listen to. There's a woman here who has a voice so shrill and piercing, it goes right through you - nothing an AK47 wouldn't sort out.

As the day drags on you can feel the atmosphere changing: animals growling, shouting getting louder and more agitated, a constant jangling of keys adding to the irritation, insecurity and restlessness. Can feel the mood taking control of me, developing into a fury. Haven't lost the plot yet, but if that silly little fuckin' bitch doesn't shut the fuck up...

Patience is a friggin' virtue, eh? Been given a cup of coffee, one of my tablets and a cup of tepid water.

It's not frightening, it's just fuckin' mad: some prick is singing the death march (*'Dum, dum, da-dum, da dum-dum-dum-dum, da-dum...'*), some woman is yapping like a parrot and the shoes are still squeaking. Sensory deprivation? No, sensory overload!

Wonder if the human race knows or cares about the mental torture a person goes through in these places. It's lonely to think not.

Just remembered about earlier on, when I got out of the sweat-box, both hands in cuffs, one gripping a bag full of piss - one of the gaolers said: 'These poor bastards are in for a long day.'

'Why's that then geeza?' says the other.

'Aint no staff, innit,' replies Silly Little Bitch.

Now I'm able to compute that little bit of intelligence and use it to my advantage - I now know that there's definitely no point in getting stressed or asking what's going on, because they simply will not know. The only option is to sit and wait whilst going slightly doo-lally. Other convicts are kicking off 'cos they don't understand what's happening - I'm actually rather pleased with myself for coping so well.

I'm not really – just trying to lure myself into a false sense of security. Trying to keep going, trying to survive, though the volcano simmers, still only millimetres from the surface. Quite scary, how close a person can come to doing some serious damage to himself or to others - having to suppress the irrepressible urge to erupt and inflict violence on the immediate vicinity, way too often, can't be good for you.

Some prick has seen that I've got a pen and some paper - he starts whining: 'Why can't I have some paper?'

Shouldn't have been born such a cunt, I think.

One of the gaolers says: 'Cos he asked nicely, innit,' and walks away, giggling like a two year old. Thanks a lot, luv - that's my street cred out the fuckin' window.

Oh, I nearly forgot – I must tell you about my time in the court; after all, that is why I'm here:

Sitting beside 'Ogre' (big, pierced motherfucker officer) at the back of the court, my solicitor Danny Crane and barrister William Wallace cannot be found - we're now running late. You could hear a pin drop; everyone starts looking round the room in a nervous silence, then at me. The judge asks me if I would 'mind waiting' while he hears another case – it should only take five minutes.

I sat through the legal exchanges between counsel, judge and barristers, and I have absolutely no recollection of what they talked about. The barristers and counsel then left and there was another brief pause, the judge scanning the courtroom over the rim of his glasses, whilst signing some paperwork - I don't think he wanted to miss the arrival of my legal team, so that he could glare at them.

When they finally scuttled in and looked over at me, I held up my wrist, tapping an imaginary watch and shaking my head. My barrister started to speak to the judge, but the latter just held his hand up, stifling a laugh; 'I don't want to hear it.'

My two boys were very red-faced and I had visions of tails between legs. I, too, pretended to be annoyed at them - the whole court was looking at the ceiling or shuffling papers, trying not to laugh; my boys thought we had been waiting all that time for them, and that they were in the cack. They weren't, but who am I to ruin everyone else's fun? Apparently situations or events of a humorous nature don't happen very often in court.

Shit, the blister on my finger has just burst.

Ogre brings me a coffee and tells me its 3.15pm. Friggin' hell - how much longer must I wait in this hell-hole?

It's during these insufferable times that one wishes one hadn't done what one did or didn't do. In other words, you start to feel sorry for yourself, or just get plain angry that you got caught; a harsh reality of life playing on your mind, 'cos all you have is time - time to think.

Could have been to Lewes and back hours ago, and, as per usual, nobody has a clue what's going on.

Need to be careful what I say and do from now on; MFI will have their spies out - I'll have to be on top form to stay out of their clutches. If I win the crowd, like today, they will have no chance.

So I must declare at this point:

'Any reference or similarities to a person or persons mentioned in this story are completely fictional and accidental. These words are completely untrue so please don't get the arse if you've been mentioned.'

Here endeth the declaration. I thank you.

Friggin' hell, they must tell us something soon; starting to feel sick - probably the same shade of green as this room.

Completed another six pages. Feel as if I'm achieving something in the old writing department - wonder if it will ever be worthwhile. It is rather therapeutic writing down these daily observations and occurrences, though way too often one hears oneself saying: 'Nobody will believe me…' Think this whole day could be made into some sort of black comedy for television or the West End?

Finding it hard to concentrate - getting agitated again; I've been up for twenty-four hours. Will I ever get out of this God-forsaken place? Still, it'll be nice to see the English countryside in the early evening.

Much talking, jangling of keys and general commotion outside. For fuck's sake, will someone please tell us what's going on? Most convicts would be a lot easier to deal with if we were treated with a bit of dignity, instead of being treated like the scum of the Earth we are presumed to be. Can hear screaming and shouting coming through the air vents now.

Fuck me – I was so content just sitting here writing; now my fuckin' blood is boiling and I'm seeing red. I swear, if I bump into that whining prick in the corridor I'll end his fuckin' miserable life here and now. No joke!

It's now 4.15pm.

Will have to take this up with the human-rights-and-wrongs-people - this just isn't cricket, old chap.

Good practice for being a Listener, though. I'm experiencing for the first time what it's like to attend court; and people wonder why everyone looks so glum when they arrive back at the nick?

All of the gaolers have disappeared and left a young, female officer in charge of this motley crew - hope another day of action hasn't been called! Don't think I can do this anymore - in urgent need of my medication, my heart thumping out of my chest. The young girl is trying her best to be helpful; it's so annoying to know that there are some good people out there in uniform - honest, genuine people who do want to help, but get called 'slags' because of the actions of others. How ironic is that?

I was told that I would be wherever I was going at 4.30pm and I wouldn't need to take my medication until I got there. They are not allowed to open your property bags whilst you are in the court building. What if I had a heart attack? Who would be to blame? Who would pay?

Unfortunately this sort of shit sticks; it's no wonder violence and anger are always just around the corner. I'm sitting here, ready to kill dead things, trying to be cool. Can you imagine what it's like for those who don't know how to be calm, or the ones who simply won't? I know *I'll* be okay, but what about the others who can't just shrug this off?

The other gaolers are back now and they are laughing and messing about, within ten feet of guys who are going absolutely fuckin' bananas. The detachment of officers to the people in their care and to their surroundings is painfully obvious when one takes a step back and sees it for the first time - we are in two parallel worlds where interaction and social interaction must be kept at arm's length, and to a minimum.

I can see why people attack the first living thing that comes through the door - it's only a simple cry for help, an attempt to be noticed, and a need for someone to pay attention, to get a question answered or to make a stand.

I make a comparison to my home country and how the IRA made people pay attention. After thirty-eight years of violence, hatred and murder they produced their trump card and announced a cessation of all military activity, producing an end to their campaign of violence – game, set and match. Even with all of the false starts, the other side had no choice but to respond and give in. I'm trying to make an analogy here but not quite getting there: what I mean is that the IRA situation was similar to that of convicts, in that they fought the system.

The system has its way - the institutional way of dealing with unruly convicts. It's easier to deal with people who buck the system - that's why countries have armies; twist them up, lock them up, impose petty and punitive punishments that create more work, more conflict and more procedure, which forms the basis of institutional rehabilitation.

'Anger Management' and *'Enhanced Thinking Skills'* are now suitable courses because the person is angry, violent and doesn't know how to cope with his particular role in the justice system. If everyone was to declare peace on the justice system - not physically fight, but be quiet and comply - the other side, the system, would have no choice but to reciprocate.

But what's easier to control: a wing full of 'Enhanced' prisoners who behave themselves, are allowed more time out of cells, more rights and privileges, or a wing full of headers, who remain permanently locked down, out of sight, out of mind, and who only need to be fed and allowed one hour of exercise?

There are three young offenders taking the piss out of three other kids in uniform, whilst in a cell not more than ten feet away a black man of forty-one years of age has just been given six and a half years in a British jail - no chance of seeing his wife and kids, a limited knowledge of English and in a foreign land. As per usual my thoughts are jumping all over the shop, but my will and determination to help others, through the knowledge I gain from these experiences, keeps coming to the fore - going to try so hard to help other inmates; even if I get set free.

Maybe I'll just stay, if only to help others. Now there's a sensible thought: commit a crime to get into prison, so that you can help people - after all, no fucker is doing it on the out.

All of the officers, about eight of them, are now singing, dancing and shouting, a bit like a primary school class - the noise is deafening, reverberating, around the room. In reply, all of the convicts have kicked off, screaming and shouting. They're both trying to see who can make the most racket, fuckin' idiots. Will I ever get out of this fuckin' madhouse? Eleven hours without a fag ain't helping matters.

A sad, emotional rollercoaster of a day.

There must be a better sort of system - this one fuckin' sucks! There must be some good people out there - the logic, jargon and reasoning don't match up, and there is no way, that I know of, to measure someone's pain. Will this well-oiled machine turn me into a bad person? I've been trying to make some sort of sense out of this, especially over the past few months.

Will anyone listen if I complain? Will wait until after my proper trial - by that time, whatever the outcome, I won't give a fuck... like so many others on the losing side.

The futility of it all - when will I accept defeat?

Once you're *in* the machine the war's already over - only *you* are too stubborn to admit it.

Time to move on.

Must explain how the system works in here:

It's taken me just over an hour to get one beta-blocker and two paracetamol from one of the more helpful children, and all my belongings are in two large, clear plastic bags, behind a large, barred gate in the reception area, not more than twenty feet from where I'm standing. The rule is: *'officers are not allowed to break the seals or retrieve any property belonging to a prison, whilst the prisoner is in transit to and from the court.'* You are also not allowed to have anything in your possession.

Fuck you! It's *my* stuff - give it to me!

I have to get permission to be escorted into the reception area to observe, in front of witnesses, a senior officer retrieve *my* goods and give me *my* property/medication. One of the many rules made by people in an office, who have never observed the result of their policies - not very practical, and, dare I say: 'illogical'? One thing you learn in prison, very quickly, is never to think logically - you're in for all sorts of heartache if you do.

The cackling and laughing continues – I never knew torture could be so enjoyable.

Let me go.

I'll go anywhere.

Just get me out of here.

I'll be a good boy, honest.

I'll never get into trouble again.

Please help me.

Want my mummy.

Imagine feeling like that. My thoughts turn to murder and mayhem.

Aha – movement! I'll catch you later.

Sitting in the sweat-box, listening to the soft elevator music playing in the background; any of you out there who've ever been to a *Motörhead* concert will know what I'm on about – twenty-five thousand decibels is the norm for the sweat-box. They turn it up so they can't hear our cries and pleas in the back. There's a song on which reminds me of my mate Gunner, who recently died in a car crash in Cape Town. I miss him deeply - he was one of the very few people I could talk to. On the night he was killed I was meant to be with him, only I got lucky ten minutes after he called me, sent him a text message saying I'd see him later and to go into town without me. Half an hour later he was dead.

That was a tough break. Locked myself in the house for three days, got absolutely wasted and beat seven bells of shit out of my fridge. My mates kept the dope and the booze coming, but they knew to leave me be - if I'd went out anywhere I would have taken all of my pain out on the first poor, unsuspecting soul who pissed me off. My fridge looks a bit like the surface of a golf ball or the moon from a distance.

Holy shit! Police custody for the night - courtesy of Catford Police station. Back to bread and water and a hard blue rubber mattress. No TV, no soft, lumpy mattress, no lovely hard pillow, no smoking, no fuckin' anything! Just 'Shut the fuck up, convict - I've had a bad day,' from the desk sergeant.

'You had a bad day when you were born, cunt.' Best to keep my gob shut - don't exactly know how this is going to pan out; I'll be seen by a doctor soon - can tell him or her my problems – and maybe get a hotel room for the night.

Can safely say that sitting here, at this exact moment in time, is another one of those defining, pretty low moments. I've got writing material because they didn't search me properly - what a fuckin' liberty! Sitting here, totally flummoxed, I don't know what to do - I'm in agony and turmoil all over again, and for all the wrong reasons; feel like crying, only I'm too numb.

Great! Just got fed - some curry-type thing and a lump of chocolate cake… oh, and a cup of tepid water. I've got bread, crisps, Pot Noodles, tuna fish, corned beef and orange Fanta in my bags - won't even bother asking, though, as a punch in the gob often offends.

When I was searched at Croydon they took my fags and my lighter - not returned; is that not theft? Maybe I'll report it, as I'm in a police station. Of course, there's 'No Smoking' in police cells either. No offers of a phone call to let my loved ones (I mean *one*) know where I am. Human rights, my bollocks.

Asked the duty sergeant to contact my solicitor. After all, you see it on the telly - when someone is in the cop-shop, they always say: 'Oi, phone my brief.'

It's around 7.00pm and the desk-sergeant has called the doctor to come and see me. The only reason I wanted my solicitor to know where I am is in case I die and they don't where to collect the body. You may laugh - I can assure you at this point in the proceedings nothing would surprise me.

Spoke to the doctor around nine; boy, was he pissed off - sharp and abrupt. No bloody wonder it had taken him two hours to get here, simply to issue me with one beta-blocker and two paracetamol; the police are not allowed to give me personal medication from my personal property (in front of an officer of the law, inside a police station), in case something goes missing and I sue them. I mean, come on - how fucked up is that?

Told the doctor I was genuinely frightened of cracking up after having had such a gruelling day - he prescribed me a sleeping tablet.

Asked an officer if the desk sergeant had spoken to my solicitor yet. Was told: 'The desk sergeant has gone off duty and it is too late to phone anybody.'

Told the officer I wasn't happy, and I was too tired to be polite. He tried to reassure me, and told me to give him a shout later if I wanted a cup of tea - a cup of fuckin' tea will make everything all right then? Anyway, *Wilson* doesn't work here, so how the fuck can I give him a shout? The cells are nowhere near reception, so I'll have to bang and kick the door to get their attention, and will probably get the shit kicked out of me for banging the door.

Undeterred, I bang the door.

Someone shouts: 'Stop banging the door!'

No fuckin' tea, then!

If I get the same sort of treatment tomorrow, I swear to God I'll end up doing life. Think about it: I've just served three months in prison, and after one trip to court I have to spend the night in a police station and sleep in my clothes, without the offer of a wash or a brush of the old teeth.

11.30pm

'Please may I have a cup of coffee?'

'Sure, no problem; give me a minute.'

2.30am

After banging the door in an attempt to get the cup of coffee I'd been promised earlier, was told to 'shut the fuck up!'

3.00am

A very young looking cop comes to the hatch, tries to be helpful and makes me laugh it off. Fair play to him - I get the coffee.

The sleeping tablet has long worn off, and I'm primed to get nasty - have had enough and it ain't going to be pretty. Still haven't had a fag. Only wish I knew where I was going - I'm now awake for the day.

As an ex-publican I still know a few guys in the Met, so I ask one of the officers to phone Uxbridge nick and see if my mate's on duty. Stupid move; I tell him not to bother. Clutching at straws; too late for me now - need to accept what's coming.

5.00am

Another officer asks me if I want some more coffee? Politely, I say yes.

Getting light - not long now until the beginning of a new day and whatever it may bring. Am totally numb, in a daze of fuzzy exhaustion. Have lost any faith in the machine - from now on they're all cunts; 'yes' or 'no' is all they're going to get out of me. I'm meant to be innocent until proven guilty, but its clear I'm already a convicted criminal in their eyes.

Enough is enough; no more Mr. Nice-Guy - give me one chance, then *bang*, and I'll be in here for a long time!

Must hold it together, must stay cool, can't lose it – fuck me, it's hard. Need to lie down, but can't - it's too sore; I just stand with my head leaning on the wall. This is it: rock bottom – staring at the floor… staring, numb, broken and empty.

CATFORD POLICE STATION

6.00am

I'd love to be able to take a shower, or simply get washed. Coffee's en-route.

I just have to sit here and chill - the madness begins all over again, like a relentless, recurring nightmare.

Asked for some toilet roll - was given eight sheets; had a pee, missed the toilet - would like to wipe it up, but can't be bothered going through the indignity and embarrassment of asking for another eight sheets of toilet paper, having to explain why I missed the toilet in the first place.

Sitting here with the biggest boner I've had since my birthday, five months previous - not the best time or place for this to happen. My thoughts turn to the librarian at Lewes again - would love to hook up with her in a different life.

Now convinced they put something in the food there - yours truly has never stood to attention like this at Lewes; *that* department has been defunct for the past three months - hardly had a sexual thought, honest. Now I find myself walking round a police cell, bollock-naked, with a raging hard-on. He looks quite well, the old John Thomas, but this is neither the time nor the place.

No sooner have I put my clothes on, than a WPC opens the flap with my coffee. Two minutes earlier I do believe I would have had some explaining to do, or maybe I'd have got lucky! Sheepishly, I sip my coffee; if only she knew. Mind you, don't all police cells have cameras in them? Oh, fuck.

Feeling invincible! Feel as if I have enough pent-up anger to walk through this wall. Lost the plot? Imagine how a psychiatrist could analyze these thoughts.

Forgot to mention, they had roused me around three o'clock in the morning to speak to my solicitor - turns out the messages had got muddled up, and they actually *had* phoned him.

Needless to say, he wasn't a happy bunny. I started to apologize, but ended up saying: 'You know what? Fuck it! I'm sick and tired of working round someone else's fuck-ups.' I'm annoyed with anyone and everyone, trying to find a scapegoat for my current situation, but not succeeding.

Out of sheer boredom and frustration I start to do some sit-ups and press-ups. Gives me time to think - to figure out who's to blame (*'Nobody's Fault But Mine'* by *Led Zeppelin* plays a mean tune in my head - over and over: *'nobody's fault but mine'*). Need to stop trying to work it out - need to simply deal with it and get on with it; get on with the rest of my life.

Shit, my gut is massive - really do need to get some sort of treatment. It's recently ballooned, as if someone was standing beside me, blowing it up with a foot pump. The timing of events in my world is a constant source of wonder.

These few press-ups and sit-ups have made me decide to embark on a fitness regime. But, as soon as I sit down, they bring me a stodgy microwave breakfast - well, I think I've died and gone to heaven: toast, beans, poached egg and sausage; culinary heaven. Mmm - healthy or what?

It was only the other day I spoke to someone about not having a piece of toast for over three months - he said it was *'something to do with Health and Safety'*, or was it *security* (razor blades could be embedded in the hard bread and used as a Chinese fighting star to attack officers with - no fuckin' comment!)? What a treat this is!

See: you whinge, moan and complain about how bad your life is and how fucked up the system is, and all of a sudden they make it all better by giving you two slices of toast. The egg looks like heaven; haven't had a fried egg for three months, either. The creative devil in me takes over and I chop up the egg, sausage, and beans and put them between the two bits of toast – result: the best toastie I've ever had in my weird and wonderful life.

Finish my breakfast and use the lav'. Fuck me! No soap, toilet paper or towel! Wash my arse in the sink and dry my hands on my jeans. No Health and Safety issues in this place, eh?

Next, I'm allowed to have a sink wash, toothbrush and toothpaste in the wee sink (bird bath) in the corridor, guarded and observed closely by two beautiful WPCs; not joking - they are gorgeous. Was going to strip off and throw my cock out to see what happened, but thought better of it - after all, I did just get some toast. I told them of my antics in the sink back at Lewes, roughly twenty-four hours ago, and they were having a good laugh (knew secretly they wanted it, honest).

Personally, I was cacking myself in case yours-truly raised his ugly head again! It's been five months since I've had a bit of nookie, and I'm standing half-naked, only in jeans, between two gorgeous women. Oh God, I can smell their perfume; forgotten how much I enjoy the company of women.

Away with ya, ya dirty, wee beast… get ye away from me, Satan.

All joking on the side; the two WPCs were very kind and helpful, in a very awkward and embarrassing situation, and I thank them for their help.

Ask the new desk-sergeant about my medication, which is long overdue. She politely, and all authoritative-like, tells me what they are allowed to do: they must phone another FME to come and examine me again, and to issue some more drugs; it'll take around an hour depending on the traffic. So, I patiently wait and she arrives about forty minutes later. She is very helpful, gives me a good check-up and listens attentively to my concerns. She then explains her own concerns, stating that she is *genuinely* concerned, which confirms *my* concerns, and also confirms her fears to the desk-sergeant, who, too, becomes concerned. Now I'm *more* concerned!

The tablets go to work straight away.

Have been struck with a startling realization, which is that I'm surrounded by beautiful women in uniform. Apart from the ones locked up, there are no men in the fuckin' station at all! There's a doctor, four WPCs and a desk-sergeant - all women and all supermodels! Not a friggin' ape in sight. Supermodels and handcuffs - oh, happy days! I suddenly develop a Cheshire Cat grin.

Sitting on my hands, dangling my legs from the bench (a bit like a schoolboy waiting to see the headmaster), when one of the models asks me if I'm okay. I bite my bottom lip and nod my head, while the slobbers run down my chin - receive a few strange looks; if only they knew what I was thinking. The wee, Irish devil and I are having a very nasty party.

Given some more paper, and my mate in the Met's phone number. Don't want to phone him - don't want to upset him, or anyone else, come to think of it; feel guilty telling anybody what I've done - they'll probably disown me, anyway.

We're not being moved until after twelve - that's nearly thirty-eight hours without a fag!

Mental note: apply for a job at the Home Office. How many Home Secretaries has the UK had in the past ten years? Seven in total - six under a Labour government.

Might be going to High Down.

Hope Carl is still there - he was my first cell-mate at Lewes.

Day one - *ground zero*! It was a bit like *'Porridge'* in reverse, as I was forty and a virgin to prison. Carl was twenty-two and had been in and out of prison since he was sixteen. We got on like a house on fire; our farting competitions were legendary! We'd a good laugh and helped each other through the early dramas. *Never judge a book by its cover*; for me, this summed up Carl. The wee shit didn't half wind me up sometimes though, able to press my buttons. He made me realize that I had no choice but to laugh and face the situation I was in. He knew all of the ropes and had a bit of savvy - if we'd stayed together we'd both be wealthy men by now. We found ourselves in a nightmare scenario, and in the end true human kindness shone through. Once he plucked up the courage to spill the beans about his problems, I listened, gave examples of how I'd handled similar situations, then left him alone to work it out for himself and decide what to do. The end result - we'd end up laughing, or find something laughable to reflect on (mostly ourselves). Hope he's well.

Will definitely track him down when I escape - I mean, after my release.

H.M.P BRIXTON
7th OCTOBER 2007
10.05pm

Well, what can I say? H.M.P. fuckin' Brixton, of all the places in all the world..!

Still on 'High Risk' - will try to stay that way for the rest of my time inside. Met the governor (not the *actual* governor, but one of the many subordinate or substitute governors), doctor, S.O. (Senior Officer), etc. For now, I'm happy.

The last two days have been hell. Just had a sink shower (not like at Catford, but a real head to toe one), made my bed up and had a nice cup of coffee and a fag.

The prison is situated a stone's throw from my old friend Basil's house. He's dead and gone now - inconsiderate git - and I miss him terribly.

Back in London; back to my roots.

Just over twenty years ago I lay on top of a bed in The Gunter Arms, a couple of miles away, over the river; remember very vividly listening to the planes on their descent into Heathrow. Now, as then, was filled with many anxieties, hopes and unfulfilled dreams.

For the moment, I'll be fine - can breathe properly again, mentally and physically.

It was strange being met by laughing officers, who made a bad couple of days end as painlessly as possible; they've made me smile again, but how long will it last, I wonder. The doctor I spoke to was from back home, so he was able to fill me in a few of the *dos* and *don'ts*.

Going back to Lewes will probably be a non-starter, so I'll have to think about my next move over the weekend. Mr. 'David Bowie' (officer) helped me steal a TV and aerial from another cell; he's black, about six-foot-four wide and takes the piss a lot.

Having to start all over again, though after the past couple of days, things can only get better. No more looking back - only forwards for me.

8.55am

Tigger was on the TV a minute ago. Got five channels now, but no Movie Channel - one hand giveth and the other taketh away.

Been awake most of the night - new bed, new room and new surroundings. On top form - can't wait to be let out into the jungle for my next set of adventures; in exploration and intelligence-gathering mode.

At the back of my mind there's always a niggling doubt: *'how long will this goodwill last?'* My change of address has put the thoughts of MI5 out of my mind; *maybe that's what they intended, and this is all part of a cunning plan to lure me into a false sense of security.*

Being here's a bit like when you start a new job: you've been up half the night with worry, but feel excited and confident at the same time. Managed to write a few letters - eight in total - simply letting people know where I am, and thanking them for being in my corner these past few months. I'm full of enthusiasm, waiting for my door to be unlocked.

If I'm not mistaken I hear the jangle of keys - is this my door being opened? *Good morning, Mr. Irwin - how are you today?*

Nope, false alarm. Must be quarter-past-nine before they open up here.

Outside, there's the jangle of keys, laughter and the sound of people who are happy going about their business. Even the atmosphere sounds and feels different. Totally positive - will just have to wait and see.

Used to love the sound of London - the city waking up, coming alive - especially in the morning. Lived over the river, in Chelsea, for many years. Now, for my first time, H.M.P. Brixton is waking up, the London hum and the roar of descending planes in the background.

Hurry up - need to get out, get the feel of the place, see who's-who and what's-what! What's the regime like? Which wings are best, or worst?

Pavarotti is on the telly singing *'Nessun Dorma'* again; feeling a bit better than the last time I heard him.

Shit, this place sounds big! Couldn't really take it in last night - it was dark and I was totally out to lunch. We'd spent the afternoon, and early part of the evening, going through the committal stage. There were thirty of us crammed into a room with our belongings, and, over the space of eight hours, we were shouted for, summoned and generally pushed from pillar to post, filling in forms and having interviews. Guys were smoking dope, fighting, throwing up… at some stage we got fed, and then there's food spilled all over the shop; it was fuckin' mad! All the time you're sitting there, trying to look nonchalant, but inside your cacking yourself, or wanting to rearrange a few people's faces *(grrr)*.

After we left Catford we drove to High Down, where we sat outside for an hour and a half before they turned us away - they were full up and the only prison with any beds left in London was Brixton, but we had to get there pronto before the courts kicked out. Arrived at Brixton around three; I got into bed around ten. Where does the money go?

2.45pm

Woke up to the sound of pigeons flapping outside my suite, the vibration of *Boom-Boom* music pulsating through the walls, and some psycho on detox. I'm going through the horrors and the noise of the mini-gym on the next landing - sounds like someone shagging (friggin' hope not – if so I'm not going out, ever!). Hope I haven't made a serious error in judgement!

Now, this is more like it - this is how I imagined a real prison looked; can half-understand the psychology behind it now. Had a wee stroll and a few chats, generally sussing the place out: officers seem to be polite and turn a blind eye to certain minor offences that you'd have been hung for at Lewes. Fuckin' hate the loud music and the clatter of pool balls! Still, won't be long before it's over and everyone is banged up again.

The noise? Only us convicts doing time, bro'.

Time to chill and do some more writing; after all, it is the weekend - there's no point asking for anything, as sweet fuck-all gets done.

Eventually, things start to become clearer, more regular - finding a routine once we get onto the main wings and a normal regime. This is 'C'-wing - the induction wing at Brixton; seems fine.

Still waiting to phone my Dad. Normally I'd be going crazy by now, especially if I didn't get what I wanted. But something tells me to play it cool - after all, this is Brixton, with a reputation; the officers smile a bit *too* much for my liking. Plus, I've achieved so much in my first twenty-four hours, now trying not to draw unwanted attention.

Think I'll put the feet up and watch Snoop Doggy, Wallace and Grommit in da Brixton 'hood; *respect, awyite* – innit?

3.52pm

Association is definitely on: can hear music blasting and YPs (Young Prisoner) flexing their still-growing muscles. Hear the buzzing of hair clippers - maybe a YP is getting shagged at the multi–gym, whilst his mate is having his pubes shaved. Must get out more often.

I'm still banged up, yet haven't yet worked myself into a frenzy. Wonder why I haven't been let out. Are MFI still involved, waiting for me to crack - waiting to step in and take another piece of me? *Let's try and see how tough he actually is!* Bring it on, you shower of shit; my conscience is clear - all I want is to tell the truth; after all, isn't the law there to protect you? Though, like the man that I am, I'm already resigned to taking whatever punishment is dished out to me.

Met up with my mate, Reno (same age as me, black Ghanaian), also from Lewes. He's in exactly the same boat as me; if we can stick together life will be a bit more bearable. We've spent three months talking about the more serious aspects of our wrongdoings, and the effect it's had on our loved ones. Can feel a good friendship developing.

One strives to have a bit of faith in human nature, even when you're neck-deep in a crock of shit. Although, like everything else in prison, we'll just have to wait and see: you simply cannot afford to second guess the machine - it'll only fuck you up.

Now that I'm in Brixton, maybe I shouldn't shave my head anymore? Maybe I'll grow some dreads; my hair used to be halfway down my back, and I smoked some radical sensimilla in Basil's, just down the road.

Take a fit of the giggles, laughing at the full circle my life has come - for twenty years I've travelled half-way round the world, meeting thousands of people along the way, and have some fantastic stories to tell, only to end up on the wrong side of the prison wall, half a mile from where I first started.

As I watch the telly, someone is giving Michael Keaton a philosophical lesson on where he went wrong with his life - spookily uncanny! This happens to me quite a lot - used to shrug it off and have another pint. Can't blame these events on the weed or chemical intake anymore. The movie with Michael Keaton is called *'My Life'*. I flick channels, and there's an advert playing *'Lust for Life'*, by Iggy Pop - the theme from *'Trainspotting'*. Wish someone could see what goes on in my head - sometimes if I think about something, it ends up happening! Here goes: *Dad wins lotto... Dad wins lotto...*

Okay, take a tablet, have a wee lie down.

Was watching one of those diet programmes earlier on... whilst eating my sausages, waffles and baked beans, mixed with a tin of ham and a Pot Noodle. Compared my tongue to the picture shown as it should be on the telly - according to the TV doctor, I've a serious liver and digestive problem, which could lead to a heart condition. No fuckin' kidding!? Want to go to the gym, but I'm too worried about my sphincter (it remains intact, by the way - had a strip-search yesterday, but they took one quick look at me, made me do a twirl and that was it. What where they frightened of? Do I look that mean? Does my bum look big? What?).

Finally got my aerial to work properly. It's a wire hanging out of the wall; apparently they are gold dust in here, getting nicked all the time.

Looking forward to phoning my Dad tomorrow, and to the England game. If England scores, cell-doors will be getting banged and kicked up and down the country. I've still got my remote, purchased from Steve - wonder if I can hold on to it until I'm free; this could be a few weeks, or ten years, depending on the outcome of my impending trial.

The S.O. (Senior Officer) looked totally pissed off when I spoke to him earlier. I was standing on the landing, trying to balance my dinner, and other bits and bobs; when I asked him about making a phone call to my father, the purple face and the point blank 'no!' seemed to suggest that I wouldn't be getting my phone call.

Don't push it, methinks.

The landing officer opens my door for the third time in twelve hours, and asks me if I'm on my own; alarm bells start to go off in my head. I know they're trying to double me up, but they can't cos I's on 'High Risk', innit? The inefficiency of the system rearing its ugly head again. Still, the officers seem cool, so I'll presume this is just the way the place is run.

'Grumpy Old Men' is on the telly; can see my Dad and me, having a good laugh making the comparisons - we're as bad as each other, but I love him to

bits. Just want to hear his voice and let him know where I am - two minutes is all it will take.

I've just realized I'm on the *twos* - a bit of a disappointment, as I'm sure the views of London from the *fours* is much better. A brief description of 'C'-wing: there are four landings on both sides, with a high Victorian roof; the suites are proper, single-man jobs, with a separate bog. On my earlier fact-finding mission, I was rather surprised at the size of the place: it's massive! Couldn't get a proper sense of it last night - shows how disorientated I was. Hope 'A'-wing's the same set up - this place looks fine.

Spoke to an Irish guy called Sean earlier - he told me it was best to stay on here if I could, even with the constant flow of junkies, weirdos, psychos and alcoholics, all going through some sort of detox (know *that* feeling all too well). Still, prison has already taught me not take on board words of wisdom that are so readily available from other cons; simply put: don't trust any fucker. Smile, look interested and do the complete opposite to whatever that particular someone mentions or suggests. Or, ask several different people the same question and do the mean, the mode and the median.

Spoke to a shrewd character called Murph. He's a frequent visitor to this establishment - knows the ropes; it's a shame he forgets everything five minutes after he's done it. Not joking; it is fuckin' funny - he has a sincere medical condition, which is why he's been in and out of prison for years: keeps going to rob the same Post Office! Every time he told me about some of his antics I was in bits. When I took the piss out of him he'd forgotten it by the next day!

11.29pm

Dave Gilmour (*Pink Floyd*) is on the telly, playing a live gig. Listening to the music brings back so many memories and emotions: remembering who I was with and what I was doing - getting stoned just *thinking* about the good times! Can remember the very first time I heard *Pink Floyd* when I was twelve, getting a BJ (also known as Felatio or fellation!) from a young girl underneath her friend's parents' piano in the front room. Hadn't yet discovered sex, drugs and alcohol then, so I can remember it quite well! Then, as now, I floated on a warm high when I listened to *Pink Floyd*. Seems like yesterday.

When I close my eyes, my memories play like a slide-show in my mind - can smell and taste every scene. Sitting, smiling, as if I was there all over again, with the people who were so near and so dear; so many have gone, and in my heart I wish they were still here to remember our innocence, our loves, our fears and sheer lust for life.

Dave Gilmour kicks into one of his hypnotic lead breaks (*'Shine On, You Crazy Diamond'*), and I float back in time to the live gig at Wembley Stadium, with Delia, all those years ago. Then, to my bedroom in Glendun, that crisp November, when I moved in with my Dad, at fourteen. The song goes: *'remember when you were young...'*

Of all the places in the world I could have been... instead, I'm sitting here listening to *Pink Floyd*, surrounded by all the drugs a person could want; all I want is a Golden Virginia roll-up and a cup of coffee.

Always wanted *'Shine on you Crazy Diamond'* and *'Bijou'* by *Queen* played at my funeral - these songs represent how I am in my true core, and the lyrics sing the story of my life. Now, I'm not so sure: sobriety casts a different spell.

This crazy diamond will shine on, and the people who are in pain because of my actions will be paid back in kind. It may take a bit of time; the world doesn't know it yet, but I'll be coming back, bigger, better and stronger than ever before, and more determined to fix the damage I've done to myself and others. Passing on my knowledge and beliefs, I know that if I can help just one person, then some good will have come out of this whole sorry affair.

Temporary feelings of guilt are taken over by an overwhelming will to be a better person - time will only tell. *'Momentary Lapse of Reason'* and *'Learning to Fly'* are now playing, bringing back horrible memories of anger I'd felt in my twenties, nearly killing my father in a drunken rage. Then, helping to put his shirt on before we hit the pub for a cure - the emptiness I'd felt when we discussed what had happened, over a few beers. Then, the disbelief, when he apologized for not being there for me when I was younger.

Another one of those turning points in my life.

Remembering watching Concorde about two-hundred feet up, on its approach to Heathrow, on a foggy winter's evening, with an old friend out in Hounslow. We were both out of it on sensimilla - one of those *'wow'* moments.

This is not the time or the place to be remembering such stuff - I'll have to write about them in another book; feel as if I'm heading in a different direction, which I need to save for another day - a day when I'm better equipped to deal with the emotions.

Tobacco getting low again - I'll have to find out what the canteen situation is. Can't believe how quiet it is - almost a still silence: they've taken Wilson away.

'How I wish, how I wish you were here... we're just two lost souls... year after year.'

I'll have to take a wee nap - starting to overload with download; getting dizzy - heart's pounding. Wish I could write to my friends and let them know where I am. Maybe I don't have any friends anymore.

Mind you, do I want anybody to know where I am? I'll have a think about it after my trial.

So much for having a good sleep. Can't blame Wilson or MI5, only myself - got nothing to read; going round in circles, way too calm - need chaos in my life. Need a lot of things - don't want to go down that road either. Starting to get frustrated again - think it's called boredom. I'll sit and flick aimlessly through the channels until I fall asleep.

No food, no milk, no books… no nothing, until Monday.

I'm being starved of activity again. Maybe I'll beat someone up, just to see what happens. Now I'm just being stupid. Or am I?

I wonder how many others will think the same as me? How many people will get up to no good, just because they're bored?

As kids, we get up to all sorts of mischief when we're bored; oh, let's start a riot, especially on Friday night - no school the next day. Anybody got any gum? Let's go rob a Post Office.

A mate of mine went to rob a Post Office once - he had a plastic replica gun, of which he had to tape the end back on, as it had snapped off; when he went into the Post Office he accidentally hit the perspex, and the end snapped off. In the end, he had to give up the venture, as the girl behind the counter was pissing herself laughing.

Remember I said about the anticipation of getting unlocked? This is the zombie hour - you are alive, but dead. Fuck, I could murder a Kentucky!

If only.

No – stop! Can't think of the *'if'* word - can only deal with now: the present; can only deal with the facts, and each situation as it arises, minute by minute, hour by hour, day by day. Glad I'm on my own.

When I was sharing, I couldn't have got up every half an hour to have a fag, or go to the bog - would have to lay there, smouldering, stifling farts and not disturbing the person above me. Was lucky before: the guys I shared with – they were cool. But not all convicts are of the same ilk, and it would only have been a matter of time before the murders would have had to start.

There is a tightrope us convicts have to walk every day: violence is only a heartbeat away.

9.00am

Woke up around eight-thirty, feeling okay.

Must go for a shower, although I'll be on sphincter alert!

Must speak to Dad. Getting angry again - not for me, but for him; still waiting for my personal phone call. My fears and anxieties are coming back.

9.15am

Still waiting.

Too tired – trembling… can't settle. Fuck, I need to get out of this room, have a shower… heart racing - can feel the volcano, just below the surface; want to start killing dead things again.

Unlock. Thank fuck for that!

No, false alarm - heard keys outside my door, then off they went again (*bang, smash, kill, wreck, hurt, pain, tears, severe anger..!).* Feel my earlier optimism rapidly slipping away. One has absolutely no fucking idea how frustrating this place is becoming.

My TV aerial is up on the left, and every time someone walks past, the picture goes all fuzzy. I'm too frightened to fiddle with it in case it doesn't work, and I end up smashing the thing to pieces; poor TV is in mortal danger, and the volcano rumbles yet again.

My heart can't take much more of this - took my last beta-blocker about half an hour ago (mind you, with the state of my digestive system, I won't get the benefit for about an hour or so).

Hear music playing, jangling of keys - some sort of activity going on.

Been banged up since lunch-time yesterday - for fuck's sake, somebody help me… *Aaaggghhh!!* My nerves are fried. Trying to roll a fag while still smoking – can't do it.

9.40am

Nothing's happening. My TV's fucked.

I'm a fuckin' Aries - what chance do I have?

Wonder why my moods are all over the place. Shrug it off - think I'm getting used to it.

This place is more intimidating, when compared to Lewes. The Education wing was opened by Frank Bruno in 2003, according to the bronze plaque. It's a long walk from 'C'-wing to the Education block, so I was able to have a good look around me. Certain areas of the prison are strewn with rubbish, and God-knows what type of debris thrown from the windows at night - I'm always on the lookout for needles and shit; realize now why the outside workers all have heavy-duty safety boots.

7.05am

It's bloody cold - my quest to buy a duvet begins today; the jungle drums tell me it'll be next winter before I receive one!

My Dad will be off to the Post Office, sorting my postal order. Hope he's okay - hurts like hell when I think about the pain I've caused him. He says he has big shoulders, but they aren't as big as they used to be.

My mate in South Africa hasn't been in touch yet - hope he's well. I'm worried about losing my house and my possessions – alas, there is sweet F-A I can do about it at the minute. Have asked my cousin to try and sort it out. If he can, he will. And if not..?

It's a strange old world: I've got Customs 'n' Excise trying to seize my assets, a property developer trying to seize my assets, one asshole and a handful of sharks trying to seize my possessions and steal my identity, and I'm stuck in here, trying to sort out a duvet!

9th SEPTEMBER 2007

I've finally managed to sort most of my bits and bobs out.

My previous problems have paled into insignificance after chatting to a fellow Irish con yesterday - he was staring at a notice on one of the boards, and stopped me to look for the chaplain's number; he couldn't read, but could recognize numbers. Turns out he was being deported - he had just killed his brother in a car crash and been done for 'death by careless driving'. A tragedy for everyone.

Constantly splashing cold water on my face - trying to cool down.

My lists are getting shorter - things that used to be important simply don't matter anymore; slowly, but surely, I'm becoming institutionalized, and going with the flow. Fuck it - don't care anymore! It's first-come, first-served in here and you never do get things sorted - being white doesn't help matters.

I'm able to clearly see how difficult this is for the staff to cope with: same-shit, different-faces, every day. Things trundle on, regardless.

My TV has become a radio, due to the lack of signal. Could have had a hi-fi by now, if I'd stayed at Lewes - I'd ordered a heap of stuff from *Argos*; suppose I'll just have to start the whole process again.

Hear a lot of heated voices outside; maybe I'll just stay in my cell - it's probably safer. Haven't fully got to grips with this place, yet - starting to get that bad gut-feeling again: seems all is not well at H.M.P. Brixton.

I'll have to have another sink shower - went to the shower once on the landing. Fuck that!

I'm at a loose end: what to do, what to do? The cleaners are out cleaning, making a racket, and the phones are ringing in the background - a bit like the bells in my head; clear out the logic and pump up the volume. Still none the wiser about this place, and how it functions (or *dys*functions).

It's ten o'clock and '*we just haven't got a clue what to do*' (*The Sweet*). Think I'll have a wee lie down, but, pumped up, I can't settle - writing is making me more agitated. Trying my best to hold it together, but the volcano still simmers below the surface; not a good place to be. I know it'll be okay, but when?

Need it to be soon - *want* it to be soon. Want this insecurity - this madness - to dissipate: not knowing the outcome of my future, my life in the hands of others, my destiny to be tried and judged...

The cons are playing pool. The music coming from the wing's plasma TV is at full blast, playing some fuckin' jungle-beat. I'm going stir - want to explode, to wreck, to hurt, to maim. Nobody can ever understand how fucked up you get when you're banged up, ten feet from others, who are having a blast. Have to keep shtum - don't upset the apple cart, don't cause any aggro, and don't get yourself into a situation where you will end someone's life, just because they laughed while playing pool.

The cravings start again: the drink, the drugs, the chocolate, the cheese, the sausage, bacon and eggs.

Ten-thirty now - presume we're out this afternoon.

Think I'll put the feet up and watch the radio. There are ghostly images of a cookery programme on the screen; want to cry.

Nothing is funny anymore. Depression envelopes me like a warm, soothing, comfortable blanket - all positive thoughts have been erased, simply out of strength. Time to switch off and try to find the numbness, without the assistance of drink and drugs. Hope I don't wake up.

'Beat It', by Michael Jackson, is blasting out from the landing, and my thoughts turn to my Grandad. At fourteen I spent most of my time staying in his house and going to school in Lisburn.

My grandfather believed in reincarnation. He was stationed in India during the war, and wanted to be reincarnated as a dog.

'Why a dog?' I asked.

''Cos you can shit and piss wherever you want, lick your own bollocks and shag any bitch walking down the street.'

He was a major influence on my life, and I'm glad he's not around to see me in prison.

Unpacking the rest of my stuff, arranging my cell and sorting out my paperwork. Don't *want* to unpack as I'm sure I'll get shifted tomorrow, but put my pics up anyway - they brighten the place up.

11.47am

All done. There's half the day gone.

Managed to put all of my odds and sods in some sort of order (not the normal state of organized chaos) - now I know where everything is. Glad I can now pack and unpack with ease (something you will be doing a lot of if you come to prison).

Have a few more letters to write, then its feet up until lunchtime, like fuckin' Lee Marvin!

At least I can look at my pics and drift off to my favourite places. The *'Serenity Prayer'* is right in the middle; it helps me through each day:

God grant me the serenity to accept the things I cannot change, courage to change the things I can, and the wisdom to know the difference.

12.36pm

TV aerial is driving me nuts!

Had my Sunday dinner - it was cold by the time I got to my cell.

I was informed by an officer that: 'You never know from day to day in this shit-hole when you are getting unlocked.' That filled me with a greater sense of urgency in the quest for a TV aerial. I remind you that I had to steal the TV from another cell on Friday night, with the help of Mr. Bowie - this is why I'm not shouting too much. Managed to rig up some spaghetti-type thing in the back of the telly, and can get three out of the five channels; well chuffed. Seem to remember, when I used to live in London, that the reception was always bad. (Mental note: put in an App for cable or satellite in the morning.)

Just been told Association is at two - I'll not hold my breath. Can't be bothered to talk to anybody anyway. Got three channels and the *Grand Prix* is on.

Did I mention that we have to pay £1 per week for TV licence?

10th SEPTEMBER 2007

8.15am

Managed to relax for the rest of yesterday. Didn't want to avert my gaze from the TV, move from my bed, fart, in case I lost the reception.

The S.O. fixed it for me – how kind? Mind you, the haste in which he did so makes me think that it wasn't the first time, and the fact that he carried a pair of pliers in his pocket was also a bit of a giveaway. Perhaps the pliers are for some other purpose (*torture, interrogation..?*).

Need to lie down and take a tablet – getting increasingly frightened with my train of thought. Can't lie down - I've only just got up!

Ready to face the challenges of a new day.

Find myself in a military frame of mind today, my army training kicking in - my suite is immaculate, and I'll be able to pack and move anywhere in the world, at the drop of a hat; just like the good old days.

The new gang and I are requesting to move to 'A'-wing at first light. It's purely a tactical move: safety in numbers. You can form friendships very quickly in prison, but, as per usual, my advice is: don't trust any fucker - follow your gut instinct, and don't tell anybody anything about your personal life; everything should be on a *need-to-know* basis. Take Reno: I've known him for three months, yet he knows very little about me; I don't trust him - he seems to be alright, but I think he would drop you in it if he had something to gain. Trying hard to keep myself to myself - my trusting nature is what has landed me *in* this predicament, so forgive me if I seem a bit harsh.

Had my first proper shower yesterday - washed away all of the stress, all of the pain, and most of the worry. It was good to get clean – all over – again.

The showers are fuckin' disgusting! When you walk in you have to wade through all sorts of crap: empty shampoo packets, discarded clothing, used, congealed soap, and God-knows what else! Glad I've got sandals on my feet.

My early optimism about Brixton is starting to disappear, very fuckin' rapidly. However, the power shower was good - it was great to get clean and my arsehole remains intact. Had started to miss the showers at Lewes - they were always spotless and there was plenty of room, unlike here.

Still, mustn't grumble. After all, it's my fault I'm here, and everything that annoys me in prison is my fault for being sent here.

Had a bit of a rant at the night-guard last night; I'd been trying to get my phone call - the S.O. said he would tell the night staff, but he must have forgotten, or was simply fobbing me off. The S.O.'s minor indiscretion has been overlooked - after all, he did fix my aerial – and have been told that he's okay, but, one thing I've found out in here is to *take as you find*: if you think someone is a prick, then they normally are.

Should be able to speak to my Dad today or tomorrow, though the letter I wrote will probably get there first. Wrote eight letters yesterday, and was able to get a lot off my chest - mostly positive. My mood has changed for the better, but there's still a niggle, and I can't quite put my finger on it yet. Fingers crossed - hope this continues.

Still think this place is too good to be true. Nothing can be done at the weekends, so I'm patiently waiting to see how much help I'll get in my first week.

Just filled in a fruit list.

Yes, you read that correctly: a 'fruit list', which accompanies the canteen; ordered twenty quid's worth. What a result! Can get healthy now, go on a fruit and veg diet, lose some weight and sort my guts out. I've ordered watercress and herbs; I have visions of a little herb garden growing in my cell.

Maybe not – might be mistaken for a different kind of herb! Even though you can order herbs individually from the canteen, the collective title of a 'herb garden' would probably be unauthorized.

The fruit can only improve my state of mind. I do hope there are no problems - feel as if it's all too good to be true! Don't risk it now: herbs and watercress rapidly scrubbed off the list. Expectations reduce joy - even more so in prison - and if the experience of the past three months has taught me anything, it's want for nothing and ask for nothing, because, at the end of the day, it's easier to be self-sufficient, and nine times out of ten you will get nothing but a headache.

Managed to suss out the *do*s and *don't*s in here - there are more *don't*s than *do*s.

If, like many, you believe that moving house is one of the most stressful things you can do in life, then whatever you do, for fuck's sake, don't come to prison! If you *do* happen to find yourself in this situation, then, whatever you do, don't get sent to H.M.P. *Brixton*! Personally, I think I'm lucky, as I've travelled and lived in many different countries, and am well aware of the inevitable delays and cock-ups; but, nothing in this world can compare or prepare you for the prison system.

Was lucky enough to be standing in the S.O.'s office, patiently waiting to phone my Dad - don't want to repeat what I heard.

Oh, fuck it - I'm going to get ten years anyway! What are they gonna do?

This place is being run illegally – there's not enough staff on duty to cover the day-to-day running of the prison under Health and Safety law. The officers were discussing this in front of me, totally unconcerned about my presence, presumably because I can't tell anyone, and, more likely, who would believe me and who would care?

These guys looked totally resigned to the fact that they were up shit street without a paddle, and seemed to have lost all interest in what was or wasn't correct procedure; on one hand you had prison policy to follow, and on the other you had one-hundred-and-fifty men who have been banged up for three days. They therefore decide to let the prisoners out and 'to fuck with the consequences'. I think they've had to deal with this type of bollocks way too often.

Now I know what to look forward to in Brixton: if I want anything done, I'll just have to sort it out myself - look after *numero uno*; take some of my own advice, for a change. If there is a way of getting something done and not going through the normal channels, do it, then fill in an App, but don't wait for the reply.

The governor can only provide with what he is given - the government wants cutbacks, then the prison gets rid of staff, the population increases, and the only people who suffer are the prisoners: banged up for twenty-three hours a day.

Being 'Enhanced' counts for nothing here, as there aren't enough staff to supervise safely. The officers have given me some free advice: 'Keep your trap shut and get the fuck out of Dodge as soon as possible' - now I can see why, but at the minute all I can do is wait.

My chest pains are getting worse; banged up in an empty cell, hungry, packed and ready to move at the drop of a hat. Found one Weetabix in the bottom of my bag - life is good.

Trying to smuggle the kettle and TV aerial with me to the other wing; you can get into shit if you get caught, but everyone does it. You have to, 'cos when you get to your next cell everything has been nicked by people moving to another wing!

12.55pm

Phew - got lunch and phoned my Dad! Believe it or not, it only took five days – all because of a simple visit to court. The phone call was in the S.O.'s office, and he had a good laugh as I was telling my Dad that Brixton was a shit-hole and all the officers were wankers. I was able to reassure my Dad, and I can't ask for more than that.

Lunch is a different set-up here.

Had three baby Viennas, a bap and eleven chips. The chips were bloody marvellous; think I'll start my diet today.

Moved to 'B'-wing (foreign nationals and 'High Risk') - I'm still on 'High Risk' and in a big, double cell on my own. I put the two mattresses together - it's comfortable, although the bottom bunk is a bit like a coffin, due to the added height of the two mattresses. Looking forward to a stress-free kip (hope I wake up!); feel the stress leaving my body as we speak. Think it's because I know what to expect now: nothing – don't expect any help, and nothing can be taken away from me; my dignity and integrity remains steadfast throughout - after all, it's all I've got left.

3.30pm

'Genevieve' is on the telly; there's a scene which was shot outside The De Burgh Arms, in West Drayton. Used to work there, and lived in West Drayton up until six years ago, when I moved to South Africa.

Oliver Skeet was on the telly last night, having a meal in *'Hell's Kitchen'*; I'd met him a few times, when I worked for Ossie, who owned The De Burgh Arms. Oliver was a *sorter-outer*, and I found it quite funny that if Jim Davidson had only known who he was slaggin' off, he would have kept his mouth shut – trust me.

4.00pm

Have asked the landing-officer twice about my canteen - won't get tobacco for another two weeks if they don't sort it out today.

'I'll get back to you' was the response - when you translate that into prison language, it normally means *'nothing is going to be done about it'*. Oh, well -

I'll have to go on the scrounge and double-up; it was to be expected anyway. I'm not bothered, but that's not the friggin' point.

I'm bored.

No, I'm not - I'm friggin' fine.

No, I'm not; this place is starting to eat away at me - too many frustrations, too many liars, too many people who don't give a shit. Think I'll have a lie down.

4.45pm

Switch on the telly: *'A Place in the Sun'*.

Oh no - it's in Cape Town! The tears and emotions cannot be held back. I know my Dad might be watching this, thinking of me - he was over there for my fortieth. The planes overhead grow louder, in a roar of sympathy. Every time I hear one I want to be on it, flying off into the sunset; if I left now I could be in my local by this time tomorrow, having a pint.

It's not going to happen, and I'm okay about it.

Bollocks! I can see my house on the shore, on the telly! They're filming in False Bay, and I can see the house in the distance. It does cheer me up though, thinking of my mates.

Still maintain I was lucky - was in a bad way before I came to prison, and in a way prison has saved my life: no doubt in my mind that I would have been dead by now.

Have just found out that I won't get Education or fruit for at least two weeks. Have to be patient: fill in more Apps and wait until I get to 'A'-wing. As Reno said earlier: 'If you're looking at a long stretch, a week or two doesn't matter'.

Think I've lured myself into a false sense of security. Maybe it's just the change of scenery - getting out of Lewes. But, still gotta go through the motions all over again here, as there will probably be different staff on duty each time -

the amount of times you have to repeat yourself in prison is infuriating.

11TH SEPTEMBER 2007

7.24am

Been up since six. Must get off this wing.

Smoking my last fag, although I've got two weeks' worth of butts to look forward to – friggin' disgusting, but necessary. Sent a letter off to 'The Jackal'; God, I miss him. It's true what they say about friendship, and counting them on one hand; I'm learning about friendship every single day - it's amazing how so many people have disappeared. Have a mish-mash of emotions regarding *mes amis* - looks like I'll have to go it alone.

Have just realized the date: 9/11. Remember that day well: waking up with a hangover in my flat in West Drayton, watching the images on TV and realizing that America was under attack. Then, heading down to the pub for the day, watching in horror as the events of the day unfolded, changing the world in which we live, forever.

Can't stop thinking about my brother, for some strange reason – keep seeing his face; hope he's okay. Got a searing pain in my chest - that's the way my life is at the minute; feel as if he's sending me some sort of message. Wonder if he knows where I am. He'll probably laugh, shake his head in disbelief and get angry, call me a prick, then try to figure out how to help me; not a lot he can do.

Can't think about him anymore - it hurts too much; my wee brother, who I respect and miss. Could be thinking this way because Northern Ireland plays Iceland tonight, and we don't have a good record against them.

The crazy hour begins again. Have a lot to do before I get banged up for another twenty-three hours - anxiety slowly creeping in.

Witnessed a pretty bad scene yesterday morning, between an officer and a convict - the officer had a file in his hand, and was trying to tell this bloke that he was moving. The convict obviously hadn't got a clue what the officer was going on about - either he didn't speak English, or he was just a complete knob. Nevertheless, the officer was calling him all the wankers under the sun, having a real go. Then, I saw him look at the photo on the front of the file, and slowly realized that it wasn't the guy he was looking for. He furtively looked around to see if anyone had noticed - of course, he would catch my eye, and he knew that I knew that he knew. I gave him a sympathetic smile.

Must get out of this prison, never mind off the wing, if this is the sort of neanderthal I have to look forward to – must get convicted quickly; might try to get back to Lewes.

10.00am

Still waiting to move to 'A'-wing. Was told to pack my stuff, but hadn't *un*packed, so I'm all ready to go. Was told it would be five minutes - that was at nine.

12TH SEPTEMBER 2007

2.35pm

What a day yesterday: had a lovely, chilled evening and went to bed early. Today has been one of opening and closing doors. At 10.00am I was off to 'A'-wing… then I wasn't - told there were no single cells.

Was then told that I wouldn't be going anywhere unless I came off of 'High Risk.' If you want something, they will nearly always say that you can't have it unless you give something up. In my case, I was giving them a problem because I was on 'High Risk', which meant they had to provide me with a single cell; because they couldn't find any they had to put me in a double cell on my own, meaning I was taking up valuable space.

However, if I came off of 'High Risk', I would never get back on it again, and would have been doubled up immediately. Would never be secure in a single cell either, as they could then move me at any time, saying: 'Well, you shouldn't have come off of 'High Risk'.'

They tried the other tactic of getting me to double up with Reno - they ask you in front of the person they think you're mates with, as it's harder to say: 'No, I don't like the wanker'. I've got nothing against Reno, but I just can't do it! I'd end up killing him or some other poor bastard! All they had to do was look at my file - I'm fuckin' sure I wasn't standing in front of half the wing, discussing my unique and personal circumstances.

Was extremely pissed off, to say the least – chest pains where getting worse, and the whole situation was getting out of hand. Getting very angry, I was going to apologize to Reno in front of everyone, but he beat me to it, saying that he didn't want to share with me. What a star - a true gent! Will miss him.

Tortured the S.O.! He was sympathetic and understanding, as I was of him; when you translate this into prison lingo, it means: nobody knew what the fuck was going on, or what was going to happen. By this stage, though, I think we both knew that *nothing* would. He told me to 'hang around, just in case' something did.

This turned out to be a rather fortunate and opportune moment, as I was able to sit and watch the movement and goings-on of the wing, and how everything worked; plus, I had the added bonus of being allowed out of my cell for the morning – no 'bang up', for a couple of hours, at least. Felt fuckin' great - was able to phone my Dad, then simply blended in with the rest of the convicts, who were going about their business.

Had a chat with Harry (a lifer), whom I had spoken to briefly the day before. We walked around the landing, laughing and chatting. What a great guy (I knew he was a bit of a head-case, but I'd lived, grown up with, worked with and drank with plenty, so that didn't bother me in the slightest). He was trying to decide who to take hostage later on – I subtly changed the subject.

Bumped into an Irish guy called Gerry; he spoke to me out of the side of his mouth, like a lot of Irish people do – as if everything is a secret – when telling you something in confidence. He was warning me about Harry.

Thought this was hilarious, and had great difficulty not bursting out laughing - yet again I find myself in a situation where two people are warning me about the other, and I know more than the two of them put together, simply because – believe it or not – I actually do listen, and try to keep my gob shut. I'm very streetwise, and I find it funny when people pretend to be clever, hip and 'with it', when they are not; all this cloak and dagger stuff - especially in prison - is a load of bollocks.

Prison is a place where people cannot be themselves, mainly through the fear of being taken advantage of if you are deemed to be weak, the pressure of being 'one of the lads', and the impossibility of admitting that you are just as frightened and insecure as the next man. Ever since I was a wee boy growing up in Belfast, I've been through this scenario in many different times and many different places, over the years. I still have my fears and anxieties, but now I know how to handle them. Some people, to their detriment, have mistaken my walking away for weakness, and have lived to regret it. I've lost that wee boy a long time ago – Belfast does that to a person.

Fell asleep.

Door opens; 'Irwin. Education assessment. Hurry up – free-flow has started.'

Rush over to Education, only to get to the gate and be sent back, because my name wasn't on their list. Spoke to the Education guy ('B', from India), who assured me that he would sort it out in the next day or two - 'Please be patient,' he said. I believe him.

Got back to the wing and rolled my eyes at the S.O.; he rolls his in agreement and understanding, and lets me wander round the wing. It amazes me how many times in prison a look or a nod is enough to establish an understanding – in fact, more often than not, *silence* is a mutual understanding between officer and prisoner.

The system works in mysterious ways, because by the end of the day I'd got my canteen and had been informed that my future in Brixton had been 'sorted out', one way or the other.

Mentally exhausted - it's been a rather useful day. Have loads of information, but haven't had time to process it all yet. It has taken me a week to get sorted out, and in prison time this is nothing short of a miracle! As a result I'll have a lot more choices, and will know how to proceed when each scenario presents itself. Happy and calm, for the time being.

There's a programme on about Northern Ireland - it's good to see my home, so near yet so far.

6.40am

Have made a few discoveries whilst sitting on the bog.

Forgot that Concorde doesn't fly anymore. When I used to live in Hounslow the TV vibrated as it flew overhead. The unique roar from that glorious bird let you know you were alive – you could feel it in the pit of your stomach.

Speaking of stomachs, I'm off to the doctor this morning.

Had a very restless night - don't know why. Haven't had a shave yet, and look a bit rough (never go to the doctor's looking healthy. And never light a roll-up at the wrong end like I've just done - nearly choked to death!)

After my chat with Harry yesterday, my thoughts turn to murder and mayhem - how callously and swiftly it can be carried out, and how quickly it can be dismissed. One of the 'benefits' of growing up in Belfast is that you are surrounded by murder and violence - you become numb to its emotional effects, as long as it doesn't affect you. Here I am talking to a murderer, but I don't care what he's done or *who* he's done - he hasn't done it to me, and it's none of my business.

13TH SEPTEMBER 2007

4.54am

Apart from my health, most of my other business has been sorted out - all that can be done has been done, and I can only move onwards and upwards.

I've always said that things take time - it's no wonder, as some fucker has moved the goal-posts and changed the rules: I've been told that my life will be in a 'state of limbo' until I'm convicted; this is because the authorities can't make permanent decisions about you until you have been sentenced.

I'm always up for a challenge, and will embrace this next chapter with confidence and positivity.

'That's Life' by *Van Halen* is playing in my head - reminds me of my old pal, Sparky. Vaguely remember bumping into him at a *Flash Harry* concert a couple of years back - my friends Speedo and Raymie played for the band. He gave me a horrible look when we were chatting - he knew I was off my face, even back then; knew I was in trouble, needed help, but couldn't quite pull myself together. I didn't want to, but I'll never forget his look, as if to say: 'Have you not wised up yet? Where's my old mate Mickey?'

Well, I'm back, Spark. As per usual it takes me a bit of time to figure things out, and I've had a little setback in the process.

Hope I see him again someday, and we can catch up and have a laugh about the times gone by… times to come - miss his enthusiasm and startling repartees; he's one of the few who would understand me.

Feel as if I want to get in touch with all of my old friends, but I'm torn by fear: the fear of getting shot, or of getting people into trouble because they are associated with me. People will also jump to the wrong conclusions. There's stigma attached to my crime, when people do find out - embarrassment I've caused my friends and family.

Still, I can't worry about friends and family now - I have to look after myself, and look after those who know; those who care. Those who don't want to know can go fuck themselves – at least for now. I've no time for them. Well, I do, but I can't make it okay for them – I have to be selfish: got to get through my prison time, my way. Can't care about how they handle it - this has to be about me, for once.

Eventually received my medication yesterday - it was a truly wonderful learning experience (being a tad sarcastic).

The nurse is from East Africa. Now the rest of the convicts say she is a real bitch. It's not her fault - it's just another prime example of a complete lack of will or even care to understand the other person.

When she has no answer to an irate question, which she probably doesn't understand, she does the African thing, which is to go quiet, look dumb and stare at the ground, not making eye contact; she will not change this type of response, no matter what you do - she will stay like that until you go away.

Now, try to take a bit of time to think about a wee girl brought up in a completely different culture to your own, who was the light of the village, with her beautiful, big, beaming smile. Remember, we *all* come from Africa - we all come from small villages; the diversity between cultures may seem alien and incomprehensible to us, nevertheless, it does exist. Where she comes from you are not allowed to talk to a man for more than a minute or two, unless you are married, you are not allowed to talk back to a man, otherwise you will be beaten within an inch of your life, and you are not allowed to make eye contact, for the same reasons. She is the pride of the village - the most intelligent girl there; the whole village clubs together and saves enough money to send her to college, where she becomes a trained nurse - the only problem is that the English she was taught is not so good. She now sends most of her wages home to her village for medicine - she has sacrificed her own happiness for the good of her village and family, and her small contributions make life and death differences to the people she loves, and has left behind. She lives in a squalid bedsit, surrounded by millions of strange and rude people, with even stranger customs, all alone, thousands of miles from her family; every day she comes to work in a prison , and every day at work she's faced with hundreds of angry, rude and evil men; all they want is their drugs - all they do is abuse their lives and other people. The amount of money they spend each week on drugs could sort out her village for a year.

Maybe I'm wrong, but all I see is a frightened wee girl. Caught a glimpse of her yesterday when I was walking back to the wing - she gave me a big smile, then covered it up quickly, but her eyes could not lie.

Harry is back down the block. MFI tricked him.

They told him he was moving to the wing he wanted to go to, and threw him in the block instead - they knew he was up to something. At least there were no hostages taken.

We have struck up an instant rapport - he shouted at me when they were dragging him away: 'Oi, Mick, I've got a cracker for your book!' Can't wait to see him again. Will I see him again? All I can do is laugh, wait and see.

14TH SEPTEMBER 2007

I've got two weeks' worth of meds and a doctor's note for two pillows and a back-board.

Achieved a small victory: I'm off to Education later on this morning – ready to go now. Managed to get Education sorted without using the prison system of Apps, etc. Instead, spoke to a Listener, who spoke to a teacher, who spoke to the head of the department, who came to speak to me. He knew I'd been a mentor at Lewes - at the minute, I don't know *how* he knew this, but I'm sure I'll find out soon enough.

Need to start remembering people's names; am great with faces, but crap with names – many years working in the pub trade doesn't help much.

This place is so quiet, it's worrying: it lures you into a false sense of security; the threat of violence and danger are only a heartbeat away. Walking around with confidence and attitude, but deep down inside watching and waiting – anticipating any sudden movements, or things that just don't feel and look right; working your way through every scenario, waiting to pounce – to defend yourself *(fuck it, bang, go mad!)*.

Lost the plot completely. It's so easy to go mental in these places.

Don't think people will ever understand how often you snap. You try not to show it, but you do drift in and out of mental breakdowns; the gaps between mine are getting longer, so I must be starting to cope.

On a lighter note, Northern Ireland have just lost the match by scoring yet another own goal. There was a joke doing the rounds in Northern Ireland a few years ago:

'What was the first thing Saddam Hussein said when they found him in the bunker?'

'Has Northern Ireland scored a goal yet?'

What the hell are the lads doing!? They needed two wins to go through and they lose two consecutive games by scoring own goals. I know everyone loves an underdog, but, come on lads!

My Dad's best mate's son scored a penalty. His poor father will be in bits – Dad's mate's own claim to fame was missing a penalty kick against Juventus in the eighties; it would have got Linfield through to the final stages of the European Cup.

Went to Dad's mate's pub one night, when I was eighteen - he hadn't seen me since I was thirteen; I'd grown up a bit now, and was with my girlfriend. Introduced myself, and we got well-pissed. Told my Dad the next day where I'd been, and he wasn't too amused; don't think fathers like sons drinking with their mates - too many secrets?

Bet you the whole country is alive with smart-arsed remarks and witticisms, as only the Northern Irish can manage. I take great delight in telling people that I beat the Northern Ireland pool champion *twice* - then I mention the ensuing six months of daily abuse and humiliation at his hands and cue.

8.00am

Watching an American sitcom. The message of the programme seems to be that you can tell your father anything and he'll make it okay. How true this is; I'm lucky: I can. Thanks, Dad. My heart goes out to those who can't. No matter how much brain-damage he has given me over the years, he is still always there to bail me out when I screw up - good or bad. Have learnt a lot of hard lessons over the years, and he has always come up trumps.

When I was fourteen, and left my Mum to go and live with him. We had nothing: I slept on a sun-lounger in my grandparents' front room. He went and got us a house. Still we had nothing - just two beds and an old, beaten-up settee; not even a TV. My poor Mum was devastated, and still I regret hurting her, but at the time I thought I was doing the right thing.

Got to get my prison head back - can't go wallowing in that stuff. Not now.

14TH SEPTEMBER 2007
6.02am

Been up since four writing a letter to 'The Jackal' - the only man in South Africa I can trust at the minute - don't have a choice but to trust him. He's moved into my house and has complete control of my future in South Africa, if I ever have one to look forward to.

Can't handle being locked up like this - think I'll have to get a cleaning job on the wing, or something, just to tide me over until I can get fully started at Education.

Apparently, there are only fourteen terminals in the I.T. department, and they're issued on a first-come, first-served basis - as soon as the class is full, that's it. So, if, like me, you live at the far end of the prison, you will always be last, get sent back, and are never able to use the computers.

The library is closed until the seventeenth – I knew this would happen.

Nothing ever runs smoothly in prison, and it's all down to management. Can't wait to make some noise once I get my foot through the door - wonder if I'll ever get to change anything. My patience is starting to be truly stretched, and I'm becoming a real pest to the officers - I'll have to tread very carefully. If I don't, and I crack up, they could send me anywhere, even before I get to trial.

Might have to go insane to be understood, then they will realize that I wasn't in the right frame of mind to be doing what I was doing.

Have tried to be patient, and am still trying to weigh up whether I should attempt to get back to Lewes or stay here.

Harry has been shipped off somewhere and I've been locked up since lunchtime yesterday - can see a pattern developing, and it doesn't look too promising. Will push a bit harder for some answers later on.

Just spoke to the night officer - he has noticed that I'm always awake when he does his patrol in the morning. Talked so fast to him – trying to swamp him with information about my predicament – I'm surprised he can understand me.

He laughs, and says: 'I'll have a word.' Think he may be genuine. A *result* even – will just have to wait and see. Hope nothing happens between him speaking to me and him speaking to someone else, to make him forget about what I said to him.

15TH SEPTEMBER 2007

7.02am

Yep, it's that time again - doesn't time fly when you're enjoying yourself?

Had a pretty good day yesterday. Had to perform much hassling and whinging – generally being a pain in the arse – but managed to get over to Education for both sessions, so I'm well chuffed. Have been told that everything should be back to normal for me by Monday - we shall just have to wait and see.

Wait and see - that's all you can do in prison: *wait and fuckin' see.*

My money has not been transferred from Lewes yet - what a fuckin' surprise!

My Dad has sent me money, and as per usual *it* hasn't gone through either. Now have to go through the ever-increasingly mundane task of telling a different officer the same story I told one of his or her colleagues earlier on.

Dad told me that he had phoned the prison and they said they would phone him back - in prison language that means that the person he has spoken to knows nothing about what is going on, and nothing will probably be done about it; you will then have to get an S.O. (Senior Officer) involved, who will then have to speak to residential governor, who will then have to contact one of the twenty-eight deputy governors, who, in turn, will have to get permission from the governor, who will refer it back to the person which said they would phone back (*'We have all the time in the world'*, by Louis Armstrong, strikes up a very apt chorus in my head).

What a stroke of luck! Spoke to a S.O. - I thought I recognized him: he was an S.O. at Lewes.

He said 'You were on 'F'-wing with Crazy Horse - he told me about you. How can I help?'

Fuckin' result, or what? You see: it always pays to be nice - to try to be on good terms with others, even if they are in uniform. He said that he would be speaking to Crazy Horse over the weekend, and would give him my regards. Hope he remembers - if he does, I'll feel safer knowing that I will always be able to call on him if I've any serious troubles.

We had a load of new arrivals last night.

Listen to me! I've been here a week and I'm already talking like an old hand.

B, the guy in charge of Education, seems like an all-round stand-up bloke. Had a very long chat with him and I'm totally convinced he has nothing to do with MFI.

Clarkie - the I.T. teacher - is also sound. Seems to be a bit of a surfer dude - wonder if he would pass an M.D.T. (mandatory drug test)! Listened to him teach and was very impressed - he encourages convicts to find out the answers to a question on their own; he won't tell them - instead they have to work it out. A cute tactic if done well, although it doesn't work with everyone.

Want to phone my Dad, but I've no pin credit as my money ain't gone through yet. Back to square-fuckin'-one again - this will start the volcano going! Know it'll be another few weeks before everything does settle down and I'll be operating with some sort of routine, in this safe, secure and rehabilitating environment.

Wanted to get a job at the weekend – was laughed at; asked about working in the morning and doing Education in the afternoon – was told to fuck off. I think Brixton is not turning out to be all that I thought it to be - starting to get those negative vibes, man. I'll make myself a list tomorrow, of all the things I hope to achieve and things that need to be done; I'll probably find the list in a month or two, with only one or two of the things on it having been done.

Going to just chill today - take in the life, sights and sounds of Brixton, and check out the new arrivals. I've already seen a few familiar faces from the out, as well as from Lewes. I hope my past doesn't come back to haunt me – I wasn't always a good boy, but not a lot of people know that.

Oh good - Tigger is on; *'The wonderful thing about Tiggers…'*

Wonder if I'm allowed to write to prisoners at Lewes.

10.34am

What a fuckin' place - there're only three officers on duty! Gerry has just informed me, as he was out cleaning the showers and the landing: banged up for another twenty-four hours – no exercise; no nothing. Well, you do get some exercise when you walk up and down the stairs for your lunch and dinner, and you get a bit of exercise in the dinner queue also - jumping out of the way of the inevitable fight or scuffle of some sort.

Welcome to Brixton.

The TV aerial is working just fine, but there's nothing on except cookery programmes - banged up for another twenty-four hours with no canteen, no kit change and I'm friggin' starving. My cell is freezing and I don't have a blanket. *Aagghh!*

I've managed to track down an *Argos* catalogue, and have ordered a duvet, sheets and a pillow – hope I get them before winter sets in. Ordered a few other items too - *Playstation*, radio, etc; anything to make the cell look more comfortable.

Starting to prepare for my future – looks like I'll be spending a few years, at least, behind bars. Deep down I'm resigned to doing some time; I need it – need time to regroup, to get my head together, to think. I'm trying very hard not to let it get to me, but when you are surrounded by so much pain, negativity, doom and gloom, it becomes so overwhelming.

Can't get annoyed – can't even get out in order to get annoyed. Was told to fill in an App for a job, but can't get out to get an App to apply for a job. When you ask one of the three members of staff who are on duty, whilst waiting in the queue for lunch, they just snigger at you - treated like a piece of shit.

Personally, I'm fine, as long as I've a rough idea of what's occurring - it's the other poor sods I'm worried about. After all, it's my fault I'm here. I've come to accept and value my situation for what it is - these other poor fuckers still think they are innocent!

Could be worse – you could actually *be* innocent!

Would love to be able to make people aware of how fragile the prison system is. They say it's running to capacity and they are coping - they are not.

11.00am

Hear one of the officers say: 'Fuck it – let's lock the whole place up and fuck off.' He then shouts out his threat to the whole wing, thinking he is clever - now *there's* a man in control.

The whole wing erupts, goading him even more.

Very fuckin' helpful!

One of the hot-plate guys starts to sing (thinks he's Craig David; could certainly teach *him* to fly – right off the top fuckin' landing! Prick!). The feeling of *us and them* starts to kick in. Vowed I would never do that – hate feeling like this. I know it's just frustration at being surrounded by fuckin' idiots - frustration creeps in every single day; the fights, the threats, the attitudes, the intimidation (and that's just from the officers!).

Two convicts are now discussing the prison system outside my door. Like I need to listen to their point of view, especially as Rick Stein is cooking a lovely bit of swordfish on the telly.

There's nothing else for it - I'll have to get into bed with all my clothes on, as I'm freezing.

It's great having a remote control, especially when you hear something kick off outside - you simply hit the mute button, and it saves you having to get up and turn the TV down, to hear what's occurring outside. Most prisoners put their ear to the gap around the door, which is what causes the draught that makes us freeze.

When you are freezing you go mad, because you shouldn't have done what you did in the first place, to make you end up in this shitty, freezing cell.

5.32pm

Fed and watered - managed to get a couple of blankets from Dave the laundry orderly. David Attenborough is on the telly, doing a programme about whales in Africa - what a pleasure!

Hear an ambulance reversing outside - wonder if someone hasn't been fed (or maybe they *have*).

For now I'll just sit and dream of Africa.

16TH SEPTEMBER 2007

3.00pm

Was doing my bits and bobs around a quarter-to-nine this morning, when the door opened – 'Association,' the officer said; a surprise.

Had a very constructive morning, and even got to speak to the wing governor - now I know exactly where I stand, what to do in the morning, and where I go after my trial: if and when I get convicted I'll be going to High Down, which is cool, because I'll inevitably bump into a lot of guys from Lewes.

Sent a letter off to Crazy Horse, so I'm now happy that they know how grateful I am for their help. Read out loud the *'Serenity Prayer'*: *'God grant me the serenity to accept the things I cannot change, courage to change the things I can, and the wisdom to know the difference'*. It seems to have more and more meaning to me as my journey/adventure continues.

This is the first time I've started to appreciate my new life on the inside - it's truly an eye-opening experience. The weekends are terrible - they drag endlessly. However, I know that in the weeks, months and years to come, I'll have plenty to keep me busy.

Had a lovely lunch. Yes, you read me correctly.

Not bothered about getting back to Lewes at the minute, provided I get my money tomorrow, and the next week goes smoothly. Need to speak to my Dad, but I know he'll be okay. Trying to take each day as it comes - every time I get a bit of positive news or information, it feels as if I've achieved some sort of moral victory. Think I'll just blend into the background for a while; could do without drawing too much attention to myself - could be detrimental to my ultimate goal, which is to get my trial out of the way and get back to Northern Ireland.

Got eight weeks to prepare myself – eight weeks to accept that I'm going down for ten years, at least; eight weeks to set the wheels in motion for my future; eight weeks to make my family okay; eight weeks to face my destiny.

8.20pm

What have I said about getting comfortable in prison?

MI5 are always at work, always working behind the scenes, even when you are sleeping. Have just had a letter shoved under my door; no explanation - nothing. Have to attend an adjudication hearing tomorrow at 10.00am, in relation to my positive/negative piss test at Lewes - a *voluntary* fuckin' piss test, to prove that I wasn't off my face, as I would be in a position of trust by becoming a Listener. Starting to feel as if I *need* a fuckin' Listener. Been told that there's nothing I can do about it until the morning.

Like the way these fuckers operate: they don't pass out the letters until night-time, when there is no fuckin' staff on duty to sort it out. You can smash your cell up if you want, bang your head off the door if you like, but there is *nothing* you can do about it until the morning, when it'll be too late.

I'll see how I handle this one.

Little do they know, I've already received a letter from the lab and the disciplinary board, stating that the result of my piss test was 'negative', and that they had 'made a mistake'. Therefore I'm *not guilty* of the charge I have to face tomorrow at ten. Was given the 'not guilty' just before I left Lewes for court, so

I'd presumed the prison service had forgotten all about it, but they have obviously fucked up, and Brixton is pursuing the matter.

Despite me being innocent, I know this is going to be another fuckin' pantomime.

17TH SEPTEMBER 2007
2.00am

That's me up, preparing my defence for something I haven't done. This situation has caused me a lot of stress. Was a mental wreck until recently - now this comes back to haunt me. Even though I know I'm not guilt and even have written proof from the authorities - I'm still sure they will fight this and I'm very curious to see what they have to say.

18TH SEPTEMBER 2007
6.05am

It's been three months, to the very hour, since I was arrested at Gatwick. Finding myself having to dig very, very deep to keep going.

Not on the free-flow list yet, so I can't get out my cell even to go to the desk - was told point blank to 'Shut the fuck up!' when I asked yesterday.

On top of that my money has not been transferred from Lewes, and my Dad's cheque has not cleared yet. Apparently it takes twenty-one days for a cheque to clear within the prison system. When I asked them at Lewes, I was told that it was still the fastest and cheapest way to send larger amounts of money into any prison. Eventually, my landing officer phoned Lewes about my money and got an answer: my money is in the ether!

This has some relevance, as I've no money or phone credit to even phone my solicitor for advice about my adjudication, which is one of every prisoner's basic human rights. Asked if I could phone my solicitor to seek advice about my adjudication – refused!

Had to fill in another set of Apps, and went through yet another round of verbal sparring with the S.O. - he said it would definitely be sorted by the afternoon; checked later at 5.30 – no joy.

My adjudication was enlightening.

Picked up by two ogres and escorted down the wing, flanked, and very military-like. Everyone was staring; they all knew where I was going: down the block. There was a buzz on the landings, and all I could hear were muffled voices: 'What's he done, then?'

Imagine all of this - like a regimental sergeant major is in your head (like Windsor Davies in *'It Ain't Half Hot, Mum'*): 'Left, right, left, right, left, right... stand in front of the governor and give your name and number.'

'Good morning - how are you this lovely day? My name is Michael Irwin: VP4677.'

Female deputy governor (very good looking): 'Please take a seat, Mr. Irwin.'

I notice the chair is bolted to the floor, about four feet from the desk - *thank you very much, don't mind if I do.* The other lady (also very good looking - turns out to be my wing governor; did I mention there were twenty-eight governors at Brixton?) is sitting behind a computer, smiling. They both look as if they have been sharing some kind of joke, and have now put on their 'serious' face for my entry. There's another ogre here, but he just looks plain angry (clearly in a very bad mood).

Q: *Do you know why you are here?*

A: *Oh yes - I find myself, yet again, having to deal with the incompetence and mismanagement of the prison service... blah, blah, blah...* I'm so angry it's un-fuckin'-real.

Q: *Do you have anything else to say?*

I give them the letter and the result of my negative piss test - the mood in the room suddenly changes. 'Please leave and stand outside.'

Had to stand outside in the cell-block area and watch some nut-case chewing the bars of his cell – he'd no teeth, and was bollock-naked. He went to sit down on the floor, near the back of his cell, mumbling to himself, whilst being watched by two ogres – obviously on some sort of supervision thing. I'd seen him on the landing a few days earlier. All of a sudden, he jumps up, runs at the bars and bangs them with his head – he ends up rolling around on the floor, shouting: 'Bastards! Bastards!'

The two ogres look at me and roll their eyes. The bloke's obviously off his rocker, or maybe he's just had a verdict from the adjudication board!

Called back into the room.

'Not guilty – take him back to the wing.'

That was it. No explanation, no 'have a nice day' – nothing.

The atmosphere on the wing has changed.

One of the servery guys thinks I was involved in a scrap the day before. He's a young, black kid, who thinks he's the dogs bollocks. He starts to jump around, shadow-boxing in front of me. He may well be the dogs bollocks in his world – not in fuckin' mine, he ain't. Am so tempted – just for fun – to let rip and beat him to a pulp. Instead, I walk back to my cell; dignified, back straight, looking cool - pull the door behind me. Then I roll the mattress up and knock seven bells of shit out of it.

The fact that I've been for an adjudication that nobody knows about gives me a bit of street-cred on the landing - the fact that the servery guys think it's about fighting gives me a bit of cred with them, and the officers will think that I can handle myself, and that I've dealt with the matter without causing them or their colleagues any harm (although I could have done the complete opposite, if I'd wanted to). Too tired to worry what anybody thinks.

Got two Rizlas (fuckin' gold dust in this place) left. Think I'll have a fag and lie down.

Asleep by nine, awake by two - restless as hell, probably due to my mental state (verging on madness).

Finally got my £5.00 phone credit, which will have to last me two weeks (did you know that a prison phone call is 70% more expensive than a normal BT landline call? If you try call a mobile, or overseas, ten pounds can be gone in one minute! No wonder people smuggle in phones: it's not to run their criminal empires or intimidate witnesses – they simply want to make a cheap call!).

My money won't be sorted out for a while, either. The post is worse here, the admin is worse here, and my brain is starting to hurt more. The only positive thing to happen is that I'm going to I.T. classes full-time, and don't have to spend my days on the wing, or banged up. And the only reason *this* has worked out is because the prison service has not been involved - the Education department and I sorted it out.

I still haven't had a reply to my application for a job yet.

Can't help but worry about my house in South Africa - another topic that's eating away at me.

Although I'm angry and frustrated, at the end of the day there is nothing I can do about it at this particular stage of my incarceration; can't plan ahead – decisions about my future are not within my control anymore. It has taken me a bit of time, but I now realize that whilst in prison, you simply just do what you gotta do. There is no point worrying, or stressing about the life you used to have; for now, it's over – you simply have to keep breathing to see the sun rise. Who knows what the tide might bring in?

Spoke to a Ghanaian guy in my I.T. class. He was severely depressed, and was telling Clarkie how hard done by he was. Clarkie gave me a look as if to say *'give us a hand here'*. I'm glad the guy was reassured by the fact that he was not alone, and that whilst he was in prison, he was part of the same boat we were all in.

He said: 'But you're always laughing and smiling.' All I could do was laugh.

He's across the landing from me now, and we always great each other with a big smile and the odd laugh – enough said.

Although I know it's a good thing to try and help others, I can't help but wonder what must I do to make it work, to make it stick, to make it last?

About to use my last Rizla. Won't be able to buy any until Friday. Of course, I'll be able to get some if I ask, but my pride is starting to suffer a bit; fed up asking for things and getting knocked back by the officers - ends up having an adverse effect, something as simple as asking someone for a cigarette. I'm out of coffee, sugar, salt, and limited to three fags a day.

All of this due to incompetence of others. No, I can't blame others. It's *my* fault I'm here. And if I'm truly honest, I'm *glad* I'm here - need a break from the world, need to heal, need to mend.

Haven't been to the Listeners course yet. Don't know if I've handled the situation properly – probably not. Don't know what to do for the best.

Another convict hung himself last week - that's four I know of in three months. These guys are not going to get the help they require in prison; the amount of people with learning difficulties and mental health issues in here is staggering! Was talking to a big, black guy who spoke like a ten-year old; he was enormous, yet all he wanted to do was get in touch with his Mum - he looked so sad and frightened. The officers ended up taking the piss out of him.

Of course, yours-truly couldn't stand back and say nothing. Hope I was able to help the big lad out. At least I was able to point him in the right direction, and, if he comes back, I'll go with him to make sure he speaks to someone who's in better a position to help. Now I understand the difference between listening and counselling - there's a very fine line. Now I know why the Samaritans emphasize the *listening* and not the *talking* bit. Can't imagine getting caught up in so many people's problems day after day.

Received a letter from Steve (Chelsea) yesterday - his words cheered me up no end.

Had a chat with a guy at Education, when we were having a smoke break on the fire-exit stairs. He reckons Brixton is an information-gathering centre for MFI, and I should be careful who I speak to. Many people have mentioned other crimes being brought up at their trials - the only place the information could have come from was inside here. If only until after my trial, I'll suppress my naturally outgoing personality - I'm already paranoid as it is, for fuck's sake!

Everything I've said has already been taken down and used against me, from the line of enquiry and questioning by Customs and Excise. If I hadn't said 'no comment' to my questioning at Gatwick, and at Brighton police station, members of my family could have been arrested - people who simply just *know* me could have been in here with me; fuckin' frightening.

The customs guy going through the arrest procedure was infuriatingly slow, especially with the paperwork; it turned out I was his first case - the prick had to read the line of questioning from a manual, and it was like watching paint dry.

The other customs officer finally had to step in and ask me if I was going to say 'no comment' to all of his questions, to which I replied: 'No comment'. He and my solicitor looked so relieved when the interview was wound up. No bloody wonder if they are on a fishing trip.

Have to get real though - when you look at the evidence, I'm fucked.

Could have pleaded guilty: get seven to eight – serve three-and-a-half to four. However, I simply will not plead guilty to something I didn't know about. I know what I had done previously, and what I was meant to do after I came back to London, but at no time had I agreed to bring cocaine into the UK!

Set up, hook, line and sinker! Couldn't see it coming – was too wasted to even care.

However, I did set out to bring cannabis back, so, in the eyes of the law, I did commit a crime and I believe I should be punished for it. Just not the one I'm charged with.

I'm enjoying the *GIMP* photo imaging software in the I.T. class. It's actually a very clever, free graphics package, and I look forward to the day I can master it. Had a good laugh with Clarkie about the name, and that scene in *'Pulp Fiction'* with Marcellus, The Gimp and Z.

'Countdown' is on the telly, and I can't help but giggle. The count-down clock is ticking (a bit like my life) - my thoughts turn to *'Peter Pan'*, and the battle Hook has with the crocodile that swallowed the clock.

Hey, I've just been talking about 'Z' and Carol has just picked out a *Z* - spooky or what? How often does that happen? *Déjà-vu* all over the shop!

The night-guard opens the flap, and I'm sitting laughing to myself - it's only a matter of time before they lock me up in padded room.

The conundrum for the day turns out to be 'PRATTLING'.

I'm off to bed.

Shaving as the dawn breaks, I'm twenty-one again. Remembering watching and listening, as the planes begin their approach to Heathrow, the vapour trails like a thin brush stroke gliding across the sky. Oh, how I've grown since then - not only in size, but mentally also.

Stamford Bridge is on the morning news - the 'Special One' (José Mourinho) has left Chelsea. When I lived by Stamford Bridge I had a ball; never looked forward - just lived for the moment, day by day, week by week. Now I'm doing the same thing, only without the hangovers and behind bars.

I remember one time waking up in Hammersmith nick, after being scooped on my way home at two in the morning for being drunk. It was my twenty-second birthday. My mate Colly couldn't carry me any further and had to take off when he saw the police coming; he propped me up in the doorway of Chelsea Town Hall. The cops picked me up, threw me in the back of the meat-wagon and drove past the house we were staying in – I saw Colly going into the house, but was sober enough not to draw any attention to him.

Even then I was guilty… of having a Belfast accent!

Back in those days, if the cops picked you up and heard your accent you were automatically IRA. So, if you were picked up drunk, they would hold onto you and try to get you to talk about something, especially as you were pissed. They could even *say* that you'd said stuff, and you wouldn't remember if you had or hadn't. Could never figure that one out, though: have you ever tried to make sense of an Irishman, even when he's sober, never mind pissed?

21ST SEPTEMBER 2007

6.20am

There's the end of another week. How time flies when you're enjoying yourself.

Need to get onto free–flow early this morning - this will not be easy, or even possible, if yesterday was anything to go by: three officers on duty (totally illegal), though later in the day they had a full quota. How they manage to cope I'll never know - if it kicked off they'd be in the shit, big time. Have spoken to a few of them (officers, ogres) and asked them how they feel - some are more willing than others to voice their opinion: many feel as trapped as we do.

If the police are able to voice their opinions through rogue officers and the media, why can't these guys? Why don't the cops and the prison officers get together and take on their employers? I know they aren't allowed to strike, but for fuck's sake! What sort of power could they demonstrate if they talked in unison? I recall the vivid images of the miners' strike in the eighties: miners screaming in the faces of police officers in full riot gear – a bit like back home. Miners ending up in prison – families being destroyed at the hands of an uncaring state. Think of the power - the police and the prison service combined: fuckin' frightening. Imagine if they did rebel.

This may sound a bit revolutionary or archaic, but the point that needs to be made is that the general public which pays for these services does not have a clue about what goes on. Spoke to a few police officers during my time as a landlord, and some told me that on certain days they have been the only officer on duty within a twenty-mile radius. How the hell can they protect the public if there's none of them there? Feel as if they would receive a lot more support from the public if they got together.

Another news article comes on about deaths in prison.

Made out another fruit order - the last one wasn't received, apparently. Look forward to starting to eat healthier.

Would use the exercise bike, but don't have the time - wanted to get over early, so I could slip into the library before lessons. The library is on the floor below me, in Education, but it's virtually impossible to gain entry - will have to try and remedy that situation; the librarian seems nice, though not as nice as 'M' at Lewes.

Need to find myself something to do at the weekends – they are so fuckin' boring.

Have finally to get some sort of routine going.

Six hundred people have died in prisons, police cells and secure hospitals. I know figures are always manipulated, but fuckin' hell - that's a bit steep, isn't it? How many of these deaths could have been stopped? All they need is some sort of risk assessment put into place. These people no matter what they had done, needed to be protected and some needed help.

I've been told that the Listeners course was postponed until the 8th November. If I'd gone back to Lewes I'd have been doing the job by now!

Been trying to get a message to Reno - I've been told that he's clammed up, and isn't coming out of his cell. But they won't let me go over to see him as I'm not a trained Listener.

23RD SEPTEMBER 2007

3.16am

Have finally developed a decent type of routine and I'm much more settled. Here's an idea of a typical day in prison:

A DAY IN THE LIFE OF - - - - - - -

6.00am

It's that time of the morning again: the five or ten minutes between sleep and being awake - the time when your brain starts to stir from its slumber, the time which slowly stirs you from the warmth of sleep. You haven't opened your eyes yet, but your ears are working - you can hear the silence occasionally interrupted by the chirping of the birds, or pigeons cooing.

If you are resident in London or another big city, you can hear it coming alive. In London, you can hear the planes starting to arrive, slowly descending, as they approach Heathrow. If you're in the country: nothing – just the birds. In London, the rumble of the trains, or the tube in the distance, and the gently increasing hum of the traffic, interrupted by the staccato of a siren - an ambulance maybe, or a cop car. In the country: nothing – just the birds.

Your brain starts to register, slowly, how warm you are, how peaceful you feel, how good life is, and all you can think is that everything is well in the world.

Then you hear the banging – metal on metal, the voices, the jangling of keys, the laughter, the different accents, the macho comments, the false laughter, and the girlish giggles.

Then, bang!

Like a clap of thunder, a punch in the mouth, being hit over the head with a baseball bat, you see stars - your body is weak, your head starts to spin, you feel the nausea creeping through your soul, and the bile fills your throat and your nostrils, as, suddenly, you realize where you are. Prison – H.M.P. or some other private institution; for me it's H.M.P. I open my eyes and my heart sinks.

Oh, God - why did I do that stupid thing?

Oh, well - no point crying. Time to get up - the forces of nature dictate so.

There is no proper time-frame for what I've just described, although, for me, the mornings are the worst part of the day. I will never get used to it, nor will I ever be happy about it - for me, these minutes are the hardest. This is the time when you have to dig deep; this is the time when you have to decide who you are, to find out how strong - how much of a man - you truly are.

Every single day you remind yourself of why you are here and what you have done – personally, I blame no-one but myself: the same dickhead looking back at me in the mirror.

'Fuck you, asshole! Let's just blank it out and get on with the day.'

6.30am

So, you do your ablutions, have a shave, a fag, a cup of coffee, meditate, say a prayer, feel sorry for yourself, try to escape, smash your cell up, strangle the budgie (or cell-mate) and whatever else floats your boat

7.30am

You hear the keys approaching. They are never the same - they always sound different; after a period of time you can tell which officer is on duty, just by the way they handle their keys and unlock the doors. They don't need to speak - sometimes you can tell who it is just by the squeak of their shoes.

The wing starts to get noisier - it generally ends up being a constant, reverberating hum; all of these places would be a sound-engineer's nightmare! If you've ever had a bad ear infection you'll know what I mean. Sometimes you don't want to walk out of your cell - the door muffles the noise.

When you do get out there, it's like Grand Central on acid. Everyone is on a mission. This is one of the most potentially volatile points in the day - there are so many flashpoints! You normally have thirty minutes to get your bits and pieces sorted out. Everyone has a frown on - everyone is touchy, edgy, and mainly homicidal; it never ceases to amaze me how arguments start over the most minor of details: I even saw a fight break out between two mates, because one of them didn't say 'Good morning' to the other! Most people in real life are nasty and grumpy in the morning anyway, so you can imagine what it can be like in here. Guys have been sitting festering behind their doors all night - the anger, the frustration, the depression, and the futility of not being able to undo a foolish act builds up inside, ferments and simmers. It's no wonder it kicks off, and it's not surprising that a lot of people choose to stay behind their doors. After a while you get into a routine, and always say 'Good morning', even if you don't mean it.

8.30am

Bang up and head count - this gives you time to have another cuppa, fag, murder the budgie, etc. and to plan your day. Some go to work, some go to Education, some do in-cell education (banged up), some people are unemployed (banged up), some people are unemployable (banged up).

At this point, I feel as if I must interject. My cell door has just been opened, so that they can check my cell to make sure I haven't dug a tunnel (I'm on the third floor), or loosened the reinforced concrete and metal windows. The unit manager is leaning in the doorway, with a cup of tea in her hand. I ask a question about getting my Education classes sorted out; it could have taken her two minutes, but she can't do anything about it - I must sort it out with the Education department.

Fair enough.

I've just moved into this cell yesterday evening. It's dark blue, so I put a football picture up on the wall to make it look a bit brighter – homely, if you like. Was told to take the picture down - pictures were only to be displayed on the noticeboard provided (I don't have one); furthermore, my cell is not allowed to be this colour and it will be painted white immediately - as if *I'd* fuckin' done it! If it wasn't repainted within the week I'd get a 'red-entry'!

9.30am

The head count is complete - sometimes it's wrong; in some places it's wrong more often than others, depending on staff intelligence. Counting is hard you see. The wing cleaners are let out, and the boom-boom of the bass starts up from certain cells. The cleaners go about their business: shouting, banging, and trying to sing, but, generally, talking bollocks. If you are trying to do in-cell work you need ear-plugs, if you're trying to read you need ear-plugs, and if you're trying to watch the telly you just turn it up.

11.30am

Unlock for lunch. You queue up, have a chat with whoever is around, and try to sort out any arguments you had in the morning. You eventually get your lunch, which is served up by the mild-mannered, helpful and ever-smiling servery guys; it has to be the most stressful job in the prison, because these guys never smile, innit. Okay, you get the odd one with a sense of humour, but if you've ever seen Godber slap on the mash in 'Porridge', that's what it's like for us, twice a day.

Must explain that the food is always monitored by an ever-watchful officer, and favouritism never, ever happens, honest!

You then go back to your cell to eat your lunch. In this particular establishment the exercise yard is also sometimes opened, so you bolt down your dinner in an effort to get some fresh air and walk off the indigestion caused by bolting down your lunch. It's pretty good here, though - you do get an hour for lunch, and you can sit at some of the tables on the wing and have a chat with your fellow convicts. However, in other places, you get let out one landing at a time, then it's straight back to your cell and bang up.

12.30am

Bang up. Time for a snooze, feet up, chill out or try to resuscitate the budgie!

1.30pm

Move to work, Education, etc., same as the morning . The only difference is that most prisons have Association during the morning or afternoon session. In here, if you're not working or at Education, you're banged up. So, if you're too embarrassed to go to Education and have a health problem, you're fucked.

The cleaners are let out, and in most places the guys are given a chance to get to the gym again, in the morning or afternoon session. Again, this all depends on things running on time, and if the head count is wrong, bang up. In some places it's a nightmare - sometimes you don't get unlocked until after three, and by that time it's too late to start anything, so they just cancel everything - no explanation given - and lock you up again. So, you end up behind your door, going mad – literally. Some of the procedures set out in certain places are a recipe for daily disaster, leading to a pissed off workforce trying to control a pissed off population.

4.30pm

Unlock for dinner. Same as lunch, although most people are more settled and in better form, especially as the day is nearly over.

5.30pm

Bang up for thirty minutes - this time is used by the officers to do whatever they have to do. I watch the news and do my dishes.

6.00pm

Unlock for Association. Everyone (apart from those on basic) is let out to play pool or chess, have thirty more minutes of exercise, or walk about aimlessly, reading the walls to find out if there are any new notices or rules - any new information will do. If there is no news, you make up your own, start a rumour, or just hang around and discuss the bollocks of a day you've just had. You normally find a bunch of guys you can get on with, so you can ask for advice, give advice or generally chew the fat.

7.30pm

Bang up. Settle down, watch the telly, write a letter, do your homework or fill in a request for a new budgie. Sometimes I forget where I am when I watch the TV - it's only when I get off the bed to walk the four feet to the toilet that I realize. Some places are an absolute madhouse at this time of night - people passing stuff from window to window, or door to door, shouting, screaming, yelling, music blaring, and people getting dragged off to the seg block for smashing their cell up; all sorts of fun. This place is cool, though - most of the guys here (like me) have long sentences, and just want to be left alone to do their time.

8.45pm

The night staff comes on - normally just one person. They do their count, and sometimes they ask if you're okay, or say goodnight - not very often, though. Then, you're on your own again.

11.00pm

You drift off by using breathing exercises and good thoughts. This doesn't always work, so you end up getting up and pacing your cell, getting more frustrated or more depressed. Sometimes people don't wake up.

Watching a documentary about Elvis - filled with tears as 'The King' sings: *'You were always on my mind'*.

It's my niece's birthday today, and I've just missed my sisters' - don't understand why they've turned their back on me. I'm sure it's only temporary. It takes some people longer than others to get over things - I'm sure they are still reeling from the shock of what I've done; then the anger will follow.

If you come to prison, you'd better believe it when I say that prison is not the hardest part - dealing with your family whilst you're in prison is the hardest part.

Can't think about stuff like that, not in here - it'll fuck you up in the long run. My Dad has told me that at the minute he is furious with me and at the trouble I've caused, but at the end of the day I'm still his son, and he will do anything he can to help me. Know my Mum will be going nuts, but she will take her time - eventually I'll get a letter saying how long it took her to get over the initial shock, the pain, the disbelief, the denial, the anger... etc. I need her now, though.

That's the trouble with prison: When you hear someone say: 'I didn't hurt anybody', they're full of shit, and haven't understood why they are in prison.

The first people to suffer are the victims and their family, then your family, and then you. Can only try not to be bitter and angry, as I know it'll all pass.

Had a good enough day yesterday. It was long and boring, but at least I'm well rested.

The day started off with a bit of drama - Gerry left me three boiled eggs, outside my door, when he was doing the landing, just before unlock. Was gagging to get into the shower before anyone else, so, I lifted the eggs quickly, set them on my bed and hurried off for a shower. Came back from the shower, switched on the telly and Elvis was singing *'Suspicious Minds'*. Couldn't find the eggs anywhere! Told the guys to put the word out.

Positioned myself in a strategic spot on the threes - eyeballed everyone;

wanted to see if any fucker had egg on their face! Was in a scrambled sort of mood all morning.

Found the eggs at lunch-time – where I'd wrapped them up in a T-shirt, before I went into the shower (or was it after - can't remember now, and couldn't remember then). When I think of the countless lives that could have been lost! As it turned out, I smashed the fuck out of my cell, made a few more enemies and was the only person with egg on his face.

This is how these places get you! Imagine, in a place full of thieves and vagabonds, you'd think something goes missing. Who'd 'ave thought it?

Lunch consisted of very-scrambled eggs, a sausage made of cardboard and a Frisbee waffle, between two bits of stale brown bread. Fuckin' marvellous! There's a video-diary on about Iraq, and one of the soldiers is saying how much he misses the simple things in life, like nipping out for a Kentucky or an Indian. Uncanny!

5.20pm

Just had a blazing row with one of the servery guys over a slice of bread. I'm tired of feeling hungry all the time - need brown bread to keep up the fibre content in my diet. In Brixton, they hand you three slices of stale bread, depending on where you are in the queue, how many people have pushed in, and how many loaves the servery guys have taken for themselves. Asked politely for one extra slice and the attitude of the little prick behind the jump made me see red. Felt embarrassed and angry, and a bit like Oliver *('please sir, can I have some more?').*

29TH OCTOBER 2007

8.00pm

Haven't been writing too much lately – was going through a bad patch; needed to switch off before I hurt someone. My trial starts next week. Whilst trying to cope with that, and all the bollocks that goes on in here, it all got a bit too much - I was in a bit of a state. I'm fine now.

Was able to keep my father up to speed. Realistically, he is the only person I'm in contact with: have written to everyone I'd regarded as a friend - no reply.

It's not their fault - it's mine. Don't blame anyone, but could sure use another shoulder.

Like most people, I've been putting a brave face on things, although inside I'm crapping myself. My solicitor's a wanker (they all are), and I've gone over and over my defence; if *I* was in the jury, I'd convict me.

Nevertheless, I'll not cop a plea - refuse to plead guilty to something I didn't knowingly do. Ten years looms ever closer. It'll be a miracle if they believe me.

Having said that, I mustn't give up hope - as long as *I* know that I've told the truth in a court of law, then I can continue my life with a clear conscience. I've come to realize that Shakespeare was right: the law is an ass.

My case is not about what is right or wrong - it's about solicitors and barristers being paid to defend someone who was caught with what now turns out to be 1.1kg of the lowest-grade cocaine in his possession - the fact that I'd agreed to carry cannabis and was duped into carrying coke is irrelevant. The fact that I'd searched the suitcase before I left the hotel, felt round the interior and tapped the steel frame of the case to make sure it was hollow, was told that the baggage-handlers would be putting the cannabis into the bag, that the bag was coated in a chemical to put the dogs off, that I was never meant to touch the bag again, and that a woman with my photo would introduce herself to me on the plane, means nothing. It's all about sentencing and money.

The fact is that Customs and Excise were waiting for me, and at the same time the guys I was working with tried to break into my house in South Africa - they obviously knew I wasn't coming back, and were trying to get my bank details, car, deeds, etc.; this would have easily covered whatever they had spent on setting me up. Still, I played with fire and… well, what can I do?

I've got loads of plans for my future - all positive. Need to get out of Brixton as soon as possible though – I'm in limbo here. Will definitely continue writing - I'll start a new piece after my trial; see how my life pans out.

Oh, God, I'm frightened.

Another new day with a new set of feelings and emotions.

Been getting up a bit earlier each morning, purely in the interest of motivation - building my resolve for next week. I'm convinced I'll be getting a long stretch, but I find it hard to write about. When I see it in black and white, it looks so final: 'TEN YEARS'.

My Education classes are coming on leaps and bounds - I've started to learn how to design web-pages. To tell you the truth, comes the night-time and I'm knackered. Eight weeks ago I could do spreadsheets, database and word–processing, as I'd already had a qualification in 'C.L.A.I.T.', gained ten years ago from Banbridge College; now, here at Brixton, I've learned about *Powerpoint* presentations and have gone on to make animations using *GIMP*. Managed to put all of this together, and, by Monday, I'd started to design my own website.

Well chuffed with what I've achieved in such a short period of time, especially with the constant aggravations of my impending trial and the day-to-day bollocks of being in prison. B, Clarkie and G have been brilliant; Clarkie has taught me a lot - not just about design, but how to help others. He has a warped and twisted sense of humour, and a real cleverness in his teaching methods; pushing the arsiest of arseholes in the right direction. I feel as if education is my saviour – it feels like my own type of sanctuary, when I leave the wing and get into the classroom; nothing else matters when I'm working. I've finally found something I would like to be good at - to take pride in something again. For far too long I've been living it up and letting my standards slip. In a weird way, I don't mind if I get ten years.

You have to be serving at least four years if you want to be considered for an Open University degree - three or three-and-a-half is no good, so I've been told. I could make a long list of faults with education within the prison system, especially the prison officers' attitude to prisoners even attending Education classes - there are so many restrictions and conditions attached to education, it makes it very difficult to deliver anything more than the basic skills. There are so many creative and resourceful guys in prison, yet very few within the establishment want to channel this creativity into something productive.

Prison policy is to protect the public, to help stop prisoners from reoffending, and to make them acceptable to the community upon release, but this is all a crock of shit: here at Brixton they want to halve the sessions in Education, so that the core day is easier to manage - due to staffing levels they find it impossible to deliver a regular regime. Apparently the solution is to have one session of Association and one session of Education per day, so the people who want to do something constructive are having their time halved, to spend the other half of the day standing around, getting into trouble!

Have a doctor's appointment this morning - need to get put on medical hold. My health is bad and I don't want to leave Brixton until I get to a hospital. It's highly likely that I'll not be returned to Brixton on at least one of the days of my trial, and will probably have to spend the night in a police station again; could end up spending the *whole week* in a fuckin' cop shop! If they send me to another prison, I'll have to start the whole process all over again - if I ever live that long. If the machine continues making me move from jail to jail, it could end up being nine months since I was first told that I needed medical treatment - nine months is significant, as I look as if I'm about to give birth to twins!

My hormones are all over the place.

I'm taking thirteen tablets per day - the last time I had to do that was when I had an accident and hurt my back; it was three fuckin' years before I stopped taking them! Had to stop, as they were fuckin' my stomach up.

After three years of scratching to stay alive, I was awarded damages (around about £100,000); that's when I started to take the heavier, non-prescribed 'medicine' - not to kill the pain or make it go away, but simply to become numb to it - the pain was always there. Even then, nobody believed me; even then, there was nothing they could do: I'd crossed the line.

People wonder why you do certain things in your life. My reasons were to get numb - only the warmth of drink and drugs numbed me to the constant pain I was in. Little did I know back then, that my pain was more than physical - something had broken in me: I'd become disillusioned with life and was on a downward spiral, clinging on by desperate measures.

I was always in control - knew exactly what I was doing.

Even when I was making the wrong decisions.

Was I always in control - even when I was sitting on the plane?

Was I always in control - even when I was transported to prison in handcuffs?

Was I still in control - four months later, after enduring cold turkey and plenty of time to face all my demons?

The booze was just an accomplice - something to hide the drug use behind. I'm now clean of drugs and booze. Now I *am* in control.

I've moved to 'B'-wing - the foreign national wing. I'm finally in a proper single cell.

My cell is pretty cool – en-suite, as usual, with one of the most sought-after locations in London, with a panoramic view of house-bricks and razor wire; not like Lewes, where the view was green fields and forests.

Have had a few laughs over the past few weeks, but they are becoming fewer and farther between. Have retreated to the safety of my own mind, my own company and my cell - don't have much time for anyone else at the moment; there's no one here I want to talk to. Though, Dave the laundry guy is cool - I spend a bit of time with him. Gerry has long gone. And the rest - who knows?

The weekends are a nightmare! I've got about forty Jamaican 'Yardies' playing dominoes outside my door - every time I go out I feel like a lion surrounded by forty elephants. Can't speak Russian, Ukrainian, Jamaican Yardie or Nigerian - the only time I mix is in the dinner queue, and even then all I want to is to *do* the fucks that keep pushing in. Remember telling a German guy to 'fuck off and get behind me' when I was in Germany with my Mum; Germans think they have the right to push in front, and he picked on the wrong boy. My Mum was so chuffed - she just beamed: 'That's ma boy', like *Foghorn Leghorn*. Can't do that here - it's not worth the aggro. By the time I get up the stairs and into my cell, I literally attack my food - I mean *really* attack it.

And if it's black pudding? Well, enough said!

The staffing levels and the morale of officers is very low here - they get nothing but aggro from the moment they unlock to bang up. I've now got more or less what I need, so I just keep my gob shut and try to stay out of the way.

Sometimes I *want* to get into an argument or fight, simply to talk to someone, or to vent my ever-increasing anger and frustration. Now that I'm back in writing mode, I'm hoping my temper will ease a bit; this is good therapy, if you think about it: where else are you able to deal with this multitude of emotions and walk away without reacting - without unleashing hell?

Received some great news yesterday: finally got contact with my brother . Wrote him a very long, heartfelt letter, via my father; we've always had a very strained relationship (that's putting it politely). Glad I got my true feelings down on a piece of paper - feel happier knowing that he will read them. All our anger of yester-year means nothing now – it pales into insignificance. I hope he can keep in touch; at this eleventh hour there is nothing he can do for me, but knowing he is there gives me some moral support.

It's all good, and only good can come of it - will gladly stay here for a few years, if it helps; we shall just have to wait and see. *'Wait and see, wait and see'* is getting on my tits - not in control of my life and don't fuckin' like it!

Can *only* wait and see. Want my trial out of the way - want to get on with my fuckin' life!

Aagghh!

(Mental note: if my story ever becomes a play or a movie, James Nesbitt or Ray Winstone will have to play me.)

I've grown my hair a bit longer, so I don't look like a complete thug when I'm in the dock. Deep down I'm dreading it - not because my life hangs in the balance, but because of the length of time you have to sit in holding-cells before and after each court session - the amount of times you slip in and out of temporary madness is frightening. It is not, and I mean *not* the way you see it on telly - physically you are exhausted, and mentally you are tortured.

Used to love the scenes in movies where the prisoner came in from the cells below, to stand in the dock - the anticipation, the excitement, the electricity-charged atmosphere… He or she would give a full account of events involving their particular crime, in chronological order - a full account of their feelings and emotions, with, of course, the assistance of their well-versed legal team, which was there to correct every slip or lapse of memory, having supported them over the past six months, telling them they would 'get off' if they stuck to the truth.

What a crock of shit.

30TH OCTOBER 2007
6.40am

Morning all.

Had been thinking about Steve, my fellow Chelsea fan – had hoped he would get in touch. He's saved me from going over the edge on a number of occasions. His trial was meant to start later this month - he's in for murder.

He's just received twenty-seven years, and is now in Belmarsh.

Replied to his letter immediately - hope I made him laugh. We've promised to stay in touch.

1ST NOVEMBER 2007

8.00am

Had a very restless night - want to get this fuckin' trial over and done with and get a transfer out of this fuckin' place. Battersea Dogs' Home is just up the road, and is looking like a better choice day by day - articulate conversation may be a bit strained for a while, but I'm sure I could cope (mind you, I'd probably get more sense from the staff and inmates in there, than in here).

I'm taking a lot more painkillers than I should, only in an attempt to stay numb. Have never tried heroin, but the thought has crossed my mind - life could be so much easier: just get stoned and lapse into a drug-fuelled haze for a couple of years.

Now frightened about how I will react - very close to throwing the towel in; as the countdown continues, the anxiety increases.

Had a horrible argument with my father - lost my composure and told him 'jokingly' that I was going to barricade myself into my cell if I didn't get what I wanted. Mistake: the whole floor on the Education department heard it; Clarkie was now able to understand why I couldn't focus on my work. When I got back to the wing I patiently waited for the S.O., who could see that I'd reached the end of my tether; he took me into the office and phoned the head of the Medical Department - as a result I'm now on medical hold. It took less than five fuckin' minutes. I'm so relieved.

Won't be leaving Brixton until I'm seen by a consultant at Hammersmith Hospital. Still in a very fragile state and I'm on self-imposed bang up for my own safety, and the safety of others. Dreading coming out at meal-times, as my volatile temper could flare up at any minute. Want and need to talk to someone, but the chaos on the wing makes it impossible.

What can I do about the poor fuckers who can't communicate or deal with their anxieties? All of these scenarios fill me with a greater urge and determination to succeed, and to help; need to rise above my own problems and use them as examples to help others in the future. In contradiction, I'll be able to look back at this time of my incarceration with such fond memories.

Better give my Dad and cousin a call, simply to reassure them that I haven't lost the plot. The problem with my family is that they know what I'm capable of doing, and it ain't fuckin' pretty.

Think I'll have a wee chat with Shandy. Mind you, he's got his own problems - he's been trying to get a desk fan from *Argos* for four months now, even in a trusted position, as someone who speaks to the governors and staff on a regular basis. Got to talk to him later on in the day and we ended up having a good laugh.

Can't wait to get this trial out of the way, get to the hospital and then get the fuck out of this place as soon as is humanly possible - can't be doing with all of these fuckin' scroungers! Jesus, you'd think they'd learn after being told to fuck off time and again. I'm in a state of mental breakdown, and all I get is: 'Got a Rizla... give us a burn... got a fag... etc.' Fuck off and leave me alone, you skanks! For your own good, just do one. Normally I'm a reasonable person, but at the minute, not so good. Got to hold it together.

My cousins are off to Hawaii today. Hope my situation doesn't affect them too much - I'm sure it won't. Know they'll be on the phone to find out how the trial went.

Know these difficult times will pass, however, one still has to go through it. Wonder if my Dad'll win the lottery tonight. Feeling the pain I'm causing him. He wants to help, but can't - a truly horrible position for any parent to be in.

Been reading *'Inside Time'* (prison magazine) and thinking about Steve's twenty-seven years. Thus far, I've overcome some serious hurdles in my life, although nothing prepares you for this. Eventually it will be over – for now I need something to focus on; I'll just try and carry on as normal. Starting to wonder what 'normal' is.

Exhausted. Want to roll over - need my strength for next week.

I'm going to wash and iron my jeans, shirt and jumper. *Déjà vu*: remember doing the same about two months ago, just before my first court appearance - seems like yesterday. Apparently I'm going to court in a people-carrier, now that I'm on medical hold. I'll have to ask again for the hundredth time if this has been arranged, and I know that the reply will be: 'Did you fill in a slip? If you didn't fill in a slip there's nothing I can do.'

'Pick up the phone you lazy cunt - it'll take you two minutes, for fuck's sake!' This is a major problem for certain officers - the very idea of being helpful is not in their make-up, and they are not trained in the use of telephones. As per usual, you have to get nasty before something is done.

'Okay,' is the reply.

'I'm really grateful,' I say, although it pains me to utter these words; still, no point shooting myself in the foot.

My shirt definitely needs an iron. Will have to set out on a quest for an iron that works - unexplored territory for me.

Keep forgetting that setting out on such a simple task is fraught with difficulties.

8.40am

It's still very quiet, which probably means we won't be getting unlocked until this afternoon.

There are notices all over the prison informing prisoners about the *'Incentive-Earned Privileges Scheme'* (IEP). Work hard, you keep your nose clean (literally) and remain (against very difficult odds) polite and courteous to helpful members of staff. Do all that and you might become an 'Enhanced' prisoner. But in truth it means nothing at Brixton.

Managed to get over to reception to collect the tops my aunt has sent in. As I mentioned before, it's a 'job' to get things done in prison – the tops were sent in four weeks ago. Asked the reception S.O. – who knew me from 'C'-wing – if there was a parcel of white T-shirts for me, since I was already here. He takes me round the back to a room full of shelves - it was like the storage room at the end of *'Raiders of the Lost Ark'*, where they put the Ark of the Covenant; 'Look, Mr. Irwin - see for yourself: there's nothing here.'

True enough, most of the shelves were empty. Signed for the letter and went back to wait in the holding cell, before heading back to the wing. Ten minutes later the S.O. comes in with an armful of white T-shirts; he looks at me and rolls his eyes. Couldn't do anything, but laugh.

I need new clothes because Dee, the laundry guy, keeps forgetting, and tumble-dries my tops – they shrink. All Dee can say is: 'Sorry, geeza.' He's about sixty-five, and has smoked so much dope in his day that he tends to be a bit forgetful. What can you say – and at the end of the day what are you going to do about it?

Still, at least I got the T–shirts.

The threes have just been unlocked; the twos (me) won't be out until this afternoon. Can only assume that it's due to staffing levels, and there is no option but to let one landing out at a time.

Hear my name being called out, so I ring the buzzer as I'm locked, to draw the attention of the officer. After what I can only describe as a 'very long wait', was greeted by an ugly mug at the flap - well pissed off and giving me a bollocking for ringing the bell. Try to explain to him that my name has just been called from the ground floor. He goes away and comes back again, then starts to tell *me* what *my* name is. He says: 'There's another prisoner with the same name: Irvine, innit.' He then slams the flap shut and fucks off.

Never opened my gob.

I slip deeper and deeper into a bad place.

Can't get the hold of an iron for love nor money - one of the female officers says she'll try and get one this afternoon; about half an hour later I hear another officer say that she's off this afternoon.

Will I now be appearing in front of the judge in a wrinkled, dishevelled white and brown checked shirt, and a Belfast accent. So much for first impressions, eh?

Find life becoming more tedious and disheartening, and I can't be bothered. Roll on Monday - want to get this over and done with; want to get on with my life, get the fuck out of Brixton and get as far away as possible. Have been assured that you get treated better when you get sentenced and sent to a proper prison.

Want to do my time.

Want to stay in prison.

Want to turn the clock back.

Want to go back to Africa.

Want to get my shirt ironed.

2ND NOVEMBER 2007

6.00am

Had a pretty restless night – understandable under the circumstances: ten years behind bars to look forward to. Know I'll get convicted; *want* to get convicted - can't face my family and my life just yet. Need time to heal - time to mend. Want to crawl into a dark cupboard under the stairs and lock the world away.

Can see how my moods affect my writing - the longer this state of limbo drags on, the less enthusiastic I become; my sense of humour has dried up, for now.

Haven't found or wanted to find anyone to talk to; find myself more and more isolated - more and more alone.

Asked, yet again, for an iron at tea-time. Was given a long and detailed explanation of the problems the prison service faces in connection with breakages, as if I give a fuck. A simple request to iron a shirt before going to court turns into an epic involving the whole prison - the outcome: there is not a functioning iron in the whole of H.M.P. Brixton; I kid you not. Said I would apologize to the judge for the state of my appearance and give him the reason why.

All in all, the rest of the day wasn't too bad, apart from an Irish guy trying to find out where I was from in Belfast, to see if I was a 'prod' or a 'taig'. He had the nerve to be offended when I tried to ignore him, and was still trying to hassle me the whole way to the dinner queue. Then realized he was off his face, so I just walked away. He's the sort of bloke you'd say 'hello' to out of politeness, because you where Irish, and end up regretting it for the rest of your life. You could be sitting in a bar, twenty years from now, and say: 'I spoke to this prick in Brixton, once', remembering it as if it was yesterday; we all come across them.

Where I come from, everybody knows everybody, and, for obvious reasons, nobody knows I'm here, for now - for my family's sake, I want to keep it that way. Things need to be handled delicately at the moment, as I want to return to Northern Ireland to serve out the remainder of my sentence; the less people who know, the better.

Sunday morning TV doesn't motivate one - you have a choice of politics, or *'Telly-Tubbies'*; they both make the same sort of sense to me. *'The Sopranos'* is on in the evening, and I look forward to that, but my options are a bit sad for the rest of the day. Roll on tomorrow and next week.

We won't be let out until 2.30, so I'll just put the feet up and do some reading.

9.00am

I've just been woken up by a load of officers running and shouting – must have kicked off somewhere. Maybe it's all the convicts who have found God in prison. Find the idea repulsive myself - the few true believers who go to the Sunday service are from the African continent, and the rest go to exchange drugs or get out of their cells for an hour – but mostly to exchange drugs.

I've had one of those moments of clarity whilst sitting on the bog again: the haste and speed to which officers respond to alarm-bells is quite commendable. Have figured it out: it's not to assist - it's a chance to unleash hell and twist somebody up, to release some of their pent-up frustration and anger on some poor convict, who's so stoned he doesn't know what's going on; he may have pent-up frustrations of his own, and is just unloading them. Must emphasize: this does not apply to every officer - just a few rotten apples; without them the world would be a better place.

My cell is outside the office on the twos, and I can see and hear (through the gap around the door) most of what goes on. Most officers don't seem to know or care that I can see and hear them.

Heard two of them say: 'Wish I'd gotten there earlier - I'd 'ave said that the guy next door was involved as well.'

'Just to have a dig at that cunt.'

'Any reason to have a pop at that fucker would have been nice.'

I know who these men are, but I'll never do anything about it. Just stay the fuck out of their way and take what they say with a pinch of salt, in the future - purely a self-preservation exercise. Still, useful information to have in case you come up against them - have also seen a few packages change hands.

Knowledge is a dangerous thing, both in and out of prison. Growing up where I did helped me to realize that if it doesn't concern you, keep your mouth shut.

I'm going to fill in my fruit form and try to continue as normal, during these difficult times; haven't received any fruit since I moved from 'C'-wing.

Bored stupid. Sitting in my cell, slowly going insane, I feel the anger rise and fall at the slightest thing - can't keep it together for much longer. The threes are out and the twos are banged up - this is a form of torture in itself.

How the fuck am I meant to relax, get on with some work, watch the TV or read a book, with that madness going on outside my door?

Two Yardies are threatening to kill one of the cleaners, his family and pet parrot if they don't get the hold of a mop soon - they only want the mop to make a fishing-pole.

Did I mention that the storeroom is beside my cell?

The smell of sausages has been wafting through my cell all morning. The officers get a fry-up made for them by one of the orderlies, and, if there is any left, the orderly gets some as well - the memories of Sunday morning fry-ups, with a big hangover, come flooding back. *'Something For The Weekend'* is on the telly – they're cooking. It's amazing the things you take for granted: fried eggs, sausages and soda-bread - have to settle for a glass of freshly squeezed orange juice. Have managed to save up several oranges over the past few weeks, and get a good mug-full out of them. Strictly speaking, you are not allowed to accumulate fruit - especially oranges - as you can get done for making hooch; this involves the fermentation of fruit - normally oranges - mixed with sugar. I believe it's fuckin' stinking, but it does get you wasted.

They encourage you to eat more fruit and veg', so I fill in an App to complain about the lack of fruit deliveries. The orange rind is saved up, and fills the cell with an orange fragrance - an old con's trick.

My final distraction is Brixton itself - it's on the main flight path to Heathrow. Sometimes, though, it's a beautiful sight, as the sun sets over the roof-tops of London, in the dusk of a crisp, frosty night, and the vapour trails of the airplanes leave their brushstrokes on the ozone. Have some great memories of twenty years ago, and I'll cherish them to tell another day.

A programme has just come on the telly about trawler-men in Scotland; there are subtitles, so I find my mood lifting as we speak (pissing myself laughing).

3RD NOVEMBER 2007

5.00am

Here we go: my big week.

Fell asleep just after ten, so I've had a good kip.

Had a chat with my aunt and cousin before they went off to Hawaii - it helped. Managed to get a load off my chest and was able to have a good laugh with them both; I'm able to speak my mind without having to argue. Understand that this will be a very difficult week for all concerned.

Think this will have to be my final chapter, though will possibly pick it up after I get sentenced. Have managed to get myself into a good frame of mind, so when the judge tells me: 'Guilty - ten years,' it will be the start of another adventure (or another fuckin' nightmare - who knows?).

If I go to court I'll try to treat it just like any other day; keep telling myself that I've told the truth and that it's up to the jury - can't ask for anyone's help. Well, I could ask, but I'm pissed off asking for things; fuck it - just convict me and let me get on with my life! I'm so tired - too tired to argue anymore.

Want to master my web-page making at Education - need to continue my daily routine as best I can. Still no sign of a fuckin' iron. No word from the Queen - no last minute pardons knocking about (maybe MI5 have put the pardon beside the iron). All I can do is laugh, but feel empty inside; comfortably numb.

None of my so-called friends have been in touch - they are dead to me now. When I eventually get out of this place, I'll get on with everything as a stronger and better person. Will not go searching for anybody - if I meet them in the future, or someone contacts me, I will simply be polite, say 'hello' and walk on by. If someone wants to fill me full of shit about how difficult their life has been, I'll turn my back on them. At this moment in time I don't care how they feel, but I do understand their actions; have discussed going to prison with friends, over the years, and also know many people who have been to prison. The general consensus has always been the same: forget about the person inside for the duration of their sentence, drop them the odd letter, then be there for them when they get out; nobody can live this for you, so they are better off out of it. If and when you eventually see them again, you will be able to look them in the eye and see the surprise in their face; surprise at how good you look, and how much you have changed for the better.

6.42am

Just had my third bowel movement of the morning; an officer opens the flap whilst I'm on the toilet – no comment. Hear them talking to a few other convicts, telling them they'll be leaving for court in half an hour - presume *I'm* not going to court, then. Fuck, it's going to be a long week.

Can get on with the rest of the day as normal, then. Only mention my bowel movements to emphasize the amount of shit I'm in (*oh, tres drole*). Think I've got some Imodium in the bottom of a bag somewhere - I'll look for them later: they may come in handy. Mentally I'm not shitting myself, but physically I am - will need them if and when I go to court; the cramp, the pain, the discomfort and the embarrassment only adds to my apprehension. Never mind, eh? Upwards and onwards. Have just taken my tablets with some orange juice, and can hear them on their journey through my intestines. Oh, what a glorious life I lead.

Smoking way too much.

It's another beautiful, crisp morning, and I've been lying on top of my bed, listening to the prison come awake: the reversing of vans, the footsteps, the muffled voices, the jangling of keys, the banging of doors and the sporadic outbursts of false laughter; time to get up - to get on with a normal day.

Have been told that a note will be slipped under my door the night before I go to court - this will have some inevitable side effects: on one hand, I'll be glad that I know what I'm doing the following morning, and, on the other, I'll have the whole night to work myself into a frenzy – sitting awake all night, smoking myself to death. For now, for another twelve hours, I'm able to put these feelings to the back of my mind.

I've made a plan to check in with my family (what's left of it). Hope my Dad hasn't gone on the piss again - my stomach turns when I ring and he doesn't answer. His weakness with the booze normally comes at a time of emotional stress. I'm well used to it by now, but it still affects me - another set of circumstances that have always been beyond my control, yet I always go back for more; sometimes I can dismiss it. This time, I will have to do just that. My aunt said that there was also no response from him yesterday, and I know he's a creature of habit. Whatever the outcome is, at least I'll only have to deal with it for this week. Want to do this on my own, but it isn't fair to exclude them.

5TH NOVEMBER 2007

5.45am

Five-forty-five and I'm comin' alive, yeah!

Some prick is roaring through his window – some foreign gibberish; he's totally off his nut. Thought there were prisons especially for head-cases like that. Poor bloke is crying, roaring and screaming to nobody in particular - maybe he should see a doctor.

I still haven't seen one, and I filled in an App last Monday, trying to plan ahead - was trying to get some different tablets, in an attempt to stop me from shitting myself in the dock, or in the sweat-box. No word yet, so I'll continue as normal. Mind you, it's not getting any easier: extremely agitated, the slightest thing pissing me off.

Last night I told one of the officers that I'd had enough of being fucked around, and if I woke up dead it wouldn't be anybody's fault, because nobody was helping me. What started out as a joke ended up having to be explained to a P.O. in great detail - he was going to put me on suicide watch, for fuck's sake. If I was going to kill myself, I'd have done it a long time ago.

Fuck it, if I die in prison, so be it. A hard price to pay for making a mistake, but, hey, them's the fuckin' breaks. After all, I am a criminal.

After all, I am guilty.

After all, I am already convicted - aren't I?

Haven't been to court yet, Sir.

Read an article the other day about the amount of suicides by prisoners on remand – especially women, think I'll devote the rest of my life to helping other people in prison.

7.00am

Haven't heard anything yet, so I presume another day will pass without going to court.

Don't know how much more my heart can take: the build up, the anticipation, the nerves and then the relief when you don't have to go. Fuck, I wish it was over.

Was watching a programme yesterday about Afghanistan, while several fireworks displays were happening in London. The old 'Bangor Reserves' (nerves) were a bit shaky on it, to say the least. Don't forget: I had the pleasure of growing up in Belfast, so, if a car backfires or a firework goes off, one tends to jump or hit the deck. This has caused much laughter over the years – normally at my expense. Was in a pub in London with my mate and several others once, having a 'lock-in' - the pub was on the crossroads of the Fulham Road and Warwick Road – when a car backfired at the traffic lights outside; me and my mate hit the floor, and everyone looked at us as if we were nuts. We just burst out laughing. At least we missed the shrapnel and the bullets over the years.

The weather has taken a turn for the worse and the heating has packed up. Even the heating works backwards in prison: it's on when it's warm and off when it's cold!

Reading a book by Robert Ludlum at the minute, and it has only managed to increase my paranoia - now convinced there is some sort of master plan, by MFI, to make my life as difficult as possible. They're attempting to break me - to make me admit to something I didn't know I was doing; their cunning plans become more obvious as the weeks and months roll on. Once you're in the system, you're fucked.

My sense of humour saves the day again - there's an article on the news about the price of excess baggage at airports: £5.50 has to be paid for each extra kilo; in my case (trying to avoid the pun), I should have just paid the £11.00!

7TH NOVEMBER 2007

5.31am

Nothing yet.

My volcano finally erupted yesterday morning. The Healthcare nurse who made the doctor's appointment for me over a week ago was on duty - she asked me one too many questions; I flipped, and refused to go over the same bullshit again.

Came back from lessons and doctor's appointment to be summoned into the S.O.'s office - thought I was going to be given a 'red-entry' for my outburst, but all she wanted to know was if I was going to be staying on 'High Risk'. I laughed, and said: 'What do you think, after yesterday?' We both agreed it would be best for all concerned if I did. She was cool, and understood my mental state, so all is well in that department.

Was able to confirm all of my previous fears about MFI, etc., and managed to get some newspapers ordered for the weekend. An officer who is a fellow countryman is on duty, and I've been able to get a more positive attitude from his colleagues since he started working; I know they've been asking questions about me. Having said that, it has taken me three weeks to achieve something that resembles a conversation. As a result, I'm in a better frame of mind.

Was able to read between the lines after my chat with the S.O.: thought that nobody was listening to me, but they were just waiting to see how far I would actually go. They've decided to give me a bye-ball about yesterday, as they realize that I'm in a bad place at the moment. In a way, I'm grateful.

At least I wasn't trailed down the block, because, she told me, I most definitely would have had the crap knocked out of me. From now on I'll make an effort to be my more normal, happy, smiling self. When I was getting my lunch, I was given a bag of chips and nothing else, as the guy giving out the Cornish pasties was day-dreaming; I said: 'Hey, pal, I know I'm overweight, but don't take the fuckin' piss, eh.' We all had a good laugh, and life rolls on. Everyone knows everyone's business on the wing - the place is rife with rumour and conjecture, so this was a good, defining moment: if you can get the servery guys laughing and on your side, you're normally onto a winner. There is always one of them who's the boss – who gives the nod: if he says 'Yeah 'e's a'wight mate', it's normally good enough, as long as you keep your head down and mouth shut.

Been inside for five glorious months now, and can see all sorts of patterns developing - people, if they are one thing, are predictable. It normally takes around three to four weeks to be accepted onto every wing you go to. For years I've worked in the pub trade, and have travelled to many different countries, so I'm well aware of this type of behaviour. For now, I feel as if things are on the up, and can only get better for me, on the wing.

But it seems to me like the whole of the prison staff is demoralized. The other morning I was on free-flow, walking past Mr. J (a big muthafucka of a Jamaican man, in his late forties/early fifties), who was leaning up against a post, smoking. He greeted me with a very tired: 'Good morning, Mr. Irwin. How are you today, munn?' Could see he was totally bored and pissed off.

I roared at the top of my voice (the whole prison must have heard it): 'All the better for seeing you, tiger.' He nearly collapsed with laughter.

We continued laughing and having a wee chat - we both agreed life was a bitch and this place was a shit-hole. Could see a lot of the other officers and convicts, who had overheard our exchange, were, too, starting to laugh, chat to each other, shake their heads and to generally cheer up.

So, you see, my friends, it doesn't take much to lighten the mood in these dark and horrible places: we are all thrown together in difficult times, only some choose to be here, and some don't.

Speaking of shit-holes, you wanna see the amount of shit you have to wade through when you pass 'G' wing, on the way to Education. It must be the cleanest wing in the prison - as all the rubbish is thrown out the windows! Vermin.

Have nearly cracked HTML (web-page language, to the uninitiated), and I look forward to getting my trial out of the way, so that I can devote my time to full-time education. Am pleased with what I've already learned and achieved at Brixton, innit.

2.30pm

Waiting for free-flow to begin.

Another fight in the dinner queue at lunchtime - officers stand by and watch as an argument develops, then jump in when the four guys are rolling around on the floor, punching and kicking the crap out of each other.

Oh yeah - forgot to mention that the doctor has informed me I may have at least two gastro something-or-other hernias; whatever it is causing my bloatedness, has also caused the hernia. This will be my third hernia, so at least I'll know what to expect. Oh, happy days!

We had to leave Education early this afternoon - turns out someone's done a bunk (gone AWOL). It's now 6.00pm, and we still haven't been fed yet. They have counted the wing several times. The intelligent roars and shouts from the windows are:

'Who is it?'

'Who's escaped?'

When we eventually get our dinner, the rumour is that some eejit is up on the roof and somebody couldn't count properly – a very, very common occurrence in prison. As a result the whole prison is locked down. Nothing surprises me anymore.

At least I definitely now know I need an operation - eight weeks of pain and humiliation to look forward to! The last time I had a hernia, my Dad flew over to look after me. Not looking forward to recovering from an operation in prison.

Managed to get some sleeping tablets from the doctor - he's given me a month's supply of beta-blockers and two weeks of sleepers, so, whatever happens over the next two weeks, at least I should be sleeping and relaxed.

Just received a letter from my mate, J 'The Voice', at Lewes. He has passed on my regards to the staff that helped me while I was there, and Crazy Horse has spoken to the P.O. about me; so, all is well and good. Unfortunately, they are not allowed to reply to inmates. It has left me a little bit deflated, because I took great comfort, and a lot of pleasure, from some of their kind words and deeds. J, as per usual, made me laugh; will make it a point to keep in touch with him.

8TH NOVEMBER 2007

7.40am

Starting to get paranoid again. Still here – will have to presume I'm going tomorrow. So much for getting my trial over and done with.

THINGS TO DO TODAY: *Don't crack up!*

Can't help but think of what it must be like for those poor fuckers who are out on bail, with a trial hanging over their head - it must be a nightmare.

Got some good news: my brother has been in touch with my Dad. Wonder how they got on yesterday; I'll find out soon enough. Hope he interpreted my letter in the way it was meant.

I've printed out the start of my book, and will show it to the guys at Education. I'll be setting myself up for a bit of criticism, but, if at least one person likes it, maybe I can start the ball rolling, and think about getting it published.

The sleeping tablets have worked a treat – ten hours kip! Feeling pretty good, considering. Think it's a combination of my family getting together, after all these years, and my worries beginning to sort themselves out. Maybe it's simply because I was able to laugh at J's letter, and went to bed feeling good. I'll draft him a quick letter in the morning, or maybe I'll be better waiting until Monday - got so much going on upstairs.

Can't wait to get out of my cell – feeling claustrophobic. My emotions are jumping all over the shop.

2.40pm

Phoned my Dad this morning – big mistake: massive blow out. It has become painfully obvious that he isn't coping well with me being in here. As soon as I get my trial over, I'm going to sever all contact with my family, and go it alone. In the heat of the moment, he said: 'It's not my fault you're in prison.'

Knew these words would come one day - was prepared to take it on the chin. Can't do it – don't fuckin' need it, especially when I'm on an emotional rollercoaster, waiting to get the nod each day. These words, I fear, will follow me around for the rest of my days. Know he didn't mean it, but it doesn't take it away. I'm totally gutted, deflated, and still don't know if my brother got my letter.

I'm not going to bother ringing again. He says he's got big shoulders – well, I hope they can carry him through this, 'cos I'm done. They say everything happens for a reason – wish someone could explain that one to me; I'm fuckin' confused!

I'm used to the rebuttals you receive in prison, but try explaining it to a family member; unfortunately, they believe that prison officers are there to help you; dream on. You don't want to tell them what is actually happening, as you're trying to protect them from getting hurt, so you end up lying yourself, and saying: 'Everything is fine.'

Late free-flow again. There is no consistency here – no fuckin' system. Still, there's no point in blaming the prison service - it's my fault I'm in here in the first place. Should not have done what I did.

6.30pm

Well, there's another day at H.M.P. Brixton over and done with, topped off by yet another fight in the dinner queue (well, I call it a 'queue' very loosely). Certain individuals think it is their right to push in and walk to the front. Most of the time I don't care - you can normally get out of the way if it kicks off – but, sometimes, you just see red. This time I got involved, as I was being forced into a corner – not a good place to be – so I decked the two guys in front of me. Four or five of them ended up on the floor - rolling around as usual - and they were unceremoniously dragged away by the ever-willing ogres.

Two seconds later it's business as usual.

Got my dinner, as I was next in the queue, walked back up the stairs to my cell, as happy as a sand-piper, and closed the door behind me. Sometimes, I just love the sound of the door being closed behind me, blocking out the madness on the other side. Ironically, this is the time when you are at your most vulnerable - all alone, stripped of your liberty and as fragile as piece of thread, ready to tear, rip, disintegrate into the void left where your soul used to be.

There are three officers to look after over a hundred prisoners, all of whom are pissed off because everything is running late, due to lack of staff - can see another familiar pattern developing. The prison system is hanging on by the skin of its teeth, and at the end of every day, someone in authority is letting out a big sigh, wondering how they managed to get through the past twenty-four hours, without serious disturbance or loss of life (phew).

9.00pm

My mood has lightened somewhat. Another week nearly over.

This week has nearly broken me - the constant state of limbo draining me. Of course, I know I'll come out the other side, eventually. For now, though, it's difficult to even think.

Only one hour to go until sleeping-tablet time, then the comfort of sleep. Used to turn to dope and booze in order to get through my bouts of pain and depression - the only difference now is that I'm sober, and I look forward to the next day.

Another day, with a new set of challenges.

9TH NOVEMBER 2007

6.00am

Looks like all my anxieties, fears and hopes will have to continue: asked the night-guard if my name was on the court list - no joy.

Holy shit! What am I going to do now?

They did tell me I 'might' be called – it seems not. I'm exhausted, drained, deflated and pissed off - have to dig deep to carry on.

Must get dressed… must get dressed. The effort involved is too much.

All I hear in my head is different voices, saying: *'Stop… start… wait… hurry up… don't know… maybe… come back tomorrow… your name's not on the list… have you filled in an App… never received the App…'* Have lost all sense of positivity.

Have filled out my third *Argos* order-form and eagerly await the outcome - recall going through the same procedure at the end of the past two months. I've been hassling the wing staff for two weeks solid - they see me coming and disappear. Finally, I got the answer I was expecting: they have no record of receiving the original forms.

I didn't bat an eyelid. What's the friggin' point?

Even one of the officers said: 'This place is an embarrassment.'

Going to get the ball rolling about my distance learning, no matter what. I've already convicted myself - received ten years - and will act accordingly. Unfortunately, there are a lot of things the system will not let you do until you are convicted - I'm just a name and number at the minute, and nothing else.

2.00pm

What a sleep. Had a weird dream: was in The George (pub) and 'K' was there (K's my ex, who was going to be a lawyer); she refused to speak to me. All of my so-called friends were there also, and they ignored me. I started to walk round the pub looking for them, and they all disappeared - one by one, they faded like apparitions.

I started running, to all the places I had visited. Then I realized I was all alone.

Ended up getting into a slagging match with some bloke I didn't know, and we ended up in a scrap; didn't want to fight, 'cos I knew I'd get barred from the pub and end up back in prison.

Woke up swinging, screaming and shouting.

I have always believed that dreams are echoes of your frame of mind - if this is true, then that dream is pretty self-explanatory: I'm fucked.

The door banging has started up again - the officers mustn't be back from their lunch yet. Everything has been late this week, including my fuckin' trial! On Thursday we went to Education at three-forty-five, and had to come back at four-forty-five; we are meant to start at two-fifteen. Not once have we started at the correct time.

Even then, you're made to feel grateful that you have been let out at all. My door isn't being opened, full stop. Not bothered: don't want to talk to anyone - not in the best of moods again. There's fuck all to do at the weekends, anyway. Plus, I speeka da wrong lingo, innit.

My newspaper hasn't arrived yet, either - no fuckin' surprise there, then. The officers read them first, before they come on duty, or whilst they are on duty. I've seen a guy go up and asked a certain ogre if he can have his paper - the one that the officer is reading.

'When I'm finished,' was the response. *Fuckin' unbelievable, Bob!*

I'm content enough to sit and read a book. What a bore.

11TH NOVEMBER 2007

8.15am

The eleventh hour, of the eleventh day, of the eleventh month - *'We shall remember them'*. Wonder if they'll do anything for it in prison - if they do it'll probably be late…

Another boring day - feel like shit. It's becoming increasingly difficult to even muster a smile, in this God-forsaken place. There is no hiding the fact that my ill health, and the constant knockbacks, are sapping my strength. Will persevere, and try hard not to give up - for today, though, I can't be bothered.

Fuck me - the smell of the ogres' fry-up is driving me nuts; the stuff you take for granted, eh? Just murdered a bowl of shredded wheat and an apple – deep joy. It's after nine - looks like we won't get out until this afternoon, or until they finish their breakfast.

12TH NOVEMBER 2007

8.15am

It's a beautiful, crisp morning, and it's bringing back some fantastic memories of when I played football as a schoolboy: the smell of *Deep Heat* rub and wet grass cuttings in the changing rooms, the frost on the pitch, the pitch of green, and the white lines cleared and drawn for battle.

Also, those of walking up my grandfather's path in Manor Park - it was always slippery, as the sun never reached it until late in the afternoon. My grandfather, who never failed to make me laugh, and who gave me help and encouragement in my young life. Of Tracy Mathers, and innocence lost.

They make me feel warm inside, these feelings of old. I keep them hidden, and I only privately hook up with them when I'm feeling low - they give me the strength and courage to face and continue another day; to be so bold.

Have many different projects to start, and have to figure out a way of focusing on one or two at a time - need the green light of a conviction to get me going. Until then, nothing - just limbo.

13TH NOVEMBER 2007

5.30am

Finished and designed my first ever website yesterday, so I'm well chuffed - I'll print it out later and send it to my Dad. Strange how, at forty, I still seek his approval.

It will give him a bit of encouragement, I hope - he'll be able to see that even though I'm in a state of limbo, I'm still carrying on with stuff and trying to be positive.

Hate coming back to the wing - the atmosphere is bad. Something is going to blow soon - can feel it in the air; there are lots of new faces, and everyone looks tense. Want to punch my way out - need to get out of this place; just fuckin' convict me and send me to another jail!

Received my fruit last night. On the journey from the office to my cell I was asked by three different people I didn't know for a piece of fruit. Why do they look at you in surprise and disgust when you say no? It fuckin' amazes me how the majority of scumbags in here really do think they are something. *I'm* a scumbag too - I'm a *drug trafficker* – how, then, can I manage to be polite, and not have to beg, or steal, or threaten others? Fuckin' oxygen thieves! Someone you have never met before asks you for a banana, and he turns nasty when you say no! I've waited for three weeks to get this fruit, in an effort to improve my health, and I ration myself to one banana a day - it costs me an extra tenner a week. Anyway, apart from that, why in the fuck should I give you any, you fuckin' prick? How close to murder and mayhem have I just come?

If I'm short of something, I'm even embarrassed to ask people *I know* for the lend of it. Respect? These fuckin' pricks don't even know the fuckin' meaning of the word. I blame the parents!

17TH NOVEMBER 2007

6.00am

Oh shit - here we go! Someone has just come to my door: 'Mr. Irwin - you leave for court in twenty minutes.'

8.00am

And so it begins: the last chapter in this stage of my weird and wonderful life.

Apparently, I'm due in the courtroom in two hours.

Slept like a log - this may have been due to the amount of beta-blockers and painkillers I took during the day. Now, my stomach is in knots – a bit like when you go to the dentist; fear of the unknown and the hernia isn't helping matters, either.

Not going to go over my defence again - have done it a thousand times already. My barrister has all the relevant information, and his line of questioning should bring out my truthful side of the story. All I can hear are his words from our last meeting: 'I want to get you off, so just answer my questions truthfully.' My solicitor has told my father that I've a good barrister, so I'm slightly optimistic. After all, if they didn't think I had a chance, they wouldn't have advised me to plead 'not guilty', would they? The only thing my solicitor has spoken to me about is 'the opportunity to plead' - in my case, he has given me the option of 'ten years' or 'not guilty'. There is a thing called a *'Newton Hearing'*, but my barrister has told me there is no need: my plea is a straight 'not guilty'.

Have been told that I'm getting a people-carrier to court - the van for Croydon has already left. This means I get double-cuffed, escorted by three officers, in the back of a converted Escort van. The S.O. has let me out of the holding cells, as there is nobody left. 'Feel free to walk around,' he says, 'we're just waiting for the van to turn up.'

Spend half an hour searching for a tea-bag, and find one that has just been used in the sink of the officers' office; make myself a cup of tea. This is the only thing I've had to drink for five hours.

It's now twelve o'clock and the van has turned up. I know the S.O. from the landing, so he tells me exactly what is going on - the fuckin' van has come from Nottingham to collect me, in London! Three different departments in O.C.A. (prison transport) have been lying to each other, and the O.C.A. guys and the officers are having a right pop at each other - it's fuckin' hilarious; I'm just standing there, watching, leaning up against the grill with a fag and a cup of tea. The prison's job is to get me to court on time - was meant to be in front of the judge at ten. Am I fucked, or what?

Have the pleasure of being wedged between two beautiful, black, female officers - one is called Rosie (she has allowed me to use her real name), and she is a wonderful, lively, bubbly, Jamaican woman (sorry if I got the 'Jamaican' bit wrong, Rosie). Anyway, we had a lovely chat on the way to court; Rosie gave me a blackcurrant lollipop, as my Polo mints were in the boot. The other black lady I was cuffed to was even more beautiful, and because of the position we were in with the double cuffing, my hand had to rest on her leg. She was rather nice, and couldn't help but laugh at the position I was in: always wanted to be cuffed between two beautiful, black women! When we finally arrived at court, we were all laughing and joking, and they wished me all the best for the future.

Sitting in the holding cells, reflecting.

It all boils down to the fact that I made the most horrible, stupid error of judgement in my life, tried to get out of it, and ended up in here. I know in my heart that deep down, behind all the façade, I *needed* to get caught; can't blame anyone for the trouble I'm in - played with fire and got my fingers *cremated.* I'm now in the proverbial shit, and will have to face the consequences. So be it.

Just been to see my solicitor and barrister. It's 2.00pm and I don't believe what's just happened: they've changed my barrister because I was late! That's me fucked, then.

Four hours late and a new barrister – fuckin' marvellous! He seems alright, but I don't like it; have a horrible feeling of impending doom creeping over me. I now know that this is not an unusual situation, and it happens way too often. Shouldn't they have more time to prepare?

Panic sets in. Take another beta-blocker, and try to answer his questions the best I can. The first part of the trial was jury selection and prosecution opening statements - long and boring.

My boyo began to ask a few questions, but the judge (bad reputation for drugs cases) stopped proceedings for the day - don't like the look of this; he says: 'I have a prior engagement in the afternoon - we will come back in the morning, finish at lunchtime and resume on Thursday morning.'

I'm fucked.

What should have been a simple, painless procedure has now turned into a four day epic - if I were on the jury, I'd be well pissed-off; come decision time, I'd want to get this stupid, boring trial over and done with, to get out of this boring place, down the pub, or off to the golf course, like the judge is doing tomorrow.

Sit in the holding cell for another eternity. They tried to take me to a police cell for the night, then someone reads the paperwork and realizes I'm on medical hold, and have to go back to Brixton. To cut a long, boring wait short: left Croydon very late, and arrived back at Brixton at seven-forty. The guys in the van told me that after eight o'clock I was 'not their responsibility' - the prison is not allowed to accept people after eight o'clock. I asked them to hang around for twenty minutes, then just drop me off outside the gate - can you imagine the fun I could have had?

Joking aside, I wonder what I *would* have done? Would I have done a bunk, and ended up looking over my shoulder for the rest of my life, or simply sat by the gate for the night, waiting for someone to let me in in the morning? The mind boggles.

Got back to my cell around eight-thirty; sat on the end of my bed, stared at the wall, and passed out with my clothes still on.

18TH NOVEMBER 2008

Back in Croydon.

It was a smoother morning today - the guys from O.C.A. were waiting for me; they've told everyone that I'm on 'drop and return'. The S.O. even phoned the court! Apparently, yesterday was a complete fuck up, and if I wanted to, I could take the matter further. No fuckin' kidding! Best let sleeping dogs lie. Don't know how often I'll have to be transported around England and Wales in the next ten years - don't want to be flagged every time my name comes up for transfer.

At least I know today will be shorter, and not as bad as yesterday. I've smuggled some tobacco in with me, but there are still too many officers around to have a fag. The holding cells are starting to fill up so, I'll just have to wait. I'm on my own because of the 'High Risk' status, and in the same cell as yesterday.

I'm well impressed with the speed and secrecy with which I can have a fag. What you do is: wait until you get a cup of coffee or tea, then light up and stand with your back to the door and window - cup and fag in the same hand; so, if someone walks past and sees the smoke, it looks like steam coming off of the coffee. This is also where the jangling of keys comes in handy: it gives you a bit of notice. The other packet of tobacco, Rizla, matches and striker are in a small, resealable plastic bag in the arch under my foot.

It has taken me several trips to holding cells in the prison to master the art of smuggling; I have one bag in my shoe, one in my jacket pocket and one in my jeans, so, if they find one, they'll think that's it, and let me leave with the other two. The laws of average predict that you *will* get a smoke. None have been confiscated yet, and if I get caught, so what.

I've still got my Polo mints. I've just had my last beta-blocker, so, hopefully, I'll be nice and relaxed by the time I get into court. It's hard to get their timing right, due to my bad indigestion.

My heart is going like a dinger, I need a pee and I'm breaking out in cold sweats. Think I'll try to have a wee lie down, but need to let the smoke settle first. These air vents are shit.

'Always look on the bright side of life' is playing in my head - hope this song will help me make it through the morning.

Made a few laps of the cell and already I'm knackered.

1.00pm

Well that's most of it out of the way. I'm back in the morning for cross-examination by the prosecution.

The barrister said I did well, but I'm not so sure - his questions did not go the way I thought they would. Don't want to speculate; saw him frantically flicking through a couple of case law books, trying to find some other litigation - not a good sign. Can only hope.

End up back at Brixton around two-thirty. Bang up.

No 'how'd you get on?' Just 'get behind your door' – end of.

I'm too sick to eat dinner - have a banana, a tomato sandwich and two sleeping tablets. The warm bliss of slumber envelopes me.

19TH SEPTEMBER 2007

9.00am

Back in Croydon for the last day of my trial. Have been awake from six, going over what was said yesterday.

Think I'm fucked - if I was in the jury *I*'d convict me.

Sure, my barrister told me that I'd done well, but his questions were nothing like the ones the other barrister had - there was so much information left out; I was waiting patiently for him to bring certain matters of relevance up, but he didn't. I glanced over at my solicitor, as the panic started to fill my throat, in the shape of bile, to try and plead with him to change the line of questioning. He was staring at the ceiling, avoiding looking at me.

He knew - the fucker *knew* - it was all a complete bollocks! I knew they were just going through the motions, and I've no chance; *thank you very much, you scheming, money-grabbing fuckers!* At one stage, I was even arguing with the barrister.

Suppose, at this stage, there are a number of things I could do, but, to be honest, I couldn't give a fuck anymore - I'm tired, and I will not admit to something I didn't knowingly do. Been telling myself 'ten years' for the past six months, so at least I'm prepared.

Sitting in the holding cell - the jury's out - feeling pretty good. Want this to be over now - my stomach is playing up big-time, and I just want to get back to the safety of my cell. Stomach is about the size of a small beer barrel; can't work it out - haven't had a pint for six months.

I'm trying to keep my mind blank, but it's not happening - all I can think about is my trip, and the bastards that set me up. Admittedly, I was wrong – admittedly, I'll have to pay. The baggage-handlers were only meant to put the drugs in the bag after - the bag was only, supposedly, for identification purposes.

Aye, to identify *me* to Customs.

Feel ashamed, embarrassed and stupid - can't believe I fell for it.

The penny dropped a long time ago - how many people had walked through when I was stopped? I recognized at least three people, when I was standing there in a drunken stupor - how many more were there? Minimum outlay, maximum profit, and, if I'd gotten through, no matter.

I'm truly exhausted, and hope this will not take too long. I've had six trips to the toilet already. All sorts of thoughts, memories, ideas and plans are whizzing around in my head.

Well, back to the washing machine again. Have reached a pivotal moment - a crossroads in my life. Which way will fate throw its dice?

Told you I was fucked.

'Twelve years.'

It's a fair cop.

PART TWO:

Prison Life

All I can hear are the lyrics of a *Stiff Little Fingers* song: '*"Well, I'd like to thank you," the consul said, "there's nothing we can do – well, you knew the risks, son, when you took the job; there's nothing we can doo-hoo. Don't call me, don't call me."*'

Plan 'A' didn't work - I'll have to go to plan 'B'; that is, when I figure out what plan 'B' is.

I'll serve six years - get my stomach fixed, go back to Education, get a degree, and, by that time, I'll be out; ready to get on with my life.

The jury was out for forty-five minutes - didn't take them long, eh? The prosecution painted a bad picture of me, and they think they've caught some sort of 'Mr. Big'.

When you put it all together, the way legal people do, it sounded quite plausible: a single guy from Belfast, with connections in London and Spain, living in Cape Town, with no fixed means of income. On reflection, I seriously believe that my accent got me the extra couple of years, and my fear came across as belligerence.

Was tricked, duped and fooled; it's of no consequence now. Know in my heart that I've told the truth - can hold my head up and continue with a clear conscience; move on - no more *ifs*, *buts* or *maybes*.

Apart from the fact that they now think I'm some sort of master criminal, they also think I've been doing this for years, and are coming after my assets - they are pursuing a 'confiscation order'. What a fuckin' pavlova!

Still, that's another story for another day.

The journey back to Brixton was a quiet one. Twelve fuckin' years – two more than I expected.

'Well, how'd you get on?' the reception S.O. asked. When I told him, he just said: 'Get out of here as soon as you can.' I knew what he meant.

They didn't even bother to put me through the formalities of strip-searching, etc. - the only thing I had to do was sign a form, saying that I was now a 'sentenced' prisoner.

Went back to the wing, and Miss McT was sitting behind the desk. She asked me if I was okay, and I just said that I was a bit tired. Another officer came along – whom I didn't know – and offered me a fag.

'Ta very much,' I said.

Took a long draw of the Benson & Hedges King Size, and inhaled deep, letting a big sigh out of me as the smoke left my lungs; was a bit light-headed, as I hadn't had a proper fag for a long time.

Miss McT was filling out some paperwork, and said: 'Take your time - I'll take you up in a minute.' The other officer had received a call on his radio and dashed off.

Leaning against the desk, I smoked and contemplated what the next twelve years were going to be like.

The night-lights were on, it was nearly dark and I could barely make out the shape of the landing. The wing was deathly quiet - everything seemed fuzzy, dreamlike and murky. I looked up and down the wing, taking in the size of the place, and imagining all of the guys behind their doors, wondering what they were doing.

I was also wondering how on Earth I felt. It was a confusing time for me - I felt small and inadequate. My mind explored the idea that it was just a small, insignificant piece of time. How many rogues had stood where I now stood, and looked up with trepidation at the rows and rows of doors, behind which another poor soul eked out an existence. At least I'd already been here for a while, and I know the ropes - the past six months has prepared me well. All I wanted to do now was to get back to my pad, have a cuppa and fall asleep.

Miss McT said: 'Okay, Mr. Irwin, let's go.'

We reached my cell, and she lifted the card out of its place by the door, and replaced it with a new one, which read: 'SENTENCED'. She asked me again if I was okay.

'You know the drill, if you need anyone.'

I just said: 'Yeah. I'll see you in the morning.'

Plopped down on my chair, put the kettle on and made a couple of roll-ups - I didn't even switch the light on, as there is always a glow from the orange wall-light outside my cell window. I lay back on the bed and blew smoke onto the ceiling.

Well, here you are, kid. You now know your fate – now, what are you gonna do about it?

Be cool, I thought - I've all the time in the world to get to grips with my demons.

The next thing I knew, it was morning. I could hear a few of the others, getting ready to go and have their day in court, and thought: *Be careful what you wish for.*

Shandy was standing by my cell when I got out; 'Well, you alright about it?'

'Yeah - I'm not bothered. Just have to tell my Dad.'

'That's the hard part,' he said

'Don't I fuckin' know it?'

Off we went, heading over to the Education department.

It was strange - some of the older, harder cons came up to me, and slapped me on the back; some gave me a nod, and said: 'Be lucky, Mickey-boy.' It was as if I had now been accepted - they could now speak to me, or acknowledge my existence, as I was, now, one of the lads; one of *them*, in every sense of the word.

Clarkie looked quite shocked – I think he'd sort of hoped he wouldn't see me again.

Sitting in my chair, I stared at the computer screen for a while, then decided to phone my Dad, and tell him the 'good' news. Again, it was one of the hardest things I've ever had to do - I'm sure, for him, it was one of the hardest things he's ever had to listen to. All I could do was reassure him that I was okay about it, and I do believe that I sounded rather optimistic and upbeat about my future.

It was now going on break-time, so I headed out onto the fire-escape for a fag.

All the usual suspects were there, and this one arrogant guy was yapping about the judge giving him six months - he went on and on about how hard done by he was, and how the cops had stitched him up, and the judge had it in for him.

The guys in my class just stood there, looking at the floor. Then, one of them turned round and said: 'That's nothing, you nonce: Mick's just got twelve and you don't hear him crying! Shut your mouth, man, and have some respect.'

Even though the guy was black, I swear he turned a paler shade. 'Sorry, Geez,' he said, and walked off, mumbling to himself.

One of the younger guys, in all sincerity, asked me: 'What does it feel like?'

I told him: 'It's shit! But, at the end of the day, I have to get on with my life as best I can. I did what I did, and I have to pay the price.

'I consider myself lucky, 'cos if I'd have still been on the out, I'd be dead by now.'

I could see that a lot of them took it on board. Could see them thinking, especially about the 'being dead' bit - I think that hit home for a lot of those guys. Where there were guns and knives involved, death was always an option, but, like anyone who becomes blinkered in that world, you simply shut it out.

Some of these young guys – came to me at different times over the next few months, and asked me questions about how I coped; they always remarked that I was always smiling and laughing. Truthfully, I told them that when I left my cell each morning, I'd already imagined that I was heading out to work each day, and that every positive thing that I did brought me one step closer to getting out. I also told them that they may never see me cry, but I have done on a few occasions, and am not afraid to admit it.

I also tried to get them to accept the fact that I was the only person responsible for my being in prison – likewise, the only person who put *them* in prison was themselves. Even though I was fucked over and set up, at the end of the day it was *my* decision, and mine alone, to get involved with those dodgy fuckers.

The choice is either to stay where you are and get fucked, or do the hard thing and walk away - take yourself out of the equation, before someone else does. Although, in my case, once I'd committed myself, I don't think I *could* have walked away; I believe, deep down inside, that I knew getting caught and going to jail was the easier option.

This also rang true with a lot of these young guys: they felt trapped, and knew they needed to walk away, but they just didn't know how to.

This is something I think we should all be preaching.

So, what have I learnt so far?

Life meanders on, and I find my mind and daily events slowing down.

After my trial, I kept my head down at Brixton, got stuck into my writing and developed my I.T. skills. I became an Education Co-ordinator, did a bit of writing for the prison radio, and also designed a logo for the Education department; I was able to encourage and assist a lot more men in Brixton with their education.

One of the hardest things to do in prison is accept your fellow man. Previously, you had choices in life: who your friends were, who you had a pint with, or what type of bar you went into. For most of my adult life, I've lived, drank and worked in bars or clubs, and I've always been able to suss people out; when you work behind the jump, you have twelve seconds to make a decision on a person as they walk from the front door to the bar. That's why bars should never have a back door – even less, if you're doing the door. But, in prison, you do not have a choice: you have to mix with the same people day in day out, whether you like them or not.

I'm of the unfortunate persuasion that I do not suffer fools gladly.

An asshole is an asshole in my book; if I'm in a bad mood, it's even worse. And, my first impression is normally the right one. I hate bad manners, I hate bullies and I hate injustices - I watch the predators in prison pick their prey, and I watch in anger as the strong manipulate the week. These actions mirror society and the lives we lead - I've watched many people in the pubs and clubs establish themselves in the pecking order, and I have been guilty myself, of fuelling, and mixing in these practices. Fortunately, as I've got older and wiser, I've learned to walk alone - to stand as an individual - and have, over the years, become reliant on the conversations and arguments that go on only in my mind; to be truthful, if a psychiatrist ever got the hold of my thoughts and feelings, I'd still be locked up for sure, in a well-padded room.

There are a lot of idiots running around prisons, thinking they're hard - the dog's bollocks - merely for the fact that they are in jail. But most of the *true* hard men I've met have been friendly and mild-mannered, yet assertive, without being menacing - this 'menacing' part only comes if you step out of line, or say or do something that is misguided or disrespectful – especially of oneself. I have found that if you 'be yourself', you will normally be accepted for the person you are; even if certain people dislike you, then that's up to them, as long as you are true to yourself. For me, the best thing is never to slag someone off - if you have a problem with someone, you tell them - if they don't like it, then tough; if they knock seven bells of crap out of you, then tough - at least you have been true to what you believe in; just because someone can beat you in a fight doesn't mean they've won.

Prison is full of prejudice, preconceived ideas, and misinformed notions about the way people should think, and how they should behave. Most of these notions are born out of fear. Myself, and some of the guys I've befriended, have leaned on the railings of the landings, on the threes or fours, like others past and present, and watched these events unfold; sometimes it's funny, but most of the time it's stupid and unnecessary.

I know what it feels like to be frightened, alone and intimidated – sometimes, you feel your stomach turn. For me, it's normally the start of an adrenalin rush, which has to be suppressed, for fear of unleashing the carnage that is sure to follow. Only time can teach you to do this, and, unfortunately, some people have made the mistake of believing that their fear is actually fear of the other person, not the fear of oneself. I wish I could teach this to some of the guys that now surround me - it would cause them so much less aggravation.

And, so, prison life trundles on.

Brixton is a crazy place, and is like any of the other London nicks, in that they are continuously processing people to and from court. Like Lewes, the weekly turnover is a conveyor belt of humanity, in all shapes and forms.

I never knew about self-harm until I came to prison.

I'd learned a little bit about it at Lewes, when I did the mentoring course, but nothing could prepare me for what I saw one morning at Brixton; it was a few weeks after my trial, around eight-thirty, and myself and Sandy were getting some photocopies in the wee office on the ones (ground floor). Next to the room is a medical room, and next to that is a disabled or PAR cell ('PAR' is an institutional term for *'Prisoner At Risk of Suicide or Self Harm'*, meaning that occupants have some sort of problem and need supervision at all times, to make sure they don't self-harm, commit suicide or harm someone else; the powers that be do a risk assessment on vulnerable prisoners, but it is something you want to stay well clear of). I was standing in the doorway of the office, and noticed something coming from under the door of the PAR cell.

I got Shandy's attention and he took a closer look.

'Fuck me,' he says, 'that's claret! Go get the S.O., Mick.'

I ran up the wing and got the S.O., who made a call on his radio - the next thing we knew, a medical team and a few officers were standing by the door. We moved out of the way, but were still able to see what was going on when they opened the door: there was a young lad lying on the floor, in a pool of blood. He was crying, and kept saying: 'I'm sorry, I'm sorry…'

The nurse said: 'Not again.' I think his name was David.

They worked on him for a while, and eventually they brought him out of the cell. Nothing could have prepared me for what I saw; the devastation this young man had caused to himself is very difficult to describe without feeling sick:

Wearing only a white T-shirt and boxer shorts, it was clear to see that his arms were a mass of deep purple, red and white horizontal and vertical lines of scarred tissue, where skin used to be; his throat was the same, and his mouth had been cut at the sides, over and over, to mimic a smile in one direction, and a sad face in the other - like Joker in the *'Batman'* movies. He was deathly-white, and what I could see of his skin was a jaundiced pallor. He looked at Sandy and I, and just started laughing, as they carried him away; it turns out that the guy has severe mental problems, and is a prolific self-harmer.

What on Earth is he doing in prison? I thought to myself.

How can the courts send someone like him to jail? He won't get the care and attention he needs in a prison cell - he should be in a fuckin' *padded* cell; the person who sent him here should be ashamed of himself or herself. Is this the idea of society's punitive justice? What is society? Where is this faceless ideology? Where can I track it down and have a good chat with it, this society?

Yes, lock people up who have broken the law, but, for fuck's sake, sort them out. These men and women will continually come to prison, serve their time, and then return to so-called 'society'. And, what has changed? Nothing.

It was at this time that I started to get a bee in my bonnet about prison.

I was seriously disturbed by what I had seen, and it will forever be etched in my memory; pure futility.

This scene, and the disbelief that accompanied it, had moved and shocked me, and I went off to my Education class feeling quite ill. Spoke to B, at the gate, and he asked me if I was alright. Told him that I'd just seen a pretty horrible sight, and he came and spoke to me later in the morning. The S.O. came over and had a chat with me, as B phoned the wing to find out what had happened, and why I was so upset. The conversation I had with the S.O. was a truly eye-opening experience:

This young fella had been a regular at Brixton, and he was also a regular at the courts; nobody knew what to do with him. They (the system) had tried everything: he had been sent to all that society could provide, and all they could do now was stop him from killing himself. But he didn't want to kill himself - he just liked to cut himself.

The S.O. was very honest and open with me. He said: 'You shouldn't have witnessed what you saw this morning'. I had to assure him that I wasn't complaining - I was just disturbed by what I'd seen. It wasn't the first time I'd seen someone with those types of scars, and it wasn't going to be the last, but it was definitely the worst.

I looked at prison officers in a different light after that day.

I remember when I used to work in my pub. We used to get a regular visit from some serious hombres, and even though I mixed well with them, I knew to keep my distance. It was strange in those days - each of the areas (manors) in London are like little villages, and everyone knows everyone else's business. I used to get cops and villains coming in around closing time, looking for a pint or two. I remember one night I was in bed with a beautiful Aussie girl called Penelope, and the front doorbell started ringing (no mobile phones in those days) - it was around two in the morning. I looked out of the upstairs window, onto the street, and there was a guy from Hammersmith C.I.D.. I got dressed, went down the stairs, and, when I opened the door, four of his mates came in with him.

'What's this, a fuckin' raid?' I said

'Any chance of a few beers, Mickey? We've had a long day.'

'Why not?' I ushered them in, poured a few pints, including one for myself, and we all sat chatting.

Penelope shouted down the stairs: was I coming back to bed? I told her to go back to sleep and I'd see her in the morning - I'd a funny feeling this was going to be a late one. About half an hour later the doorbell goes again, and I opened the door. Only, this time, to the gangster, and four of his mates.

'Come on in - join the party,' I said, thinking to myself: *Fuck me - this is going to be a bit of fun.*

''Ello, John – how's it goin'? What can I get you?'

‘‘Ello, Jack – no, I’ll get you one.’

I stood behind the bar and started to pour the drinks, as they argued over who was paying for them. Of course, *I* ended up paying.

I’d just sat down, when the door goes again. They all looked at me, as if to say: ‘Now who?’

It was two of my mates from Belfast, who were staying out of trouble and needed to be away from Northern Ireland for a while. And I kid you not, twenty minutes later another two guys from the opposing team turned up.

What a fuckin’ night that was!

I remember, at one stage of the morning, standing on my own behind the bar, just laughing my head off. They all stopped and asked me what was so funny.

I just said: ‘You should see what I can see.’

Here were twelve very serious blokes, from different sides of the fence - and the law - all sitting together, having a laugh and a beer; all of their rivalries, egos and animosity had been left at the door. They had all come to see me, and they all knew that whatever was said would stay within the walls of my pub. They all felt safe, and free to be themselves in my company, and because of my company. There aren’t too many people who can say they have sat in the same room with such people, and come out of it unscathed.

They all left around six o’clock in the morning, and I went back to bed, pissed as a fart.

I would see them all at different times over the coming years, and they would always ask about the others, laugh and say: ‘That was a good night, Mick - cheers.’

CHRISTMAS DAY 2007

11.20am

I’m typing this in a wee room on the ground floor of ‘B’-wing, H.M.P. Brixton.

'The Snowman', by Aled Jones, is blasting out, and the lads are playing table-tennis.

I'm holding back the tears… not. Phoned my family – everybody fine, and life is okay.

Was offered a drink of Bells this morning, by my Maltese neighbour - one of the officers had brought it in for him. Took one sniff and said: 'No thanks.' It was very tempting, but I've stuck to my word: *No drink or drugs whilst I'm in jail.*

I'd mentioned before about Brixton being on a short fuse, and this all became evident when there was a mass riot on 'A'-wing - the authorities were minutes away from losing the wing completely. It was a bit rough, and a few of the governors were hospitalized, but not nearly as bad as it was claimed in the newspapers:

'MUSLIM AND IRISH GANGS RUN WILD IN BRIXTON,' the headlines read.

What really happened was an Irish guy and a Muslim guy got into a row over drugs, a couple of the Muslim guy's mates went for the Irish guy, and then his mates piled in. When the ogres came to break it up, it kicked off, and the whole wing went on the rampage.

Subsequently, 'A'-wing was locked down for a few days, and forty or fifty cons were shipped out. It didn't hit the papers until two weeks after the event, when most people inside had forgotten about it.

I'd started to get settled in Brixton, and ended up on the fours on 'B'-wing – a single cell, with all the mod-cons, and a fantastic view of London's rooftops.

Myself and Shandy had become good pals by now, and Mr M. (Irish officer), was always there, with a laugh and a joke about everyday life, and bullshit in general. He called me over one day, and said: 'Mick, you're one of the more sensible ones - do you want to go to a meeting next week in the chapel?'

'Sure, no problem,' I said.

Next week rolled up, and, to be truthful, I'd forgotten all about the meeting, and was heading off to Education for the day, when I got directed towards the chapel.

Inside were fifty inmates selected from the population (of 900), and we met people from *'The Howard League for Penal Reform'*. It was great - I met Lord Carlisle, Francis Crook, and a few other people from the business world and general public, who had an interest in stopping re-offending and offending behaviour.

One lady in particular made such an impression on me, that I suppose if it wasn't for her, I wouldn't have realized that there actually are people out there who want to make prisons a better place. Her name is Pauline Campbell, and she told me the story of how her young daughter - who had learning difficulties - hung herself, whilst in custody in a woman's prison. I could see how badly this had affected Pauline, by the trauma etched on her face.

She asked me if I had any problems here, in Brixton - after what she had just told me, I didn't think that I had anything to complain about. I told her we had problems getting to the library.

The next thing I knew, she'd called some guy in a suit over; 'Tell this gentleman what you have just told me.'

So I did. I didn't know – at that stage – that he was the governor.

He rolled his eyes, and said: 'Okay, point noted. Give me a couple of weeks, and stop me when you see me.'

Pauline had a big smile on her face, and so did I – or more accurately, a stupid grin. She said: 'Do you not know who that was?' I just shook my head. When she told me, we both had a good laugh, and we continued chatting.

Like all of these things in prison, it was over all too fast; Pauline and a few others gave me their business cards, and I promised to write to them.

Was heading to work one morning, about three weeks later, when I spied the governor heading in my direction. He looked stressed, and in a hurry, so I didn't say anything, walking past. I'd walked a few steps, when I heard: 'Excuse me,'

I turned round.

'I spoke to you at the meeting a few weeks back, didn't I?'

'Yes, governor - about the library.'

'I've sorted it,' he said, 'you should all be getting word next week; if you don't, please get word to me as soon as possible. What's your name again?'

I told him my name, and off he went - it took less than a minute.

Popped into the library and told the librarian, and a few others at the Education department.

The following week, there was a notice stating that anyone could attend the library; if you made the landing staff aware at unlock in the morning, you should be able to attend the library that afternoon, if not the following day.

I saw the governor the following day, walking across the yard.

'Governor,' I shouted.

He scowled in my direction.

'Nice one,' I laughed, and gave him a big grin, and a thumbs-up.

He then recognized me, and, with a big smile, he said: 'My pleasure, Mr. Irwin. I'll be sending for you soon.'

My face dropped; *Oh shit - that's me fucked!*

Summoned to see him a few weeks later in the library.

I was cacking myself, but everything was cool: he's asked me to make some contributions about how things could be improved within Brixton - specifically the Education department. It was unbelievable the level of productivity which came from such a short meeting in the chapel.

I kept in touch with Pauline - she was pleased to hear that things were starting to work out for me. She was full of determination, and gave me lots of encouragement for the future.

Still, Brixton was only a local nick, and, for my life to progress within the system, I had to get to a proper jail.

Customs and Excise were still pursuing a confiscation order, under the *Proceeds of Crime Act* (POCA) – which, loosely translated into English, meant that the state were coming after me to take everything I possessed. They came up with a figure, which in my case was the street value of the drugs I had on me (they always go for the upper end of the figures); on further examination, it turned out that I was only carrying 1.1kg of the weakest (47%) grade cocaine, which would have cost around ten to twelve grand. They worked out the value at £87,000.

Never knew about a POCA, and, to be totally honest with you, I don't think too many budding criminals do, either. When I was told some of the horror stories from other inmates, I simply could not comprehend the intricacies in legality, and blatant robbery by the state of anything of value that was in your name, your wife's name, your granny's, or the cat's.

I had to provide my bank statements from South Africa and the UK, dating back six years, but all of my stuff was in a box in Cape Town – how in the name of Christ was I going to get in touch with The Jackal, and get him to go through my personal stuff and get it sent over to a prison in England? I didn't want to contact him, in case the South African authorities started looking at him - he is, after all, a gangster, and although he has nothing to do with what I've done, I didn't want a pile of shit landing on his doorstep. Not to mention the fact that he was now in control of my house, my car, my I.D. - everything. Sent him a letter, telling him to do as he saw fit and that I hoped to see him when I got out.

I later heard, from another friend, that two bastards (it's easier if I just call them 'bastards') tried to break into my house while I was still in Trinidad. They knew I wasn't coming back, and the money they would have got for the car, house contents, my paper I.D. and other personal items would have easily recouped the outlay for the 1.1 kilo of coke. The manner in which I'd been set up by these bastards became all too clear, through time and events, as they unfolded. What a fool I had been! My relationship with cocaine had dulled my powers of reasoning and sensibility, and I was well and truly shafted.

Being 'shafted' seems to be the theme of the day: just got twelve years for a crime I didn't knowingly commit, the developer who built my house wanted my property, the 'bastards' wanted my property, the British authorities wanted my property, and, with my consent, The Jackal had taken my property; in my eyes, every fucker was after a slice of me.

H.M.P. RYE HILL

I'd been told, by nearly everyone I knew, that H.M.P. Rye Hill was the place to be, and after a few very busy and productive months, I got the nod that I would be heading there. But, alas, in order to do so I had to come off of medical hold.

Fuck it, I thought, *let's get out of Brixton and start afresh at Rye Hill.*

So, off I went, and duly landed at H.M.P. Rye Hill on 5th February 2008.

It was fuckin' freezing.

What a contrast - what a place: unbelievably friendly and hospitable. Was greeted by a couple of trustees in the small, modern reception area – after being uncuffed – and given a piping hot cup of coffee. They went through my property bags, whilst a female officer wrote down the items on a property card.

A very pleasant young fellow popped his head round the corner, and said he'd see me when I was done. Got my mugshot taken, and my photo I.D. was printed out whilst I waited for dinner, which had just been brought in on a trolley - they had guessed I'd arrive over the dinner period, and made sure that I had a decent hot dinner to eat whilst I was still being processed - unheard of! I'm lovin' this place already! Fish, chips, peas and gravy, and another cup of coffee.

Another officer came in and took my four bags away. 'Don't worry,' he said, 'they'll be waiting for you when you get over to your cell.'

Officers carrying your bags! Another novelty.

Was then ushered into a room, where the cheerful chap from earlier was waiting. 'Good evening, Michael - welcome to Rye Hill. I hope you're not too tired. Won't keep you long - just a few formalities, and I'll take you over to

'Hastings' (induction wing); you'll stay there for two weeks before moving - probably to 'Edwards' - it's the 'Voluntary Drug Testing' (VDT) unit; I can see from your record you don't dabble in the weed or anything like that.'

'*'Hastings', 'Edwards'*?' I said; 'Don't tell me all the wings are named after rugby players.'

'They are indeed,' he said: '- the first governor here had a great love of the game.'

'Had?' I asked. 'Did he die, or something?'

'No, he just left suddenly.'

'Suddenly, why suddenly?' Jokingly, I said: 'This place looks brand new - who would want to leave? Has it been open long?'

'Six years.'

'So, the governor has been here for almost the whole time the place has been open?'

'Uh, no.'

'How long then?'

'Uh, she's been here two months.'

'Two months? How many governors have there been in six years, then?'

'Uh... six,' he sheepishly replied.

I thought to myself, right there and then: *Get the fuck back on the bus, my son - you have just landed in one hell of a fuck-up.*

Like is my nature, though, I shrugged it off, and 'Mr. Ever-So-Cheerful' escorted me over to Hastings, where I was greeted by Al, a guy I knew from Brixton; Al was a true cockney villain, who introduced me to a few other hard-looking men, all of whom were in their late fifties and early sixties. Now, this is more like it: proper hard-men who look as if they've been around the block a few times.

It turns out most of the guys on the wing were, like me, sentenced to twelve years and more, or were on their way down from 'A'-cat prisons, with 'A'-cat time.

Al got twenty-six years for drug trafficking. J was also in for drug-trafficking, and it turns out he knew me from London; I vaguely remember him - we were acquainted through a very serious hombre from our old manor. There was also John, Ray, Steve, Pen and Big Tony.

There was also this one guy: Dicky - he had an Irish brogue and he heard mine when I spoke to J.

'Another bandit,' he says, 'how ya doin'? Is there anything ya be needin', Belfast? Coffee, tea, burn or a wee dram, if ya prefer?'

Dicky was a Republican, and was still 'at war' with the British, this time in the form of the prison service. The years behind bars had also taken a toll on his sanity - he used to walk round the yard in the opposite direction, like the guy in *'Midnight Express'*, laughing and mumbling to himself. He was a great chess player though, and you would always see him engrossed in a game with anyone who was good enough to last the distance; he would always end up winning, so I don't think he was quite as daft as he made out.

Most of the guys I met were in for some sort of drug-related offence, and all had been, or were in the process of going through the POCA.

Was shown to my cell – number 11; I'll never forget it as long as I'm alive (there was nothing special about the number - I'll just always remember it). All the officers in this place have to be called by their first name, so I'll just use an initial to address them from here on. 'B' comes into my cell with two brand new duvets, four big, fluffy pillows, pillow-cases and duvet covers.

'Are you going to a party?' I ask him.

'I wish,' he laughs, 'these are for you. You're only meant to have one set of each, but they saw on your record you needed extra pillows and decided to give you an extra duvet as well - say nothing.'

Couldn't believe it - myself and Shandy had been trying for four fuckin' months to get a duvet at Brixton, with our own money! Here they were at Rye Hill, issuing them as 'in possession' property/bedding - what a result!

I made my bed up, made a cup of coffee from the full, unopened jar Richard had just given me, rolled a fag and walked out to the yard to smoke it.

They yard was a strange set-up; one side of each wing faced onto the yard to form a 'V' shape, and, at the other end, was a very high mesh fence, which looked onto the prison allotments and gardens, forming a triangle for the guys to walk round.

It was around seven-thirty in the evening, cold and foggy, and I was dazed from the hassles of moving from one prison to another – it felt strange. Aware I was in the country, I really started to fill my lungs with the night air - mingling with the smell of freshly brewed coffee and cigarette smoke, it felt good.

Pen came over to talk to me. Pen was a Scouser with a rare trait of being able to communicate like a dictionary, and with his intellectual command of English, he abused the spoken word to its fullest at every opportunity.

'So, you're from Belfast den, Mick? Do ya know *such-and-such*?'

'Well, now, I might and I might not - you know as well as I do, Pen, it all depends on who's doing the asking.'

He burst out laughing and said: 'Sownd, Mick! You'll do me.'

We had a good old blarney for a while, and the next thing I knew it was time for bang-up.

''B' says you've time for a quick shower, if you want one,' Pen says.

I looked at him; 'Are they for real here, or what?'

'Aye. Just don't take the piss and you'll be fine.'

The showers were right beside my cell, and I stood there for about ten minutes, watching the shit - the stresses of Brixton, and the ordeal of the last few months - disappear down the plug-hole in a clockwise direction (it goes anti-clockwise in the southern hemisphere). Got dried and lay on top of my bed.

B comes to the door; 'You set for the night, Mr. Irwin? Have a good rest and I'll see you in the morning - all the best.'

How kind was that? How thoughtful and how appreciated those few little words were - the manner in which they were delivered was not only sincere, but made me feel real… feel good… feel human, again.

Slept like a log, uninterrupted, and was woken the next morning by the key turning in the door.

Got some breakfast – another luxury I wasn't used to – and headed out into the yard with a coffee and a fag. It was still cold and still foggy.

Dicky walked past me and said: 'Hey, Belfast, is your head not cold?'

'I'm alright,' I replied.

Two minutes later he comes over, shoves something in my hand, and says: 'Say nothing, kid.'

He had given me a black, cloth beanie to keep my head and ears warm - stuck it on, and immediately felt the difference.

Al appeared at my shoulder and said: 'Fancy a few laps, Mick?' I put my mug down by the door and we headed off, as the daylight was starting to break through the mist.

He gave me a roll-up, and as we were walking, he looked at me and said: 'What have we done, Mick?'

'I hear you, Al,' I replied.

Those words will never leave me - the more I thought about their meaning, the more I realized how profound they were. This wasn't a question: it was more of a declaration - a statement, an admission of defeat and an acknowledgement of futility: we had fucked up - all the people, all the contacts, and all the money in the world could not change the fact that we were destined to walk around a prison yard for the foreseeable future. In Al's case, it might be the last thing he ever does.

'Do you reckon you could land a helicopter on the other side of that fence?' I asked, with a big grin and a twinkle in my eyes.

He burst out laughing, and slapped me on the back; 'You're alright, Mick. I'm off to make a few phone calls - is there anything you need?'

'I'm fine thanks, Al.'

The next day I was woken at six-thirty, and was told that I'd be leaving for court in twenty minutes.

'What are you on about?' I demanded; 'I only got here yesterday - I don't know anything about a court appearance, and I'm fucked if I'm going back to London to wait for another six months before I can get moved again.'

'So, you're refusing to go, then? If you refuse to go you will be given a 'red-entry'.'

'Do what you gotta do mate - I ain't going back to London,' I said. 'I know nothing about any court appearance.'

He tells me to relax, and that he'll get the unit manager to come and see me at some stage during the morning.

I was fuming, pacing up and down the cell. What the fuck was happening? I'd only just got here and I hadn't heard from my solicitor since the trial - that was over three months ago.

Mid-morning, the Unit Manager turned up and took me over to the office. We sat down and he gave me my 'red-entry' to sign.

'I'm not signing that.' I started to explain what had occurred.

He started to shake his head, and said: 'Okay, hold on - calm down, Mr. Irwin: you won't be going anywhere, except the seg at the minute, so take it easy. Do you want a cup of coffee?'

We had a long chat, and he ended up telling me to: 'Forget about this morning'. Then he ripped the 'red-entry' up, and threw it in the bin. Cool.

All I had to do now was find out from my solicitor what was going on. I got my Dad to phone the solicitor's office, and the solicitor claimed that he didn't know what jail I was in, despite speaking with me when I was at Brixton, a couple of weeks after my trial. Alarm bells started ringing, so I decided to get rid of this guy, who had failed me at my trial (staring at the ceiling), and try to find a new one.

This POCA hearing is a real monster - if you think your troubles are over once you are convicted, you will be in for a horrible reality check.

It was round about this time that Fin, my ex from South Africa, got in touch.

Fin's brother was my next door neighbour over there. Fin and I got together after the Ireland v France rugby game in 2005; she could hear me shouting and roaring at the TV while she was sunbathing on her brother's lawn. I was being a good boy that day, as I had to go to a friend's birthday party in the evening, though I'd had a few, and I couldn't help but notice her. I put on some *AC/DC*, and, after the game – which Ireland completely turned round and won - decided to give the car a good clean, as is standard practice in South Africa. Peaked my head over the wall, introduced myself and asked her if I could borrow a hose – forgot to mention I already had one hanging in the garage! She was wearing an orange thong, a pair of sunglasses, a beautiful smile and nothing else; she had the body of an angel, with long legs, beautiful, long, dark hair and the most glorious ass I'd ever seen.

A couple of minutes later she popped round with the hose, wearing a baggy T-shirt, and I offered her a beer. Turns out Fin loved *AC/DC*, and we instantly hit it off – I invited her to the party, later that day. The rest is history.

She left to go back to the UK after a few days, but we kept in touch. About a month later I had to go back to Northern Ireland on a business trip - stayed with her in London, introduced her to all my mates, and invited her over to Belfast for a few days. Before I knew it, I had quietly and unexpectedly fallen in love – I didn't say anything, because I knew that she was a career-minded business woman, and I was involved in all sorts of mischief at the time; she was based in the UK and travelled all over the world - we kept in touch, but as my loneliness, insecurities, and fear of commitment increased, so did my intake of cocaine, alcohol, women and any other type of chemical that was going: crystal meth, speed, blow, mandrax…

Eventually she stopped calling, and I was glad: now I could be left to self-destruct as I saw fit. We met up a year later, but she took one look at me and disappeared again - I was *gone*: off my face, and had become something and someone that she definitely did not need in her life.

Now, though, here she was, asking to come and visit me the following Saturday. Of course I said yes, but I was full of fear, longing and embarrassment in the days and hours leading up to her visit.

Then, there she was, standing with open arms and a beaming smile.

I crumbled in her embrace - all of my fear and trepidation dissipated, to be replaced by gentle warmth; a bit like when I'm writing: I feel safe in the page, and take comfort in the embrace of my emotions and my memories. All of those short memories - of love, laughter and passionate moans - flashed in my mind's eye, like a slide-show in fast forward. I could feel her heart beating, her body trembling, and as our bodies unwrapped themselves from that warm embrace, all of a sudden, I felt safe. Something had been said, but was unspoken; barriers were crossed, and niggles erased, to be triumphed over by well-being, and sanctuary of a sort.

We sat holding hands, facing each other - the table a welcome barrier, the ever-watchful officers and cameras our inhibitors.

'Well?' she said.

'I'm sorry,' I said.

'Please do one thing for me, Michael: do not insult me - please tell me the truth, and do not try to hold back, or the reasons for my being here will be pointless.'

So I told my beautiful Fin what, why, where, and who - didn't try to blame anyone, and my confessions were only punctuated by the occasional tear running down my cheek, the spontaneous gulps, and gasps born of anxiety and fear of truthful interaction.

When I was done she squeezed my hand and said: 'Thank you. What do you need me to do for you? I will come and visit you once a week for as long as I remain in the UK - this matter is not open for debate, and the minute you try to tell me not to will be the last time you hear from me; end of discussion.'

Holy fuck - I really do love this woman.

We stared into each other's eyes for what seemed like an age, each one waiting for the other to break the spell, to crack a nervous joke or make light of what had just been said, and *not* been said. Then I leaned over and we kissed - it was enough to seal what was done; enough to break the stalemate; enough to break the hold we both had on our fears.

And the next thing I knew, it was time for Fin to go. She said she would see me the week after next, as she would be in Hong Kong the following week, but would write. We were nervous again as we hugged, kissed and said adios. *'Never look back - it's a sign of weakness'* John Wayne and my father used to say.

I saw her through the window, heading towards the reception area - she had her head down, arms folded across her chest. I could tell she was relieved, yet upset - it broke my heart.

I went straight back to my cell and started to write to my lovely Fin - the letter started: 'Wow!'

Received a letter from Fin the following Tuesday; it started: 'Wow!'

Life was getting better.

Met a guy called Steve Wilcox - a tall, quiet, unassuming sort of bloke. He heard I liked to write, and approached me with an idea of helping him with telling his story, and maybe sending some of my work to his website. *Website?* What the hell would this guy have a website for?

Steve told me his cousin worked for a local solicitor in Leicester, and that since he had come back to England, he had been visited a few times; the guy seemed to be very good. So, I duly gave him a call and he took on my case; the other guy in London was now gone. After a couple of weeks, he too came to visit, and explained to me all that needed to be done.

Told Fin, who immediately, without any hesitation, took over, and told me that she would deal directly with the solicitor if I gave my permission.

'Of course,' I said, 'but be warned: you might not like what turns up.' She told me that if I'd already told her the truth, there was nothing for her to worry about.

To cut a long story short, it is because of Fin, and all of her hard work in London and South Africa, that I was able to get all of the paperwork for the prosecution. I believe that the Crown issued a court-order to seize my assets in South Africa, and were told by the South Africans that: 'South Africa is not a police-state, and unless *I* walked into a bank in Cape Town and signed over any so-called assets, they could whistle.' Or that was the general gist of things. Fin told me not to concern myself, so I didn't. All *I* had to do was wait until I was asked to go to court, or was summoned by my new solicitor.

Steve and I became good pals, and he gave me some of his writing to spruce up, and maybe help him with his grammar.

My God – I could not believe what I was reading:

Steve had been living in Thailand, and was caught with a couple of grams of heroin and a few 'e's. His story was truly horrific - when we talked the next day, I could see in his eyes the true horror of the scenes he'd tried to describe; how he had the will to carry on living is beyond me.

Steve ended up in Bankwang (*the 'Bangkok Hilton'*). He told me of having to go to the toilet in a queue, all shackled together, and having to squat over a hole in the ground, while the Thais would laugh and jeer at him because he had a jelly-belly. He told me of shuffling through the court-house after sentence was passed, not understanding a word, and shouting: 'What I get? What I get?', while the other prisoners laughed and mimed being choked by a noose, and drew fingers across their throats, in a country with the death penalty. It was only when he got back to the prison, did someone tell him in English that he got thirty-three years; he would have received two to four years for the same offence in England.

He told me of sleeping head-to-toe on the floor, with forty other men in the same room - the heat, the sweat, the smells and the noise, at times, drove him completely mad. I asked him why he didn't top himself.

He said: 'I don't know - I just didn't want to die.'

He told me how everyone spent most of the day cleaning their shackles, as the slightest bit of rust could cause an infection in the open wounds caused by metal on skin - everyone was petrified of infection, as there was no medicine. You could bribe the guards for certain things, such as medicine, but trying to hold on to personal possessions was very difficult. Food, too, had to be bribed and bought through the guards, or brought in on family visits; it was cooked by the lady-boys, who performed other services as well.

Steve eventually got a transfer back to Blighty, where he has to serve the remainder of his sentence (twenty-nine years) in an English prison, because the British government has a treaty agreement with Thailand, that if any prisoner is sent home to England they will not be released and must serve the full amount of the sentence, as handed down in Thailand.

So, every day Steve is surrounded by guys who've committed murder, robberies, dealt and trafficked massive amounts of drugs, and will serve only a third of what he has to do. It beggars belief, and I don't want to misquote, but Steve has challenged the establishment regarding his sentence, and the last I heard he was making some sort of progress. You can contact him at *steve@bankwang.com* or just *Google* 'Steve Wilcox'.

NOVEMBER 2008

To say that H.M.P. functions at a snail's pace is fair comment. Private jails - at least here at H.M.P. Rye Hill – are worse: they fool you with politeness and political correctness.

There is a group of individuals among the middle management here, who are rotten to the core: they spend their time covering up the mistakes and bullying tactics of a handful of their subordinates.

Was transferred to Edwards unit - the V.D.T. wing. There I met Angel.

Angel was the editor of the award-winning prison magazine, and was also the founder of the prison radio. One of the staff members had seen that I was always writing, and instigated my pass from Hastings to Edwards, with the idea that I would meet Angel, and he could help guide me to work in the radio and magazine. What a great idea!

What a fuckin' mistake.

Nothing to do with Angel.

The problem was I had to go to the Education department, where the person in charge of assisting prisoners (my job at Lewes and Brixton) was a civilian member of staff employed by Manchester College. When I'd gone through the induction process it took me four weeks to speak to this person, and, when I did... well, to say that we didn't hit it off would be an understatement of the greatest magnitude.

The problem was that I had overheard this person interviewing a young lad, whilst they sat at one of the tables situated outside my cell door, and this person was the rudest, most arrogant, patronizing piece of work I have had the misfortune of meeting within the system - I've met some nasty individuals, but this person topped the lot.

To make matters worse, the officer in charge of the well-being, security and assistance of prisoners in the Education department was one of the most reviled in the prison - this officer had been 'shitted up' on no fewer than eight occasions (a process in which inmates will save up their excrement in a large container for a couple of days, then throw it over the appropriate person). To be honest, I actually believe that she was proud of the fact!

Angel had warned me to stay well clear of both of these individuals, because they have destroyed many a man, and, short of committing another crime of a very serious nature, there wasn't much you could do against them, because they were protected by the little clique inside the management. It was only a matter of time before I fell foul of these people.

Still, while it lasted, it was pretty good - working on the radio and magazine most days, myself and Angel got on like a house on fire. Angel was an ex-marine and 'Hell's Angel', and you certainly wouldn't think him an 'Angel' by the look of him. He was five-foot-six, balding and built like a brick shit-house - I'd always associated Hell's Angels with long, greasy hair.

Whilst I was on Edwards I only associated with Pen and Angel, calling over to have a chat with Angel most evenings. He always made me laugh, and it wasn't long before we became good friends, confiding in each other and discussing our futures, families and fears. Angel had been stationed in Northern Ireland in the bad old days, and was always winding me up about being a foreign national - after a while I stopped biting, but he still tries his best.

Angel is another one of us who has to go through the POCA. He told me how it had affected him and his family, and it really did put the fear of God into me.

By now I had realized that the simplistic idea of being caught committing a crime, being sent to prison and serving your time behind bars as the sole punishment, was somewhat rather naïve. Furthermore, being sent to a private nick was turning out to be a further punishment *within* a punishment. I'm not going to rant on about individuals, and how delusional they are when they think that they contribute to society by turning up for work each day, to antagonize, demean and bully men.

The very idea of prison is one of subversion and dominance. A well-known psychological experiment, conducted in the United States by Philip Zimbardo and his colleagues in 1971, shows how they 'set up a simulated prison situation and randomly assigned a group of male participants to the roles of "guard" or "prisoner".' Their experiment, scheduled to last for two weeks, had to be stopped after only six days, because the participants had taken their roles too seriously: the 'guards' became increasingly brutal and abusive, while the 'prisoners' became passive and showed signs of emotional disturbance. These findings seemed to show how quickly apparently 'normal' people – individuals neither prone to violence nor emotionally disturbed – could change, simply because of the roles they had been assigned.

I remember a guy in the cell next to me losing the plot and throwing a jar of Branston pickle at the closed door; the female Unit Manager had been shouting at him through a closed door, and he basically told her to go away and leave him alone. This is how they would operate. They would wait until you were behind your door before informing you of any misdemeanour, or get four or five strapping lads from the security team to ghost you off the landing when everyone was locked up.

Angel told me that he was going to leave the radio and magazine, which he had worked so hard to set up. When I asked him why, he simply said: 'It isn't worth becoming another statistic'. To fall foul of these individuals was to screw up an otherwise faultless prison record; at the end of the day there was too much to lose - your sanity and family had to take precedence.

So, Angel left and got a job in the prison gardens, where he became a more content person.

Foolishly, I thought I could take over where Angel left off, even though Angel had been there for three years, and me only three months.

I'd arranged for Fin to send in some CDs, for use on the prison radio. I asked for permission and received a reply from the relevant governor, stating that there was no problem, as long as they went through the proper procedure. In an attempt to make everything clear and above-board, I asked the guy in charge of the radio if I should address them to him and not to reception, as anybody could claim them.

Oh dear - what a mistake. The little clique had been waiting for a chance to pounce, and pounce they did.

Was sitting in the radio room, putting a programme together, when an officer from the security department came in and told me that I had been sacked for trying to illegally smuggle CDs into the prison, undermine a member of staff and undermine the prison.

That was the start of a seven month war with H.M.P. Rye Hill, a prison already under investigation over a death within its walls and its covering up illegal practices.

I'd asked for permission and received it in writing from the Head of Residence. When I showed this to the powers that be, they said that I should have addressed it to the prison radio or reception, and not to the person in charge of the radio, and that I could re-apply in six months; I was now under security surveillance within the prison.

This was only the beginning. They would come and sit beside me if I was talking to a fellow inmate, go through my cell day after day, or just come and stand beside me for no reason. Well, I say 'no reason', but it was clear to me that their intention was for me to snap and swing for one of them.

Within the space of one week, I was ghosted off the V.D.T. unit to 'Carling' - the worst wing in the jail - when the reviled officer, who had been in charge of the Education department, was made temporary manager of 'Edwards' for five weeks. Myself and Angel had a good old laugh about it, and the guys started a book on how many days it would take for her to find a reason to get rid of me; she started on Monday - I was gone by the Friday. Three times that week I had to walk past this person - each and every time she ordered me to do something; she spoke to me in a way that can only be described as antagonistic.

The fourth time it happened, I was standing beside Angel, outside his cell, having a break from what was now in-cell studies. As this person walked past, she told me to get behind my door or she would bang me up permanently and remove me from my Open University studies. I flipped, and demanded to see the prison chaplain, as I was sick and tired of this intimidation and bullying.

The chaplain came over, and for the next hour this person hid from him - she would see him coming through one end of the wing and disappear out the other - it was very childish and comical.

The chaplain said to me: 'This has become ridiculous, Michael - I've got better things to do with my time. Just do me a favour: keep your mouth shut and don't give this person any excuse to cause you harm.'

They came at lunch-time lock up - six of them.

I won't say what happened.

But I decided to register a formal complaint. It went to the prisoner ombudsman, and no fewer than twenty-eight members of staff made statements. But not one member of staff in that prison would help me.

I'd reached an all-time low; it was only when I spoke to the prison chaplain did things change for me.

I'd been asked to write a piece about bullying in prison, for a charitable organisation, which would be mixed with music to create a CD for young offenders and prisoners, who felt vulnerable on the inside. I wrote my piece, and the lady in charge told me I had to go to the radio room the next day to record my writing with the sound-engineer, who'd come in to record and mix everybody's work.

'Do you honestly think they are going to let me into the Education department, after what I've been accusing them of?' I said.

She laughed, and said: 'Don't worry - I've cleared it: you'll be escorted there. Please, for your own sake, don't say anything to anyone - just walk in, record your work and leave.'

Could not believe the reception committee I got the following day - there were three big lads escorting me through the prison to the Education department, the head of security, the head of Education, the acting governor (the usual governor was in the process of leaving), and several of their minions waiting in the corridor by the radio room. The acting governor nodded at me, and I just looked through him - I did the same with each and every one of them: looked directly into their eyes; those who tried to stare me out saw nothing, as I felt nothing.

When I walked into the radio room it was just me, the guy in charge of the radio and the recording guy, the latter of which looked at me and said: 'That was a bit intense, wasn't it? Are you going to be okay to do this?'

I just beamed at him, winked at the guy in charge of the radio, and said: 'You'll understand once you hear my piece.'

'Okay,' he said, 'what music do you want me to mix with this?'

'*'Amazing'*, by *Aerosmith*.'

'Okay, cool. If you're ready, you can begin. If you get muddled or make a mistake, just continue or repeat the same sentence over again - you can do it as many times as you like: I can chop it up at the end.'

Here's my piece on bullying:

MY PIECE ON BULLYING

'Hello, I'm Michael. I'm forty-one years of age and I'm from Belfast in Northern Ireland. I've done quite a bit of travelling and exploring in different parts of the world in the past thirty years, and I can safely say: 'I've been around a bit'.

'I've ended up in jail, through nobody's fault but my own - I made a terrible error in judgement and I've ended up paying the price for it: namely, twelve years for drug trafficking. In a way, I'm glad: I got stopped in my tracks! I would probably be dead by now - I was taking three to four grams of cocaine per day, accompanied by roughly half a bottle of brandy and ten to fifteen beers. I was getting into some very serious situations and it was only a matter of time before I ended up in serious trouble or a wooden box.

'So, when I ended up in prison, it took me a month or two to get my sensible head back on.

'I was determined to give something back - to contribute something - and to help myself, by helping others. I went back to school! I became a mentor at my first jail, where I listened to other men's stories, and I witnessed some truly heart-breaking, and, mostly violent, sights.

'I grew up with violence, murder and bombings - I grew up with being told to hate, murder or harm someone, because they were a different religion, and I listened to men of the cloth incite violence towards their fellow man, all in the name of religion!

'I started to speak with men and young lads from many different cultures, religions and faiths, and I found a common theme in most of our conversations: it was intimidation, victimization and bullying. *Well, let me tell you: I was over the moon to hear this! I was definitely on home territory. After all, I grew up with all that crap - if anyone understood it, and why people did it, it was me. I built up my confidence and I started to receive a bit of support from certain individuals within the system. Before I asked a question, or sought permission about certain issues, I always explained to those concerned what my intentions*

were.

'I could see people's eyes widen as they grasped what I was trying to achieve. And with widened eyes they would let out a deep breath, as the penny dropped! I used to grin from ear to ear when I looked at a person's face, as they finally got it.

'What I wanted to do was "talk" - to share my experiences with others; talk to fellow inmates, both young and old, about a situation or circumstance that may have been similar to any experience you had when you were growing up. By doing this, myself and others could explain why certain rules were in place within the system, that we were all in the same boat, and that when you impressed upon a person that these rules were not a personal attack, nine times out of ten they would accept it. They may not agree with it, but they would accept it. I moved from jail to jail, slowly gaining the trust of others and watching people benefit from these actions.

'Then, the bullying started.

'I have found out, to my cost, that some people do not like change! Some people do not have the education, the understanding or the will to even listen. I was left alone, devastated and very vulnerable.

'I developed a fear - a fear of me*; a fear of the anger that was building up inside me - a deep, festering fear of what I could and would end up doing. I was frightened to talk to anyone, in case I snapped. Inside, I was a gibbering wreck who had been pushed to breaking point. I cried myself to sleep and stayed awake for days. My family was frightened, as they knew I was in a very dark place.*

'I spoke to the chaplain – a kindly man – and he suggested that I came to his service. "I don't believe in all that crap," I said.

'"It doesn't matter," he said, "at least we can have a chat for five minutes after the service."

'Aye, aye, *I thought* - here we go: more bullying; he'll try to brainwash me with God first, before I get my five minutes.

'Still, off I went. For some reason or other there was a break in the

service, and I got chatting to a young man I had spoken to on a few occasions before. He told me that he had heard about my problem and that the same thing had happened to him. Then, someone else – who had overheard us – said: "Same thing happened to me, mate!" The next thing I knew, there were four or five of us sitting, laughing, with wide eyes, and shaking our heads in disbelief. We all had a chat afterwards and several others joined in, then we all headed back to our separate wings, laughing and joking. Personally, I felt about ten feet tall.

'The next day I was placed in a very bad situation: I had to walk past the two bullies, only from behind. Everything was in slow motion - the venom oozing from every pore in my body was overwhelming: I could have changed the course of our lives in a matter of minutes. When I reached my cell I was shaking with adrenalin and was physically sick.

'After that, I stopped going out, I stopped talking to anyone and even stopped going to the library. The fear was back - not the fear of the person or the people doing the bullying, but the fear of what I *might end up doing. I couldn't sleep that night. I started to say the* 'Serenity Prayer' *over and over in my head, until I fell into a restless sleep.*

"God grant me the serenity to accept the things I cannot change, courage to change the things I can, and the wisdom to know the difference.'

'When I awoke the next day I wrote letters to a few people, explaining how bad I felt and how determined I was not to become a victim. I explained how I knew that all this pain, all this anger and all this hate would eventually go away.

'And that's when my penny dropped - I listened to my own advice. I knew that I could not give in to my fears - I knew that if I confronted my fear it would go away. I tried to talk to the bullies, but they just ignored me. What a result - they ignored me! I started to laugh again.

'I then began to get replies to my letters, and one person came to visit me. When we talked, it was as if a great weight had been lifted. I went to the church the following week and managed to speak to a few of the lads - within minutes

we were all laughing, joking, nodding and shaking our heads in disbelief again.

'This was when I truly stopped being angry. I didn't feel sorry for the bullies - I didn't try to understand them; they simply didn't matter anymore, because I realized that they would only be in my life for a short period of time. They would always have their problem - mine was gone - and thanks to their bullying of myself and others, they will eventually be found out. I eventually found safety through their bullying. I had a few more run-ins with the main culprits, but, after a while, they just gave up.

'Further down the line, things have changed for the better - some of the lads have moved to different jails, but we still keep in touch. It was a very dark chapter, and I was in a very bad place, both mentally and physically, but it's over now.

'There's a song called 'Amazing' *by* Aerosmith. *I sing it all the time. To me, it sums up what has happened in my life and it makes me smile. I will always thank the bullies when I hear this song, although I will also laugh, shake my head and grin, thinking of all the desperate hearts that may be going through the same thing I went through.*

'Oh yeah. Did I mention the bullies were wearing uniforms?'

Only had to repeat two lines, as I didn't have enough venom in them.

The recording guy started to clap and the guy in charge of the radio just whistled. We said our goodbyes, and I was escorted past the ensemble outside and back to the wing.

The lady in charge came to see me the next day, and told me that security had listened to the recording, and had taken the last line out - if I objected, the whole piece would be removed.

I just let it go, as, after I had read my piece, I, too, had let go.

It was out there - the message would be out there. I hope it helped some poor young guy sitting in his lonely cell, or made someone change their train of thought in difficult times.

Carling wasn't so bad, as it turned out, and a couple of days after my arrival, Pen turned up. He too, had fallen foul of another smiling assassin, and had been whisked away of a lunch-time lock up ('smiling assassin' was the name we used for all of the unit managers – some were worse than others, but none of them were better).

Had to find something useful to do with my time and, as I'd been helped by the chaplain and a few of the other Christian workers, I decided to start going to church. It wasn't that I'd found God, nor was I going to in the foreseeable future, but I found that the service gave me comfort, and I enjoyed listening to some of the guest speakers.

The services were of an evangelical nature, or *'happy-clappy'*, if you like. Sometimes they would bring in a band or some gospel singers, as well as ex-cons and bad guys who had found God and changed their ways. A lot of prisoners could relate to what these guys had to say.

They all had a similar story, in the respect that you had to be 'down' to get back 'up' - the alternative was death or prison. There was one guy - a Manchester man and real hard bastard - who had left prison after ten years and become a minister; he had us all in stitches, and invited us to follow his path.

He asked me face-to-face if I would accept the word of God.

I said: 'No, but I will still listen.'

He then asked Angel, who said he would speak to him after - turns out Angel had been making some very serious decisions in his life, and was going to be baptized in a couple of weeks. The following week Angel asked if I would come to his baptism - I truly felt honoured and was proud of him: it takes a lot of balls to stand up and speak in front of a room full of hard, cynical bastards (well, maybe not so much a roomful - maybe just me). We had a good chat one night in his cell, and I asked him how genuine and truthful his actions or beliefs had become.

He told me a story of when he was a serving marine in some west African country: he was walking down the road towards a bus and the rebels opened up on him; he just kept walking, laughing and letting off the odd controlled tap or burst from his own weapon - he could feel the bullets whizz past his head and see them dancing around his feet. He ended up pretty close to the bus, and the guys inside just abandoned it and ran away; they had spent their ammunition and couldn't believe that this mad soldier was still alive.

Angel explained that he used to think he was invincible, made light of the bravado and the machismo that soldiers attain to. For years it troubled him and, after, he read a verse in the bible he came to believe that, that day, it was, in fact, God who was looking after him. I could see that he meant it and I was touched by his sincerity.

At the baptism, Angel stood up and gave his testimony, which included the story about Africa. He choked up when he told everyone about God looking out for him, and when I looked around the hall I could see many people coughing, fidgeting and rubbing their eyes. Like me, they were moved by his story, and it had a profound effect on everyone there.

The ex-tough guy from Manchester was conducting the baptism, and when it was all over and done, I couldn't help but give Angel a hug. It was cool - everyone saw it and recognized it for what it was: a mark of respect and of friendship.

Still not my cup of tea, religion, but if you believe and that's what floats your boat, then good luck to you.

My every move and conversation was being scrutinized and monitored by the prison security team. It turns out that the most reviled officer was the girlfriend of the woman who was head of security; they wanted me to crack - to give in and start smacking all around me.

I cannot explain how difficult it was not to do this. People watched me from afar, and could see how I struggled sometimes to keep a grip of the demons inside me – guys would just come up to me and say: 'Don't give the bastards the satisfaction, Mick, you're better than that - they mean nothing to you.'

Had a conversation with a senior member of staff, who told me that they were only acting on security information received.

So, I sent off for my security file, which every prisoner has a right to see under the Data Protection Act. It cost me ten pounds, and I was warned by some of the guys not to expect too much - what an understatement that was! Received a covering letter and two pages, one of which was blank; the other contained one paragraph which had three sentences blacked out, just like this:

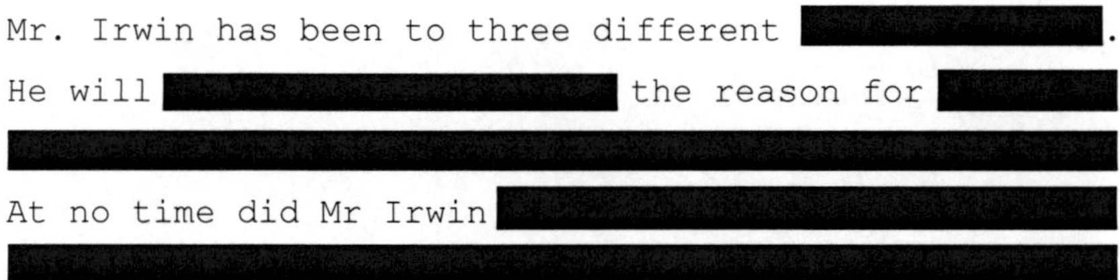
Mr. Irwin has been to three different [redacted].
He will [redacted] the reason for [redacted]
[redacted]
At no time did Mr Irwin [redacted]
[redacted]

Ten fuckin' quid for a blank page and that! I roared with laughter when I received it, and when I showed it to some of the guys they just shook their heads in disbelief.

Even though I had been moved from Edwards I was still able to see Angel when I went out into the yard, as he now worked in the prison gardens, which where situated beside our yard. We always had a laugh.

He told me that he had spoken to the person who was the instigator of all my problems. She was laughing and smiling, and said to Angel: 'I believe you're off to work in the prison gardens then, Angel?'

'Yes,' he replied, 'much safer than working with you!' Apparently her face was a picture.

Events became more stressful when I got word that my father was in hospital with renal failure, for the second time. It was awful – again, I felt truly alone and helpless. For the first time since I was child, I prayed and meant it.

I was summoned to the office and one of the members of staff said to me: 'Who do you want to tell you when your father passes away, the prison or the chaplaincy?'

I couldn't believe what I was hearing.

I managed to talk to my brother, my aunt and my cousin - they had all been to see him and they told me to prepare myself for the worst. What a nightmare.

Whilst trying to come to terms with the fact that I was never going to see my father again, I was glancing through a newspaper and read that Pauline Campbell - the lady from *The Howard League* - had killed herself by her daughter's grave, on her daughter's birthday; Pauline had given in and taken her own life. I just sat on the edge of my bed for hours, staring at the floor.

Went to the service on Sunday, and Angel told me that there was another guy from Belfast on 'Garforth'. He told me that the guy seemed okay - was 'awight' - and was looking for some help with his education, though not from the Education department (which had now been labelled the 'Kiss of Death Department'). Angel arranged for us to meet the following week at the service.

George turned out to be a great bloke and we became good friends. We made request after request for George to be moved onto my wing, so that I could help my fellow countryman with his education, but no luck: security blocked it every time. By now the whole prison knew how petty and childish their issue with me had become, and if this wasn't so serious it would have been funny.

Still, there are many ways of skinning a cat, as the saying goes. Myself and George had a good chat with the prison chaplain, and he arranged for us to come over to the church and speak with each other, where I was able to give advice in regards to his education, and my transfer back to Northern Ireland.

For me, getting home was my one and only target.

George was in a similar boat, and because I had made my initial request to return home when I was at Brixton, I was able to help him.

In relation to George being in prison, you could say that he'd had a bit of bad luck: George was a lorry driver, who had been unknowingly carrying copious amounts of illegal class-'A' drugs, mixed in with his cargo. He had a European judge sitting in on his trial and was granted bail – unheard of when dealing with drugs trials in the UK – as the judge had stated that in his country this man would be 'no risk of flight', etc. George was out for nine months and flew back to England for his trial, where he was led to believe that he would be let off. On the morning of his trial they changed his barrister, and the judge, which meant that the European guy wasn't able to witness the trial. George was duly convicted and is appealing his sentence, hoping for a retrial.

I've told him not to hold his breath, but I'd help him in any way I could.

My father was on the mend and I sent my condolences to Pauline's family via *The Howard League*. My problems, again, started to feel small compared to the people around me, and when I had a long hard look at myself in the mirror, I decided that life wasn't so bad. Okay, I was in a bit of shit, but at the end of the day - if I'm honest - I picked a fight and got it.

My only concern now was to get back home to Northern Ireland, and as a result of this change in attitude it no longer mattered or concerned me about the idle threats and obstacles - all I had to do was not react: don't physically attack anyone and I'll be fine!

Angel had been lucky: he'd received his 'C'-cat status ages ago, and, with the help of the chaplain, had managed to get to where he wanted to get to: H.M.P. Erlestoke, near Bristol. Angel would now be near his home, and it would be much easier for his wife and grandson to visit. Before he left he told me not to give up fighting, and not to give anyone an opportunity to screw me over - just be cool and say: 'Yes Sir, no Sir, three fuckin' bags full, Sir,' for as long as it took to get the fuck out of Dodge.

There was a man from Ghana on Carling, who we called 'Father', or 'Papa John' - a big man and an even bigger Arsenal fan, who had lived in England for years, and was also in for drug trafficking. His confiscation order was worth over a million, and he had lost all sorts of property and business premises; as a result of his actions, his wife and daughter were in the process of losing the very roof over their heads.

'Papa John' had a strong, African-based belief in God - he had the idea of becoming a minister and going back to Ghana. The only trouble was he didn't fully understand the bible and its meaning, because it was in English - he would hear the words but not fully understand the context. He asked me for help.

I wasn't allowed out of my cell by this stage, but a few of the officers allowed me to sit with him at a table in the corner of the wing, and to sometimes use the study room if none of the other guys were using it.

This was a strange time for me - Papa John had enrolled for a couple of religious courses - what he had to do was read certain scriptures from the bible and translate their meaning, according to the word of God. I decided to use these courses as a basis for teaching him English; this meant that I had to explain everything twice or ten times, depending on the particular sentence in the scripture. During this time, I found that I had a better understanding of the bible than I first thought, which caused me to rethink my attitudes and views towards myself and my fellow man.

At the end of every month I submitted the coursework, and myself and Papa John eagerly awaited the result and explanation from the tutor. Sometimes it became a battle of wits, as the tutor thought she was dealing with an African man, but was actually dealing with the teachings of a heathen from Belfast who always had a conflict with his attitude towards God. Again, to my surprise I found that I could teach quite well, and it wasn't long before the chaplain had me attending bible studies and meetings with other religious groups in the evenings.

Who was I to complain? It got me out and about, and I was in kind and caring company. This, in turn, helped to soothe the anger, pain and frustration I was dealing with on a daily basis. I came to the decision that the bible was still a mystery to me, but I understood the message it was giving to others; I was able to help other guys – mostly African – with their studies, and I received my biggest boost ever from Papa John: unbeknown to me, he wrote his first ever letter in English (he was sixty-two) to his wife. He received a reply and showed me his original letter - it wasn't going to win a Booker prize, but for me it was the most rewarding letter I have ever read; a letter of love, as opposed to a *love letter* - a letter from a humble man to his wife, stating how sorry he was for the trouble he had caused her, how much he missed her and how he still felt like a little boy when he dreamed about her. He was very nervous when he showed me, and said: 'Please don't laugh at my English.' He wasn't worried at all about the content, which proved to me even more the worth of his efforts. I honestly could have burst, and walked around for days with a permanent grin, which not even the smiling assassins and their most reviled could alter.

Looked forward to seeing George each week, and together we soon became regulars at the religious services. We would disappear into the back room, make a cup of tea or coffee, and chat until the rest of the lads came in. George had made several requests to be transferred to Carling, and after a very long period of time and continual moaning from George and myself, he was eventually allowed over.

The same week I received word I would be going to court in November for my

POCA hearing. Fin had managed to retrieve my bank statements, and if it hadn't been for this wonderful woman and all the running around she had to do, I would have had no chance in the up-and-coming hearing.

Fin had now left the UK to live and work in the United States. In a way I was glad, as I'd been through the mill emotionally, and it wasn't easy to face her most weeks – trying to put a brave face on things when the walls were crumbling around me. Her penultimate visit was strained, to say the least, and she had to leave early.

I could tell there was something wrong, and when I spoke to her at the last visit, she confessed that she felt as if she was letting me down by going away. It broke my heart to see her like this, and in fact nothing could be further from the truth. I told her that without her I would not have had a fighting chance in my trial, and that her presence had given me nothing but hope and encouragement over the past few months. I asked her to get on with her life, be happy, and not to worry about the future - if things worked out, then they worked out; if they didn't, it was a pleasure to have had her in my life. We left on good terms, and our last hug felt good, for all the right reasons.

It was time for me to start thinking about moving on, I knew that by going to London for my court case I'd have to leave Rye Hill. Didn't want to let the powers that be know that this had indeed now become what I wanted: to leave this place and never come back.

I started to make noises about staying: as anyone who has been in prison will tell you, if you ask for something you want, the exact opposite will normally happen; I didn't tell a soul, not even George.

I've just been for my Category Review Board, and at least I've learned a bit more about how they think I should be behaving. I'm not allowed to be aggressive.

Fair enough - let's just see if they will allow me the chance.

Just received a letter from Angel, in Erlestoke - he reckons he's made a bad move; it sounds pretty bad. Think I'll write him a letter.

I've applied for a job as a Listener and I've also spoken to CARATS (drug counsellors) about working with them. The girl in charge has given me a written letter - which will go in my file - explaining how I had already previously been considered for a post with them. As usual, the prison knew nothing about my ideas or the work I had already been doing with some of the other guys.

Wish to fuck the ignorant person next door – a Jamaican, pretend-Yardie, Muslim trafficker – would turn his fuckin' music down - he's downstairs using the phone. Think I'll have to smash his hi-fi to pieces or throw some water over it when he's out. He leaves his door open and struts around with an arrogance which obviously masks his fear and insecurity; I know Yardies, and he ain't one of them.

God grant me the serenity to accept the things I cannot change, the courage to change the things I can, and the wisdom to know the difference.

I'm sitting out on the wing by George's door – he's just sat down. Life is okay.

We're heading off to the chapel to see Charlie the chaplain. No, not Charlie Chaplin - the prison's Catholic chaplain is actually called Charlie!

What an up and down sort of day it has been.

I've just written another letter for 'T' (Open University administrator) concerning my funding for further O.U. courses. Was turned down for the last one, as I hadn't completed an A-level Business Studies course: they have told me that unless I finish the course I won't be getting any funding. This seems a bit pointless - a business studies course will be of no use to me in the future, mainly because I will be classed as a convicted criminal. When I get out, even in my previous trade I will no longer be able to hold a licence in the UK; not that

I care about this, considering my whole attitude has changed towards this line of work: I no longer want to eke out an existence by knocking my bollocks in twenty-four-seven, in a set of rooms above a public house. Sure, you can save and get your own place, but the idea of having to listen to all the crap that goes with running a pub is something for younger people to do and, frankly, I have no interest in doing it any longer.

Couldn't help thinking about the guy at Brixton who'd been drunk, killed his brother in a car crash, couldn't read or write and was trying to get back home to Ireland. The amount of young and old men in prison who can't read or write properly is frightening, and, like George's situation, dyslexia is a common complaint. I know that when I was growing up, if someone was a bit slow they just got kept back a year.

My conversations with George and my bible studies with Papa John made me realize how lucky I was, and how much more I had to offer.

'K' (a very lovely female officer) has just had a chat with me about what I've been doing with Papa John. She could see how pleased I was, as he's just received 97% out of 100% on one of his bible study courses. K has said that she will have a word with the Smiling Assassin about the positive effect all of this is having on myself and others.

From what I can gather, things might be looking up in that department, and the management may be starting to give me a bye-ball. I'm not holding my breath, and, as per usual, will just have to wait and see.

K is in her late twenties, and is a very attractive woman with a great personality and is one of the few people who has helped me in this place - she has kept her distance, but was always good for quick chat and gentle reassurance. I never got the chance to thank her - I do so now.

13TH NOVEMBER 2008

I've managed to buy myself a digital hi-fi and a set of cordless headphones -

what a bloody luxury! I don't think I've listened to music properly - or sober, come to think of it - since I was a teenager. I've just been listening to *Planet Rock*, blasting in my eardrums; lovely - warm and content.

Was brought out of my trance by the sound of someone rapping on my door - it was George. He's just received a letter from National Offender Management Service (NOMS), and he was unable to read all of it. They have informed him that there are no spaces back home, and that he will be in for a long wait. I reassured him that this is just a standard response, and we'll be back home as soon as the system processes our relative requests.

I'm still waiting to go to court. Just woken up so I'm a bit grumpy.

Think I'll definitely pack my gear up tonight.

Pen is complaining about the music. He says to one of the officers: 'Why do you let these people get away with it, day after day? It's driving everyone mental! You are a bunch of cowards and should be ashamed of yourselves.'

I agree with him, and chirp up: 'If you don't do something about it, I will, and people will get seriously hurt.' I knew I'd be going to court, so I just let them stew for a while.

I can't wait to get out of here, even if it is only for a day. I've been lucky in a way, as I've been to the hospital a few times, and have got to see the outside of the prison. Some people *never* get outside, from the beginning to the end of their sentence. It's all a bit of a palaver, to be honest, and they really make a big deal out of it. I have no intention of trying to escape - the thought would never actually cross my mind, as it is illogical: there is absolutely no purpose in escaping, or even in *thinking* about it. Fact is, if they gave me the taxi fare I'd be there and back as soon as I could.

The amount of time and effort it takes for a prisoner to be taken to hospital is ludicrous; normally, three members of staff have to go with you - one to drive and two to escort you. You are double-cuffed the whole time, to an officer. I heard one story about a guy who was going for open-heart surgery: the officer had to scrub in, and was only allowed to take the cuffs off when the surgeon made the first cut in the guy's chest.

On my last escort to hospital, I'd already fallen out with the prick I was handcuffed to, as he'd said to me: 'All you fuckin' paddies are the same to me'. I told him he was prick, that the English master-race still thought they had an Empire, and that they were solely responsible for the rape and murder of many a country, in the name of said 'Empire'. It was a tense journey.

At one point, approaching a roundabout, as we slowed down, a beaten-up, old, white Transit van pulled in front of us and the back doors flew open.

I shouted: 'Here's my boys comin' for me now!'

The guy beside me nearly shat himself, and the taxi-driver nearly crashed the car, he was laughing so hard.

Fuckin' wanker!

The last time I went to hospital it was for a double endoscopy (a camera in both ends), which was extremely embarrassing. The staff nurse asked me to slip into a hospital gown, as is hospital procedure, and the five-foot tall, twenty-year old female officer I was handcuffed to said: 'We are not allowed to take the cuffs off him.'

'Well, unless you get him into a gown we can't follow procedure.'

The second officer went and phoned the prison in order to get permission from a governor to put a chain on me. They then had to phone another member of staff to find out what the procedure was - nobody knew.

The nurse had already given me an epidural: by this point I was ready to evacuate my bowels.

I said: 'Can you just drape the gown over my shoulders, tie it at the back of my neck and pull my pants down?'

This seemed to please everyone, except the surgeon, who asked me if I didn't consider this somewhat degrading. I told him I found the whole process degrading, but I'd rather get the procedure done if it helped to resolve my stomach problems.

It was one of the most embarrassing, humiliating and degrading experiences of my entire adult life: that I had to sit with the toilet door open, chained to a male officer (they had to change officers as I could not be attached to a female whilst being on the toilet), as I let loose the contents of my bowels is something I'd rather forget. The nurse then had to come in to wipe my arse; this is the first time I'd ever had this done to me, and I pray that it's the last. I shrugged it off, but it was excruciating.

I was then led into the room where the procedure was to be carried out, attached to a four-foot chain; everyone was staring at me, and I had to suppress the urge to start barking at them. They pulled my pants down, as my hands were still cuffed in front of me, and I manoeuvred myself onto the table. I had been given a tablet to make me drowsy, but by the time they'd finished sorting out how to proceed, the effects of the tablet had worn off completely: I was fully conscious, and I felt and saw everything going on in the monitor above me.

It was very weird lying on my side - I could feel the draught around my nether regions, and a little thud of pain where the camera was proceeding through my gut, intestines and anal passage to my bowel; at one stage I could see these yellow, mushroom-like things in my intestines.

I heard one of the medical team saying: 'Are you getting all of this?'

To which someone else replied: 'Oh, yes'

It was over as soon as it had started, and I knew what to expect next, as I'd had an endoscopy done years ago, in Belfast: I had to sit on the toilet, letting my body continue to evacuate itself, and at the same time get my head near the sink in order to violently retch and be sick – basically, contracting and convulsing from both ends, which was horrible, and lasted about ten to fifteen minutes. The nurse then came back to wipe my arse again; to be on the safe side she gave me an adult nappy to wear until I got back to the prison, and the safety of my cell. I took it off as soon as I had my cuffs removed at reception.

15TH NOVEMBER 2008

It's time for me to go to court for my confiscation hearing. I've been told by my solicitor that it's going to be a formality, but I must attend.

Need to pretend that I don't want to leave this horrible place, so I'm telling everyone I see that I'll be back and will see them soon. The reception manager has told me that if I don't return today, I'll be back within three or four days - I asked her if she was sure.

'Look,' she said, 'you have to leave some of your stuff here, as they will only let you take four bags with you to court.' She labelled the rest of my belongings and wrote on them: 'NOT TO BE SENT TO BRANSTON' ('Branston' is a general storage place for prisoners' belongings, and if you have the misfortune of getting your stuff sent there, you can kiss goodbye to it for at least two years).

'What about my CDs?' I asked.

'Don't worry,' she replied, 'they are in your stored property.'

'May I see them with my own eyes before I go, please? I want to be sure they are there before I sign any forms.'

She headed around the back and returned with a big basket containing all my stuff. There was a lot of stuff in there - stuff that I had asked to be thrown out ages ago. 'Get rid of half of that crap,' I told her.

As we went through all of my stuff, and she filled out a new property sheet, one of the officers, who was standing behind me, said: 'Is this going to take much longer?'

'What's your problem?' I said. 'The transport isn't even here yet.'

He was obviously late for his breakfast - he just wanted to get me processed and back to whatever he *should* have been doing. I'd met him on a few occasions on the wing - he was new, and a bit of an asshole; he knew I didn't like him, but I didn't care.

After a very long wait, the transport turned up - it was half-past eight, and I was due in court, in London, in an hour and a half - there was no way we were going to make it, so I said:

'They don't need me at the court - I'm sure if you ring them the judge will carry out the hearing without me.'

I remember, at my trial, that the judge said that he thought a confiscation hearing (in my case) was a waste of time, and of taxpayers' money. This is another thing you get labelled with in prison: if you're a criminal, you've obviously been one all your life, have never had a job and therefore never paid any taxes. Let me tell you, I've paid more taxes in one week than some of these guys earn in a month; the way I see it, I have paid for my fair hearing.

Just before I left, the officer sorting out my property said: 'Don't worry if you're not back within a week - we'll send your stuff on to you; as you can see: it's all here.' I thanked her, headed off into the back of the van and plonked myself down in the seat. The door was closed by the driver, and I was locked in the cell in the back of the van.

The impatient officer got into the back, beyond the glass, and started to go through his procedure, saying: 'Are you Michael Irwin, and do you know where you're going?'

I replied: 'Yes. I don't know why I'm being sent to court so late.'

To which he replied: 'Shut the fuck up, you cunt!' He put his face right up to the glass; 'I hope they take all your money off you - your family's too. I hope they make you suffer, you bastard.'

And with that, he was gone.

I just sat there, dumbfounded.

The van door was slammed shut.

When the driver got into the front seat he said: 'Fuckin'ell, mate - he's calling you all the names under the sun out there. Do you want to make a complaint?'

I asked them if I could take their names, and whether they would back me up if I did.

The passenger shouted: 'Don't worry, mate - our names are on the log; if anyone asks us we will remember what he said.'

So, off we went, heading for London.

On the way we pulled into the car park of H.M.P. Onley, a young offenders' centre next to Rye Hill. 'We've just got to pick one up here,' the driver shouts. Now I definitely know there is no way we are going to make it in time.

Forty minutes later we leave HMP Onley - I ask them to phone control, and ask if I'm still required in court; if they can sort it out fast enough, I say, they can take me back to where I just came from.

No such luck.

We're half-way to London, when they get the phone call saying that the trial will be going ahead without me, but they still need me at court. Bollocks! I bet they don't need me: someone just wants to speak to me.

Probably just as well, as I could have gotten into some serious shit the next time I saw that officer. I don't mind having to deal with abuse, but my family has done nothing - this man knew what he was saying. There is no excuse for what he did. I just wish I could remember his name.

We have to take the guy we picked up at Onley to Southwark Magistrates first. It turns out that he's being released, knew fuck all about it, and has left all of his gear back at Onley.

We arrive at Croydon Crown Court at twelve-thirty-ish. When I get into the reception area, one of the officers comes up to me and says: 'It's okay: they've already had the hearing and they've dropped the confiscation order.'

What a relief! I felt a lot lighter.

Asked him why I was still brought to court.

'Oh, your barrister wants a quick word.' I bloody well knew it! Why on Earth couldn't I have spoken to her by letter, after the trial was done and dusted?

My solicitor had already left, and I spent ten minutes with the barrister, before being taken back to the same green cell in which I'd spent the days during my trial. *Déjà vu!*

Not quite, but it did feel as if I was going to have to endure another long and meaningless day.

The barrister wanted to talk to me about appealing my sentence, as it was now painfully obvious that I wasn't the massive drugs baron Customs and Excise had previously thought. The barrister did say that she thought my sentence was a bit excessive, but the judge - the right honourable 'Judge Josey

Wales' - was the same which conducted my trial, so it was unlikely that he would change the length of my sentence; that which he had handed down was still well within sentencing guidelines for the offence with which I was charged.

I hear all of these prison 'experts', inside and out, slagging off judges, but have they ever stopped to listen to themselves? Agreed, there are a lot of miscarriages of justice, but these stem from the police, and from Customs, not the judge. In my case (as indeed in the majority of cases) it was *me* who got into trouble; I know that a judge has to do his or her job.

So, for fuck's sake, if you're guilty be a man, dry your fuckin' eyes and get on with it.

I still hear guys five or six years into their sentence, saying: 'There's another day up the judge's arse!' Is the judge also, on that particular day, thinking: *Oh, good: there's another day done for wee Johnny - I hope he suffered*? I think not.

Wise up and stop trying to attribute blame.

I digress.

My barrister went on to tell me that if I appealed and lost, I would have to start my sentence all over again.

'The Law' is mad!

I can see how they play their games, and *justice* has nothing to do with it. I told the truth, but I didn't follow the correct procedure: I didn't *admit guilt* at the earliest opportunity - if I had, I would have received around eight years, instead of twelve. Levi was right

It's okay looking at these things in hindsight, but, at the time, I knew that my family would be connected to what I had done, and for me that was totally unacceptable. At least I'm free from POCA now, to get on with my time, and my life, as best as I can.

It's around two-thirty, and we're on the off again. We're stopping at Southwark again, where we pick up seven or eight guys, all gang members, all around eighteen or nineteen. The gang culture is crazy in London - you really have to be on your guard at all times where these young men are concerned.

NEXT STOP: H.M.P. HIGH DOWN

I remembered being here – sitting outside, in the sweatbox – just over a year ago. All the building work which had been going on seems to have been completed. I wonder if young Carl is still here, or Mick ('Martin McGuinness') - if they are, I'm quids-in.

We're let off the bus one at a time, and escorted into a largish room, with a bench round the wall and a bog in the corner: the reception holding cell - I grab a piece of the bench, in the corner, near an open window. Everyone is smoking – I've been off them for six months now.

The room starts to fill up – courts are kicking out – and it is getting very claustrophobic.

Just in the nick of time, I hear my name being called out. I approach the desk and the S.O. says: 'Well, well - what have you done, to come from the relative luxury of Rye Hill to this dump?'

'Confiscation at Croydon,' I replied.

'How'd it go?' he asked.

'No-brainer: case dropped,' I said.

'Woohoo - lucky boy! I've seen some horror stories coming through here. How long you got left? Never mind - I can see it here: twenty-thirteen; you'll be with us a while, then.'

'I'm waiting for my transfer back to Belfast - it couldn't proceed until the confiscation hearing was out of the way.'

'Don't you get any visits, then?'

'Nah: my girlfriend has moved to L.A. and all of my friends and family are in Belfast. Is it possible I can stay here until I get sent home? It would save a lot of time, effort and money if I got sent home from here.'

'You're probably right, but you should know by now that things don't always work out the way they should. I'll make a note of it and have a word with the P.O., who deals with the transfers - if you're still here, he'll be able to help you; he's a good bloke.'

'Great, thanks very much,' I said. 'What's the craic now?'

'You'll be stuck on 'HB3'- new arrivals - until you go through the committal process, and you'll probably move to one of the house blocks by Tuesday. I see here you're on 'High Risk' - you'll have to see the P.O. before you go anywhere.'

'No problem,' I said, and went back to the holding room, which, by now, had filled completely.

I waited for about an hour, listening to the gang members recruiting some other young, black guys - establishing who was from where, and who knew who. One young guy, who was obviously scared, said he knew such and such, and he was a big face in their world.

This other guy chirps up: 'How do you know him? You're full of shit: you don't know him.' His mates were starting to giggle, and I watched them all start to get in the young guy's face.

'I'll ask you again: how do you know him?'

'He's a mate of mine, innit.'

With that, the gang guy slapped him across the face and said: 'You're talking to him, you prick! I'll deal with you later.'

They all started jeering at the guy, who ran out of the room and told the officers he couldn't stay in there. They just pushed him back in the room, and the young lad went and sat sheepishly in the corner.

The gang member went outside; about ten minutes later he came back in, and approached the young lad, who was sitting on the floor; 'Look, it's cool. I'm going to HB2, and you're gonna be on my landing. Join up with us and we'll look after you.'

And that was the end of that.

As the room slowly started to empty - I just sat there, minding my own business.

Eventually, I got called in to see the P.O. - a large woman, very well spoken.

'You know that single cells are not a given, and you have to earn the right to have one?' she said.

'I didn't make the decision, and I'm not coming off of 'High Risk' until I get back to Belfast,' I said, as unthreateningly as possible.

'Okay,' she said to the S.O., 'where are we going to put him? We don't have the space.'

'There's plenty of room on 'H5' after he's done the induction - look.' He pointed to something on the computer screen.

'Okay,' she said, 'it'll do for now. But I want to review this in a couple of weeks.'

An officer then came and said: 'He ready to go?'

'Yes,' the P.O. replied, and off we went, to the area where property was checked and searching was carried out. I could see there was an X-ray machine, with about twenty bags beside it, waiting to be processed.

'How many of these are yours?' an officer asked me.

'Six, and those two boxes,' I replied.

'There's no way we're going to get that lot done tonight - you'll have to come back in the morning.'

By this stage, I'd been through enough receptions to know that if you didn't leave with your property there and then, it would take you weeks to get it back onto the wing. I would have to go through the endless daily routine of lies, bullshit and having to hassle officers, just to get off the landing to reception and collect my own gear! I asked him if I could, at least, take my bedding with me, and he agreed; they stuck my bag through the X–ray machine, and off we went.

It was now dark, and there was a frosty mist in the air. I'd come into the reception on ground level, and had now just walked up two flights of stairs to a walkway - all of the wings were connected to walkways. It was spooky: I couldn't see that far in front of me, and the walkways were closed in with wire mesh.

We took a left turn, a right turn, another right, then a left, and I had absolutely no idea where I was. There were sign-posts everywhere with arrows on them, which was very helpful, I thought - especially for those who can't read.

Was handed over to the wing officer. He showed me to my cell and said: 'You're the 'High Risk', are you? Do you want to take a shower?'

'Yes, but not with you, thanks.'

'You got ten minutes, and no more.'

Was done in five, and back in my cell, getting dried off. That's when he came and said: 'Look, it's getting late and I'm bollocksed - any questions will have to wait until tomorrow. I'm 'Mr. O' - I'll see you in the morning.'

'Don't worry,' I said; 'this is my fourth nick in a year - you won't be hearing much from me.'

'Good to know,' he replied, and off he went, slamming the door shut behind him.

There was a welcome pack on the table. I brewed myself a cup of tea, fiddled with the controls for the telly and made my bed up. The bed was bolted to the floor - an old metal-framed type. It wasn't flush with the wall - there was about a foot of a gap – and I felt the euphoria, the anticipation creeping through my body, as I lay down flat, buried my face in the pillow and was able to spread my legs, causing each foot to slightly hang over the edges of the bed; words alone cannot express the joy I felt at that particular moment in time. This little bit of space made up for a year and half of bullshit.

I buried my head and started laughing into the pillow, letting out a few '*yee-haw*'s. The beds in my last four cells had been bolted to the wall, and were just about wide enough to lie on your back - you most certainly could not spread out. If you meet someone in a bar, ten years from now, who's carrying a bit of a limp, it's probable because they've been in prison, and caused by a sore hip, from hours of sleeping on one side all the time.

I got up and sat by the table, in one of those chairs made of metal legs and frame, with a plywood seat and back - rejects from schools - and quietly observed the stillness. I was sure the next few days weren't going to be quite so quiet.

The cell was roasting – the two blue pipes running through each cell again – yet I felt strangely relaxed. I hoped that this would be my last stop before I went back to Belfast; with that in mind, I decided to stay out of the way and ask nothing – to keep myself well and truly under the radar.

Got into bed around ten o'clock and slept like a baby.

Couldn't quite remember how it felt, being new to a prison: cracking up because you don't know what's going on. Well, it's slowly starting to come back! I've been awake since half-seven, with the sound of pigeons cooing on my window-sill - one of them came inside, looked around and walked back out again.

I've been listening to people coming and going all morning. I'm determined not to ring the buzzer - will try my very best to ask for nothing; I'm in a single cell and on my own, which is all I really need, for now.

It's now three-thirty. I'm banged up, and everything I own is in reception - they told us last night that it would be sorted in the morning; famous last words, me thinks.

I'm sitting here, in prison clothes (too small), without my medication. The nurse has tried to get it for me, but the doctor won't prescribe it as my charts are in Rye Hill - they didn't send them with my paperwork (at least, that's what they're telling me). I gave all of my medication to the nurse on duty last night, but the fact that she started to fill in *my* details, on *someone else's* chart leads me to believe that there has been some sort of fuck-up, and that I will not be getting my meds. It's the same story in nearly every prison you go to: they are overwhelmed by the amount of people being processed in and out of jail on a daily basis, and the way the system is set up leads to inevitable fuck-ups.

I'm resigned to the fact - there is no point screaming and shouting about it, so I'll just have to suck it up.

Three of the spurs are out on Association and three are banged up - guess which one *I'm* on! I'm remembering how this felt when I was at Brixton: all the orderlies, out laughing, shouting, etc.... Still, I know it'll only be for a couple of days or so.

I can tell by the attitude of Mr. O and his colleagues that this wing is the mad one, where they have to deal with a constant flow of nut-jobs in and out, day after day, listening to the same questions, the same complaints and the same bullshit. I haven't bothered any of them yet.

Went down and collected lunch, then straight back to my cell. Grabbed a few of the information leaflets and a few job application forms (back to fuckin' Apps again). We will have our induction on Tuesday - that means nothing is going to get done until then, so I'll just put the feet up and try to be as cool as I possibly can; without my tablets.

Mr. O has confirmed that Rye Hill has not seen my file, and as far as he is concerned I'm not 'Enhanced' and not 'High Risk'. I'm not bothered: I'm in a single cell, nothing will be done until Tuesday morning, and I'll move to another house block after that.

Not used to this bang up again, though: we were spoilt at Rye Hill, for the amount of time we had out of cell. Suppose I'll just have to sit and soak it all up, do a bit of writing and get reacquainted with life at H.M.P. - a stark contrast from the likes of 'Ever-So-Cheerful', way back then.

If the public in general ever wonder why it costs so much money to run the prison service, they only need to look at what happened to me yesterday. One of the main purposes of the prison system is to keep and produce prisoners for court - the problem arises when a prisoner inevitably moves because of 'progression' through the system.

I know going back to Rye Hill won't happen, as I prepare myself for the upheaval of settling into a new prison. I now have to be re-processed and dealt with as a new prisoner in a new jail, before they can figure out what to do with me, whereas a trip back to Rye Hill would have saved the duplication of resources. This induction process happens nearly every time a person goes to court and ends up in a new prison - some people can be in three or four different jails in the space of a month.

17TH NOVEMBER 2008

It's really weird sitting here without wearing my earring - they made me take it out at reception.

Don't say nothing - keep thy gob shut and wait... watch and wait... watch and wait...

This is my fourth nick, and by now I have the tools, the ammunition and the experience to get me through the three month 'induction'; three months is the average time it takes for a prisoner to get fully established and accepted in a jail - people in general are wary, other prisoners, senior officers and ogres alike. Everyone treads carefully, and it doesn't take long to suss things out. I reckon by Christmas I'll be alright (or as near as - makes no difference).

2.00pm

Everybody is off to work. I had my (real) induction earlier this morning - the usual thirty minutes in a room, with loads of different coloured T-shirts sitting behind tables, ticking boxes. Maybe I'll have a go at getting a T-shirt once I get settled.

There seems to be a lot more opportunity here: a better atmosphere - you can feel it in the air, and see it in the way certain people carry themselves. There is the usual bollocks, of course, but I really can feel a difference here at High Down.

The buzzer system is back, with such a vengeance that I can't even summon the humour to revive Wilson from the dead; but I will find out who's on it and give them a slap - I'm in no mood for assholes; I'm an old hand at this prison malarkey now, so cross me at your peril!

H.M.P. 'bang up' / H.M.P. 'no staff' is also back - alive and well, just like I left it nine months ago. The officers have all fucked off and ignored the buzzer; ho-hum - here we go again.

At least I have learned to give myself a chance - to be quiet.

Daytime TV beckons - not much else to do at the minute; *tick-tock*.

19TH NOVEMBER 2008

It's around 9.30am and I'm sitting in my new cell, overlooking the exercise yard (*'House Block 5 - A spur, level 3 - cell 30'*. Or *'5A, 3-30'* - easy when you get used to it). *I* didn't go out for exercise as it's brass monkeys - I haven't got a jumper or coat (gear still at reception), and I'm waiting to go to the gym induction.

The regime and layout is completely different here at High Down: there's a desk on the twos, where an officer gives and takes Apps in the morning - the Apps are then taken to an office which overlooks 'B spur', and the adjoining 'A spur'; it houses the S.O.s, and keeps them protected from inmates asking too many questions, and from having to give answers. This desk is where it all happens in the morning, and it is a good idea to strategically place yourself within earshot, as you will pick up loads of relevant information by listening to others getting fucked off – this, then, enables you to *not* make the same mistakes, and the officers to *not* go: 'Oh, no: here's that prick coming again!' You have learned at someone else's expense - tough old world, innit?

Met a guy (Dec) from the Falls Road last night - he seems alright, though he looks permanently off his head. Dave C (one of the landing orderlies) had heard me talking and said: 'Come wif me geeza - I'll introduce you to another paddy.'

Myself and Dec both agreed it was great to be able to talk 'Belfastish' at our normal speed, and that if we did it right no other fucker could understand us - a useful trick when taking the piss.

I was able to phone my Dad last night as well, which was a load off; he received my letter and he knows I'm alright. The phone cuts off after ten minutes here - at least he now knows I'm not hanging up in bad temper.

My new cell is brand new, clean and compact - a bit more modern than Rye Hill. Mind you, the people who designed these things should be shot! I slept badly last night: back to a crappy metal shelf/slab they call a bed! This particular one is just wide enough for my shoulders - another foot either side would be fine.

There were alarm bells going off and on all night, and the brand new, state-of-the-art underfloor heating doesn't work - mid-November in the Surrey countryside: effin' freezing!

Dave C has handed my details to Joe, a kitchen orderly who knows the lady in Education that deals with new arrivals - she will in turn give it to the Education department head; this should speed the process up a bit. I did my own Education assessment yesterday - I'm still level-2 English and level-2 maths; funny, I don't think that has changed, or that I have been taught anything different in any of the other three jails.

Still no sign of my clothes and 'Enhanced' status being sorted - I'll just have to keep pestering officers until somebody decides to do something (when they realize I won't be going away). I'm trying really hard to teach myself how to be more patient - using this time as an experiment; wonder how long it'll last?

The ole cockney accents have become stronger and more distinguished - it makes my skin crawl. I watch certain individuals watching me - trying to suss me out. Wankers! I know I've mentioned this before, but they are so easy to spot, these guys who think they're tough - plastic fuckin' gangsters; wee boys trying to be hard. I can see their fear - it's in their eyes. Still, I'm cool, and I let them play their little game - they mean nothing to me.

I overheard a story when I was in reception about some young lads getting raped. I asked Dave if he knew anything about it, as this was the first time I'd heard of such a thing. Apparently, it happened the week before I arrived: some young (twenty-one year old), black gang leader had been raping two other young, black men for a couple of weeks, when they were transferred from 'Young Offenders' to adult prison. When the perpetrator was interviewed by police, he said that this is the way he'd thought he had to act in adult prison, to establish dominance over his subordinates.

I know rape and the like is meant to be a big problem in America, and over here we all joke about it, but nobody *really* believes that adult men rape or get raped in prison. Do they?

But it's a fact of prison life and its one that is not taken seriously enough. I wonder how many of the suicides in prison are from the trauma of such experiences.

The whole business leaves an unpleasant aftertaste, and it makes me wonder what goes on these young men's minds. Are they so out of touch with reality? Is our society so fucked up that it is producing such dogma from the youth in our cities.

20TH NOVEMBER 2008

My right arm is getting stronger! Not how you're thinking, dirty beasts! I've just finished copying the latest batch of notes from a notepad onto A4 paper.

Declan has lent me a radio, Joe is dealing with my Education Apps and Eugene is sorting my laundry out; the Irish connection - works every time. Eugene's a member of the travelling community (or in slang terms: a 'Pikey') and is always up to some sort of blaggarding.

Elton John is singing: *'It's sad... so sad... '*, and it's a really weird feeling, because 'sad' is something I am not - for once in my life, I'm starting to feel a bit upbeat, and surprisingly the *opposite* of sad. Something in me is changing - maybe it's my new surroundings, present company, change in routine, or maybe it's just High Down. I'm not sure, but there is definitely something going on here - something I *like*; can't put my finger on it yet, but I'm sure if I stay long enough, I'll figure it out.

Was summoned to reception earlier, to collect my belongings. They have decided not to allow (and stored to Prop) my hi-fi and cordless headphones - the P.O. actually got me to take the padding out of the headphones and searched them, but then still said he refused to take the risk as I could hide 'things' in them in the future. Fuckin' unbelievable!

The *Incentive Earned Privilege Scheme* (IEP) is totally different here, even though nothing has changed with my security status. Every prison has its own IEP scheme and security department, with its own slant on what is and is not permissible. I'm starting to wonder if there is any point in being 'Enhanced'.

Justice department regulations are set up in such a way that each governor, in each prison can defer to local rules and local policy; it is so general that if anybody complains about an issue involving staff, it is referred to the justice department, who refer it to the local governor, who refers back to local rules, and all legislated by government policy.

The sun is setting behind the trees and the wall - it looks stunning; I feel unbelievably peaceful - a rare and infrequent occurrence.

I just received a compact for living on the VDT Unit (*Voluntary Drug Testing*), and Joe has told me I've got to attend Education tomorrow morning. Can hear the guys showering - the water splashing on the floor; my cell is right by the showers, only this time on the top floor: the threes.

The buzzer is a constant background noise. It's been turned down, and the prisoners are trying to get it shut off completely: if it can be turned down, it can be turned off; but new building, Health and Safety and all the crap that comes with it... suppose they're finding their way.

Shame. It was peaceful, there, just for a moment, as the sun set, clouds rolling across the sky, in different hues of yellow and orange; a crisp, winter evening - a bubbling, frothing witch's cauldron.

Looking forward to tomorrow. Where has the past week gone?

23RD NOVEMBER 2008

Back from church, waiting for lunch. Church was annoying: there were four or five guys behind me, talking away, sorting out their deals, then singing out of tune, loudly, on purpose, as they giggled away, stoned. Fuckin' pricks!

I've got this happiness creeping over me again – can't shake it (don't *want* to); but it's not always advisable to look happy in prison, because some arsehole will always go out of their way just to fuck you up.

Spoke to my father again and he seems happier - glad that things have worked out and that I'm away from Rye Hill.

Stood at the end of the landing, at the big glass windows looking out over the wall, at the trees and fields. We're on the outskirts of Croydon, but it don't half look and feel like the countryside. The view seems strangely hypnotic, as the trees sway gently in the wind, totally devoid of clothing, and silhouetted by clouds, travelling by at high speed.

Think I might put my name down for the 'Writer in Residence' class - feel stirrings.

Dec is into his poetry - deep stuff, but good.

It snowed, lightly, this morning, but the rain has washed away the little that was there. I'm thoroughly enjoying this moment, sitting quietly, writing and looking out of the window at the yard, the walls, the wire, the fence and then the trees, so close yet so far; *tick-tock*.

Reading another Wilbur Smith book: *'A Time to Die'*. Think I've read it before, but who cares? Need to drift off to distant shores, to fading memories and rekindle romantic dreams. Not sure if I'll go back to South Africa - don't know if I want to. All I know is that Mr. Smith makes me feel warm, in this cold, dark place in winter, and that's all that really matters at the minute.

Certainly didn't get any inspiration from the church service. The church is actually quite big, but more impersonal. I felt for the minister - seventeen years he's been here; no wonder he's extremely grey on top.

24TH NOVEMBER 2008

Back to the wing – bang up. H.M.P. hasn't changed, though *I* have. Managed to walk away from a confrontational situation, then stood and watched as a young lad got seven red entries:

'Fuck you!' gets one...

'Fuck off!' gets two...

'Fuck you!' gets three... etc., etc....

He's lucky he didn't get 'twisted up'.

Looks like I'm locked up for the rest of the morning and afternoon. Don't mind - I can head off to Africa for a while.

Watched a movie last night, starring Peter O'Toole and Lesley Philips - think it was called: *'Venus'*. It was very good – deep and thoughtful. The movie was about a failing actor getting old... ready to die. Made me smile. I felt for the old guy: all he wanted to do was get to the seaside and feel the sand between his toes before he passed away. I must have enjoyed it because I slept like a brick.

25TH NOVEMBER 2008

Slept well again.

'No movement' this morning, due to 'essential staff training'; this normally means there are no staff – a regular occurrence at H.M.P.. My name wasn't on the free-flow list, anyway.

I've given Joe a note to give to the Education woman, Carol-Anne - bypassing the ogres normally gets things done quicker. That's why you should never fuck about on the wing, and stay well clear of trouble: because you never know when you might need a little favour; everyone has a very long memory in prison. If you are genuine, and people see that you are, then you will achieve a hell of a lot more, and a lot faster.

Watched another movie last night, called *'This is England'*, about a group of young skinheads growing up in Thatcher's 1980s - brought back some great memories. In 1983 I was sixteen - I remember feeling the excitement of the Falklands war, but the rest is a bit of a blur.

Waiting for Mark (Writer in Residence) to come and see me - Dec says he's a good bloke; can't wait to show him my book and some of my writing. Not much else to do.

So, me and my mate Wilbur are off to Africa - don't want a repeat performance of yesterday.

Fell asleep and nearly missed lunch.

28TH NOVEMBER 2008

Friday morning - not a lot going on. Sitting in my pad, listening to the buzzer, and to some a-hole going on about *'Strictly Come Dancing'*. I mean: come on! This is prison: full of hard cases, who should be talking about blags and cons, not Anton's fuckin' sequins!

Been watching this little prick run around the landings when we eventually get unlocked. Apparently he's back on recall and has ten days left - thank fuck: don't think I could put up with him for much longer. He'll be back - a longer stretch each time; it's written all over him - a complete wrong-un. Myself and Eugene said the same thing at the same time: 'Wanker!'

The Education centre here is like a warehouse, with screens and partitions put in place to give a little bit of privacy for individual classes. There is a class there, twice a week, for classroom assistants to develop learning activities; I started my job as 'classroom assistant' with essential skills and learning difficulties - was thrown in at the deep end, and feel as if I've done well. The teacher, Nina, is a lovely woman - softly spoken, with the nicest manner I have come across thus far in prison; I've met some good people, but Nina just oozes caring. We'll get along fine.

I also started a *Photoshop* class, with Simon – this, too, is rather enjoyable. Simon's class is up on the balcony, and depending on where you sit, you can observe everyone else going about their business down below.

Had a nice chat with Carol-Anne when I was at Simon's class. She was telling me that she was the person who employed Tony (my boss) at Brixton, and as I was the first person Tony employed, in an indirect way Carol-Anne has had an influence in what I was doing. I hope she remembers to pass on my regards. I've found out that teachers and staff can't reply to letters, as it can be and will be used against them: inappropriate relations with a convicted criminal. Fuck 'em - I'll still keep sending my Christmas cards.

All in all, it's been a fairly hectic and disruptive week. I've been thinking about Brixton quite a lot, and regret leaving there now, if only because Rye Hill was such a mistake. It's all been a bit of a rush – hopefully next week will be a bit more organized and settled.

Roared at *'The Simpsons'* last night, and Mr. Burns's gay assistant saying he had a 'rocket in his pocket'; some of these kids' cartoons are so close to the knuckle, you have to be an adult to get it.

19TH DECEMBER 2008

I know it's the 19th, but I'm not really sure what day it is - they are going by so fast, they just seem to blur into one another.

I've become a very busy tadpole over the past few weeks: I'm now working three days a week with Nina as a classroom assistant for Learning Support, one day at *Photoshop*, and one morning a week with Mark. Mark has read my book - he's given me lots of encouragement, and I'm going to keep making time to write down the daily occurrences I find myself in. The help and encouragement I'm receiving here at High Down only further highlights how much I didn't get at Rye Hill - I'm definitely not going back. Next stop: Belfast.

I also did a course called *'Prison SMART'*, taken by Adelita - 'SMART' stands for 'Stress Management and Relaxation Technique'. What a difference - it's fuckin' great; I feel like a weight has been lifted. Finally, I've been shown something that I can do on my own, which will help settle my overactive soul, help me make sense of myself and find out who I really am. Adelita is a really small woman of retirement age, but she oozes confidence and has an aura about her.

The course is related to teachings by the *'Art of Living Foundation'*, founded by a guy called Sri Sri Ravi Shankar, and I've been sworn to secrecy. I'm still in the process of practicing my breathing and meditation technique - should last for another forty days. But the course doesn't just teach you how to breathe and meditate - it's much more than that: it teaches you about alternative thinking and being honest to yourself, loving yourself and giving yourself some positive back-slapping every now and then. We've only skimmed the surface, but I know I'll definitely hook up with it again when I get out. I feel a weight being lifted, and my mind being unlocked. This really is a magical moment - a defining one, perhaps?

I've suffered from gastric reflux for years - could never lie on my back, and always had to have my head propped up; felt anxiety if anyone went near my stomach - even a girlfriend lying on it, during quiet, intimate moments, would give me the heebie-jeebies. Now I can lie flat on my back, with my jumper for a bit of neck support, and meditate for nearly an hour. Still get the regular attacks of reflux at night, but I never thought I'd be able to lie flat on my back for any length of time.

I've received Christmas cards from Angel, my aunt, uncle and cousins, and Dad, as well as letters from John and Gigi - nothing from Fin or Mum; Mum is obviously still angry, and Fin is simply getting on with her life. I wish Fin well - I'm sure she will think about me from time to time, but I have to let go: I feel it's better for all concerned if I stay out of sight. Maybe I'm wrong, but I do feel that all the negativity which surrounded me would test even the most optimistic of people.

There is so much more to say, but I'm hungry, and they've just called hot-plate workers, so lunch will be ready soon.

1ST JANUARY 2009

Happy New Year.

It's been a quite a Christmas period for me. My only trouble was at the last day of Education - one of the young gangsters wouldn't keep quiet during a DVD we were all watching. When I told him to, he really went off on me, screaming and cursing - calling me all the names under the sun, inches from my face. The teachers were about to hit the emergency alarm bells – 'twist-up' time! And over Christmas? Fuck that.

I just sat there and tried to breathe. Outwardly, I showed nothing – inwardly, I was a mess, torn between sorting him out, or putting to good use the stuff I'd learned with Adelita.

Mark came and spoke with me afterwards, and said he was proud of me for letting it slide. The young lad has lots of problems: all of his so-called 'posse' are getting bumped off, one by one, and it looks like it won't be long before he gets his; at least it wasn't by an ageing paddy. Can't believe how much it bothered me at the time, though - was it my pride fuckin' with me, or was it something else? Not so long ago, it would have been no contest: I'd have emptied him without a thought for me or anybody else. Something has changed in me.

I've tried to forget about it, for now.

Received a lovely letter from my mate Davey, in Belfast, and a card from my Mum, yesterday - there are no words to explain how this has lifted me. I've now learned not to get annoyed if I don't receive a birthday or Christmas card -

the post is slow, and it also sometimes takes a little bit of time for a card to get from the prison mail-room to the landing; they are all very busy over the holiday period, so I just let things slide - no big deal. No point getting yourself worked up over something you have no control over.

I passed my O.U. openings course, but, unfortunately, I'm still waiting to get started proper on my O.U. studies. Received word that I've been cleared by security to work for *The St. Giles Trust* - a London based charity which tries to find housing and education for offenders, upon release. All *St. Giles* workers wear bright, day-glo orange T-shirts, so at last I can truly say: 'the future's bright', which normally gets a rise out of my Irish Catholic colleagues. You normally get put on hold for six months, if working for *St. Giles*, but I haven't been, which leads me to believe that I'll be moved back to Belfast within the next six months.

I've persevered with my breathing exercises, and the feelings of melancholy, that I once had around this time of year, are replaced by a relaxing warmth - *it is what it is, man*. There is definitely something afoot, as I didn't even buy a TV guide for Christmas! Now, for all the TV I actually watch, I'm reading and relaxing, though not necessarily in that order.

Dec is good craic, and I go and visit him for half an hour every day – he's normally found in his flea-pit. 'Flea-pit' is a good, accurate description of what his cell is like - if he had a dog or a cat it'd be fuckin' mingin', and I try not to sit down or touch anything when I go in. He doesn't give a shit. Eugene has had a word with him about showering and stuff, but I think he's frightened of going near the showers, but won't admit it; hopefully, he'll snap out of it one day.

There's one year and six months done – gone… finished! Time to get me some proper work to do.

Don't get me wrong: I enjoy helping others, but if I don't help myself now, I'll be no good to anybody in the future. I don't want much, just purposeful study time, a place to study, a bit of work and the gym - if I can get that sorted my days will be busy, the weeks will fly by and, before you know it, home time.

One day at a time, and keep the head down - that's the plan for 2009.

It snowed heavily here the other night, and it's been absolute chaos, as the officers have to park at the end of the lane and walk the mile or so to the prison. Some abandoned their cars on the first morning after the snow-fall, became martyrs for making it into work, and haven't been able to dig them out yet.

Mark has been encouraging me to write more - to write down the little things that happen, make me wonder or make me laugh. Mark is a very enthusiastic man - he's one of those guys who looks unflappable, running around all the wings on a Friday afternoon, making sure he speaks to all the men he said he would. I don't know how he does it, but he finds time, and that little bit of personal interaction goes a long way.

My first ever poem:

SIX MAGPIES

The sun sets behind the naked trees of winter
And a soft, hypnotic glow fills my room.
The air – cold, but not quite freezing -
Fills me with a quiet pleasure...
..the pleasure of being alive.

I count six magpies
Sitting on the dark grey mass of the prison wall –
Like me, they are surrounded by barbed wire and fencing,
Yet they are free.

I think: How often in your life do you see
Six magpies at the same time?
The rhyme says: 'Six for gold,
Seven for a secret, never to be told';
I feel as if I have to let you into a little secret.

I have travelled half-way round the world,
Partying and having a ball.
When I came to prison, I wanted to die...
I should have already been dead;
I was living a lie.

It is only now, when I breathe in the air,
I realize I was never really there.
A lady taught me how to breathe,
Through Sudarshan Kriya.

I had been searching for something to set me free
Most of my adult life.
Who would believe that one could be set free in prison?
I have lost my guilt, my shame,
My pain and my angst.

My metal door has just been locked
With a resounding, metallic thud,
And the shouts and roars of men in prison
Pale slowly into the background.

It's now deadly silent, and I sit and smile,
As the sun sets, with its bright, golden glow -
A glow I can feel in my heart.

I can rest my head and dream at last,
Because I know this day has nearly passed.
I know it's this glow that keeps me warm,
And I know it'll be there tomorrow.

14TH JANUARY 2009

I purchased another set of headphones and a new hi-fi from the *Argos* catalogue, something your allowed to do if you an 'enhanced prisoner'. so that I can use them to listen to the TV or radio, they help block out any superficial noise coming from the landings; this helps me forget where I am, and it is only when I get up to use the toilet that I realize I'm in prison. Well worth the forty bucks.

29TH JANUARY 2009

I know it's been a while, but I really am a very busy bunny.

Had a bit of a setback with my Open University: Adelita was the O.U. co-ordinator, but is in the process of retiring, and the lady who took over isn't too sure of herself - to cut a long story short, my application to register remained in her 'in' tray over Christmas, and I missed the cut-off date. The head of Education was very apologetic, and they could all see that I was gutted, especially Nina, as she watched my shoulders slump and head go down. She wrote me a little note and slipped it under my door during lunch-time lock-up - actually came to the wing and to my cell; this is not a common occurrence, and it made me perk up a bit - when I thanked her later, I had to hold back the tears; as I said earlier, she oozes caring, and it meant a lot to me. So, I dusted myself off and continued to teach within her class, until starting proper with *St. Giles*'s.

I bumped into the young gangsta (not literally) who'd threatened me just before Christmas, on several occasions, and, after our third curt nod, I approached him and said: 'Do you mind having a chat sometime, and not just a nod when passing on the walkway?' We arranged to get to Mark's class early on Friday, and we'd talk then. It was cool: he'd calmed down and said that he was sorry for being so rude, but he'd a lot going on in his life, and I said the wrong thing at the wrong time. We had a good chat about things, life in general and how the incident between us all boiled down to saving face, in his world.

He knew what I was capable of - some of the other guys had warned him that anybody who could sit so quietly and not react when someone was screaming and spitting in their face was made of bigger stuff - they also pointed out that I was from Belfast. It was funny, because when we discussed Belfast and growing up there in one of Mark's classes, he actually commented on how similar certain aspects of our lives were, if only at different times - so, I became a bit more enlightened as to the inner-city gangland culture of the young black man in London.

We watched a movie called *'Babylon'*, about racial hatred in the late-seventies and early-eighties. In one particular scene, young white guys were travelling around certain areas of London in a car, looking for black men to bash - the black guys in the class couldn't believe this. I chirped up and told them that in my day, in Belfast, we tended to stay in our own areas, even though there was no black and white - if you were unlucky enough to come across a car like that in my day, you'd be dead. I told them that I knocked about with guys who'd be in the car, doing the business, so to speak.

Mark loved it, as this started a whole debate about gangs, culture, religion, stigma and beliefs. Some of the older black guys in the class told the younger ones what it was like in their day, and we collectively brought up the issue of the pub signs that read: 'NO DOGS, NO BLACKS, NO IRISH' - the youngers couldn't believe what they were hearing; we described how the black man and the Irishman living in inner-city London had an unwritten affiliation and mutual respect for each other's identities. I told them about some of the pubs I used to frequent off All Saints Road, by Notting Hill - the older guys knew who and what I was on about; I left them to explain it to the younger ones.

After that there was no more aggro.

As usual, Mark lapped it up. He told me his goal was to try and instil the seed that there was a world outside of their postcode, and to realize that they needed to walk away from false dreams of quick-fix money, drugs, violence, cars and women - that all led to classes like this on a Friday morning, at Her Majesty's pleasure.

4TH FEBRUARY 2009

I've been teaching this young traveller how to read - his name is Sean, and he's just turned twenty-one; he's only been here for a while. It was the end of November 2008 when we started with the alphabet, and was just released at the end of last week - on his last day he made his first sentence. When he left, he smiled and shook my hand; the way he walked, and the way he carried himself, was a far cry from the slumped, mumbling, frightened *Lenny-esque* character I'd originally met.

He said: 'I can't wait to tell my mum.'

Nina smiled at me and said: 'You did that. Now you know why I come to work each day: it's for moments like this.'

I understood - it made me walk tall.

5TH MARCH 2009

I'm ready for work: got my bright orange *St. Giles* T-shirt on.

Standing, talking to Al (my next door neighbour), when Mr. Murph approaches me. 'Where you off to then, Mick?' he asks.

'I'm off to work, as soon as they call 'freeflow',' I reply.

'No you ain't, mate.'

I'm startled.

'You're out of here,' he adds; 'you're being moved.'

'Where to?' I demand. 'I ain't going back to Rye Hill.'

'No, no,' Murph replies: 'Some place called *'Magga-berry'*.'

'Bollocks!'

'No, Mick – honest. Go and pack - they're coming to get you in half an hour.'

Holy fuck! I'm off home!

Before I do anything, I rush to the phone and call the old man. He's chuffed, but full of questions as usual - questions to which I don't have answers, and I have to pack.

By the time I get back to my pad it's all round the wing. Poor Dec comes up and says: 'Ah, fuck - what am I gonna do now?' He really looked sad, and I felt sorry for him.

'Don't worry: I'll write and tell you what to expect - if it's bad news, I'll let you know, so you can stay put.'

The usual vultures appeared: 'Oi, Mick - give us your-'

'Fuck off, the lot of ya! Give me five minutes to get my head together.' Not that I've got five minutes.

Murphy comes back and tells me: 'Right, you're off to Woodhill, and then to Forest Bank for the weekend - then you'll fly to Belfast on Monday, to H.M.P. Magga-berry.'

Most people who aren't from the north of Ireland can't pronounce *'Maghaberry'* – it's 'Ma-gab-ry'.

'How the hell am I gonna get my gear down to reception?'

Murph says: 'Leave it with me, paddy.'

Again, I rush to the phone and tell my Dad what's happening; as time is short, I say: 'I love you - one way or the other I'll be speaking to you from H.M.P. Maghaberry, or face to face, next week.' He's pleased; I'm pleased, too, and at the end of the day, that's all anyone can ask for.

Get back to my pad before everybody nicks everything, pack up all my gear and give a lot of shit away. I then shout: 'Fuck the lot of ya!', with a big grin to all my mates and the finger for everyone else.

Dec and a couple of the lads help me down to the exit with my belongings, and no sooner are we there, than Murph appears with three reception orderlies - they all know me from my previous visits to reception. Last week, I finally managed to get all of my belongings from reception, including my earring - I'd made at least one visit every other week for the past three months, and I was on first name terms with all the staff and orderlies; what a palaver!

'Okay, Mick - you got anything in there you shouldn't have?' (I have six prison-issue, clear plastic bags).

'Just the love-letters from you, honey.'

'Fuck, am I glad to see the back of you, paddy?' said the S.O., coming out. 'Only jokin', fella - be lucky.'

Then, it was all a bit of a blur: next thing is I'm in the back of the sweat-box, heading out of the gate. My mind flashed back to that day after court, over a year and a half ago, when I sat outside, sweating my bollocks off, and there was no room at the inn.

Time really does fly when you're enjoying yourself.

Belfast, here I come.

For the obvious Health and Safety reasons, prisoners on transfer are not allowed to travel more than sixty miles per day - at least, that's the general gist of things.

I get to H.M.P. Woodhill around half-eleven, and I'm the first to arrive in the holding cell.

'Shouldn't be too long,' the reception officer says. 'You're only here for the night, anyway - off to Forest Bank, then Belfast on Monday: H.M.P. *Magga-berry*, or *Mag-bree…* Fuck it, all your mick names are the same, innit?'

'All you officers' I.Q.s are the same,' I mumbled.

As the day dragged on, the holding cell got fuller and fuller; all the dregs - the throwaways of society - seemed to congregate around me on this particular day. There were guys in the toilet, crapping out the gear they had stashed before they went to court, some were smoking crack, one guy injecting and the others just skinning up - the place smelt of two or three different types of shit; fuckin' horrendous! I sat in the corner and did my breathing exercises and meditation with my eyes closed, for at least thirty minutes – they all gave me a wide berth.

To top it all, I was the last one to be taken out, and over to the 'First Night' centre, where the officer says: 'You'll be doubling up in cell number... *(blah, blah, blah...)*'

'Please read my file and you'll see I won't be doubling up,' I told him.

The next thing I know, I'm being interviewed by the doctor - he looks like he's had a hard day. 'Sorry,' he says, 'this is just a formality.'

He asks me a couple of questions, and then I'm stuck in the medical cell - the windows have no glass or Perspex, and I'm given a sheet, a blanket and a fire blanket; kept all my clothes on and tried to sleep. It was a long, uncomfortable night, and I never got a wink, shivering all night.

The next morning, I had a shower, and then off to pastures new. The reverse reception process took a matter of minutes - they made sure I had all my belongings with me, and put me into the back of a *G4S* (private security company) van.

The guys in the van were dead on - Sean and Sean. They started to have a chat with me as we were heading up the M6; well, we were shouting at each other over the roar of the van and the noise it made on the tarmac - the 'highway roar', as I call it.

Sean (driver) says: ''Ere, Mick, you're off to Belfast on Monday morning from Forest Bank, and two mates of ours will be escorting you. Will you do us a favour?'

'If I can,' I reply.

Sean tells me that his mate Tommy managed to leave the paperwork for a Belfast prisoner at the airport, in Manchester the previous week, so there was a whole pandemonium when they couldn't make the handover because of no paperwork. He said the guy was getting some stick about it, and if I could wind him up, it would be great.

I thought about it for a minute, and said: 'Okay, no problem - Monday morning I'll put on a bit of a show. They'll shit a brick!'

The two Seans were wetting themselves - they said they'd back me up if things went pear-shaped. Sean (back-up driver) says: 'We don't often get a chance to have a laugh in this job, Mick, but if you pull this off we'll be forever grateful.'

We got to Forest Bank just after lunch and the lads wished me well.

I was now used to the waiting process at reception, and set about doing my breathing exercise.

The girl at reception saw that I had talcum powder in my bag and said: 'You're not allowed that in 'ere.'

I made the mistake of asking why, and was dutifully told that some prisoners poured it into the air-vents, causing the whole system to shut down. So, typically, the prison service removes the item from the canteen list, punishing the general population, instead of denying the perpetrators.

This time reception wasn't so bad, and I got over to the induction wing about six o'clock. The S.O. who escorted me over to the wing said: 'We get a lot of Belfast lads through here, and we all get along. Do you know-' and he proceeded to mention a few names.

I told him that if he really dealt with those men, he should know that I couldn't possibly say if I knew them or not.

'Cool,' he said; ''nuff said.'

We entered the wing, and he asked me to wait for five minutes outside his office, before calling me into the office, and making a cup of coffee for himself and one for me - very civil.

'Okay,' he said, 'I want a simple life and I don't need any bollocks - tell me now what you need for the weekend and I'll sort it... within reason, of course.'

After the experience of freezing my nuts off in Woodhill, I said: 'I need at least two duvets, three pillows, a couple of towels, my toiletries, three changes of clothes, my writing material and my meds.'

'Okay. I'll take you up to your cell in a minute, where you'll be locked up for ten minutes, until Association, then I'll let you out for Association - to get a shower and that - and I'll send someone along to sort your gear out.'

'Fair enough,' I said.

As I sat in the cell, I thought: *What a fuckin' tip - glad I'm only here for the weekend!*

Sure enough, ten minutes later, unlock, and an ogre tells me to go and stand by the grill.

As I'm standing there, minding my own, I suddenly hear: 'Oi, paddy!' I'm not biting and I ignore it.

'Oi, Mick.'

I looked up, and there on the twos was a guy I knew from Rye Hill: Wayne. I called him down, and he duly arrived at my side. 'What's the story here?' I said.

'Don't worry: you Irish boys get special treatment, no matter what side. They'll take you back to reception to get what you need. Got any snout?'

'I stopped, you twat.'

'Fuck, yeah,' he said. 'I'll see you when you get back.'

I stopped smoking in February 2008. I'd a horrible flu, and at one stage my temperature was 102° - pretty fuckin' rough! At some stage during my illness, I decided to have a cigarette - not a good idea: I was coughing and retching so hard, I thought my lungs were going to burst, and my eyes were going to pop out of their sockets. In bad temper, I threw my tobacco into the bin, and when I got better, said: 'That's it - no more.' I'd already spent two weeks without one, so the worst of the withdrawal was over, and my illness left a bad taste in my mouth, as far as the ole nicotine sticks were concerned. I was now totally without vice.

Next thing, the S.O. appears and takes me back over to reception. I got all I needed, thanked him and went back to my cell. Wayne and I were sitting, chatting, when another officer turns up with two brand new fluffy duvets, covers and pillows - just like Rye Hill; these private nicks don't half know how to treat a body. The officer looks a bit out of sorts; I say nothing, but he can hear Wayne and I laughing our heads off when he leaves.

We go for a gander and Wayne introduces me to a few of the lads. Turns out Wayne is still serving at Rye Hill, and has been sent here to receive his accumulated visits.

Maybe that's what I should have done after Fin left: accumulated my visits and flown home for a month every year. Hmm - don't think they would have worn that one for long. Still, I'm going home, and that's all that matters for now. I make a request to go to church on Sunday morning, as there will be nothing else for me to do.

It's soon lock-up, so I get back to my pit and make up the bed. What a luxury - I swear, if you'd listened outside my door you would have heard purring. Woke up in the middle of the night, sweating my bollocks off, and had to sleep with half the duvet over me - that'll teach me.

Get unlocked in the morning, and there's a whole commotion going on in one of the cells across the way - a guy has flooded his cell; blocked up the sink and toilet with his clothes, and kept flushing the toilet and pressing the tap buttons. It turns out that it was the same weird guy that was in the holding cell - Wayne tells me he's a regular, and, as per usual, should be in a mental facility, because the prison doesn't know what to do with him.

Nothing much else happening, so I head off and put the feet up. Go to church on the Sunday morning and that's about it. I write a few letters and contemplate my last night in English custody.

MY LAST NIGHT IN ENGLISH CUSTODY
8TH MARCH 2009

How do I feel? Grateful, thankful, and mostly relieved - this is silently what I've wished for from day one, and it has worked out. I'm a little bit apprehensive, though not nearly as much as I expected.

If there is one thing that does register with me, it's the English accent - I'm fuckin' sick of it, and I mean *sick*. Over the last wee while it's become a real effort to listen to it; I don't have anything against the English, but I've had enough - need to be home, back amongst my own.

Suppose my attitude has come from the company I've been keeping – let's face it, there are some scumbags knocking about. I'm not judging in any way, though I have had time to sit and reflect, take a step back and look at the bigger picture. When I get home I'll be living with either terrorists or joy-riders from west Belfast, who believe their little part of Northern Ireland is the centre of the universe. Deep down, I know I've got much of the same to look forward to, but at least I'll be home. At least I won't have to repeat every sentence, and, if I stay true to myself and keep my head down, things should tick along nicely. I won't be wishing my life away - I'll live in the present and take each day as it comes. It's been working for the past few months, so there is no reason why I shouldn't do more of the same when I get home.

Tonight means everything, yet means nothing. I'm happy today… now… and I'll just have to see what tomorrow brings.

9TH MARCH 2009

'Here we go, here we go, here we go-o. Forty-two and I'm hitting the road - here we go-o: rockin' all over the world.'

I say goodbye to Wayne and tell him to 'look out for George when he's coming through'. Also, spoke to the S.O., and he said he'd keep an eye out for George as well. George should be heading back shortly - I'll write to him and let him know what to expect.

I'm standing in reception, filling in the paperwork and I spot the two *G4S* guys coming in - definitely Tommy, from the description Sean gave me. I waited for the officer to finish writing, and it was my turn to sign the paperwork.

Here we go:

'Right,' I said, 'before we go any further, I'm going nowhere until my solicitor has gone through my paperwork!' I could see the four guys in the room tense up; somebody must have hit a silent alarm bell, because within seconds the four became eight.

'What's your problem?' the officer says.

With the most sincere and apologetic face I could muster, I said: 'Look, lads - no offence, but I ain't going anywhere unless I see all the paperwork in front of me, because (pointing at Tommy) this buck eejit keeps forgetting to bring the paperwork to Belfast!'

The whole room burst out laughing.

Until one smart-arse says: 'How do you know about this?'

The whole room fell silent again - you could have heard a pin drop. They all had their security heads on, and I could see the wheels of industry ticking over.

'I'm from Belfast, lads - it's my business to know these things.' I winked, signed the paperwork and sat on the bench with a smug grin on my face. A deathly silence fell over the ensemble. Everyone was quiet and sombre, as I was escorted out and into the back of the van.

As I sat there, looking out, one of the officers was leaning with his hand on the door-frame. Davey, the co-pilot, didn't see him, and slammed the door shut with the guy's fingers still in it.

The officer started punching the passenger window, screaming: 'Open the fuckin' door!' There was a bit of a commotion as the all the officers came running out - they must have thought I was kicking off; they soon relaxed when they saw this poor guy had caught his fingers in the door.

We had to leave, and my last image of English prison custody was of an officer in tears of pain - how ironic is that?

We get outside the gates and Tommy shouts in: 'Okay, Michael – really, how did you know about the paperwork?' That's when I told him the two Seans said 'hello'. Davey started laughing.

Almost on cue, the walkie-talkie goes - their control room, asking Tommy if he's got the paperwork. A minute later Tommy's mobile goes - it's the two Seans, and they're having a real good laugh.

Tommy tells them all to: 'Fuck off!' as we all have a giggle at his expense.

Sean shouts to me: 'Hey, mate - can you hear me?'

'Yo,' I shout back.

'You're a star,' he says. 'Be lucky.'

We arrive at Manchester airport and park up outside the police station. Tommy and Davey are dead-on, apologizing for having to keep the cuffs on, but saying it would be more than their job if they took them off.

I said: 'Look, I'm the one who put myself in this position, lads - it's my fault, not yours.'

They're only following procedure, although I do feel double-cuffing is a completely unnecessary and inhumane way of treating an individual. Besides, where in the hell am I going to run to - the world is not big enough anymore? All I want to do is get home, see my Mum and Dad, do my time and get the fuck out of England - I don't need to be looking over my shoulder for the rest of my life. Let's face it: they *will* catch you. As I've said before, the whole notion of escape is something for the TV and movies; in real life, for most, it's a no-brainer.

The cop on duty was in plain clothes, and was also dead-on. We all sat in an interview room with biscuits and hot coffee, which warmed me through, until it was time to head to the aircraft.

No checking in for me - we drove out to the rear of the aircraft, where there was a set of portable steps laid on, especially for me! Davey told me not to feel embarrassed: I'd be the first one on and the last one off. My coat was draped over the cuffs, but that didn't take away my vulnerability, and I didn't feel much like a rock-star at this particular moment in time. The plane started to fill up, and Davey told me that as soon as the wheels left the ground, he would disconnect himself - as soon as we touched down, he'd have to hook up again. I kept the set of handcuffs on.

When the stewardess came round with the trolley, I spared her the cliché:

'Don't suppose you could stick a large one in that?' My can of Pepsi tasted absolutely magnificent, on its own. I prefer Pepsi to Coke - I can't believe it's been nearly two years since I've had a can. The stewardess never made any comment about my cuffs, although I could tell she was aware of the situation.

Was in the window seat, and I managed to shut myself off for a while. I thought to myself: *Oh, my God - what a horrible way to come home*. Although, when I tried to remember, I couldn't recall a flight where I didn't have a hangover, or wasn't half-shot.

We crossed over the tip of the Isle of Man, bang on schedule, and the east coast of Northern Ireland soon loomed into view.

Davey asked me if I was okay, as I'd been a bit quiet. I told him it felt weird - mixed emotions: happy, frightened and sad, all in one; I had to take a moment, as I became overwhelmed by the whole situation. It soon passed, though, and I dutifully watched the coast go by, as we passed Ballywalter on the left-hand side, where my Mum lived. Wondered if she could hear her son coming home - I'd sent her a letter explaining what was going on. My heart skipped a few beats, and again I had to gather my composure; *Shit,* I thought, *I hope the whole day isn't going to be like this.*

Millisle passed slowly by, triggering a thousand images of caravans, hamburgers, football on the beach, swimming and Ellen Carmichael, my one teenage, true love - would marry her tomorrow. I'm smiling now, thinking about her and the head-games we used to play. If only life could be more simple, like when you're young. My Mum met her at a band parade in Lisburn many years later, when I was living in London - Ellen told my Mum I was the best boyfriend she ever had, but she didn't know it at the time. Me too, but what are you gonna do? Life goes on, with little pangs of regret that become easier to suppress over the years. Bloody-hell – twenty-nine years ago! Can remember some of it, but not all. Maybe it's nostalgia, but I think not: I used to ache when I saw her - *really* ache. Big hugs, Ellen - you'll always be part of my now fragmented and fractured heart.

The landmarks fly by much faster, as we pass Donaghadee and Bangor - I can see the golf courses I used to play with my Dad: Clandeboye and Helen's Bay. The plane banks, and we take a left down Belfast Lough, past Hollywood, the Oval - where I played football as a lad - and the dual carriageway, running parallel with the runway to Belfast city airport.

And there goes the bump: touchdown.

Snapped out of my dreams by Davey, hooking me up again.

I said: 'Have you got the paperwork?'

We waited for the aircraft to empty. I was nearly the last off, and was met by a few stares from the remaining passengers - walking through the airport was horrendous.

We eventually get to a side room, where there are two plain-clothes guys waiting. They say they've just got a cup of coffee, and can we wait a minute - they don't even acknowledge me. Davey just shrugged. They went through the formalities, and eventually Tommy and Davey came over to shake my hand, saying: 'It was a pleasure meeting you - good luck for the future.' It never ceases to amaze me how human kindness can be found in the bleakest of situations - all you have to do is let it be. I told them to remember to keep an eye out for George, and with that, they were gone.

I'm now shackled to the Northern Ireland Prison Service (NIPS), or are they plain-clothes cops? I don't know - they haven't spoken one word to me; no friendly banter - just the hackneyed poker faces of the system. *Welcome home.* I pray they're not all going to be like this - feel a sense of oppressiveness and a definitive change in attitude... for the worse, I might add.

I'm stuck in the back of a freezing cold prison van, still cuffed - at least they take the cuffs off you in the van, on the mainland.

This is Northern Ireland - we do things differently over here - if only I had known how this attempt at self-enlightenment - at personal humour - will haunt me in the years to come. *What have I done?*

I thought of Al at Rye Hill, out in the yard on that cold, misty morning: 'What have we done, Mick?'

I felt it now.

A sense of tiredness swept over me, as we trundled through Belfast; a wave of despair, as we approached the Westlink exit to the Grosvenor Road roundabout, and the start of the M1 - my final stretch of tarmac before H.M.P. Maghaberry. As we went under the motorway bridge at Dunmurry, my heart sank - I looked at the cuffs, then out of the window to the wee track leading from the bridge to Lady Dixon Park; childhood memories.

So close to my home, to my Dad – yet, strangely enough, I thought: *Where is my home?* It's certainly not with my Dad. The last family house I lived in was sold long ago, yet I still attach myself to there - to that place in time. Or is it just the *memory* of there. It was from there that I headed out into the big, wild world - I had a flat in Areema for a while, when I was about twenty-two, but I left that and headed back to London, and I never really stopped, until now.

Was he sitting at home, wondering where I was? I started to sob. They weren't sobs of self-pity, just sobs of emotion - an overwhelming realization, and an accumulation of circumstance. It didn't last long, and in a way I'm glad I got it out, as I felt I little bit better - I am only human, after all.

Driving up the road to the prison was also a bit strange, as the last time I drove past it was a few years back. Was with my wee brother - he'd taken me up to his then-new house, and made me a burger for lunch, then he showed me around his pad, and I was so proud of him. He showed me one of his boys' rooms, with all the budding rock-star regalia that befitted a fifteen-year old; I'd never met his boys - I silently hoped that one day I would.

One of the guitars propped up in the corner was just like Eddie Van Halen's: red, with white crisscrossed stripes - something my brother attempted to learn when *he* was fifteen. I wonder if he ever chooses to remember that he, too, was once a boy, with dirty socks and stripy guitars. I didn't pursue it, but I did recognize that my bro would live on, in his boys.

But what about me?

Fuck that! I've bigger fish to fry at the minute.

H.M.P. MAGHABERRY, NORTHERN IRELAND

9TH MARCH 2009

Holy fuck! The reception area here is massive - big glass rooms, holding cells and loads of open space; you could house a bloody wing in here.

The officer on duty, looking at my bags, says: 'We aren't going to get through all of that today - we'll call you over before Friday to sort it out.'

Now, where have I heard that before? Is it ingrained at training for officers to deny and dehumanize from first point of contact?

'Excuse me, but I've been through enough receptions in the past two years to know that isn't going to happen,' I chirped, 'so please just let me sort out my clothes, bedding and meds and I'll be out of your hair.'

I'm then taken off for a strip-search and a shower. When I get back, there are a couple of large, brown paper bags sitting on the desk - brown paper bags are indicative of NIPS.

'What's this..? What's that..? You can't have this… Who the fuck do you think you are? This is Northern Ireland, fella… We don't allow that here…'

The endless droning of the officer - he really enjoyed telling me what I couldn't have, and at the end he said: 'Take you're earring out: it looks too expensive.'

I wasn't going to give him the satisfaction.

I could tell from the off that this was not the most friendly of prison environments I'd come across.

I'm escorted over to the committal wing: Roe House, and I think I might want to consider rowing myself back out of here. All I've seen so far is a security team in riot gear, guard dogs and officers who take great delight in telling me what I can't have. When I get on to the landing it's immediate bang-up.

I have some dinner, and this is another new experience: the food is dished out from a trolley, on the actual landing, a couple of feet from my cell - I grab my dinner, and it's straight back into my cell again, an officer standing by my door the whole time, keys in hand.

'What - no Association then?' I ask.

'Yards or lock-up,' comes the reply; 'not for you, though - you're too late.'

I receive an emergency pack of biscuits, tea and crisps: Tayto cheese and onion! If it hadn't been for the fact that I'd received a pack that morning in the van at Manchester, I'd have been drooling.

I'll see my Mum and Dad soon - I think of them and dismiss my impending feelings of doom. Fuckin' hell - this place reeks of oppressiveness. Is it only done to intimidate me, or is this what it's going to be like for the next four years? Fuck that!

I've experienced a few nasty bastards in England, but there seems to be a general atmosphere here. Very frightening!

I shouldn't be feeling like this.

What a day - don't think I'll ever forget it.

PART THREE:

Back Home

10TH MARCH 2009

9.00am

My first night was spent munching crisps and watching local TV - good to hear the accents again. Paul Clark is looking very grey in this weather; I wonder how his brother is getting on - we used to knock about in the same crowd, many moons ago.

What was last night all about? I get a torch shone in my face every hour on the hour and told to move. What a nightmare! I'm fuckin' exhausted, instead of being full of the joys of spring. Came out of doze around five-thirty and stayed awake - no choice. I then hear an officer walk round and wake everybody up; how kind - an early morning call. Maybe it's just a first night thing.

As I speak, I see a couple of guys walk past my window with guard dogs - an 'A'-cat prison with 'A'-cat rules; I seem to remember the 'Troubles' are over, aren't they?

13TH MARCH 2009

8.50am

It's *'Red Nose Day'* and I've a visit in about an hour's time. I've also got to attend a 'fire drill induction' at 9.15am, clean out my cell and have a shower. H.M.P. drill and routine - such is life.

I'm extremely relaxed at the minute, and all the efforts of the officers to piss me off are falling on deaf ears - I'm doing a lot of breathing exercises and mucho meditating. I can't express enough how much the *'Prison SMART'* course has changed my life - without it, I don't think I'd have made it this far.

Haven't had any officers freaking out yet, thinking I'm dead - it just goes to show you how thoroughly they carry these checks out; every hour, on the hour, all they do is lift the flap up, shine a torch in or turn the light on. Half the time they don't even look in the cell, but as far as any camera is concerned they are seen to be carrying out their duty.

Their duty of care is a constant bombardment on my senses and my sense of right and wrong - they aren't doing these checks for my benefit: they're doing them for themselves. If anybody wants to kill himself, he will, and will start as soon as the officer checks his cell - that will give the person a good fifty-nine minutes to carry out the deed. So, don't give me your bullshit about 'my health' - *you're* fuckin' with my health by keeping me awake. Takes a bit of getting used to, this old twenty-two hour lock up.

Spoke to a guy from the *Christian Fellowship* yesterday, and he told me that H.M.P. Magilligan was my best bet, so I've put in a request for a transfer - better to go now and get settled for my last stint, rather than to up sticks again in six months or a year's time. I've only got four years and a bit left to serve; I fit the criteria for Magilligan, and everyone I have spoken to so far has said: 'Get out of this place as soon as you can'.

My Dad came for a visit on Tuesday, which was great - he looks good, but old.

And this is something I never thought I would say: my Mum is coming to visit now, too.

Looking forward to seeing her. I'm sure a hug and smile will end the tension between us.

Or is it only in my mind?

I'm sure we'll be fine.

11.40am

I've just seen my Mum.

What tension? No tears, no anger and definitely no guilt. We had a damned good chat and I think I managed to put some of her demons to rest.

I had a bit of extra time on the visit as they couldn't find an officer to take me back - every prisoner in here has to be escorted everywhere by an officer:

'B'-cat, 'C'-cat, 'D'-cat, remand, fine-defaulter, drunk, swearing in public - makes no difference. This is a Northern Ireland - we do things differently over here.

Where does the money go, eh?

On the way out of the visit I had to get searched - I started to take my clothes off.

The officer growled at me: 'What the fuck do you think you're doing?'

I'm ready to let rip, but I take a deep breath. I've come to the conclusion, in the space of a less than a week, that the NIPS have problems. I can bitch and moan about officers until the cows come home, but over here there is definitely a difference - it's not actually *what* they say, but the *manner* in which they say it. They loathe having to deal with prisoners, and they make their presence felt as menacingly as possible during every interaction with an inmate.

This might subside after time, but I doubt it - I can understand their mind-set: they have control of the prison population again, and they don't want to give an inch; they can freely bully, intimidate and threaten prisoners, because there are no longer paramilitaries involved. Well... there are, but minor infringements such as bullying and bad manners won't lead to their house being petrol-bombed.

Most of the men and women I have seen so far have been fifty-plus, meaning they were all around during the days of *The Maze*, when brutality and torture were par for the course in H.M.P. Northern Ireland.

I hear all these young lads saying they'll go on hunger strike if they don't get what they want – a lot of good that did Bobby Sands and his brigade. The state let those men die - terrorists with the backing of public opinion amongst the nationalist community and the political wing Sinn Fein, as well as the misplaced sympathetic ear of America, with the coffers that backed them – so why on Earth would that very same state listen to a car thief from Andytown, who's throwing his toys out of his pram?

It's the same hierarchy with the same politicians barking the same old rhetoric; what has changed? There are approximately sixty separated political prisoners in Maghaberry - less than one percent - yet this still dictates policies and procedures for the majority who want nothing to do with them.

Being back in Northern Ireland reminds me of why I left. If I was younger and more impressionable I'd be developing an anger problem - an anger which could so easily have been avoided if the people whose care I'm under spoke to me as human being, with a bit respect, and allowed me to keep hold of some of my dignity. I'm sure if I'm around in twenty years' time, I'll be reading stories about men appearing in front of judges who'll have developed their beliefs from this time, and the hatred and anger they felt for the people within the system.

They say: 'We're here to help', but for fuck's sake, don't pluck up the courage to ask for any - you will experience sneers and jeers before you eventually get through to someone, and, for most, by that stage the damage is done.

Anyway, I'm taking my clothes off and this ogre starts barking at me - he didn't know that I'd been strip-searched in and out of four different prisons in the past week, hadn't had a proper night's sleep since I came back, have just spoke with my mother, whom I hadn't seen for two years, and was simply working on automatic pilot.

Fuckin' prick!

I've just had my dinner - a curried chip.

Well, it was meant to be a chicken curry with chips, but you know how it is when nobody knows your face yet. It was a very pleasant change, I must say, and I'll make the most that the old pounds won't be long building up - I'm already well overweight.

Can't wait to get off this induction unit and onto the wings - time is really starting to drag; if it wasn't for the visits I'd be on a serious downer.

15TH MARCH 2009

8.15am

Went to church yesterday - Jim greeted me with a strong handshake and a big smile. The service didn't last very long - about half an hour - and, again, all I see are officers and dogs everywhere.

There is no let-up - this place is all about the officers, and how they carry out their perceived public duty - it has very little to do with prisoners. The officers are dinosaurs of the worst kind: those that see change coming and can't cope or know how to be different. It was a bit strange only seeing two black blokes at the service - I've spent two years in places where the opposite happens. There is a strong Chinese contingency here.

Can hear the breakfast trolley being wheeled round the landing, and a bowl of cereal is delivered to my door - how quaint. I must emphasize that this is not an *act of kindness* on the part of the prison service, but a method of control which results in prisoners not being able to communicate with other prisoners during meal times; at Brixton I used to enjoy the chats on the way to and from the servery - they were a welcome break from the monotony of twenty-two hour bang up, or one hour yard-time (weather permitting, of course).

I've been to the 'yard' twice - fuck that! You're allowed to walk round a cage, within a cage, within a cage - maximum security? Not for us! On the inside, you are allowed to mix freely, in a big room with a TV, microwave, and a few tables and chairs, where there are no officers present: they, apparently, observe these rooms by CCTV. Again, you're locked in a cage, and I have never felt so unsafe in all the prisons I have been in - if someone were to attack me, or vice-versa, the damage would be done and finished long before any officer got near the trouble; I suppose they look upon it as: if they're attacking each other, then they're leaving *us* alone.

Didn't go to the yard much in England, and it doesn't look like I'll be going much here.

Also, if you do go and end up getting bored to death by some fucked-up junkie who's always on the scrounge, you're not allowed out, and have to stay there until they say you can leave. Fuck that.

The officers keep asking me what I'm in for - I'm sure it's just small talk, but I was *never* asked by an officer in England, ever. I'll be polite and answer them, but I don't actually *trust* anyone; besides, I'm only a number to them, so why all the interest? It is not normal for so many members of staff to be asking me why I'm here: they only have to look at my file - are they not privy to my details, so they have to go searching elsewhere?

Rumour and gossip is rife in these places, normally started by inmates. But, alas, it seems 'this is Northern Ireland, and we do things differently here'.

I know everything is written down and recorded, so I'll play along, be polite and get the fuck out as soon as possible. Where have I heard that before? The only trouble is that now I'm running out of options or places to go – H.M.P. Magilligan is my last hope; if that goes tits-up, I'll have to break a lot of rules and get sent back to England, but that brings with it possible extra time, stripping of status and recriminations from on-high.

ST. PATRICK'S DAY
17TH MARCH 2009

Moved to 'Erne House' yesterday - what a drama that was. I got to the landing and the officer says: 'Right, you're in here with *such-and-such* - he's out at work at the minute.'

Can't these fuckers read?

I said: 'I take it you haven't read my file - I won't be doubling up.'

As per usual, this minor correction is taken as a personal insult, and the officer says: 'Oh, are you going to be a problem fuckin' cunt? Are you?'

As we were about to get to it an alarm bell goes off, and he forces me to go into the cell. I said: 'I'll leave my belongings on the landing as I won't be moving in.'

'You'll do as your fuckin' told, you cunt! Now, get in there before I charge you with refusing a direct order.' The venom and ferocity with which this command is delivered has to be observed to be believed.

I'm standing, leaning against the sink, fuming, as I try hard not to lose control; the breathing exercises don't seem to be working.

Shortly, the guy who resides in the cell comes in and says: 'Aw-ight, mate?'

Another fuckin' Englishman - that's all I need!

After a while, we're let out again and the officer is standing, waiting for me. 'Are you going to be a problem child?' he asks.

'There wouldn't be a problem if you read my file - I'm sorry if my circumstances offend you. Do you have my extra pillows and duvet?' I swear on my life, if I'd stuck a pin in him, he would have burst; his face was purple with anger and he had to bite it. We walk to the store room and I get my extra bedding.

Aye, a fuckin' idiot! Still, who am I to judge ?

I'll leave it for now, but I'm sure my card is well and truly marked.

I'm in a cell, right at the far end of the landing. These landings are the worst I have ever experienced - the guy in the opposite cell is only ten feet away from me. The officers fold the doors right back, flush with the wall, and you have no privacy whatsoever. In my case, the two guys across from me are at the gear all the time, and then their mates, who are also at it, come and stand in my doorway, smoking and chatting.

I tell them to fuck off and close my door.

'What's his problem?' I hear one of them say.

I'm glad my door is closed: I'd show him what a problem is.

This place is a fuckin' nightmare! It's too small - it feels like a dungeon. I'm on the ground floor, but the ceiling is low, and there is no daylight or windows on the landing - only in the cell. The attitude of staff and prisoners is disgusting: there's so much anger, and music blasting out from nearly every cell. The guy next to me must have got some seriously good shit, because he hasn't shut up for nearly two hours! The conversation (well, you can't really call it that) is about not meaning to upset someone.

'Shut the fuck up, then you won't be upsetting *me*!'

The music here, too, seems to be on a completely different level: maybe we're stuck in a time warp! I'm listening to Phil Collins's *'Another Day in Paradise'* and *'The Fields of Athenry'* - I mean, come on lads, get a life! The only positive comment I can make about my current situation is that at least the music is not *boom-boom-boom* gangsta-rap crap.

Get me to Magilligan! At least they have the brand new drug-free wing there - read about it when I was in England; I called over to see George, and we decided that this is the place we should aim for as soon as we get back to Northern Ireland: get to Magilligan and apply for the drug-free wing. I wonder if it'll pan out that way.

20TH MARCH 2009

Can't sleep in this fuckin' place! Not allowed to - keep getting woke up by night-staff. It's become intolerable.

Maybe I'll just live with it until I get to Magilligan - after all, this is an 'A'-cat jail and every one of us is a danger to national security and public order.

In the wee, small hours, I sat staring out my window; a rabbit appeared, and started digging at the mossy grass, as rabbits do, about fifteen to twenty feet from my window. My eyes had adjusted to the darkness after the glare of the light being switched on, and I could see quite well.

I didn't budge, like a wolf ready to pounce on my prey - an ambush. I swear that rabbit could read my thoughts: it stopped foraging and scraping, looked left, looked right and then looked straight at me.

'Hello, little bunny rabbit. What big ears you've got - are you a hare, perhaps?'

He flapped both his ears, as if to answer my question. He was a rabbit, no doubt.

I stopped breathing, my heart beating faster, thumping in my chest - it felt like a Mexican standoff: man and rabbit; the rabbit and me. *Don't move a whisker or the rabbit gets it!*

Can you really see me, sitting here in the dark, or can you just feel me?

I wish you no harm - you're safe.

Like you, I wish I could feel the mossy grass between my toes.

Now hop off home and make love to the missus.

One day soon, Mr. Rabbit - four and a bit more years to go.

You be safe, Mr. Rabbit.

I'm going to try and catch some zzzs.

The rabbit whipped its face with its paws, flapped its ears again, then paused - I do believe it then nodded at me and hopped off.

I started laughing, thinking about Jimmy Stewart and Harvey, the invisible rabbit.

Don't need any more imaginary friends, after the loss of Wilson. It's still funny, though.

I've been moved to the other side of the landing, which houses the lifers. Think they now realize I'm no trouble and want a quiet life.

Everyone is at it in here - I mean *everyone*: the whole fuckin' place is stoned, and the smell of dope is a constant companion. I walk into one of my neighbours' cells to ask a few questions and he and two others immediately skin-up. They offer me some, and I say: 'No thanks - I appreciate the offer, but my dope and booze days are over.'

They're cool, and don't force the issue.

They answer my questions, but also warn me that the officers have long memories - one guy tells me he still gets shit for something he did twelve years ago. I'll not get into the details, as these guys are all probably still serving and I wish them no further harm; they treated me well and even though I wasn't a lifer they accepted me and spoke to me quietly and politely.

This is more than can be said for the others - the ones in white shirts.

'Who does he think he is, that Irwin fella?' I overhear one of them say outside my cell – well, to be honest, they don't do anything to quieten what is said.

'More like Er-*whine. Ho-ho-ho.*'

I want to crush them, but I know if I spill blood on their starched white shirts there'll be hell to pay; keep it shut and just get the fuck away from this horrible place.

The food here is great - a real shock! Remember saying ages ago that each prison manages to get one part of its regime correct – well, at Maghaberry it's the food; the rest isn't worth a flying fuck, but the food is great. Well, for me it is, anyway - maybe it's because I'm used to English grub.

Had a hot Scotch egg the other day, and can't believe how good it tasted. I'm piggin' out on Tayto crisps, and will have to watch myself - I can feel the gut expanding already. Must be all the stress of this place: the only thing that gives me pleasure is food. No wonder everyone is stoned - it's the only way to cope.

Maybe I'll give it a go again… only for a wee while.

Can't get to the library - there is some sort of 'industrial action' going on with the Prison Officers' Association. Well, they call it 'industrial action', because if they called it a 'go slow' nobody would see any change!

Dad came up on Wednesday and couldn't wait to get out the door again - can't really blame him: if this place feels oppressive to me, then what on Earth does it feel like for someone who doesn't experience it every day? In prison, you do get used to your surroundings, and the people therein - you might not like it , but you do get used to it. Wish I could make it better for him - he's hard work sometimes, but I love him, and without him I'd be a lot worse off; not just financially, but emotionally as well.

Or would I? Did I really come home for my Mum and Dad, or did I do it for me? Did I do it out of misplaced loyalties? Did I use them as an excuse to get what I wanted? Do I really need them in my life? 'Need' and 'want' are two totally different things.

Do I get a big whack of whacky-baccy and slip into comfortable numbness?

I know I have to think of myself first, but I also need my parents. They have stood by me now, and I will make the effort to be included in their lives; after all, we're all not getting any younger.

When I was walking over to the visits, all I heard was: 'Michael. Michael.' I look up and see George, squeezing his face between the metal bars in an upstairs cell.

I shouted: 'Put your name down for church.'

Cool - he's made it home too. I'll see him next week, or after.

Waiting for my hi-fi to be cleared by reception - they have to take it apart, and check it for bombs, drugs and things (did I mention this is Northern Ireland and we do things differently here?)

Can't believe it: one of the officers came up to me and asked if I wanted to get over to reception to get my gear sorted out once and for all. Have to be careful when they mention 'gear': might think the officer is asking me if I want some drugs (something that *never* happens in prison, honest!). I'd been putting requests in on a daily basis, and someone has actually taken the time to ask me what I want for a change. The officer takes me over to reception and they wheel all my stuff out.

The reception guy looks totally put out, but the officer who is helping me says: 'Look, we get this done now, and it'll be over and done with - no more requests.'

So, they're not actually helping me at all - just doing what they should have done in the first place, and because I keep putting in requests, someone of rank has said: 'Why is this man still waiting for his belongings?'

Every item is a chore. We eventually get to my earring and the reception guy says: 'You can't have that.'

No sooner has he said it, than two prison orderlies walk past - one is wearing a thick, gold hoop in his ear, just like mine. I look at the two officers, and, pointing at the other prisoner, say: 'What's the difference between him and me?'

I can't quite believe the reply: 'You fuckin' cunts, who come over from England, think you know it all and can have whatever you want!'

'Yes or no?' I say, gesturing towards the earring.

He manages a positive grunt.

'Thank you very much, officer.' Big grin on my face.

I'm walking back with some of my stuff, and I turn to the helpful officer and ask him: 'Has everyone got attitude in this nick?'

He tells me: 'Your problem is that you've got a brain - you've been in the system and you know how it works - especially outside of Northern Ireland - and people don't like it.'

If these guys are so worried, it makes me wonder what the hell are they doing that's so wrong. Why are they so worried? I start to think about waves and ripple effects, and paranoia sets in.

No more requests - I'm officially worried.

When I get back to my cell, I open a box full of my Education paperwork and notes. To my surprise, sitting on top of the paperwork is an official H.M.P. plastic bag containing my whole prison file from day one - *everything*, including passport-size photographs used for ID cards at Rye Hill and High Down, governors' comments on adjudications, my security information, and comments by officers in Rye Hill – basically, all the juicy bits: good and bad. I spend the whole of lunch-time going through my official file, and use the last twenty minutes to rip up and flush every bad or negative comment made about me down the toilet.

When I'm unlocked, I take my file down to the landing office and say: 'I don't think this is meant to be in my possession.'

The S.O. says: 'Where the fuck did you get this?'

'Reception, just before lunch-time - it was on top of the rest of my paperwork. Do you want to see what else I collected?'

He turns a funny shade of purple and escorts me back to my cell, where I show him all my stuff and mention my earring.

'What's the problem with your earring?'

'I was told I wasn't allowed it, though it has taken me two weeks to get it back; the only reason I got it back is because another prisoner walked past, wearing something similar, when we were discussing the issue.'

'Okay, Michael, I can see what's going on here: you're waiting to go to Magilligan, aren't you?'

'Yes, please,' I replied.

'Okay, leave it with me - don't make any job applications and I'll get you away next week. Okay?'

'Thank you S.O., I'd appreciate that - I'd like to start getting on with my life, instead of being bullied.'

We nodded and off he went.

The next thing I know, I'm told I'm off to Magilligan next week. I phone Mum and Dad, as I know they have both booked visits for next week - it'll be harder for them to travel, but I need to get out of this horrible place and think about my future.

I'm just back from my last visit in Maghaberry.

Nearly had a heart attack! My Mum and Dad are both sitting there when I walk in; the last time the three of us were in the same room together was my 21st birthday party in London - it was my 42nd birthday last week.

Twenty one years! Doesn't time fly?

How do I feel about this? Not too sure; it was definitely an experience. I'm sure it can't have been easy for them, and they both put a brave face on things. It went well, and there wasn't even a hint of atmosphere - they both looked and felt at ease, and for that I am grateful.

If I'd have known coming to jail would have gotten them together, I'd have done it years ago! Only messing: I gave up on *those* dreams a long time ago; the pain, confusion, frustration and anguish that went with it all played a part in who I am today. It's a shame, but what can one say? Such is life.

19TH APRIL 2009

That's me off to Magilligan. Forgot to pack my bucket and spade!

Asked at reception for a piss-bag, like they have in England. The response was standard NIPS: 'You'll hold onto it like everybody else.'

I told the kind officer that I'd be pissing all over the floor of the van, as there was no way I'd make it - as if on cue, the purple face appeared, then he disappeared round a corner. He came back a couple of minutes later with a nearly-empty, 5-litre, plastic container. 'There used to be bleach in that - I hope it stings your knob,' he said.

This is what I love about the NIPS: the men and women who work in it are so polite and helpful. There are a few good ones, but I must emphasize the word *'few'*. NIPS really are a different breed from what I've been used to - I think that years of dealing with terrorism has resulted in them losing grip on what their job entails: it no longer includes torture, segregation and humiliation!

Oh yeah, I almost forgot: this is Northern Ireland…

With that, the door of my cubicle in the sweat-box was firmly slammed shut, and off he went, muttering to himself. I poured the remaining bleach out on the floor, spat on the sleeve of my top, and rubbed and cleaned around the rim of the container as best as I could.

The sweat-box pulled up at the lights by the Antrim Forum - this image triggered a flood of memories and emotions from childhood: trampolining, canoeing, football, and the *Meat Loaf* concert, when I was about fourteen. I recall the sweet taste of Woodpecker cider, and the even sweeter kiss of Donna… was it Donna?

I can't remember if it was Donna, Tracy, Lesley, Allison, Karen or Linda – fuckin' sound like a bit of tart, but at that age, mixed with the cider, it feels like they were *all* there, because at that time they were all part of my early teenage discoveries of the opposite sex; mostly innocent fumbling, but, boy, did I love kissing? Especially after a shared mouthful of cider. It was erotic - for me, anyway - and made my head spin; soft, luscious lips… mmm.

Snap out of it, boy: you'll go blind!

As the van cleared the crest of 'the hill' at Magilligan Strand, I could see the sea and the marching line of white-tipped breakers - like waves of Roman legions, crashing relentlessly upon the cream-coloured sand. A bit like my beach at Muizenberg, in South Africa, only Magilligan is a smaller beach, with smaller waves and much less heat. We drove parallel to the sea, and through my window I caught glimpses of the tiny, wooden holiday homes, shacks and waterfalls flowing from the hills and cliffs round Binevenagh, which marks the western extent of the Basalt Plateau of Northern Ireland, from where the legends of Irish kings and giants emanate; I think of the story of David and Goliath, and compare it to my battle with the system, as I spot the old army turrets – cast-offs from the 'Troubles' - guarding the entrance to H.M.P. Magilligan.

Tried to pee a couple of times on the journey, but, for the life of me, I couldn't manage a drop. Is it nerves? Is it fear? Perhaps, it's excitement, or a mixture of both.

I remember NIPS is on a 'go slow', and we sit in the van, outside the gates, for what seems like an eternity - this causes much mumbling and grumbling from the inside of the sweat-box.

'Keep the noise down or there'll be trouble,' shouts some faceless officer. They're pretty good at that over here: waiting until you're locked up or out of reach, before calling you names or making derogatory comments. Four more years of this crap.

Another reception, another induction process and another new beginning.

Hopefully, this will be my last port of call, unless I go bananas and get sent back to England.

The reception S.O. looks at the cover of the box containing my cordless headphones, with the word 'APPROVED' stamped on it by H.M.P. Rye Hill, H.M.P. High Down and H.M.P. Maghaberry.

'You're not allowed this here,' he says.

Foolishly, I ask the doomed question: 'Why not?'

'Because I fuckin' say so - that's why.'

My expression and my mood blacken in a flash - I'm seething; 'What is your problem? You can see it's been approved, and I've just came from a maximum security jail where they're allowed - all part of the NIPS,' I spit out, through clenched teeth.

He just smiles that fuckin' hateful smile they all have, when they know they have you over a barrel.

'So it's like that, is it?' I said. 'Do what you gotta do.' Nothing like getting off on the right foot, eh?

It's lock-up by the time we get over to the wing - 'HB1' (or 'H1', for the initiated). The 'H' stands for 'house', but for those within these walls, the 'H' represents the shape of the accommodation block - an instantly recognizable image of Northern Ireland. As a child and young man it instilled fear - fear of where you could so easily end up if you were in the wrong place at the wrong time, hooked up with the wrong crowd or decided you wanted to stand up for your country of birth. The H blocks at Magilligan were built at the same time as their more infamous brothers at The Maze (Long Kesh).

The blocks here were designed to be a temporary solution to an escalating situation in Northern Ireland, back in the seventies. Those at The Maze have long been condemned, declared 'not fit for purpose' and torn down, although one or two remain standing as a reminder - a museum to the past. Yet, these very same buildings are alive and well in 2010, holding over three-hundred men at a time, on the continuous conveyor belt of 'the system' - they too have been declared 'unfit for purpose', but nothing is done about it.

Unlocked after an hour and I'm immediately looking for an officer; 'There's no toilet in there, I need a toilet in my cell.'

He looks at me as if I'm mad, and says: 'None of them have toilets.'

If this seems hard to believe it is another fact of prison life. Prison cells without toilets or a sink. Where prisoners have to piss and shit in little more than a bucket.

Apparently, 'slopping out' (the term given to prisoners when they empty carry their bucket out of the cell in the mornings to empty,) has been an ongoing problem, with no in-cell sanitation at Magilligan for years - something which is banned under the European convention, yet is still practiced in around two-thousand cells within the UK, with Northern Ireland accounting for three-hundred of them.

'I think you'd better look at my file. No offence, like…'

'Okay leave it with me,' he replies.

Here we go again, I thought. What is the purpose of having a file or documentation on a person if you're never going to look at the fuckin' thing?

After a while I'm told to grab my gear, and they stick me in the Listener's cell - the guy who had to move out wasn't well pleased, by all accounts. Ended up chatting to him later on, though - we knew the same people from Lisburn, and end of story.

They still keep checking us every hour, on the hour, during the night, so I don't get much sleep. When we're unlocked in the morning, it's not for long, and I feel impending doom creep over me.

Northern Ireland thus far has been a bad fuckin' move – prison-wise, that is. Though seeing my Mum and Dad again has been great.

I ask around about the drug-free wing, 'Halward House'. Have to wait two weeks until I finish induction, then pass two piss tests and join the waiting list. Okay, that's not too bad, but I seriously need to get the fuck off this wing. I can't believe I'm saying this, but it's worse than Maghaberry.

After two weeks, I'm granted my wish and sent off to H2.

Holy fuck! What a shower of shit!

I'm not even going to waste time and effort discussing these vile creatures.

Three weeks later, I'm off to Halward House.

Now, this is more like it.

The same set up as Rye Hill and High Down - bloody marvellous: wide open spaces, with loads of natural light and high ceilings, a skylight, and communal areas with tables and seats; admittedly, these are made of metal, bolted to the floor, and as uncomfortable as hell, but better than nothing.

I'm in cell number eight, on the ground floor, overlooking a massive exercise yard, which is surrounded by numerous fences, as per usual; I think this is a Northern Ireland thing: you are unable to see any great distance anywhere within NIPS' cages, within cages, within cages – they are designed to disorientate and confuse you, and remind you of why you are here. Row upon row of razor wire - totally over the top! I suppose they needed it back in the day, but, come on lads - get with the fuckin' programme.

I've only done two years, and even though these years have been eventful, it's now time to settle down and get something constructive sorted out. I'm going to keep trying to make a note of the eventful things that happen in my life, but for now I'm going to take a break from all this writing malarkey, as after a while it feels as if it is becoming a bit too repetitive and boring. Maybe this is just a sign of me shutting down and keeping the real world and reality at bay.

OCTOBER 2009

I've initiated a complaint about the night checks - it has gone to the prisoner ombudsman and I'm sure it's going to be a long time before the NIPS will admit any wrongdoing, or will consider that their policy designed to help all prisoners is, in fact, fuckin' them up!

I'm doing a C.L.A.I.T. (*Computer Literacy and Information Technology*) course, O-level English Lit., Open University degree in *'Criminology and Psychological Studies'* and am the new servery orderly - who says life in prison is dull? I haven't got a fuckin' minute! It will end up taking its toll, I know, but I need to keep myself busy and not think about where I am.

Mum and wee sis started to come and visit together. It's been great, but my Mum still insists on forcing her religious views on my life, and I hate it - didn't like it when I was wee, and don't like it now; it still manages to muster the same sick feeling in my stomach, resulting in the same ferocity. I know Mum means well, but this blinkered view of righteousness does not work with me - it only drives me away. *Leave me be - I'll believe if I want to believe.* All her goodness gets drowned out by this one annoying trait.

Tried to explain it to my sister, but that seems to have gone tits-up as well: no more visits or letters.

It's probably upsetting for all concerned, but, in the close environment of a prison visiting room, I cannot be seen to have any weakness, embarrassing or emotional moments - a person cannot have the same arguments or discussion that they would on the outside: raised voices receive sideways glances, and, if one thing is certain, it will be all over the wing by the end of the day.

This alone is not the problem: the problem is that there are those in here who love to push your buttons, and a wee dig at the appropriate time can lead to all sorts of eruptions. I've seen it done all too often, and I watch the perpetrators laugh as their target gets twisted-up, or worse. These places are not normal - *life* is not normal, and the only time normality comes into it is when you speak with a loved one, face to face; even then, you are under constant pressure to be on your guard - a simple request can lead to all sorts of grief.

I'm sorry I've caused this grief in the first place, but I will not lie anymore about my feelings, or things that hurt me. Lying fucked me up, and I ain't doing it anymore - if my truth is too much for you, well, tough; I'm the one in here - not you - and I am the one who wants to lead some semblance of a normal life upon release, preferably with you by my side.

The summer has been and gone - my friend Hans has had a good laugh at the Northern Irish summertime, basking in all its two-week glory.

I keep company with Hans and Mick - Mick is an older man, from Lurgan. Even though we are from different sides of the political divide, we always manage to have a laugh, moan and gripe about our daily lives, normally trying to explain to Hans (German national) what life used to be like back in the day, and how, if he thinks it's bad now, he would not have wanted to be in prison in Northern Ireland from the seventies onwards.

Mick hasn't got long left, and Hans has another two years. I'll stick with Hans - he's good company; knows what the real world is like, and isn't one of these people who think Northern Ireland is the centre of the universe. By the time Hans is ready to leave (June 2011) it'll be time for me to move to Foyleview - our resettlement unit - then town visits, home-leaves, and out of this place.

CHRISTMAS DAY 2009

Woke up this morning, full of Christmas cheer.

Was behind the servery, getting things ready for the breakfast. The officer on duty is one of the better ones; I've known him for nine months now and we discuss prison life on regular basis, and are in agreement on many things.

But when I held my hand out to wish him a happy Christmas, he left it hanging.

There was brief awkward silence, then I just got on with my work as if nothing had happened.

This man has managed to destroy any feeling of respect I had towards any member of the NIPS. The gesture might have seemed a simple one, but the way it was refused made my gut lurch: this man does not see me as a human being, worthy of any type of physical contact. Shaking hands is one of the basic forms of respect in our society.

One of the little proclamations I have posted on my wall reads: 'Always be the first to offer your hand'. But not here, I'm afraid - not to the men in white shirts; never, ever again will I be made to feel so small and insignificant as the dirt on your shoe. I'll never hold my hand out again.

Served up Christmas dinner - there was loads left over. Some guys didn't want it, so myself and Pat kept the extras in a couple of big Tupperware containers; Hans and I had too much - we sat around the table on Boxing Day, laughing and complaining about how painful our stomachs felt. It was terrible - my guts were killing me - but it was nice while it lasted; pure gluttony.

2010

The new year brought me a concerted return to physical exercise - I haven't been to the gym for a long time.

Went to the doctor's, to attend a 'well-man clinic', where they checked blood pressure, cholesterol and stuff like that - I weighed in at twenty-one stone, nearly had a heart attack, and a wee voice went off in my head: *No more lies or excuses, boy - this is fuckin' serious!* My blood pressure and cholesterol are fine, but I need to have a serious pop at the old weight.

Started going to the gym three times a week and was also put on some tablets - they take all the fat out of everything you have eaten, and it is passed in the form of an oil slick from your back passage (my days of farting are long gone, as a fart can often be... not a fart, if you get my drift). My early gym sessions are met with *'whities'* and dizzy spells, but I stick with it, and by the summer I've lost two and a half stone - as a result I feel fuckin' great. I've also been cycling and doing a bit of weights, though not too much, as any tweak of my back will have me laid up and back to square one. I plod along, and sometimes get a bit jealous of the young lads, bouncing around in their prime, as fit as fiddles, ripped and buffed: they make it all look so easy - I think it's called 'taking things for granted'.

I remember a time when I, too, used to play football, badminton, canoeing and bodybuilding, all in the one week, and then go out and get trashed, sleep with the girlfriend, get up the next morning and ache, but shrug it off and carry on regardless. I'm now in a position where - as my new friend Pat says – I'm 'in a marathon, not a sprint'; I'm going to the gym so that if I attempt any of the previous activities when I'm released, I won't die on the spot.

29TH JULY 2010

Decided to start writing again. This long break has been worthwhile: I found it helpful in the past, and hopefully it will ameliorate some of the hidden and not-so-hidden stresses that are slowly creeping back into my life.

My main bone of contention with prison life – at the moment – is the night checks. I've been on mirtazapine - a mild anti-depressant - for a couple of months, and my dosage has been increased to 45mg. I've also decided to make sure I'm awake, sitting up, watching the TV around 7.00am in order to withdraw the satisfaction certain officers get when they bang your door, call you names, or threaten you if you are sleeping and do not immediately move on their command.

Nobody within the system wants to admit that these checks are causing me and my fellow inmates harm. Their only purpose is to protect officers, and ultimately the governor, from accusations of culpable manslaughter, when - not *if* - someone commits suicide.

I was called as witness to another prisoner's adjudication a few weeks back. The officer concerned was under the influence whilst on duty, and I believe the incident between him and the prisoner would not have happened otherwise.

The rumour going around is that because of the impending shake-up within NIPS, certain officers are trying to get themselves assaulted, so that they can leave on a medical ticket, or serve out the rest of their time on the sick. This sorry state of affairs is so indicative of the prison service within the UK - not just Northern Ireland – where, although everyone knows what's going on, they do nothing about it.

The officer hasn't spoken to me since; I'll need to watch my back: he can be a vindictive bastard, and I'm sure some of his colleagues will also bide their time, waiting for an opportunity to fuck me over. I fell into a similar trap in one prison in England, although I must admit I did handle the situation rather poorly. I'll need to keep a low profile for the next few weeks; the officer is on duty now, and he just glares at me - baiting me and waiting for me to bite.

When they came round to see if we needed hot water last night, after one of the regular and frequent early lock-ups, he just flung my cell door open, banging it off the wall with a considerable amount of force and a look of venom - obviously tanked up and finding it difficult to contain himself. With the agility of a coiled spring, I leapt from my bed and flung the door closed with a similar amount of force. Didn't say a word - it's not worth it; instead I just sat.

Some of these 'brave' men and women in uniform continually think they can get away with bullying and mistreating prisoners - they seem to think that they're invincible.

I'm glad I'm not the sort of person who holds grudges, but I will say that some of these men and women tread a very thin line, and I'm actually surprised acts of revenge do not occur more often.

Enough of all this depressing stuff. See, this is how prison gets you: it ropes you in, seduces you, and before you know it you're as bleak and as depressing as your surroundings.

Had a lovely surprise visit from my Mum and my sister yesterday - it was great to see them. I sometimes forget how fantastic a simple hug can be, how a smile can wash away all of your fears, doubts and insecurities in an instant, and how someone saying 'I love you' can make all the difference.

My sis has promised to send me the letters she's written but hasn't sent yet - I won't hold my breath. Ah – my wee sister. Can't believe she's living at Millisle - this is where we had a caravan when I was a kid; I'd love to live down there. Who knows, maybe I'll be able to when I get out?

Getting out - what will that entail? Where will I be? How will my marbles be holding up by then? I'm making plans for my future, but, as per usual, I don't know what it might hold for me.

I always used to have this foolish notion of returning to Dunmurry, going to The Stagecoach, seeing all my old friends from twenty years ago and picking up where I left off. I always wanted them - my friends - to share the adventures, places and people I've met over the years; I used to sit in bars and clubs, and think *Bill would love this... Sparky would laugh at this... Bimbo might like that...* These thoughts have gradually faded (*'Dreamer'* by *Supertramp* in my head).

I suppose I just wanted to impress people: *the prodigal son returns, broken but not beaten.*

The Stagecoach has gone now, and so have a lot of my friends. Where has all this time gone? What on Earth was I thinking? I just kept running, kept getting up, dusting myself off and running.

No more! Time to settle down and come to the party. Think I'll try and be close to Mum and sis.

Of course, they have their own lives, and maybe I don't fit into their plans: maybe I'll be home, but alone again... Maybe I'll never get what I'm looking for. It's hard to achieve an emotional goal if you don't actually know what it is.

Pat and Craig are sitting at the table by my cell, having a chat and a cuppa. I'm in cell two - a perk that goes with being servery orderly; it's a disabled cell, with its own shower. I have told the doctor and the medic that I could do with being in a medical cell permanently, because of the pain in my feet, and the difficulty I have walking, towards the end of the day - I have to sit down to take a pee, my feet are that bad; I've got *plantar-fasciitis* - a condition where the ligament in the heel gets inflamed and hurts like hell.

Suffer on in silence - grin and bear it.

Officer J is running around, being officer J, and I can hear officer S letting the odd chirp out. Life trundles along.

Purchased *'Slash'*, by Slash, and over the past weeks the album has grown into one of the best I have ever listened to; it features different singers, and he plays the song like the band the artists have their roots in, but puts his own individual spin on it. Some of the singers are new to me (Myles Kennedy, Andrew Stockdale…), but I do know Ozzy, Dave Gröhl, Fergie from the *Black-Eyed Peas*, and others. I look at Gigi's photo on my cork notice-board, and the lyrics from *'Gotton'*, featuring Adam Levine, remind me of our friendship, and how cool it was to be around her: *'I can't save you if you don't let me… you just get me, like I've never been gotten before.'* Sent Gigi a letter last week - haven't heard from her for a while.

Haven't heard from Fin at all. I suppose it was inevitable. People and time march on, and best intentions and promises fall by the wayside; people have lives to live, and if you're out of sight, then you inevitably become out of mind, whilst us prisoners try to hold on to false hopes and conditional love (*'I'll love you and be with you, as long as you are with me!'*). It's only now that I fully realize what *un*conditional love is.

My sis summed it up nicely, when she said: 'If this situation was the other way round, I'm sure Michael would be coming to see me, no questions asked.' She is so beautiful, my wee sis - reminds me of my Mum when she was twenty-six or twenty-seven, and I was about eight or nine.

I've just came back from the podiatrist (chiropodist), and he didn't do the procedure he said he was going to do (namely, cut out half my toenail to stop it from growing back in). He's put me down to see him each month - as long as I see him each month, there won't be a problem. However, nothing in prison ever runs smoothly, and healthcare is a different animal altogether. Still, it isn't as haphazard here as some of the places I've been in.

Spoke to a guy from *'Alcohol and Drugs: Empowering People Through Therapy'* (*AD:EPT*) earlier, and he's very interested in my idea about a 'Prisoners' Advice Centre'. I hope someone picks up the gauntlet and I'm given the opportunity to put my ideas to use.

So, what had started as a shit day has brightened up already - all because I've done a wee bit of writing.

I'll go and phone my Dad in a minute and let him know I've received the shorts he sent me.

30TH JULY 2010

Was awoken by night staff at 7.00am - the big, tall fella, accompanied by the bald guy with glasses. I'm a bit miffed, because normally I'd be awake by then and not give them the satisfaction of waking me by banging my door and flicking the light on and off.

The only reason we are woken is so that the night-staff can go home knowing that everyone is alive, and hand over to the day-staff, who then go round and do exactly the same thing.

Or maybe they're just being bastards.

1ST AUGUST 2010

August already - I can't believe it! It seems like January was only a week or so ago.

Had a nice, relaxing afternoon and went to the gym this morning - no speed wobbles this time. I've reduced my tablets, cut out a lot of shit in my diet, and am starting to feel the difference.

This time yesterday we were all banged up - the alarm bell went off around 4.30pm, and we're normally unlocked about twenty minutes later. I put my dinner in the fridge and went straight to my cell. Something had occurred upstairs, and, as I'm busy working away in the servery, I'm unaware of a lot of the goings-on around me.

Every time an emergency button gets hit, the alarms go off the whole wing is locked down. Not only that the whole prison is denied movement and a security team is sent in their vans to the location of the alarm. We are normally locked at 5.15pm at the weekends (this being a Sunday), but by six o'clock I realized we would not be getting out again, and I hadn't had my bloody dinner. I rang the bell and told the officer my predicament - he came back fifteen minutes later with the S.O., and they let me out. They weren't saying much I guessed that the incident earlier had been a bit serious.

The officer said: 'You're lucky we know you, and you were polite about getting your dinner, or you wouldn't have got out.'

It takes all of my strength, sometimes, to keep my gob under control. I mean, this fucker is making it seem like it's *my* fault I'm locked up, and I'm being granted a massive favour in being fed, because something out of the ordinary happened.

It turns out the incident was a bit more serious than the normal handbags at dawn: prisoner 'A' hit prisoner 'B' over the head with an iron, splitting his skull; there were pool cues involved, as well. Apparently, there was a bit of history between the two - it was only a matter of time before it kicked off. One of the blokes is due out in a couple of weeks - why on Earth would he jeopardize this, just to save face? I guess it takes all sorts.

I've seen worse and heard worse, but this is the most serious fracas I've seen since I came back to Northern Ireland. I just shrug it off - forgotten by the end of the day; by next morning, completely gone.

In complete contrast, I've just received a card and a letter from Mum, which leaves me in a much more happy mood.

TV will stay off until *'Sherlock'* at 8.30pm - think I'll spend the rest of the time reading. My TV hardly ever goes on during the day anymore.

6TH AUGUST 2010

I've been having the strangest dreams recently, mostly, and most vividly, about Anne-Marie. On Thursday morning I woke with tears streaming down my face and an ache in the pit of my stomach - no, it wasn't just wind. This morning I woke, after dreaming I'd bought her old house in Areema, and made a deal with her mum that Anne-Marie's daughter could come and stay any time she wanted - after all, it was her home.

Anne-Marie has been dead for fifteen years now and I can't believe how clear the images in my dream were, and how real it felt when I kissed her. I wonder how our lives would have turned out if she'd lived, or if Basil hadn't also died soon after; my two best friends gone within a matter of months. God, I miss both of them terribly, and I'm glad I could call them my friends. Smiling now, thinking of the laughter; seeing their laughing faces - *real* laughter, only fittingly experienced between friends.

I meant to sit down and write this earlier, but got caught up in another Lee Child novel.

Officer 'A' and Al are back on duty after their holidays, and I feel safer knowing they will be around on a more regular basis.

There's just been a huge downpour - it looks and feels spectacular; the temperature is changing, and the smell in the air is of rain drying on soil, and evaporating on tarmac. The sky is a light grey - almost white - and I can't see Binevenagh - only as far as the house block (HB3) on the other side of the yard.

This is the first week I've managed to get to the gym three times in a row. Because Halward House is a supposed drug-free wing, you have too many blokes who are interested in looking after their health and not getting whacked all the time – consequently, there are nearly thirty guys daily, who want and need to go to the gym. So, in an effort to please everybody, the two landings take turns with days of preference, and the first fifteen get selected.

Feeling good about life - gonna go finish my book and watch *'American Chopper'* later on.

I've allowed myself to have our 'sweet of the day' from the menu; sounds exotic: it's a sweet mince pie about the size of teabag - bloody luxury, lad.

9TH AUGUST 2010

It's a lovely morning. I've just finished my servery chores, and life is cool - ticking along nicely.

Wrote to my Mum; enjoy where we are now in our relationship - I find it easier to talk, now that I've knocked down the walls that held me back in the past.

Can't wait to start my O.U. course in October. Killing time at the minute - treading water - doing a lot of reading.

20TH AUGUST 2010

Torches are now being used on a regular basis by night staff. There are still a few who insist on turning the light on, but I must admit it's a step forward.

I've just received the results for my final TMA (*Tutor Marked Assignment*) of DD101: 62% - gives me an overall mark of 60%, which has earned me my first sixty points toward my degree. Spent a whole afternoon with Mr. Yeats, discussing the structure and set up of an academic essay; he makes it look so easy. I'm sure, given enough time and practice, I'll eventually master it.

I've treated my success with some modesty, although I'm getting pleasure from the fact that this is the first time in my life that I've actually finished anything of meaning, not cut corners, nor given up as the end came near. I'll also get my O-level English Literature, and am thinking about doing an A-level as part of my O.U. studies - undecided as yet.

Self-doubt creeping in, and I keep hearing Adelita's voice: 'Just do it.' Maybe I will.

Fuck it - I will!

Dad is up tomorrow and I'm looking forward to seeing him. Received a couple of letters from my wee sister - one of them had been written last September and she'd just found it and posted it anyway (there's logic there somewhere). She did make me laugh, and I wrote back immediately; glad I've finally got her new address - can write, now, whenever I want.

Received a report from the prisoner ombudsman, stating that we will be getting a new library and we will be able to go once a week. I wonder how long this will take. Watch this space.

Read an interesting article in *Inside Time*, by two solicitors, about drug trafficking. It says that if *A*, *B* and *C* agree to import cannabis, but *A* and *B* change their minds and import cocaine, and *C* is unaware of it, then *C* has grounds for appeal (I'm *C*, by the way). Sent them a letter, but won't hold my breath or get my hopes up - don't think there is anything I can do about my past, and, at the end of the day, I'm here now, and will probably be ready for release by the time it would get anywhere.

26TH AUGUST 2010

What a day! Early lock-up - thank God! Some of the lads blast out their music from a couple of cells, as they believe they have a right to; they think it's the done thing in prison, and staff just ignore it because we're on early lock-up.

Was meant to see the chiropodist/podiatrist this morning, and, despite six different members of staff telling me I was on the list, I didn't get to see him -

filled in another complaint form.

On a more positive note, I've decided to write a blog when I get out, and I've achieved a B in my English Literature O-level. The prison had arranged a little presentation, and the dignitaries arrived thirty minutes late; there were six of us and six of them: one was the governor, and one was the deputy of operations, soon to possibly become the Director General - the rest are a mystery. That's what happens in here: you see all these suits, but none of them tell you who they are. If they are inspectors, they are accompanied by an officer, and nobody wants to say anything derogatory, in case they get bullied by staff and management

The lady from the *Jaily News* wanted to take everyone's photograph - I declined the offer. She tried to persuade me, and I got a funny look from the governor, but I refused and said: 'I'm still in South Africa, thank you very much.'

I'm the one standing behind the photographer.

Dinner has just arrived - I'm having a bowl of porridge and a banana; being a good boy, as far as the old diet is concerned.

It's funny how notions dawn on one - never in my life did I ever consider eating porridge, whilst *doing* porridge, at four in the afternoon.

Looking forward to the door getting locked, and getting stuck into another Lee Child book.

Officer Al and I have been having good discussions, and a laugh, about the madness of the system; the real world - the public - does not know, and is not privy to what it gets for its money. Officers and staff in general, within the prison service, are frightened to make any sort of decision, in case they are hauled over the coals, and even if and when they do make a decision, and it is a mistake, nothing will be done about it; there is no accountability - they'll probably just get a bollocking and decide never to make a decision again.

30TH AUGUST 2010

It's an overcast bank holiday Monday. August is nearly over, September just beginning, and I still think it's January or February! Time is well and truly flying by.

Made the mistake of sleeping in this morning, and had the usual key rapped against my door, and door handle rattled and shaken - so that it makes a bang in the locks metal housing - in order to wake me up. Lay awake, listening to see if I could hear any of the others getting the same treatment, but couldn't.

The alarms are being reset and tested for the day - it's the same every day, and totally unnecessary - all about bodies, and making sure prisoners don't sleep in.

Wonder what the atmosphere will be like on the wing today; one of the guys is threatening another bloke, and a few of the others want to empty the guy doing the threatening. Oh, the joys of life behind bars.

2ND SEPTEMBER 2010

I've been wrestling with the idea of sending a letter to my old English teacher, and telling her I finally managed to get an O-Level in English Literature - the only thing holding me back is that I'm embarrassed about telling her I'm in prison. But the more I think about it, the more I want to do it. Keep hearing Adelita's voice: 'Just do it.'

Are my motives real? I'll get the address and think on it a little bit more - maybe I'll ask Allison her opinion.

All the orderlies have been moved upstairs again, though myself and Pat have been allowed to stay downstairs… me, because of my bad feet, but Pat..? Probably because he's my back-up. The powers that be have decided to remove six guys from general population and stick them upstairs, renaming it 'The Harm Reduction Unit'; none of the other prisoners are allowed to talk to or associate with them.

Is Queen Victoria alive again? I mean, this is fuckin' scary.

Some of the guys are from west Belfast, and went to school together. How the hell can you tell one half of a landing not to speak to the other? Madness!

Started to grow my hair again; a notice has just been issued, stating that disinfectant spray can be found in the class office, and must be used in line with Health and Safety instructions, after every use of hair-clippers - the first time I actually *see* spray being used, I'll cut my hair. I've a funny feeling I'll be getting a trim when I get out on home-leave, in about two years' time! My hair's at the spiky stage, and I'm able to use gel; feels weird - been a long time since my hair had any length. Fuck it - I'll just grow it long, and get it cut when I get out.

Can't get a hairbrush from the tuck shop yet; I'll keep trying - the old plastic comb won't do it for much longer.

Received a reply from the two English solicitors who talked about *A*, *B* and *C* and drug-trafficking in *Inside Time*. They sent my letter back, very kindly, and said they couldn't look at my case, as they only represent those people they originally represented at trial. Oh, well - that's the end of that, then.

Haven't been to the gym for a week; here goes - I bet it hurts.

4TH SEPTEMBER 2010

Slept well, though very windy outside.

A group of people from the 'Prison Arts Foundation' had a little get together yesterday, and some of us from Mr. Yeats's class were asked to read the first page of our *'Postcards from…'* stories. I was fine when I got up, but started shaking as soon as I started to read - thank goodness, it subsided enough for me to continue. This is the first time, in my entire life, I have stood in front of a group of people and read to them, and I couldn't believe it: they actually laughed at the bits they were meant to, and at some new bits. Was trying my damnedest to speak calmly, loudly and clearly, and all I could hear was these people laughing with me - I was genuinely taken aback; my chest puffed out, I took a deep breath and I kept going. When I finished they all started clapping enthusiastically.

On the way back to my seat, one guy catches my eye and says: 'Well done.' Found out later who he was: Mike Moloney.

I must apologise to Mike: I've gotten his name wrong on a couple of letters I sent. Anyway, Mike is an Antipodean who ran away to join the circus and see the world, at an early age. He's a now much-travelled gentleman, with boundless energy and enthusiasm, and the head of the Northern Ireland Prison Arts Foundation. His two little words will always stick with me; they have given me the courage and strength to pursue my writing endeavours, and, with the help and guidance of Mr. Yeats, I'm sure I'll produce some decent stuff in the future.

Mike's words may not seem like much to some people, but in a prison environment, when you're constantly have to scrape and cow to authority, it feels good sometimes to have a bit of dignity, and take a bow yourself - a feel-good moment.

The rest of the guys got up, but I found it really difficult to make them out - hope I was clearer than they were, or my feelings of triumph are short-lived.

Another group of guys (I think they were ex-prisoners from Italy) and an Italian lady got up and did a short skit. The lady was really hard to understand, but she was very funny, and exuded confidence, passion and humour. It made me think about how much I've forgotten what it's like to be in the company of the human race - I'm not saying that we're all animals, and that all prison officers are bullies (they're not), but at moments like this it becomes painfully clear. When one looks at the expressions on the face of someone who doesn't live under the glare of the system, one realizes how unnatural our life actually is - in our case (prisoners *and* prison officers) every word, every action, and every reaction will be scrutinized, taken down as evidence and used at a later date to fuck you up. This observation, for me, only exposes how the system unwittingly creates 'us' and 'them' - society vs. the excluded, and never the twain shall meet

– that it's not deemed natural, and we (the *system*) can't allow these men to associate with the society from which they have been removed.

The reason I say this is because we were escorted over to the event half an hour late, and removed half an hour early, before any purposeful interaction could take place. Mr. Erwin James, from *The Guardian*, had just got up to speak, and I was only starting to get into it, when we were asked to leave – early lock-up again for Halward. We've got toilets on our wing, so it's easier to lock us up.

And, it was a lovely Friday afternoon (barbecue weather), so, all of a sudden, no staff.

Still, the little bit I did hear Mr. James speak about was enlightening. He's a person who has been to prison, served twenty-odd years, and he was telling the ensemble how much energy it took for a prisoner to get through the day. I did laugh when he noticed us being removed and was told it's an early lock-up; he quipped: 'Oh yes - the sun is out... Friday afternoon - officers won't be knocking off early to get to the pub.' Bang on the money, as usual, Erwin.

There is no doubt in my mind that not all prisoners or officers should be allowed to attend such gatherings - some people do not possess the life-skills, manners or social awareness to interact with others, and that's just the staff I'm talking about. I do get on well with most staff; however, at the end of the day, it boils down to a simple statement: 'I'm a prisoner and they are *the system*.'

We all play the game - put on the mask of the role, which we act out on a daily basis. It was only when I watched the faces of the ensemble, who are not entrenched in the daily political shenanigans of prison life, did I feel a realization of my own being; for the first time, since I'd been inside, I forgot about people watching me - I laughed, and remembered *how* to laugh in the company of others, without inhibition. It reminded me of what it was like to be me the *real* me; I found the whole experience touching and liberating.

Need to be careful of that word: 'liberating' - after all, I've lost my liberty, and can't be seen to be getting some of it back. These gatherings are all well and good, but inside they are also few and far between, and, as I've already said, they start late and finish early.

I've discovered that education is my sanctuary inside prison – my safe space; nowhere to hide, nowhere to run and no-one to make excuses to. Just me and a pen and paper, or me and the screen. Wish it could positively affect others the way it has me.

28TH SEPTEMBER 2010

'Progress' is what my stars say, in today's paper - if only this could be true.

It's been a busy and eventful few days: first of all, I've made it back into the eighteen-stone bracket (18st 12lb) - I've been stuck around the nineteen-and-a-half mark for what seems like forever. I'm feeling pretty good, and am up to thirty sit-ups every morning, although I tried to do a push-up on the bars at the gym, and couldn't even support myself - this is something I shall have to remedy. I'm now able to say that I've lost two stone. *'Progress'* - yes, but I need much more.

They didn't check me at all last night - couldn't sleep because my sleep *wasn't* being interrupted. It's a funny ole world, innit?

My daily chores have changed: I'm back studying, and going over to the Education centre every day now - gets me out for a bit of fresh air. Made another complaint to Healthcare about not being allowed foot powder - my feet are killing me again, especially my toes.

Started doing the 'Victim Impact Programme' (V.I.P.) again. What I've discovered about men in prison in Northern Ireland, compared to those in England, is that men over here can't comprehend that the people who want to help them in jail are other prisoners, and not part of the system. They are paranoid, and think that everyone is out to get them, including all sorts of intelligence-gathering agencies, even when they are only in for nicking a couple of T-shirts, non-payment of fines, or smacking some fool when they've been off their faces on booze, or drugs, or both - not exactly national security issues.

They all think they are the dog's bollocks, and that they are the main men.

You're not: you're a tool... a dick... a legend in your own lunchbox.

One particular bloke kept giving me daggers every time I made notes in my wee book. Asked him what was wrong, on his way out, and he told me he didn't want anybody writing anything about him. After I explained that I was making notes about previously unasked questions, and possible future topics of discussion, he lightened up;

'Oh. I wondered why you - another prisoner - were taking notes about me, for them.'

I laughed, and told him it wasn't all about him.

I do hope this one guy does come and speak to me, though (HM) – I can see him searching for answers, but he doesn't know how to ask for help. He's already asked me, once or twice: 'Why do you keep doing this course.'

I've told him that when the moment arrives, I'll tell him. He thought I was joking at first, but looked at me funny, when he saw I was serious. I know what's going to happen, especially with him: he's been in denial for a long time, and as soon as he stops lying to himself, he'll feel about ten years younger - I know because I've been there. Only experience can teach you this.

Hope he gets it.

9TH OCTOBER 2010

9.40am

Saturday morning, and I'm listening to Slash, in an effort to drown out SJ, who's walking around the landing, slobbering, as usual. He's permanently fucked up, and waffles on and on; some people make excuses for him, because he's had a serious car accident which has made him a bit slow, but he's nobody's fool, and plays the game.

It's been a strange week, full of ups and downs. The night-checks carry on regardless; they were brought up at the last 'Prisoners' Consultation Meeting' -

when the HMCIP recommendation that all night-checks should stop was mentioned, the governor said: 'Yeah, but they're only recommendations - we don't have to obey them.'

I'm gonna go round his house and flick on his lights every hour, to see how he likes it.

The V.I.P session today was the best yet - a hard crowd: plenty of alpha-males. HM had his *'eureka'* moment - it was brilliant; he was discussing the rights and wrongs of his crime, all the denying it, the making excuses, the being *the big lad.*

All of a sudden, officer 'A' said: 'Are you guilty?'

I held my breath, and everyone looked in his direction. He tossed it around for a second, nearly choked, but did it.

'Aye, I am guilty,' he said.

Not easy. Especially with this mob - a room full of hateful, self-centred individuals. The type of courage it takes for a person to admit to what he did is one of the hardest I know of. HM then went on to tell about having to explain his crime to a family member - the moment he spoke of this, to this room full of people, was the moment that he realized he had taken his family member's innocence. Yet that same realization will be the making of him - now he can move forward.

I'm sure there are plenty of psychologists out there who know all about this type of thing, but, for me, unless you've experienced it, you can't feel it. For me, the day you stop lying and be *real* to yourself is the day you set yourself free; this is the day you take back control of your soul, and of your destiny.

He came to my cell later, and when I looked him right in the eye, he was able to look back.

'Do you remember you asked me why I help out on this course?' I said.

'Aye,' he replied

I jumped up and stood a couple of inches from his face, telling him: 'It's for what you're feeling in here (I tapped his head) and here (and his heart) right now, at this minute. Look at you - you've grown about six inches; your whole demeanour has changed.'

He nodded.

I sat back down, smiling, and said: 'How light do you feel now, since you said what you said this morning?'

'Fuck, aye – you're right. I cried a bit when I went back to my cell, but I feel fuckin' great,' he said.

I replied: 'Well, H, now you know why. Now you know how you can help others, if you want to. Only *you* can experience what you're feeling now, but you know that I do know what it's like.'

He pulled out the chair and sat down - this is the first time he had ever sat in my company. He relaxed a bit, but I could tell it was all a little overwhelming for him, so he just stared at the floor for a while. I said nothing – I just waited.

Then they came: the questions, the conversation, and the relief - the avalanche. And I fed off his buzz - it was great to see that the penny had finally dropped. He stood up, made a fist and invited me to do the same. Then off he went.

I felt like bursting, if only because I had played a small part in helping him reach his understanding, just by listening and being there.

Yet again, I have seen hope and happiness arise from the darkest of scenarios - this guy had been written off, and, indeed, had written himself off. It'll be a long road back for him – I hope he makes it.

These moments, although rewarding, are physically draining – I slept like a brick.

He always says hello now. I've just lent him my *'It's Amazing'* piece, and the CD by *Aerosmith* - he gets it.

Our Open University computers have now become a security issue.

The latest words of wisdom from on-high are that we're not allowed to have a printer, as we 'can smuggle things out on a visit'. As opposed to words written with a pen!? *What do they have to hide?* is what I keep asking myself.

What planet do these people live on? We are not terrorists, fighting a gagging order - as a serving prisoner I'm allowed to write to journalists, as long as I don't mention anyone's name, quote or make any money from the exchange (though, upon release all bets are off).

The fact that I hardly know anyone in Norn Iron anymore is neither here nor there; my only regular visits are from my Mum, my Dad, my sis and my cousin - if they (the system) knew of their backgrounds, they would recognize how ridiculous their claims are. Fuckin' unbelievable, honestly!

Each time Magilligan is mentioned in the news, or in a report, it describes Magilligan as 'a medium to low security establishment, housing men who are approaching the end of their sentence'. The problem is: the people in charge are all of The Maze/the 'Troubles' ilk.

Hans is laughing at my flabbergastedness. He, too, keeps shaking his head, and saying in his inimical brand of English: 'I just can't believe it.'

He's just written a letter to David Ford (the Justice Minister) about why the early release or resettlement of foreign nationals (like the rest of the prisoners) has not been implemented in Northern Ireland - he'd be out now if he was in England.

Think I've got a cold coming. Hope I can get to the gym tomorrow - been doing well lately.

Managed to see the podiatrist. He's given me stuff to stop my toe from sweating, but says there's no medical reason for which to allow me foot powder - he says using foot powder is not NIPS 'best practice', which he has to obey. So what have I been using for the last twenty years?

Does the pharmaceutical industry know that its future in foot powder is in jeopardy, because the NIPS say it's not 'best practice', and can be used as a cutting agent for drugs? Here's a thought: stop letting the drugs into prison! They spend more time blanket-banning and enforcing unenforceable logic, than they do in stopping the drug flow into prison. Every prison is the same - all you've got to do is look closely at certain staff members: I'm not making any implications, but I will say it is a very lucrative and easy game to get into.

Mum and sis came up and we all had a bit of a moment. I tried to tell my mother that I wasn't interested in God, and to stop sending me quotes from the bible, and little religious tracts. It was horrible - I felt like shit having to explain this, but I did have to: I feel worse each time I get one of these quotes.

Wrote a letter to my sis, trying to explain why I think the way I do, and that I don't want to hurt anybody, but it has to stop, or there will be no more Michael around. I hope she gets it. Tried to explain to her that Mum and Granny forced me to go to church, so my feelings run deep where religion is concerned – I didn't just wake up one morning, and decide to feel sick every time someone I loved mentioned religion; I'm *scarred.* It's weird: I can talk about this with others, but not my mother or father.

Managed to achieve another little victory today: I've managed to get proper-sized envelopes issued. The normal prison-issue envelopes are small, brown, square ones - they're okay if you only write one page, but I don't, I write four or five; if you fold that it won't fit in the envelope. Besides, I've started to write a lot of letters to officialdom, so I would like my well-structured and well-worded letters to arrive in the comfortable attire afforded by decent stationery.

Still haven't been allowed the envelopes my mother had handed in on a visit. I presume it's to do with 'things' inside them: perhaps a secret, hidden message, written in invisible ink, which will overthrow the system.

1ST NOVEMBER 2010

Turned my light off around nine, and by nine-fifty my gastro reflux had started to make my throat burn - it's been a while since this gave me any jip. Had to prop myself up, and fell asleep in a sitting position. What a kip!

I knew I needed it - had a bad day: I snapped at officer A, and he deserved it. I lost my temper - he thinks that security justifies everything; they have taken the computer used by Hans off for analysis, and removed the printer from the room we use.

Received a letter from my mate Davey - as usual, he's made me laugh and smile, but some sad news, also: an old friend has passed away, after a long battle with throat cancer. He was one of the founding members of the band *Sweet Savage*, and I'll always remember him propping up the bar in The Stager.

I'm a bit shocked by how unfeeling I have become, where death is concerned – I think these places take away your caring nature, and crush your natural emotional state; maybe it's self-preservation, as any sign of emotion shown in here can be mistaken as sign of weakness.

Officer Al hijacked me when The Samaritans came onto the wing, looking for new recruits for the Listeners scheme.

'How long have you left?' the lady asked me.

'Two and half years,' I replied.

'Oh, good,' she said – then added: 'Oh, sorry - I didn't mean it like that; good for us, I meant to say.'

'It's okay,' I laughed.

We ended up having a good chat, and it looks like I'm going to finally become a Listener. It's strange how things arrive when one least expects it - it's only been four years since I made my first application, at H.M.P. Lewes, in September 2007.

16TH NOVEMBER 2010

Three years, five months and one day since my arrest at Gatwick airport; three years and one day since my conviction at Croydon Crown Court. What a joyride!

It's a beautiful morning, and the air is crisp with frost, the sun is peeking over the distant hills, and dark clouds (with possible silver linings) are scattered all around. Just out of the shower, fresh and relaxed, I'm thinking about how I felt when I was at Brixton, the morning after my conviction: it was a mixture of tiredness, relief and excitement.

Yeah: *excitement*! I was now labelled, classed, judged, and found guilty by my peers - now I just had to get on with my life, to get real and come to the party; to start anew. Even though it was a hell of a lot more manic at Brixton, I was much more relaxed than I am here.

I know it's a mistake to relax here: you can't show it, as someone will make sure that it doesn't stay that way. Can see it in some of the more vindictive officers, when they look at you: *'What's he looking so happy about? I'll soon sort that out.'*

I was actually warned about smiling too much at Lewes by Miss Chewing Gum: 'Your problem, Michael, is that you've got a lovely smile, and some people will hate that.'

Will have to keep an eye on my ass, or, as sure as be damned, something will come along to bite me in it.

The alarm bells are being checked - my cue to put my shirt on, dish out the milk, then go and give the kitchen a clean.

Waiting for the V.I.P. course to start again - not looking forward to it: not in the mood to listen to some of my fellow inmates. I don't get on with, or like, some of them - they are not good people, and I can't listen to their bullshit. There's a rumour going round that I made a statement against another inmate; I know this guy, and I hope he doesn't make any trouble for me - I don't want or need to go down that road. It's bollocks, of course, but this place is full of nasty, bitter and twisted people, some of whom will do anything to make your life miserable. They can try, but I'm not biting. They need to grow up.

17TH NOVEMBER 2010

Mr. 'A.N.' - R.I.P.

Knew something was up - the officers have come round our cells giving out the cornflakes, and the wing is on lock-down. It's 9.00am, and I've just been informed that A.N. has died. Hopefully it was peaceful, and in his sleep.

Makes me wonder why the night-checks didn't pick this up. Still, I'm not aware of any of the facts yet, so I won't jump to conclusions. What I do know is that A.N. was terminally ill, and had already been diagnosed with cancer when he came to prison. He was from overseas, had no family or friends, and was a heroin addict - this man, a foreigner, didn't want to die in hospital or a hospice, and told staff that he only had friends in here, so he wanted to stay on Halward.

10.40am

A note is slipped under the door from the governor, expressing his regret and sympathies for Mr. A.N.'s family, at this difficult time. What a crock of shit - the man had one child who wanted nothing to do with him, and, other than that, nobody; that's what I'd been led to believe.

12.00pm

We've been let out for five minutes to get our lunch. It was an early lock-up yesterday, so we've been in our cells from 4.30pm until now.

It's strange being locked in our cells with a dead body on the wing, it willl be there until the coroner and the police turn up to take it out.

No, it's not been a pleasant day.

20TH NOVEMBER 2010
9.45am

Watching the gusts of wind shape and bend the grass outside my window, like an invisible hand, smoothing down green suede cloth. Listening to *'Back to Calais'*, a track from the *Slash* album, with Myles Kennedy - this bloke's got some voice, and I'm loving the song.

Waiting to be called for a visit - Mum and sis en-route. Can't wait to see them - unusually excited: maybe I just need a hug.

Another early lock-up yesterday - apparently for *all* the wings. This was originally a staffing issue over the summer holidays, but it's now become a regular occurrence: at least once a week for each wing. The P.O.A. really does have the authorities by the balls. How can this institution, which has *four times* as many members of staff, compared to its English counterparts, still run out of staff on a daily basis?

28TH NOVEMBER 2010

Had a lovely surprise yesterday: my mate Davey appeared for a visit. It was great talking to him. He left me thirty-quid, a book and a magazine, God love him. He'd also bought me sweets, toothpaste, deodorant and other knick-knacks, but wasn't allowed any of them in - it must be awful when a person who lives in the real world comes to a prison. He didn't know what to get me, so he just bought a bit of everything; didn't know the rules, but for me it was a very moving gesture.

Oh, I nearly forgot: was given an 'adverse' ('red-entry' in England), first thing on Friday morning by a member of the night staff 'care and reconciliation committee' - they didn't hang around to do it in person, of course.

They accused me of using foul and abusive language to a member of staff.

Fuckin' cunts!

It snowed again last night, and it looks quite tranquil out. I'm sitting here in my jogging bottoms, lovely and warm, after a nice, hot shower. Did I mention I'm in cell number 2: a disabled cell, with a shower? This is a big deal in prison. The perks of being servery orderly.

30TH NOVEMBER 2010

All I want is to have an uninterrupted night's sleep. I've been allowed to do just that, for two years, in four different prisons on the mainland, even when I was a 'B'-cat. They woke me again this morning, shortly after midnight.

1ST DECEMBER 2010

4.15pm and another early lock up.

The V.I.P. programme has been dragging along; it's a bit like pulling teeth sometimes - you think you're making progress, then it's back to square one. However, we did have a bit of a wake-up call, in an unexpected way: Pat, my neighbour, fellow servery worker and co-facilitator, let loose about an incident in his life which is happening today - for confidentiality reasons I cannot, and will not, repeat it; I know *he* won't mind me telling it, but others might... All I can say is that if it was an officer saying this, or someone else from outside the group, I would have said: 'That's tough, but fuck him!' The fact that it's another prisoner carries a bit more clout, and I know Pat will have gained a lot of respect from what he said; it was not his intention to gain favour, to lose the plot or become so emotional, but I know that this incident will allow others to approach him, and me to talk about more personal stuff - it would be much more difficult to get this respect from an officer.

It's okay for everyone to keep hammering the message home, but when moments like this arise, they are defining ones, and I hope it sticks. Maybe some will think of this time when they're about to commit a crime - hopefully they'll remember this moment before they go to harm someone, and think about how their actions can affect many people in different ways. I know it affected everyone in the room - I know it'll make a difference to some.

Oonagh has given me some stuff to read, which can be linked to my business plan. She's been great, and I don't think she realizes how important it is for us to have someone from Victim Support at V.I.P. gatherings. Without their presence, these would be about a bunch of men - cons and officers - discussing rights and wrongs, being all macho and manly about it; an outsider, who has experience with victims, makes it real - not a game, and keeps it grounded.

It takes a while for men in prison to accept who they are, and why they are there; some will not even look at the Victim Support people when they speak. For me, this only proves I'm right: if someone can't look you in the eye, it is because they know they are wrong, and no amount of bravado will hide it - they are exposed and weak, and they don't even know it. Eventually they'll come around, but it isn't easy, this unfamiliar territory. Some have even said: 'Are my victims going to be there? I can't fuckin' deal with that.'

Lost another kilo - well chuffed! I'm now doing thirty minutes on the push-bike: fifteen flat-out and fifteen slow alternately, with a wee breather on the ten-minute marks. Feeling good.

This place gets on my nerves sometimes, but it is what it is, and it's good to be alive.

7TH DECEMBER 2010

It's now 10.22am and I've got the ear-plugs in. Watching the snow fall, silently, in thick, heavy, slow-moving flakes.

There's been no movement again this morning, because of the inclement weather - it's the same every year: they know it's going to snow, but when it does, it takes two or three days to get it cleared and salt put down; always reaction instead of action.

According to the new regime, everyone should be unlocked by now for Association, but, as is always a problem with the NIPS, the governors issue orders, and the staff defy them and do what they want.

12TH DECEMBER 2010

12.30pm

Phew! Just back from the gym - feeling great! Had at least nine hours of uninterrupted sleep last night.

Yes, you read right: nine hours! They have amended the governor's order in relation to the night-checks. They did not officially tell us what has changed - nor will they. This is what happens in prison: if the management have to concede on a contentious issue, they will change the rules and not tell the inmates - we are left to find it out through the jungle drums, or, if we're lucky, a notice will be issued.

A lot of notices get issued, but never make it to the notice-boards, as the S.O.s believe it is in the best interests of smooth running of the wing that prisoners' morale should not rise above a certain level. No victory will be gloated over, and they will make sure that the transition from old to new is as low key as possible.

17TH DECEMBER 2010

One of the officers has just given me a small key-ring hoop. The zip on my coat had bust and I couldn't get a proper grip; this little hoop fits perfectly. He'd seen me struggling a couple of times, trying to do my jacket up on my way to work. It really surprised me that this officer took the time to bring this little item in - this officer gets a lot of bad press; his seemingly small and insignificant gesture has moved me.

Spoke to my cousin last night. He's dying with the cold, but apart from that, all is well with him and the rest of the family. He's a good lad, and I'm glad he makes time for me - I appreciate it.

Want to get stuck into my third TMA on DD208, but can't, for the life of me, get focused. Suppose it's that the more I learn about *'Welfare, crime and society'*, the more I get wound up.

No movement again this morning, so I'm stuck on the wing.

18TH DECEMBER 2010

8.30am

Saturday morning, watching the dawn break and listening to *Queens of the Stone Age*. It's snowed again - even more so than before - and it's quite deep; not that I've been out in it, but I can see how it has formed drifts in the yard, and built up on the mesh fencing. As per usual, the whole country has come to a standstill! The newsreader tells us it's been the heaviest snowfall since 1963.

This affects me how? Sure, it looks lovely, but I'm still locked up.

The world outside means less and less to me these days.

All of the officers left work early yesterday, in order to make sure they got home at their normal time - the downside of this is that none of them have managed to make it in on time this morning. I'm sure these underpaid, overworked individuals find it much harder to get *into* work than they do making it home. How many cars wouldn't start in the car park yesterday afternoon, on the way out? How many people couldn't make it to the main road on the way home? None, methinks.

When there's an early lock-up, we normally get let out at around seven to get our flasks filled (no kettles in Magilligan). Didn't happen last night: no staff. Bet they had to run last night's shift on a skeleton staff.

We've been banged up since 4.20 yesterday afternoon: no cover - no staff. It's mad, but what are you gonna do about it? God knows what time we'll get out today.

Is there anybody out there?

Is there anybody… out there?

20TH DECEMBER 2010

Nearly lunch-time - been studying for about an hour. My head was hurting, so I stopped.

No movement today again. Outside its foggy, icy and overcast - the snow and freezing temperature makes for a pretty bleak picture.

25TH DECEMBER 2010

The only other Christmas I can recall at the minute is when I was at Brixton, in 2007 - oh, how things have changed since then.

Slept like a brick - turned the lights out around 10.00pm and woke at 6.30. Not bad, eh? My fourth sober Christmas in a row. There was nothing worth watching on the telly - watched *'The Chronicles of Narnia'* until 7.00pm, and then I just listened to music for the rest of the evening. The song which sticks out the most from last night is *'Woman in Love'*, by Barbara Streisand - I've been humming it all morning, and will have to catch myself on, before I get caught-on; some of these boys will have a field day if they catch me humming this song. The thing is: she has such a beautiful and powerful voice.

It's in stark contrast to *'God is in the Radio'*, by *Queens of the Stone Age*, which I'm now plugged into: *'You come aback another day and do no wrong - you come back another day and do no wrong'*. How apt. I think the message is ever so subtle; what the song is saying is: *now please fuck off – you're doing my head in, and if you do come back and do my head in another day, I'll rip your fuckin' head off!*

You see how the Christmas cheer is alive and well in H.M.P. Magilligan?

The dawn is just breaking and there's an icy fog in the air. Apparently it was -15°C yesterday - brass monkeys, or what!?

My head's in a much better place compared to last year.

I've got two O.U. courses going on at the minute, plus the V.I.P. course, so life is a bit chaotic - think I'll back down come the new year.

29TH DECEMBER 2010

Lights were switched on at 2.00am.

One of the day staff has told me that the noisier night staff detail will be on duty soon. How do they know they are noisier? If they do know, then why the hell don't they do anything about it? The day staff have to work with us, when we are grumpy and angry from having little or no sleep.

Must keep my gob shut.

Sent a letter off to Mum, apologizing about upsetting her over the God business. I thought it was me who had the problem, and I'm the one who ends up feeling bad - I'm sick to death of the whole sorry affair; think it's a cross I'll just have to bear *(oh, tres drole)* if I want to have her in my world. Such is life.

We've had no running water for a couple of days now, although we seem to be the lucky ones: some people on the out have had no water at all over Christmas. I can see a big scandal lurking, as they are having to open leisure centres for people to have showers, and are distributing bottled water. Welcome to Northern Ireland 2010, where there are seventy-seven towns without water, caused by burst pipes, and all the shops and supermarkets are sold out of bottled water. Robbie and I have been driven over to H1 twice a day, to fill fifty-five 5-litre containers from a tap in the laundry room, which is still working.

'So here it is, Merry Christmas - everybody's having fun...'

31ST DECEMBER 2010

Been to see the quack about my right ear - slowly been going deaf over the past few months, and it's now become really painful. The doc said: 'Oh, my God: your ear is completely full of wax - it needs syringing, but I'm afraid that the head of Healthcare will not allow me or my trained staff to syringe it.' New rules and best practice, according to NIPS healthcare policy.

He's asked me to put in a written complaint, and who am I to turn the man down? One of the most productive meetings I've had with this man: more than two sentences have been uttered, *and* I got to see his face! Normally one talks to the back of his head as he types into the computer. I even detected a slight hint of humour - must have got himself laid over Christmas.

He's given me a bottle of drops to use. It says on the bottle: 'Use to gently soften ear wax prior to syringing by a doctor or nurse.' I'm in fuckin' agony. *Undue pain and suffering* vs. 'best practice' – fuckin' nightmare!

I've just written the complaint in the form of a letter, as per doctor's orders, to the head of the Healthcare; it won't get posted until Monday. Made the mistake of asking officer G for a photocopy - he's had a quick read whilst doing this… off the record, of course - no doctor/patient privilege here, then?

I'm working behind the servery and he comes in and starts to tell me about procedures, and that Healthcare won't answer letters - they'll only reply to the blue complaint forms; he ends up giving me *more* earache.

How we got onto the subject of the 'Independent Monitoring Board' (I.M.B.), and of him telling me that he was going to knock the crap out of four prisoners with his truncheon, throw another inmate off the landing and 'adverse' another guy for having a coffee cup in his possession, from when the prisoner came down from Maghaberry, is beyond me. Had to go back over to Healthcare to get some paracetamol.

3RD JANUARY 2011

Happy New Year! I've been sitting here for the past half hour poking the wax out of my ear.

God grant me the serenity to accept the things I cannot change, courage to change the things I can, and the wisdom to know the difference.

I've had to come back into my cell: couldn't get near the microwave to make my porridge - everyone is up and at 'em this morning - so instead I had my melted choc-ice, apple pie and custard, left over from last night; that's the last of the festive fare. No more now - diet well and truly back on course. I've started taking the fat expelling tablets again (only for a month, though), and my toilet has started to look like an oil slick again. Apparently, the gym rats who take steroids will pay fifty-quid for a box of these tablets - there's a market for everything inside a prison. Not that I would ever do anything illegal, of course.

Finished my third TMA of DD208 yesterday, and feel as if I could have done more. I've left out the quotes on this one - tried to put most of it in my own words - and only referenced my comments to the course material; I wonder if it will improve my marks.

Ready to get stuck into the next one - I'll have to get cracking with this one, as I'm starting another course: K101 in Psychology, in February; hope I can cope with the two courses over the next five months. Should be okay - at least I'll get plenty of practice writing essays.

9TH JANUARY 2011

Been keeping the cold at bay for about three days now - it's lurking there, although it hasn't blossomed into a full-blown cold yet; a lot of the guys are dropping like flies! That's another thing about prison: if an officer comes into work coughing and spluttering, you can be sure that the whole population will catch it; poor Pat has been in bed since Thursday.

Finally received all of George's paperwork - I'm helping him appeal his case. I've asked him about a dozen times: 'Are you sure there is nothing else?' He tells me this is everything he or his mother has in their possession. Hopefully, I can get his case to the 'Criminal Case Review Commission' (CCRC).

The solicitor is a very methodical worker, based in England; she's also representing Pen, the Scouser I met at Rye Hill; we've been corresponding, and he put me onto this lady.

George has a fair chance of a re-trial, but I've told him that the law is fickle and not to expect too much. I've always believed him, but nothing is ever set in stone in these places - some guys have told the same lie so many times, they end up believing it's the truth.

12TH JANUARY 2011

Thought I'd finished TMA 03 last week - Mr. Yeats persuaded me otherwise; he's a great influence. *Now* I've finished it. He's teaching me how to nail down the question and focus on answering it academically, cutting out the waffle. He also tells me that I've improved dramatically in such a short period of time.

I'm pleased with myself, and I now know I've nailed it; hope the tutor thinks so, too, and doesn't burst my bubble.

Got a letter from my mate Davey - he told me that when he came to visit he'd got lost on the way here. He also left his lights on in the car, rendering his battery flat when he got out; managed to get away around three-thirty, and was home just after six that night. Nobody would help him because he was a prisoner's visitor, though eventually someone came to his rescue. Poor Davey - it could only happen to him.

Mind you, I did laugh.

Keep thinking about Mum and sis, the God incident and subsequent letter - think I've hurt them; can't keep on like this: it's left a lump in my gut. Can't keep worrying whether they're going to be coming up or not. I've been looking longingly at the daily sheet, which tells us of the next day's activities, and have become disappointed when my name is not on the visits list - disappointment I can do without.

I remember what Gerry said to me, way back, at Brixton: 'Walk away from friends and family - block them out, and do your time on your own; tell them you love them, and that you'll see them when you get out. But they cannot do this for you, and you cannot help them.'

Can't do that to my family, though: don't think it's fair. They're the real ones who suffer in all of this - the true victims of my crime.

Another late unlock - it's now 8.30 - just two months after they told us there would be no more staff shortages. They're always early when it comes to lock up, but they never *un*lock early… ever.

13TH JANUARY 2011

How easy it is to have the wind taken out of your sails. Got up full of the joys of spring and went to give Pat a hand, but I managed to piss him off, and he lost his temper with me. Feel like shit and now have to go and sit beside him in the V.I.P. course. He's a complex man – I don't want to alienate him – but he probably just got out of bed on the wrong side.

I'm sure we'll be fine. It normally wouldn't matter that I pissed someone off, but I like Pat, so I must make an effort.

It goes to show you how you can never let your guard down - the moment you do, rest assured, something will crop up and ruin the day.

This exposes how fragile I am. I've got all these emotions flying around and all I really want to do is let rip - not with Pat, but rather the system; Pat is just a catalyst, which could be anybody. My tiredness and frustration is showing; maybe because I'm reducing my medication.

Decided to wean myself off the beta-blockers, and had to have a follow up interview with the mental health nurse, which was fun. They think they can compartmentalize everyone, but they can't. Missed the gym because of it – grrr!

20TH JANUARY 2011
2.23am

Just woken by a light being switched on and a torch being shone in my face - very nice.

Received my K101 course material on *Health and Social Care* - it's now time to come to the party, as far as studying is concerned.

Am I taking this seriously, or am I just playing at it? I've decided to take it seriously - who knows where it will lead? Two courses and two exams over the next five months - I'm sure I'll be alright. Have you ever heard a dog whimper? That's me, right now: *yip, yip, yowwww!!*

My tutor is up in the morning - looking forward to seeing her. She's a breath of fresh air, and I thoroughly enjoy talking to her. A bit like my probation officer: a lovely person - great to chat with. I appreciate them in my life.

Dad and my cousin came up on Saturday - seems like a long time ago already. A fairly full agenda of late - don't much need the sleeping tablets prescribed me: I'd sleep right through if they'd fuckin' let me.

Here's me, trying to avoid officialdom, when the P.O. asks me to go over to the P.O.'s office at 9.30am.

I'm thinking: *Oh shit - what now? 'Into the lions' den - into the valley of death - rode the eight hundred...'*

Turns out they've got a brand new plasma TV and wanted me to tune it in for them.

21ST JANUARY 2011

It's only 9.00am, and an early lock-up has already been called for later on, just one week after we've been told that they will not be happening anymore. They really are a bunch of lazy bastards - totally frustrated and dejected; prison is a hopeless place, sometimes.

Heading off to the Listeners training course this morning - a bit of fresh air, a stroll, some chocolate biscuits and interaction with half-intelligent, like-minded individuals. The course turns out to be extremely enlightening and informative.

Need to think about why I'm doing it, and need to adjust my attitude: not sure if I've the patience or integrity to stay the course. I'm doubtful that I could sit in-cell, all night, with someone who keeps going on and on about the same thing.

Need to remember, I'm only there to listen - my role *isn't* that of a counsellor; I suppose that's the hard part: not doing anything. But by not doing anything, you're actually doing a lot more.

Makes one think and ponder… a lot!

23RD JANUARY 2011

Just replaced the plastic ink refill in my biro - such a simple task, you might think. Not in here it ain't!

I have a clear plastic container, full of pens and pencils - it was originally the packaging containing a yule log at Christmas-time; it brought me a lot of pleasure and a lot of pain (pleasure at eating the chocolate, but pain working it off at the gym), a bit like this writing malarkey: no pleasure without pain. Anyway, I removed the ink cartridge from another biro (on my fifth attempt I found one that works), but it was 3-4mm longer than the original cartridge and needed to be trimmed. We're not allowed scissors.

Up to the officer's station, where the hairdressing equipment is kept.

There's a new directive that all cupboards must be locked, and I wake the dozing officer, watching patiently as he unwraps himself from his key chain, which has got tangled up in the chair.

'What the fuck you want the scissors for?' he politely asks.

I hold up the pen cartridges and smile.

Get the scissors, back to my cell, snip, quick scribble to make sure it works, then back to the officer; he's now talking to one of his colleagues about retail profits and consumer rights – I patiently wait for them to acknowledge my existence.

The officers stop their conversation completely, as if it could not be continued in the presence of a master terrorist/criminal, and national security depended on it - don't they know that I can hear every word they say from my cell?

Return to my suite, put my music back on and do a bit of writing, happy and relieved that I didn't have to go through the whole pantomime of the questions normally asked when a primary school kid borrows scissors.

I start writing and three lines later the ink runs out. Pick up a pencil and keep going; the lead breaks. Don't have a sharpener as it contains a blade - used to have one, but it was removed on my return to Northern Ireland. Put the feet up and listen to some music - some things are just not meant to be.

29TH JANUARY 2011

Spoke to my probation officer yesterday - she's lovely. I mean, very beautiful and a very nice person. Well, she is with me.

Haven't spoken to her for ages – actually thought she'd left. She said there was no need to bother me, as there are no issues with me. I asked her about my licence, and travelling to different countries when I get out - I'll have to wait for a wee while before I think about going off for a holiday; need to let the person who is dealing with me on the out get to know me, and be confident that I don't pose any risk. I'm not too sure, as yet, where my studies will lead me.

One of my colleagues has been shipped off the wing - he claimed he was drinking the cleaning detergent. Nobody believes he actually drank the stuff.

Turns out he was in a bit of debt, and it's canteen / tuck shop / pay day.

31ST JANUARY 2011
8.15am

The clouds have a flame-red to golden hue, and are silhouetted in dewy haze. There's January nearly over - time's flying by; hope it slows down a bit when I get out.

Mum came to see me on Saturday afternoon - it was a surprise, and great, but too short. We were just getting into our stride, and they come round, saying: 'Finish up now, please.' Bang on time, or just before. Not a word about Mum being at the gate from 1.30, and not getting seated until 2.40!

Mum shrugs it off, and I admit that they do treat people a bit better here than in some of the other places I've been.

This is the first Mum has been up since the God thing, and, noticeably, without my sister.

My Mum and I have always had this weird connection (well, I suppose it isn't that surprising, considering I'm her first-born) - she looked a bit anxious, and I asked her what was wrong; she can never really hide her emotions from me, and, most of the time, we are frank and honest. Mum tells me that two nights previous, she had a dream that I was stuck in the middle of the wilderness in Africa, caught in a fast-flowing river, being swept away - she was on an island in the middle of the river, and caught me as I was swept past, saying: 'It's okay, son - I've got you.'

Mum told me that she was going to McDonalds in some shopping centre yesterday with my niece, and when she glanced at a TV in a shop window, it had an image exactly the same as in her dream - she freaked, but didn't say anything, and booked a visit as soon as she woke this morning.

I squeezed her hand, kissed her cheek, and said: 'It's okay - I get it. I'm safe now - you've caught me.'

She just stared at me, unwritten signals of understanding passing between mother and infant.

I've mentioned how difficult it can be to show too much emotion in a prison visit hall - today was one of those days. We hugged and kissed, and Mum left happier and content.

I got back to my cell, closed the door behind me and screamed into the pillow; didn't have the heart to tell her that I'd made a mental decision, and said 'goodbye' to her two nights previous.

But I'm okay with all of it now.

She heard me and came - my beautiful Mum heard me and came running, like the true lioness she is.

Similar occurrences have happened over the years, but this time it's as clear as day. It makes me question our consciousness - some might call it an 'act of God'; the Lord does move in mysterious ways. For me, it's more than that: my Mum *made* me, and I'm part of her. Some people inherit looks, temper, ego, and stuff like that; I've inherited consciousness - a part of my mother's being - and it will always be there. My Mum's got my back, in this world and the next.

It's Sunday morning and it's my day off. All I can hear is the officer's C.B. radio blasting from the circle.

Came flying out of my cell at unlock and asked officer G if he would mind asking the officer in the circle to turn the radio down - there was no need for the whole landing to listen to the noise, which is similar to a sonic ping on a submarine.

Officer G's face went purple, and he said: 'Right. You - out to the S.O.'s office now!'

I replied: 'Don't want to see the S.O. - don't need to see the S.O..'

He purples up a bit more; 'I'm not arguing with you, Michael, and I'm not asking you, either - I'm *telling* you.'

Woo-hoo! Here we go; need to keep on my toes if I'm going to get through this one. This is the same officer who took great delight in telling me he attacked four or five prisoners with his baton, and was going to throw another one off the top-floor landing.

We get to the office, and I look at the S.O. and say: 'I didn't want to be here - he made me.' I nodded toward officer G.

Officer G starts off by saying: 'Our young friend Irwin here is complaining about the noise of the radio.'

I flipped and said: 'I ain't yours, and I sure as hell ain't young!'

Officer G goes: 'Oh, okay then - if that's the way it's going, I officially request that M.R. Irwin - C7874 - be removed from Halward house, as he is obviously not happy here.'

This line is an age-old tactic used by prison staff who want to force their will onto a prisoner - I'm not biting, as I've had it done to me before on several occasions on the mainland. I look at the S.O. and laugh.

The S.O., fair play to him, says: 'Look, I'm not threatening this man with removal from the wing, just because he's making a verbal observation - the days are gone when you can do that. Are you making a complaint, Michael?'

I'm well steamed-up, and reply: 'No. Are we done? Well, *I* am - I'd no wish to see you, S.O., and, as far as I'm concerned, this conversation is over.' I walked out of the office.

I'm back in my cell and by now the whole wing knows what went on, because some of them could hear it coming from the office.

I know this will come back to haunt me one day - no way does an officer like G get taken down a peg in front of a prisoner. I could see the hatred in his eyes when he realized the S.O. was not going to back him up. Come to think of it, the S.O. will probably need to watch his back too.

It reminds me what happened to the English governor they sent over to sort out Maghaberry: the prison staff planted his personal details in a dissident Republican's cell, to make it look like the boyos were coming after him. In the end the man fled, because he had never come up against so much resistance from his staff. We do things differently in Northern Ireland.

I've been and had it out with the medical officer (M.O.) and the S.O. - they have both said that I 'have not made them aware of any reason why I should be in a disabled cell'.

They have me doubting whether or not there is anything wrong with my feet.

I've phoned Brian (my solicitor), who says he'll send a letter to the governor asking why my medical needs have not been considered or documented - there have been two occasions when all the orderlies have been moved up the stairs in the past year, and on both occasions I have been allowed to stay downstairs because of my feet; yet, all of a sudden, nobody can remember this happening. Despite this it looks like I will be moving cell.

As luck would have it, I'd forgotten that the guy from *AD:EPT* had arranged to pop in for a chat - it was a well-timed and well-needed conversation. He's been giving me a bit of advice on where to go with my studies and my future - he's a good bloke and I enjoy our little discussions. We met when I was mentoring young 'T'.

T is a young man I was asked to help when he decided he wanted to come off of drugs and turn over a new leaf. He has been set up in a rehabilitation community in Armagh and has, at the least, been given the opportunity to change his life – if he doesn't, he'll be straight back into prison. He was a good lad, but hard work - he'd been in prison, more or less, since he was twelve. A problem child, with as many convictions inside prison as outside.

I've had some communication with his mother, and she has thanked me for taking the time to listen to her son; T's problem is that he's still fourteen, in a twenty-four year old's body - he doesn't know how to grow up, and if doesn't get his finger out, he's going to spend the rest of his life in jail. I don't doubt his good intentions, but if he isn't constantly monitored, he'll slip, and be back in here. The last time was his last chance - the courts and the NIPS will write him off if he re-offends.

I feel for T's mother - her heart has been broken time and time again, and, like any mother, she knows that her son is a good boy, deep down - it's just a pity T can't see this.

Apparently, this Armagh place is a new project, so T has a lot riding on his fragile, young shoulders. Still, talking with the guy from *AD:EPT* has left me in good spirits.

I've been taking a bit of stick about being forced to move cells - this is prison. There are more people approaching me and giving me encouragement.

11TH FEBRUARY 2011

My initial hearing for my judicial review regarding the night checks was held this morning - Brian has informed that it went well. The NIPS will present their argument on 1st April 2011, and the actual JR will be held a week later, on the 8th. He doesn't believe we will win, but he does reckon we'll shake things up a bit; even the judge suggested that there was an argument under 'Article 8' of the Human Rights Act: the right to privacy and family life. As a result, I have now become *persona non-grata* with a certain element within the NIPS.

Officer D made a joke about having a great night's sleep. I didn't bite.

8TH MARCH 2011

7.50am

Can't believe it's been a month since I last wrote something down - thought it was last week that I last spoke to you lot.

Listening to *Queens of the Stone Age*, and I'm waiting to get the call to go and see my Mum, only this time it's not a visit - our family members have been allowed to come into the prison and attend the presentation being held at the 'Prisoner Development Unit' (PDU) for the newly trained prison Listeners. Nearly four years and six different jails have passed since I made my first application to be a Listener.

I've also arranged, through governor B, officer A and officer Al, to have our families take a tour of our accommodation at Halward - a great opportunity for the prison to demonstrate its commitment to openness. How reassuring will it be for our loved ones to see, with their own eyes, that where we live is not so bad, and to see what our gripes are about? Officers A and Al have agreed to stay behind and escort our visitors around the wing - I'm grateful to them both for making the time and the effort.

I'd sent T's mum a letter, it was a letter about hope and the future. But what I got back knocked me for six: after a few weeks, he threw the head up and left his bungalow - he's now back in his area in Belfast, running amok. His mum is in bits, and I feel for her - it won't be long before he's back inside, only this time he'll be totally out of friends; he's not a well-liked boy, by either staff or prisoners. When he does come back it'll be for a long time, and it's going to be a lot harder for him - he'll get no more chances.

I've made a business plan for a 'Prisoners' Advice Centre' (PAC). It's well put together, by myself and a few others. I'm going to start torturing officialdom; hoping that someone will be embarrassed into picking up the gauntlet. Why does this idea have come from guys who are locked in prison?

27TH MARCH 2011

The fire alarm has been set off by the toaster again, and we're all locked up - the ogres are running around, screaming: 'Lock up! Lock up!' They really do go overboard, some of them - we all know it's the fucking toaster setting it off.

Had a incident on Friday morning: caught a bloke stealing some Weetabix out of the cupboard behind the servery; no other prisoners, apart from me and Pat, are allowed to go behind the servery, where food is served. Don't like this bloke anyway, so I flipped - he's a big bloke, but I pushed him up against the door; he took off, calling me all the names under the sun.

I retreated to my cell, in order to calm down a bit. But then he was talking about me outside my cell, and I flipped again; I flew out of my cell and got right in his face. I never swore or threatened him - I just asked him to say what he'd just said to my face. He couldn't; I'm glad he didn't.

When I get back to the wing at lunch-time I'm confronted by officer A - he asks me if I thought it wise to take six months of servery duty, as I already had a lot on my plate.

I reluctantly agreed - I'm now on a sabbatical. I'd been thinking about giving up the servery, so this was now my chance.

Oh, I knew that officer G was stirring the pot behind the scenes, and he will think I'm upset, broken and downcast, but the opposite is what's really happening - this will buy me some time.

If I had *asked* to give it up, so I could go to Education to study O.U. full-time, they would have found some reason not to let me. But now *they* have come up with the idea. I know it always has to be their idea; I have become quite clever at manipulating - this has been taught by the system.

1ST APRIL 2011

9.10am

Another late unlock - another *Prison Officers' Association* meeting; there've been quite few of these in recent times. There's a new sheriff in town, in the shape of a devolved government, with a new justice minister, who has hired some people from the English system to bring the NIPS out of the dark ages; think there will be a lot of toys being thrown out of prams - especially that of the P.O.A. chairman. Well, he's had it too good for too long - times they are a-changin'.

Somebody's been ringing their cell bell, but it's being ignored, as all the staff are standing in the circle having a good laugh.

Still waiting to get the fan in my toilet fixed. Got some extra ear-plugs from a guy who works in the metal shop, but they are slightly smaller than the previous ones, and I can still hear the in-cell toilet fan going off every ten to twelve seconds. They came up from Trades yesterday – I tried to speak to the guy, but he just blanked me; complete cunt!

Shit - George has just gotten into a fight outside my cell!

Heard some words being exchanged and looked out to see what was occurring - George had some guy in a headlock. I could see what he was trying to do: standing up and facing downwards, he was attempting to lift the guy up, snapping his neck in the process; I pleaded with him not to do what he was going to do: 'George, you don't have to do this!' I shouted.

Thankfully he heard me.

I took one look at the other guy's face, and I think he knew how close he had just come to not being here anymore; the blood vessels in the whites of his eyes were all shot - another minute would have done it. *Do not pass go; do not collect £200* – a lifetime behind bars for killing another prisoner, over nothing.

After he let go we were all locked up, as we are when there has been an incident. George, who has just been made a Listener also, will be taken down the block.

I hear one of the officers jokingly say to his colleagues: 'Does anyone need counselling? Does anyone need to go to sick bay?' They couldn't give a fuck.

Managed to speak with the P.O. when I came back from my O.U. studies - he's getting George out of the block and back on the wing. He realizes this incident was out of character, and he wants to know why George snapped. As he said: 'He's not a thug.'

We all had a good chat later on, and the P.O. says he's going to look into the reasons behind George's frustrations - can't see it somehow. It's not that he doesn't want to help - it's more to do with the ridicule he will earn in trying to make our lives more bearable. I believe him.

He actually said to me one day: 'I don't know how you do it.' This from a man who's spent more than thirty years in the service.

I realize the futility of it all; I've decided to go into hibernation for a while.

13TH APRIL 2011
4.30pm

Seriously pumped up - just back from the gym, showered and getting stuck into a tuna sandwich. This is my third gym session this week, and another bloody good workout; starting to reap the benefits - can feel my body starting to change shape: my whole posture has changed. Still a lot of work to do, though: need to lose another four and a half stone.

Good stuff. Sleeping a bit better too.

Talking of which, my JR was held on the 8th, and the judge has reserved his decision. As per usual, Brian doesn't think we'll win, but we will be appealing the outcome. I think they're arguing about damages.

If this had had anything to do with money it would have been sorted by now! All I want is to be treated with respect, and allowed to have an uninterrupted night's sleep!

Can't stand the sight of the people on this wing, and feel as if I need a change of scenery - the sight of some of the officers here makes me feel physically sick. I know it's not a good way to be, but I can't help it, and can't keep shrugging it off - my recycle-bin is full.

Think I'll put in a request for Foyleview, as my last two years will start soon.

19TH JUNE 2011

Four years served - two to go.

More accurately: twenty-two months. Sounds good when I say it out loud.

I'm now forty-four years old. When did that happen? I was only forty half an hour ago! Where has the time gone?

Remember being told at the start of my sentence that I'd do two years at 'B'-cat, 'C'-cat and 'D'-cat. We don't have a 'D'-cat in Norn Iron - just Foyleview, with its semi-open conditions.

Foyleview is a group of Nissen huts, originally built as temporary housing for the army, and taken over by officers in the seventies – it is falling apart, by all accounts. Magilligan is an old army camp.

I'm torn between what I'm used to and change: there are big changes afoot in the NIPS - you can feel it in the air - and I'm frightened of moving and not liking it; then these fuckers might not let me come back to Halward, or I'll be forced to go back to the 'H' blocks. Halward is the only registered unit safe and fit for purpose in the whole prison. Don't know what to do.

Hans is leaving soon; he's starting to make his preparations - they've given him a scanner to copy all of his work onto a couple of CDs. Know what'll happen: when it comes his time to leave, they will lose the CDs.

I'll miss him - he's the only person I share anything with, though we don't have deep and meaningful conversations; he, too, is a very private man, and he has let me in, in part only, to his private life. Even though I get on well with Pat, it's not the same.

I've become quite comfortable with my own company, and I no longer seek the approval or conversation of others. Some might think that I've got a spoon up my arse, but that's not the case - I have time for everyone, and my door is always open; I just don't feel the need, anymore, to search people out and spend time with them.

Whilst on my *Tour de Cape Town*, on the static bicycle over at the gym earlier, I could hear Jim counting out the number of lifts, as George was doing his bench presses. I thought: *Fuck me, that's annoying.* If someone did that to me, I'd have to ask them politely to desist: *You're not really helping - just annoying the crap out of me! I know you mean well by shouting: 'One more... one more... push, push, push-' But please fuck off and leave me alone - I'll push one more out if I feel like it, thank you very much.*

Suppose that's how pregnant women feel during child-birth: 'I know you mean well, but fuck off and pass me the gas on your way out.'

Maybe that's why I stick on my own: I don't need encouragement; weight training is not a team sport.

Well, it is for those who keep pumping themselves full of steroids, all trying to outdo each other. Wonder who'll be the first to have their heart explode.

Think I'll get stuck into my O.U. work tonight. I've been tottering along, doing a bit here and bit there, but other things on my mind of late. Now time to concentrate, focus and get busy again. I'm on my last Tutor Marked Assignment (TMA) of DD208: *'Welfare, crime and society'*, with an exam to follow on 18th June, and I'm also working on a TMA of K101: *'An introduction to health and social care'*. Starting to find that, collectively, it's all rather interesting.

Will have to stop doubting myself and get stuck in. As soon as I get this exam out of the way, I'll be fine: the subsequent result will prove whether I've got what it takes or not.

My second exam in twenty-seven years! Would you be crapping yourself? Me - most definitely.

Oh yeah - I nearly forgot: old Mick came up to visit Hans - this is Hans's first visit. Mick left me a tenner for my tuck-shop - well he left Hans twenty pounds and said: 'Please give half of that to Michael.' How kind and considerate was that?

It proves a somewhat contested point within me: I strongly believe that there is good in everyone, and if you treat as you find, it will always come back to you. This is why I'm now selective of whom I choose to have in my company - if you surround yourself with idiots, then more fool you; I can normally spot an asshole a mile off, though I still don't be rude, just dismissive - you never know when you might bump into that person again, or you might need his help, so always be polite; it costs nothing.

Was on the phone with my Dad last night - he told me that big Stevie had died. I've written a little note to his Mum and Dad - didn't say where I was, just passed on my condolences; hope it means something to them. I've known them since I was old enough to remember, and Stevie went to the same school as me; he was five years older. I know his Dad will appreciate my note.

My Dad said: 'I wouldn't bother.' But he's not me, is he?

It's 5.00pm and I'm gonna put the feet up and chill for thirty minutes - just breathe, nothing else.

EASTER MONDAY

25TH APRIL 2011

11.30am

Time to start a new chapter in my life. I'm not doing the servery any more, or the V.I.P. programme - my O.U. studies will be my sole, full-time occupation. I'm still a Listener, and will make enough noise to get the P.A.C. off the ground.

I've just been for a walk around the yard - fifteen minutes' worth; my hip and back started to get bit sore. Feel like a hamster on his wheel - boring as hell. I've never been one to go to the yard - it's demoralizing; could never get my head round the psychology of it. I've seen pictures of the treadmills they used to have in Brixton, at the turn of the century - think there are plenty in here who have lived in that era. Don't mind cycling over at the gym - I'm up to ten and a half miles; I've had two weeks' worth, with five sessions per week, so the weight is slowly starting to trickle away. Not sure of the exact amount - the scales are out being mended again – but definitely changing shape; feel great, mentally and physically.

My old pal Gary has been in touch, and has told my father if he's home over Easter he'll definitely make it up to see me - it's only been twenty years! Need a good laugh - Joe's father has just died; he's been allowed out to attend the funeral.

Wonder if Joe'll see my other old friend, Colly. I've written a few letters to Colly, but he's a very private person, so I'll back off - don't want to him to think I'm pestering him.

4.20pm

Another early lock up.

Spoke to Joe - he's just back from the funeral, and well-loaded, which is understandable, under the circumstances. A local Sinn Fein councillor had come to collect him, and take responsibility for him. He tells me that he had a good morning at the funeral - all went well; no big upsets. It turns out Joe's father was on pureed food for over a year, in a nursing home, when he'd nicked a sausage roll from the food-trolley, and subsequently choked to death. It's a strange old world, eh.

Phoned Dad earlier. Apparently Gary won't be able to make it over - something has cropped up at work. It's cool - I know he's got a fairly responsible job. Ah, well, I'll see him sometime, I suppose.

Going to go and do a bit of reading, until *'Indiana Jones and the Crystal Skull'* at seven.

29TH APRIL 2011

Royal wedding day.

Received a postcard from Gary - he's apologized for not getting over, is in Hamburg, and will see me as soon as he gets back home. At least he's sent a card - he's a good bloke.

One of the night-staff officers turned my light on at 2.13am - I turned over, and he didn't switch the light off. My temper got the better of me and I sat up, and said: 'Why are you turning my light on?'

He replied: 'Can't see without it.' Then he slammed the flap down and fucked off.

Tossed and turned for the rest of the night - my anger wouldn't allow me to sleep, and a thousand arguments proceed to interfere with my sanity; can't believe how it still annoys me so.

The latest jungle-drums tell us we're getting doubled up next month - can't wait to see how *that* pans out.

Think I will ask to go to Foyleview. Sometimes I get so fed up, I say to myself: *Right, you need a change of scenery, boy.* But the thought of change and bad reports about the regime at Foyleview stops me - the thought of the unknown reduces my resolve.

Nearly finished my final TMA of DD208. Find it strange that other guys, who are also studying O.U., are coming and asking me for help, as if I'm all-knowing; the actual truth is that I've just finished learning how to write an academic essay, and am in no shape or form a qualified voice. Still, it makes me feel good, and if I think about it, I suppose I do make a bit of sense.

All of this learning is finally starting to sink in. Or is it?

I'm ready for the gym - all revved up and ready, baby; looking forward to another ten miles on the bicycle.

Don't, however, feel too revved up after about fifteen minutes, although I do enjoy the last minute, as I try to go as fast as I did in the first minute. This opens the pipes - I'm normally sucking like hell, and watching the puddles of sweat widen on the floor, beneath my nose and elbows.

A couple of the guys have commented on how well I'm looking. But good old Pat brought me back down to Earth, when he said: 'You still have a long way to go yet.' You gotta love him - not.

1ST MAY 2011

Listening to *Magic FM*, having a honey sandwich, without butter.

I sent a poem in to *Inside Time*, and it was printed - did get a bit of stick from my fellow inmates. One guy said: 'Fuckin' hell, Michael, I thought *I* was getting it rough.'

When I explained what the poem meant, he looked at me for a minute, and I could see he was trying to say something. Then he choked and said: 'Fuckin' nice one, son.' And off he went, shaking his head.

A few of the idiots started giggling, but they're just that: idiots; they only appear fleetingly in my psyche. Maybe I'll write a poem about *them* one day.

There's a twenty-five pounds prize for 'Poem of the Month' in *Inside Time*, and I'm determined to get it before I'm let loose on the world.

Inside Time is distributed free to all prisons, and has gathered a substantial readership over the years. It's good when you open it, and see the odd letter or poem from someone you know, from way-back-when. Pen has written some class letters - I wasn't joking when I said he had a unique command of the English language - he really does.

2ND MAY 2011

Osama Bin Laden is dead!

Have told officer A to put my name down for Foyleview; fuck it - just do it!

God grant me the serenity to accept the things I cannot change, courage to change the things I can, and the wisdom to know the difference.

7TH MAY 2011

Had my interview for Foyleview last night, by a very pleasant S.O.. He informed me that I'd received a glowing report from officer A, and that he didn't see any reason why I shouldn't be over there next Sunday, pending the Foyleview board on Wednesday. I was shocked to discover that if I go to Foyleview, I could be getting town visits by January 2012 - six months before my first parole; only seven months from now! Bring it on!

According to the S.O., I'll be working in the print-shop, and will be allowed to do my O.U. - they're looking at full-time education being included in the criteria for resettlement.

I'm told I'm on the *'working out scheme'*, and could be working with adults with learning difficulties. This will be good experience for me, as I'm learning so much about society, people, exclusion and inclusion - first-hand experience could be adding another feather to my cap. It would be good to see the difficulties experienced by disabled people and use it for research, whilst helping out at the same time.

It's at a riding school, though. My problem with this? I'm shit-scared of horses.

I've a funny feeling that all this talk about education being accepted at

Foyleview is just that: talk. The resources are *this* side of the wall, and I know they will not let prisoners come back into the prison to work (to stem the flow of drugs into the main prison).

12TH MAY 2011
8.00am

Waiting to be unlocked. Outside it's damp and cloudy - a day of heavy showers in the offing.

I've never been one to concern myself about the weather, though a lot of people start off a conversation this way - I only mention it as it's what I see, through the three-foot square gap that I have left between curtains and shirts, hanging from the curtain rail. The weather, for others, dictates their mood, but not for me – for me the weather just *is*. Sometimes I love to walk up the phase ('the phase' is prison slang for the road through the main prison, which we have to walk along), coming back from a visit, with wind and rain howling all about – it reminds me of Cape Town, and makes me feel alive; doesn't dampen my mood in the slightest.

It doesn't really rain here anyway - you should see it in Africa! Wow - now that's what I call rain! Never figured out why the kerbs at the side of the road are so high - when it rains, the roads become like rivers in some places, and it needs to be channelled, or floods will ensue.

Waiting to hear the result of my Foyleview board - it was meant to have been held yesterday. As it stands, at the moment, the Education department don't want me to go, as I will not have access to the current support network when I get there. Although Mr. Yeats has agreed to come and see me on the last Wednesday of each month, to help me go over my TMAs.

Didn't want to ask any of the officers on duty yesterday - didn't want to give them the satisfaction of saying: 'No'.

George has requested a move back to the blocks - he's got the hump about doubling up. I've told him 'they can't make you', but he's also concerned about his gym sessions: they were meant to be looked into after his incident, but, alas, nothing has been done.

The NIPS have installed another shelf/bunk in cells 3-14 - I'm in 8. Everyone is freaking out - there are complaints going in left, right and centre; the foreign nationals upstairs have all lodged one each.

Brian is up tomorrow - Hans had his judicial review for racial discrimination yesterday, and will find out tomorrow how he fared. He has spoken with a guy from the 'Equal Opportunities Commission' about prisoner wages: why does the rest of the UK prison population receive a maximum of £25, and Northern Ireland only receives a maximum of £20? Northern Ireland really is a law onto itself.

2.00pm

My Foyleview board will now be held next week. I think the S.O. from Foyleview is treating me like any other prisoner, but the governor-in-charge doesn't want me over there, because I'll disrupt his little empire. I've been studying my nuts off for four years, only to be told that in order to receive resettlement I must do without the resources you have, in order for me to go and paint fences, or work in a garden centre. Don't think I'll be going to Foyleview - they're being too hesitant: normally a prisoner gets interviewed at the weekend, and they are gone the following weekend.

Was walking down the landing earlier, the P.O. and S.O. heading in my direction, when they both started laughing and pointing at me.

'What?' I said.

The P.O. jokingly said: 'How are you going to handle being doubled up?'

I asked: 'Can you read?'

'Yes,' they replied, their faces becoming more serious.

'Then I suggest you read my file, and don't make assumptions,' I laughed.

They walked away, muttering to themselves.

Not many prisoners like sharing their cell with another. Most of the cells were only built for one person and are simply too small to accommodate two people.

Not only that but Hans was attacked and beaten by a former deranged cell-mate in Maghaberry, for which he was awarded a substantial amount in damages.

A notice has also gone up telling us that 'Sperrin' is fully operational again, six months after it was to be razed to the ground – a facility in which sixty-four sex offenders are held in dormitory conditions, with bunk-beds. The notice also states that 'doubling up' will be introduced.

I've been in eight prisons, fourteen different landings and over forty different cells. I was doubled up for six weeks at the start of my sentence and one weekend at Rye Hill, before I was put on 'High Risk' by the staff at Lewes and Brixton, and have never agreed to come off it; it wasn't relevant before, as all cells at Magilligan are single-cell accommodation. Will have to wait and see how things unfold - this is why I want my medical files.

Had a productive chat with the Head of Learning and Skills this morning. Mrs. M arrived at Magilligan just under a year ago, and has tried to drag prison education into the 21st century; my heart goes out to both Allison and Mrs. M, as they strive to give us the support we need, but keep coming up against powers that be, who cause more obstacles than are imaginable in 2011. The Education department should be given cartè-blanche.

Received ninety-three percent for my final TMA on DD208 - over the moon, or what!? Can see Allison and Mrs. M are pleased for me - they can see that my hard work is paying off, and that the things they try to achieve in the job they do make it all worthwhile, when somebody like me uses it and does well out of it. Nailing the references pushed my mark up, and my tutor only made one minor criticism.

It's another milestone for me. Good stuff.

14TH MAY 2011

Mum came up yesterday afternoon - one of her surprise, spur-of-the-moment visits. Of course, I'm waiting patiently to go to the gym, unwashed and unshaved, and, none too pleased, took it out on poor officer C, as I rushed back in and got changed. But on the way out, this other prick stuck his oar in, and I got called into the S.O.'s office.

The S.O. says: 'I take it was just a misunderstanding, Michael?'

'Aye,' I replied, 'stop holding me back from my visit.'

The guy working alongside officer C is a right bastard - the hatred hangs out of him; he wears a moustache, like a badge of honour, this relic from the past (mind you, a lot of our lovely officers are stuck in a time-warp). He goads prisoners into answering him back, and then gets them up on charge.

Fuckin' oxygen thief!

It's weird, this old prison life: one minute you want to turn someone's head into pulp - the next minute, you're kissing and hugging your mother, with a big smile on your face, as if you didn't have a care in the world. As Erwin James stated: 'You will never know how much energy it takes to get through an average day.'

George and Kenny have had enough, and deserted the sinking ship: they've requested a move to H1, and got it.

Poor George - he's been having a rough time of it lately. I'm waiting on word from his solicitor in England - think he's got a good chance of getting his case to the 'Criminal Case Review Commission' (CCRC). They will only investigate if there's new evidence, or a miscarriage of justice - George has both, in my opinion. Fingers crossed.

16TH MAY 2011

Woke up this morning, mad with my father - Dad and my cousin came up on Saturday morning for a visit (busy boy this week); my Dad always seems to get one dig in about something. We are as bad as each other, as I take his words as ridicule, and bite back – then, even if just I roll my eyes, I get a bollocking. Sometimes his words come across as hurtful and spiteful, and I think: *If you've got nothing nice to say, why say it at all?* He gets nasty, lighting a fuse in me – red rag to a bull territory.

I look over at cousin, and he doesn't flinch. I can read his eyes, though - they say: 'I know, but what are you gonna do?'

The rage passes, but it leaves a sour taste in my mouth; it comes back at moments like now, to play on my emotions. I hate to say it, but I will: knowing my father comes at a price: he hurts me, but I love him. I'd have been up shit-creek on many occasions if it wasn't for him, and I respect him for that.

I suppose, if the boot is on the other foot, then I've hurt him more than he has me.

Families, love and emotions - a bag of tricks, if ever there was one. I've been lucky enough to read some psychological theories on being the *Adult Child of an Alcoholic*, and I'm old enough and stupid enough to let it all slide - he's my father, and that's it.

Hate feeling like this, but I won't lie to myself anymore: it hurts, it's real and I deal with it.

Look forward to getting out for six hours on a town visit, but six hours with my Dad? What the hell are we gonna do? Oh, dear.

17TH MAY 2011

Spoke to officer C this morning, and apologized for getting off my pram the other day. He's cool - he understood – and, as usual, we ended up having a laugh about something unrelated. Officer L has given me a *'Classic Rock'* magazine to read - such a minor thing, yet it means so much; she just opened my door this morning, and said: 'Good morning, Michael. Would you like to read this?'

Some people might think this is inappropriate behaviour - and that is what you have to be careful of: innocent remarks and conversations will be misconstrued. The general thought is that a prisoner - a deviant - and you have no principles, and therefore no morals; you have been removed from society, are a non-person and cannot conjure rational thoughts.

It's 8.45am, and I'm beaming from ear to ear. Watched a wicked programme about Strangeways last night - forgot what it was like over in England. Although I hate to admit it, as much as I bitch about Northern Ireland, I'm much better off over here.

18TH MAY 2011

Feel like shit - had words with Pat last night. Didn't shout, or give off - just said: 'Ah, fuck it,' and walked off.

Apparently, the prisoners from Foyleview do not want us to be part of the V.I.P. programme. We know it comes from the officers over there, but Pat forgets to tell me relevant stuff, and I'm left hanging when trying to argue our point. For me, the whole thing is getting out of hand: the course is becoming departmentalized, and if that happens, it won't work - it'll end up being a programme in which officers go through the motions and dictate to prisoners. Pat told me he knew all about what was going on, but neglected to tell me earlier when he was telling me all the positive stuff. Instead, he waited until I was in heated mid-discussion with an officer to tell me - it took the wind out of my sails, made me feel stupid.

Don't need that sort of shit anymore - think I'll make myself unavailable for the V.I.P. programme - it's a good course, but I'm way too emotional about the politics in here, and I need to take a step back and regroup.

Some arsehole keeps flicking my light on and off, after I'm locked at night. The first couple of times I go: 'Funny – ha-ha,' but now it's getting on my tits. Woke up this morning at 5.30, in bad twist.

Everything is annoying me - need to get off this wing before I have a moment. The sight of the bunk-beds being installed each day is making my stomach turn - keep thinking they're going to force me to double up, and are going to deny, or conveniently lose, the relevant part of my file which says I 'must not be doubled up'.

Convincing myself I need to go to Foyleview, but my heart isn't in it.

20TH MAY 2011

Spoke to Pat for the first time since my little outburst - he said he wanted to talk to me.

I've given him my bundle to read, as he's been following my progress throughout.

Sat up to watch *'Question Time'*, from Wormwood Scrubs, in London. Was looking forward to a good debate from inside prison, with prisoners included in the audience, but it was overshadowed by the comments Ken Clarke made about some rapes being worse than others.

Got bored and went to sleep.

21ST MAY 2011

The guys from *'Tough Talk'* came to the prison last night – 'Arfur' and Ian, a couple of proper cockneys.

The group is made up of ex-body-builders, doormen and serious blokes, who have all found religion - all have been bad boys. They are big blokes, and command respect, because of where they have been. They travel around the world, telling their stories in a unique way: through weightlifting demonstrations.

Enjoyed what Arthur had to say, about not seeing a blinding flash of light on his road to Damascus, nor hearing a heavenly chorus of angels - for me, he eloquently described the 'moment of clarity', when you say 'enough is enough': by a skip at the back of Smithfield fish market in London, on a freezing cold morning, after beating the crap out of some guy. He asked God for help, and, according to him, he got it. He also described how a lot of his answers came from within, and this resonates deeply with my own beliefs.

They had a mini bench-press competition, and this guy got up.

Arthur said: 'Right, I want you to give this guy all your support. Does this guy have any mates here to back him up?'

The whole room, in unison, including the officers, said: 'NO.'

Arthur looked a bit stunned, and laughed it off, thinking it was a joke - it wasn't.

All in all, it was an extremely enjoyable hour. They're in H.M.P. Onley next week and they have promised to say hello to a lovely lady who works there for me.

23RD MAY 2011

8.45am

A wet and windy morning. *Ooh-arr* - can't wait to get out and feel the fresh sea air filling my smoke-free lungs.

Nearly three years off the fags now… another two years to get rid of the weight I put on since I stopped smoking. I didn't put the weight on just as a direct result of stopping smoking - more a combination of boredom, stress, frustration and inactivity. Working hard now.

The air-vents on the roof have been flapping all night, and everyone is whinging about them.

Hans is clearing out his belongings, and has given me a load of newspaper clippings about the prison service and the people in it, which he's been saving since 2007. I managed to go through them all last night, but binned quite a few, as the people involved might not take too kindly to someone collecting material on them and if the security people got hold of this, they could make a big fuss out of an innocent situation.

Paranoia is the fuel that drives them; every person in this country is, after all, a terrorist, or has a connection to a terrorist…

4TH JUNE 2011

Had to move fast this morning - didn't stir until they unlocked my door. Not like me - I'm normally tossing and dozing from around half past five. Was in a deep dream, and I woke up to the keys rattling in the door. Know I tossed and turned a lot last night, and I imagined both my hips were sore with muscle-ache? I feel nothing now, though.

It's 10.40, and I'm in the downstairs classroom, doing some revision for my exam; at least, I was *trying* to, until they have just announced that we will have another early lock up today. Same old story, same old crap: no staff. It's not even lunch-time, and they're telling us they can't cover the rest of the day; the kitchen already knows to bring the food up early. We'll get fed at 4.00pm, and do not have the opportunity to eat anything hot again until eight-thirty in the morning.

We start work late and finish early, every single day, then we get locked early, every single day - we lose out on 'purposeful activity' and 'time out of cell' every single day, and when it comes to meeting targets, the prison governors get paid their bonuses for achieving them.

Must get back to my studying; blank it all out - none of my business.

5TH JUNE 2011

It's funny how one's moods lighten and blacken in this place.

Asked a young fellow if he'd had any problems with the night-staff lately - he just grunted at me.

No word yet on Foyleview - patiently waiting for the governor in charge of Learning and Skills to reply to my letter.

6TH JUNE 2011

Wondered what the hell was going on after lock-up last night – grills being opened and closed, and cell doors being locked and unlocked, on the upstairs landing. They normally only open a cell door after lock-up in an extreme emergency. Found out a few minutes ago that seven of the foreign nationals cut themselves (self-harmed) at around six o'clock - they say it's because the NIPS is threatening them.

The problem is, the NIPS will never bow to, or reward, such behaviour. It's bad, I know, but I don't feel one bit of compassion for them.

In a coincidental vein, I watched *'The Shawshank Redemption'* last night, whilst all of this was going on, oblivious. Although I've seen the movie many times, I see it differently each time I watch it; it seems ironic, and I compare the attitude of the men in the fictional 'Shawshank' to the men in here - it's not that different. In the movie, when they found out that the 'new fish' had died in the infirmary, Andy said: 'What was his name?' The inmate who won the bet (Heywood) gets angry and says: 'What's it matter? He's dead - that's just how it is in here.'

I've just been thinking about this, sitting here, writing about what happened - about how uncaring and selfish us prisoners become - when I hear someone out on the landing say: 'At least we'll get to the gym this week - seven less on the list.' The ignorant whore chirps up, without batting an eyelid: 'Sure, it's our turn today, anyway.'

I see what he means: that's just how it is in here.

7TH JUNE 2011

All of the foreign national self-harmers have been split up - one on each wing and three back to Maghaberry. This is an age-old prison institution remedy: split them up and disperse them; instead of finding out what the problem is and dealing with it, they move it, hoping it will go away. Nothing has been achieved, and, in my view, nothing ever will in these places, as long as you have the present hierarchical rationale in place; the British government's politics is all about deniability, and accountability to the gutter press - the NIPS fits in lovely.

One of the guys tells me that George and another guy were asked by one of our S.O.s if they would like to come back to Halward - I believe they both laughed and told him where to go. Halward is getting a lot of bad press of late, what with the threat of doubling-up, antics of the night-staff, mass self-harm, and problems getting gym sessions for 'Enhanced' or well behaved prisoners; why behave yourself when you can fuck about and get the same or more privileges on the blocks?

The one thing Halward does have going for it is 'in-cell sanitation', and it is a bit more relaxed during the day; not at night though, even with the cameras and intercoms.

A lot of people might think that doubling-up is all part of prison life, and you have to do it. Not so, and once you have been on your own for four years, in the sanctuary of a single cell, trust me, you ain't ever giving it up. Send me to the block - back to England, even - you will *never* get me in a cell with another person.

Thought something might change - they've changed the times of our gym sessions: we get to use the gym three mornings out of five - two of them are nine o'clock starts. Wonderful - it's hard enough motivating oneself to exercise when you've been up all day, but first thing in the morning? My toilet routine alone will just about let me make it; I have no choice in my bowel movements in the morning (something I said a long time ago that I wasn't going to mention again – well, four years and six different prisons later, I'm still in the same boat).

I cycled eleven miles just over twelve hours ago, so I'll give this morning's nine o'clock start a miss.

10TH JUNE 2011

Friggin' dreams are getting worse! Shook my head and giggled to myself.

It's nearly nine, and time for the gym. I've had my cursory three dumps; maybe I'll squeeze another one out before I go over – fuckin' pain in the arse, if you ask me.

12TH JUNE 2011
3.00pm

I'm ensconced in the computer room on the downstairs landing.

Didn't get any lunch today: they were one short - not an uncommon occurrence. Depending on the staff, I might or might not get fed: certain members of our caring staff simply refuse to open a prisoner's door to give him his food over lock-up. I'm not bothered, because I've got a self-replenishing bowl of porridge in my cell.

Didn't say anything after unlock - can't be arsed. What's the fuckin' point, anyway: nobody gives a shit. Anyway, I like the officer on duty (officer B) and there were new bodies after lunch, so I kept my gob shut.

When we get unlocked, officer B says: 'Aren't you hungry?'

I look at him, a little incredulous; 'Well, I didn't get any lunch, did I?'

He just grins; 'That's terrible – maybe you should check your cell.'

'Bastards!'

The other officer had sneaked into my cell after I came out of it, and left my lunch on my pillow, and we all laughed like school-children. Some of these guys are sound.

Now that I think of it, I thought I'd heard someone open the flap about one-ish, but I was snoozing.

16TH JUNE 2011

DD208: '*Welfare, crime and society*' - mission accomplished. Put to bed after a three-hour end-of-course exam, yesterday morning. Know I've done enough to pass, and am quietly confident; I'll have a little post-mortem later on.

Got into bed at 8.20 last night, and emptied my mind of all thought - dozy and relaxed; feel well rested this morning. I've managed to get a bit of peace from most of the night-staff, but some, bastards that they are, still keep turning the main light on.

Apart from the usual bollocks, it's a beautiful morning and I feel as light as a feather. I'm going well at the gym, and the pounds are starting to slip away, which is giving me another psychological boost.

It's been a while since I listened to music in the morning, so I've got *Queens of the Stone-Age* pumping away.

17TH JUNE 2011

One of the guys won his appeal yesterday - *Time Served: pack your bags, son – you're free to go!*

How cool would that feel?

Was at work when it happened - didn't get to see him go; at least he remembered to leave my CD behind. As predicted, the whole place has got a bit of a buzz about it. He's a good lad, and I'm happy for him - good luck to you, mate.

Was chatting to one of the officers about it last night - you should have seen his face go purple when I said: 'Just goes to show you how the law - the system - is always correct. Makes one wonder how many other poor souls are in here because of wrong decisions, wrong advice and poor representation.'

This poor officer's look was like the weather today: black, wet and windy. I walked away chuckling inside.

I've got to go to meeting this morning with the 'Northern Ireland Association for the Care and Resettlement of Offenders' (NIACRO) - I've been instructed to bring my business plan with me.

Just said cheerio to Joe: time served - another rat deserting the sinking ship. They're leaving frequent and regular now - I'm becoming the one constant; after Marky leaves in September, I'll be the longest serving member on this wing. Anyway, Joe knows my old mate Colly – hopefully, he can persuade him to come up.

Hans is also leaving on Monday. I watch him saying his goodbyes with strange feelings - I'll miss him, but I wish him well.

Thinking about getting a day out in January, if they let me go to Foyleview. Can't see it happening, and still not sure about Foyleview - when S.O. BE told me I could get a town visit six months before my first home-leave, it made my mind jump.

19TH JUNE 2011

Sunday morning. Overcast and showery, but not in my world - Hans is out in the morning, and I'm more excited than he is (well, he *is* German, and doesn't show his emotions). He's all packed and ready to go.

We've already had a wonder whether his journey/deportation will go according to plan - the Borders Agency, and the people attached to it, are an even bigger fuck-up than the NIPS. Hans has shown me his flight details: he leaves here tomorrow morning, flies to Heathrow in the afternoon, then gets an evening flight to Munich; can't see it myself.

Hans has served five years of a ten-year sentence - no home-leaves, no town visits. He's fought to get to Foyleview ever since he got here, but they refused, and dragged it out for so long that when Brian eventually got his appeal to a judicial review last month, they had run out of time. So much for foreign nationals getting the same rights and privileges as a Northern Irish prisoner. If you, the general public, knew how many people were involved in Hans's two-year battle to get equal treatment, you'd be frightened: the cost, time and effort to keep him inside will have far outweighed the cost of letting him out for one day a fortnight. The powers that be fight for the unattainable - they get paid big bucks to enforce the most petty of laws, that they make up.

Hans's situation isn't one that's just been pulled out of a hat - UK legislation in 2006 states that 'the likelihood of deportation cannot be the sole reason for a foreign national held in the UK to be denied open conditions'; we don't even have open conditions, for fuck's sake - we've still got a ruddy great wall, and are securely locked in the Nissen huts at night.

They think that once he's gone it will all be over - they will be mistaken: this man will not let it rest. He's meticulous, and will never forget why he's been denied the same rights as anyone else: they have been unjust because they *can*, and it will come back to haunt them.

Taking a week off from studying to catch up on writing this book. It's strange when I type up stuff that I wrote over two and half years ago: I can recall my exact feelings at that particular time, and so much more.

There go the alarms - bang on quarter-past-eight. Nothing doing on Sunday for most people, but hey, what the hell - we'll wake everybody up anyway. Prison sucks. Tired of this place now - need a change of scenery.

Managed to get to my meeting with NIACRO, and also spoke to some people from the 'Prince's Trust' - they all seemed interested in my P.A.C. concept. Wonder if I'll be going to the same meeting this time next year, and saying: 'Remember me from last year?'

Pat and I are waiting for a guy from the 'Prince's Trust' to come up and see us - he runs a mentoring scheme from Hydebank, for young offenders. I've kept my relationship with Pat, despite my bad mood - we've never discussed my annoyance, so I think we'll both be a bit more grown up about it, and not say anything more on the matter. Pat's a good bloke, and I have a lot of time for him, although, after Hans leaves, that's me done: no more attachments - I'm sick and tired of saying goodbye to people I befriend.

Two years left today. Sounds good when I say it aloud.

22ND JUNE 2011

Been informed that my Foyleview board will be this week - now positive I'm getting led the merry dance. Will keep telling them that this is what I want, even though the opposite is true. The whole wing has changed, and I'm sick of the sight of most of the people in it; this is probably a side effect from convincing others that I want to leave: I get caught up in the convincing, and end up believing it myself.

Spoke to my aunt last night, and told her all the ins-and-outs of my days out. Don't know if my family members can cope with me getting out on a regular basis, and this makes it easier for me to stay where I am.

Dad is up on Saturday, with my friend Gary - looking forward to seeing them.

Officer L just gave me another *'Classic Rock'* magazine, and told me about his visit to Glasgow to see *Foreigner*, *Journey*, *Def Leppard*, *Thin Lizzy* and *Alice Cooper* - not bad, eh? It's times like this when I wish I was out. Still, it's getting closer.

24TH JUNE 2011

Got my third TMA back yesterday - tutor (I get a different tutor for each module) says he's disappointed with my lack of understanding; I'm not amused, but he's probably right. However, I'm over the moon about my level-2 course.

It's strange, though: my attitude to this psychology module is considerably less than to the criminology ones: I treat it with a bit of contempt; a level-1 course is for beginners, and I find it hard to reign in the progress I've made at level-2. My tutor says I'm trying too hard and need to make my essays more simple. Well, he's got my full attention now, and I intend to dot every 'i' and cross every 't'.

Typing up my diary is good therapy - I've reached the point where I've spent my first night at Maghaberry, and I notice I didn't write anything for nearly a year! Did coming to Northern Ireland hit me that hard? Did I really stop writing for that long?

25TH JUNE 2011

4.00pm

Waiting for dinner - trying to calm down: Gary and Dad are up in the morning - don't want to do anything to fuck that up.

Earlier this morning I asked officer A to unlock the downstairs classroom for me. Knew he was going to say something.

'Why can't you use the upstairs, like everyone else?' he asks.

Here we go.

The fact that this room has been turned into an Education classroom doesn't bode well with this man. He starts mumbling about being too busy to open the door; 'We've got a long term SPAR on the wing,' he yaps.

What the fuck has that got to do with me? 'If you don't want to open the door, then don't,' I say, with a bit of venom.

Then he brings up if I have permission to use the room.

I've already asked permission from the Head of Learning and Skills, but I now know he's going to make an issue of it.

Officer G, who tried to have me removed from the landing, is back on duty, after a long spell of holiday leave - six weeks; not bad, eh? He makes me feel physically ill. I'm not alone in my thinking - I actually heard one of my more unscrupulous fellow prisoners go: 'Oh no, not him again,' when they saw this man on the landing.

We were unlocked at 2.40pm - no reason given.

Everyone is getting on my nerves.

27TH JUNE 2011

Well, I was correct about the classroom: first thing yesterday morning I'm called in to see the S.O. and officer A - had massive blow-out with them both, and flipped the lid completely; told them they should be ashamed of themselves.

Now I'm not allowed to use the computer room downstairs - I now have to apologize to Mrs. M for asking *her* for permission to use the classroom: apparently, I should have asked the wing staff.

The S.O., being his usual deflective self, has twisted the whole issue, and, as normal, managed to get me to bite.

Was really sad before I went to sleep last night - felt drained, like the days when I was at my lowest and didn't want to go to school. I'd lie awake in bed, making up excuses not to go - feigning illness and concocting all sorts of weird and wonderful schemes. Even thought about going 'sick in cell'.

The M.O. was dressing my toe, when I said: 'I feel depressed today.'

He said: 'Ah, sure - you get days like that.'

Just like the dressing on my toe: spray some disinfectant on it and make sure it survives the next twenty-four hours; if it gets through the next twenty-four hours, then that's another twenty-four hours out of the way. Another twenty-four hours.

Need to snap out of this - need to get my act together. Just feel a bit disenchanted - doubting myself; working hard, but, as yet, with no real direction. Need to get something to aim for - only two years to go.

On the other hand, it was great to see my old friend Gary - we'd a good laugh and a good chat.

Felt sorry for my Dad - he looked so vulnerable. It hurts me to see him in pain with his hip, but it's like talking to a brick wall. We ended up talking about diabetes: Dad has 'stage 2'.

I asked Gary if he'd any major dramas or upsets in his life - could see him thinking. He left it for a minute, battling with himself, then says: 'Okay, apart from my partner, Mum and Dad, you're the only two I've ever told-' He then proceeded to tell us about his own problems. We had a long chat about it.

I ignored my father's little quip about my weight - it's just his way of saying how worried he is. I do get it, but I can only go at one speed without giving myself a heart-attack in the process - it all takes time. The pounds are dropping off nicely, so I'll just keep doing what I'm doing, thank you very much. Having a little dig every now and then does not endear one.

The trouble with me not saying anything is that the next time he mentions my weight, I'll more than likely pounce on him.

1ST JULY 2011

8.40am

When I (a prisoner) come out of a visit, I have to go through a security room, where I get randomly strip-searched or patted down, and collect my jacket and card. On this occasion, I checked the door handle to find it was locked - the officers normally give you a shout: 'hold on', if there's someone already in there.

'Come on ahead,' came the voice from the other side of the door, so I tried the door again, but it was locked.

After a bit of a pause, the officer opened the door in fits of giggles; 'Sorry, I couldn't resist that.'

I gave them a look, and the other one sitting at the computer stopped laughing immediately. 'You must be bored stupid, boys.'

When I was in a side-room, waiting for a legal visit with Brian, I overheard these same two officers addressing a succession of prisoners, as they left the visits hall; this prick said to one guy: 'I know who you are, I know where you're from and I know what you did; you're a cunt - now fuck off out of my sight.' I don't know who this prisoner was, but I heard them abuse several more prisoners after this guy.

I did have a lovely chat with my Mum. We were kindly allowed to move table, after much frowning by the security staff, as Mum's hearing-aid picks up a lot of background noise. It's always good to see her, and when Mum gets a hug, and sees my smiling, content face, all is well with her world again, too. Deep down I am content – I just get fed up with my surroundings and the people in it, every now and again.

Received some good news concerning George's appeal: looks like it's going to investigated by the C.C.R.C. This is all I'd hoped for, and the solicitor has done her bit. I'm pleased for George and his family, though I don't think they fully appreciate what a milestone and achievement this is. Fingers crossed now; the process will take a further twelve to twenty-four months, but, hey, we ain't going anywhere.

Now that George is on another wing, the NIPS will not let me attend to him or help him with further communication.

2ND JULY 2011

Somebody has just hit the alarm… and lock-up. Officers react differently to this. Generally one officer shouts: 'Lock up,' and when everyone hears it, they know to immediately head to their cell, if they are not already in it. However, some start running around, squawking: 'Lack ap! Lack ap,' and proceed to try and fuck prisoners up, if they are not seen to be running back to their cell at the pace and intensity required to match the officers heightened state of alarm and officiousness.

It's probably just the toaster setting off the fire alarm again.

As I write this, our doors are being unlocked - false alarm: toaster again.

Most cons just raise an eyebrow, and get on with their business.

You should have seen it in England: alarms went off several times a day, and if you were on your way to work you just stood still - out of the way of the response teams flying down hallways, walkways and landings; if you were unfortunate enough not to jump out of the way in time, you got steamrollered, flattened and left to look bruised and embarrassed.

Spent all of yesterday afternoon watching the tennis - Murray lost.

After my gym session this morning, I headed over to Education, as per normal - there was only myself, Mr. Yeates and Paul present. Paul had been talking to an officer for ages, but no sooner had the officer disappeared, than Paul arrived by my side with a plate - on the plate was a toasted bacon soda (for those of you who are not familiar with Norn Iron fare, 'soda' is not a fizzy drink, but our traditionally baked soda-bread)! No sauce… no salt and pepper (pepper is banned, remember) - just virgin bacon and soda-bread. I haven't smoked for over three years now, my taste-buds are in fine fettle, and the last time I had bacon soda was too long ago to remember. Fuckin' unbelievable - if I was a cat, you'd have heard me purring! Sat and considered how grateful I was to Paul for sharing his breakfast with me, and how appreciative I am of the simpler things in life - less is definitely more.

Received a letter from Davey Wilson last night, and he tells me that Mervyn McCabe has passed away, after a long period of illness - God bless you, Mervyn.

Always remember Mervyn slagging off his son - my mate Trevor; he used to say: 'Thon is one eejit,' whilst shaking his head. Mervyn was a large man: Don Connelly (the *'Fox Hunter'*) christened him 'Calf', so my mate Trevor became 'Half-a-calf'.

One morning, Trevor was giving me a lift to school, and I was waiting for him to get ready - Mervyn was struggling to put one of his socks on with an elongated shoe-horn. I was about fifteen, doing the body-building, and as fit as a fiddle, with not an ounce of fat on me.

'For God's sake, Mervyn, give me the bloomin' socks,' I said, and sprang to my knees, with the cocky spring-chicken ability that my youth allowed.

Mervyn said: 'Thanks Mickey. You may smile, but mark my words, son: one day all of this (clutching the folds of his belly) will be yours - when it does you'll look back and think of me.'

We had a good laugh, and I said: 'That'll be the day.'

Well, that day, my friends, has been and passed!

True enough, today I look back, remember and smile; 'Good luck, and cheers to you, Mervyn, wherever you may be.'

5TH JULY 2011

Waiting to go to the gym. Did a terrible amount of tossing and turning last night, awake for all the checks, and I heard and saw each one - all without the use of a torch. The 5.30 one was well noisy (on purpose, of course). I could also hear the officer's radio, squawking away in the background.

Need to move. Had a chat with Mrs. M yesterday - trying to decide what is best for my future. The governor in charge of Learning and Skills is meant to be giving me a reply about my future studies, so the DG tells me - I've patiently waited for six weeks now, and still no sign of him. Funny: he's always around when he's after something – strange, that.

I told Mrs. M I'd withdraw from O.U. studies if it held me back from getting out for a day or two in January. Constantly trying to stay one step ahead of a system which continually moves the goal-posts is physically and mentally draining - nobody would ever believe the amount of bullshit and bureaucracy a body has to wade through in the institution of prison, time after time; day after day - it's relentless. You must never relax, or it will swallow you up.

Apart from that, I'm fine. Back on the Orlistat (fat-repellent pills), and my bowels are continuously on vacation - deep joy!

8TH JULY 2011

8.20am

Had a lovely row with one of the information-technology consultants yesterday afternoon. I'd just started my afternoon tutorial, when Allison asked him to come and explain why I wasn't getting access to certain internet sites – namely that of *The Guardian* newspaper.

Apparently, the Northern Ireland minister in charge of education in prison has threatened to withdraw all computers from prison and sack the I.T. guys, if another inmate is caught using a porn website.

He said that it was *The Guardian*'s fault that I could not access their pages, because they have not categorized each page, and he told me that I should contact the person who designed their website, to tell him I can't access their pages. This poor guy doesn't know me very well at all!

After checking the prison rules regarding contacting a newspaper or journalist (I'm allowed to), I took the I.T. guy's advice, and I wrote a letter to Mr. Erwin James (can't repeat it here, for legal reasons).

I've just been privy to a conversation between another prisoner and an officer - the prisoner requires a new fuse for the plug on his radio.

The officer laughed, and said: 'I doubt if you'll be allowed a fuse.'

Rules and regulations normally come from the 'Denis Irwins' at H.Q. (who I may have mentioned before), who have never set foot on a landing in their lives.

12TH JULY 2011

Another night of rioting in Belfast, and across the rest of the country - I see some of it's in the Oldpark area.

18TH JULY 2011

8.40am

No sign of life yet, though I see lots of officers in little groups, with their heads down, discussing some written paraphernalia. I recently read a report that mentioned officers' 'attitudes' – they were not shown in the best of lights.

On a brighter note, yesterday Darren Clarke won the British Open! It was held at St. George's, and the weather played its part. Darren recently returned to

Portrush, and it looks like the links golf has paid off; I've been glued to the TV for four days, and my nails have become somewhat manicured - it was great to see, and a *'feel-good'* moment for Northern Ireland; it's such a pity that this year's generation of rioters make me remember why I left, all those years ago.

Things don't look too good on the old job front in this country: I recently read in the *Belfast Telegraph* that a new cinema complex was built in Londonderry, employing thirty staff; over two-thousand people applied, including post-graduates and under-graduates.

19TH JULY 2011

7.15am

Sitting with my empty, plastic milk bottle, waiting to go to the Royal Victoria hospital, in Belfast, to see about my hiatus-hernia and gastro-reflux problem - not sure if I'm being operated on, or it's just a consultation. I have the bottle because in this civilized country of ours, they (prisoner transport and medical department) have not heard of a bag in which one can piss on prisoner transfers; *You'll be there in an hour or two, so just hold on to it like everyone else, or we can stop at a police-station on the way and escort you to the toilet.*

Mr. Yeates and I both spoke to the I.M.B., but, as usual, there is nothing they can do about it - it costs too much money to buy these bags, and it's easier to get the four escorts to stop at a cop-shop.

I'm sitting here, staring at the back of my hand - my skin is starting to age: faded scars of untold and unremembered battles, from God knows when; hundreds of lines, forming diamonds and shapes - some stretched, some compact, and the cells contained therein, dying… slowly passing.

Suppose I'm at that age now where things start to stutter a bit: betwixt and between - neither young nor old; hair going grey, waterworks playing up, guts starting to fail like old, industrial plumbing, and headlights starting to fade (glasses, though only for reading at the minute); the natural march of time.

Tick-tock.

Half-seven and another head-count - the night-staff did one fifteen minutes ago; are they reverting to old tack? Maybe they're just checking on me because I'm off to hospital, and not normally up at this time.

We had a situation yesterday, where a young lad was taken to his dying mother's bedside, and the whole wing was locked down because there wasn't enough cover. They must maintain high staffing levels in order to maintain the high levels of security; if they are one short, they will shut the whole wing down - lock up fifty men.

19TH JULY 2011

My light was left on this morning by the head-count officer - wonder who it was. It woke me up at ten to eight, and (for once) I will not complain, as I was completely out for the count - was in bed for half-nine last night, and the next thing I knew, it was ten to eight, with no pees in the night, some kip, and well pleased.

My trip to hospital in Belfast was uneventful. My back and shoulders ached when I got back to the prison: the cells in the back of the van are small and compact, with hard seats, plus one must remain cuffed - makes for very bad posture; in total, I spent nearly four hours in handcuffs - completely unnecessary, but hey - this is…

I've got to go back and have a wire inserted in my gut, to measure my pH-levels over a twenty-four hour period - an overnight stay in hospital! Wonder how that'll pan out.

The hardest part about yesterday was that I was only four miles from home: Dunmurry - my wee place (although I don't *actually* have a home anymore - my home is in my memories, my imagination, and not my future). Grappled with that thought for most of the day, and it left me so deflated.

26TH JULY 2011

Been awake since 4.30am - got a lot going on at the minute.

Managed to corner the governor in charge of Learning and Skills yesterday - I asked him when he was going to reply to the letter I'd sent to the DG, concerning my future O.U. studies, and move to Foyleview. His smirk and reply toppled me over the edge.

He says: 'I don't have to reply to that letter: it was not addressed to me - the DG must give you the information as it was him to whom you wrote the letter. I'm not prepared to discuss the matter any further.'

We ended up having a right old go at each other - this is one of the men in charge of my progression through the system, and of helping me to achieve my goals. The problem is that he is not interested in me, as I am above level-1 English and maths - *his* goal is to get as many men processed through basic skills, to assist him in achieving his targets. I applaud this - welcome it - and I support it, by helping other prisoners with writing letters, poetry, etc.; I used to be a classroom assistant, so I know how much illiteracy is out there. But the bottom line is that I have been told by this man that I have to choose between education and resettlement, and if I choose education, I will not be allowed to return to this side of the wall and use the facilities.

'I'm not getting into it with you,' he told me; 'it's up to you what you choose.' Then off he went, looking a bit disgruntled.

There were two young lads sitting in the room completing an education assessment - one of them chirps up: 'Mate, you should be a politician - we'd vote for you.'

I was more concerned with these young men starting out on their possible education journey, and what they are hearing: that when you approach the end of your sentence, you will have to give it up if you want to go to Foyleview. Well, not necessarily 'give it up', but lose all of the present resources at your disposal. How does this motivate them?

I know of one guy who will be going out on home-leave in a couple of months; he's doing O.U., and intends to download as much information as possible onto paper, then post it to himself in here. Where's the fuckin' logic in that: a system which lets you out, so you are able to access everything that is banned in prison?

I've written a letter to a guy at a charity called 'Unlock' - he's an O.B.E. ex-con, a prison reformer, and a big noise in England, by all accounts. I've been reading an article in *The Guardian* about him - wonder if I can get them involved over here?

2ND AUGUST 2011

George's Mum's birthday today (83) - sent her a wee card on Sunday. I've got George hooked up with Brian - hope he can advise him on relevant matters within Norn Iron .

Made my mind up about the Foyleview business. The governor in charge of Learning and Skills forced me to make a choice, and I said that I no longer required resettlement - think they're breathing a sigh of relief, now, because they knew I'd make their life a misery over there.

My father breathed a sigh of relief, also, when I told him I wouldn't be going to Foyleview, and allowed out every couple of weeks - he's right, of course: it's okay if you're from this neck of the woods, but to travel back and forth from Belfast and beyond is too much to ask. Still, I'll get my first home-leave in June, only ten months away, and would like to get the weight down a bit more. Allison is over the moon that I'm staying this side of the wall.

Another probation officer came to see me, as my regular one is off - he's an MFI agent if ever I met one! Definitely part of the system defence league: *Let's make excuses about how difficult the present political climate is.* I started work and grew up in the Thatcher-era mate, so fuck off and get a life.

A lot of these guys' heads are up their own arses; unfortunately, I have to bow to them for another while - I've seen too many people recalled to prison, simply because they can't communicate with their probation officer. Mind you, the people being recalled, I suppose, were not the most sociable of blokes.

Well, maybe - I don't know enough yet. I do know that my regular probation officer is fantastic, and the world would be a better place if there were more like her;

Thanks for everything - I know I haven't given you much to be concerned about, but I will say that your smile, honesty and integrity lit up the world on some of my darker days.

Received another letter and book from Gary: *'The Girl with the Dragon Tattoo'*, by Stieg Larsson. Well chuffed with the book, but when I saw it, I had an overwhelming sense of *déjà-vu*. I've been in touch with Gary for a couple of months, and the only other people who have sent me anything have been Mum, Dad and Davey.

Officer G is back on duty, and I can hear a lot of *'oh no'*s being muttered, as guys walk out of their cells and realize he's on the wing. I refuse to ask him for anything anymore - wouldn't even acknowledge him if I didn't have to.

One hundred and twenty-three kilos, and I've got another month's supply of Orlistat (bloody hell - is that a month gone already?). There's a difference of five kilos between the reading on the scales in the gym, compared with the scales in the medics' room - no matter: as long as the reading is less on both, every time I weigh myself, I'm not too bothered. If I get down to one-hundred and seventeen I'll be well chuffed.

Think I'll knock the bread and butter completely on the head, and no more sneaky chips - just the meat from the dinner; glad I'm not doing the servery anymore. Spaghetti and porridge for a couple of weeks, and see what happens. Okay, Michael, no more excuses: a concerted effort, please!

3RD AUGUST 2011

I've had few good reviews from my fellow inmates about some of my writing.

I'm pleased with myself, and have posted them off to Dad, Mum, and a few others.

Maybe I'll write a novel; I will, as soon as I get this exam over and stuck into my new psychology course in October.

I've discovered a whole new plethora of websites, originating from the 'World Health Organisation' (WHO). I've got four weeks to finish my final TMA for K101: *'Health and social care'*, and then my tutor will be up. Looking forward to chatting with him - our two hours usually fly by; hopefully, he won't have to be subjected to my arguing this time.

My regular probation officer is back; she came to see me, and assured me that I had nothing to worry about as far as probation are concerned: I'll have no conditions on my licence. Blasting away a bit of *'Slash'* at the minute - good for the soul!

6TH AUGUST 2011

8.10am

Waiting to get unlocked, on a thundery day. My mood? No – the weather.

I'm not in the slightest thundery today – more relieved. The reason? Sitting in Education yesterday afternoon, miles away as I typed, when I notice Allison has a big, beaming grin on her face. Then, she tells me she's just received an email from my other criminology tutor, stating (and I quote): 'Please congratulate Michael on receiving a distinction on his DD208 module: *'Welfare, crime and society'*.'

Well, slap ma thighs - what a result! This has given me a much-needed boost, and has erased my self-doubt - now I know I can go on to bigger and better things; I'm considering a Phd. Why not? This is an opportunity for me to lead by example: by the time I'm fifty, I could be travelling the world, making a difference to prisoners and their families' lives.

I'm purring like a kitten… a kitten which, when armed with the proper qualifications, will come back to haunt the criminal justice system, with a resonating roar of the beast it has become. *Its first hurdle – self-doubt – now out of the way, it smiles… and it plots…*

My hair has gotten quite a length now, and, being *me*, I asked for permission to have some hair-bands left on my next visit from my father - security have refused, saying this item is like an elastic band, and therefore prohibited.

I spoke to the P.O., and he just rolled his eyes, saying jokingly: 'Get it cut.'

So, I applied to the tuck shop to have two hair-bands - the tuck shop sent the request to security, who again refused.

I consulted my legal representative, and, as per usual, a prisoner must exhaust the complaint procedure before any action can be taken. I'm at the first stage of the complaint procedure, and will have to see what happens.

8TH AUGUST 2011

Wrote a couple of letters yesterday: to Mum, Angel and a guy called Shadd Maruna, at Queens University.

Angel's brother recently died, and I can tell by his letter that he's not in good place - he's struggling; hope my letter hits the right spot. I miss old Angel.

Can also see PI struggling a bit at the moment - his father has had another stroke. He mentioned it to me last week, but hasn't said anything since. Confidentiality and trust stops me from divulging too much, but I hope his father stays well enough until PI gets out to see him.

Spoke to my aunt on Saturday - she's busy being a granny, which is great.

10TH AUGUST 2011

Allison has asked me if I will help out on one-to-one mentoring at the Education department - happy days. Have started to mentor and assist a guy who's recently come to our wing - he's been on SPAR a few times, and is finding it

hard to get on with this life in prison. He's a good enough fella, but he keeps going round the houses and back to the same point each time I talk with him - some people just can't 'do their whack', as we say in Norn Iron.

Hope he stays level-headed. I've made an appointment for him to see the guy from *AD:EPT*, and he's got his name down for AA meetings next week; can see by his arms that he also self-harms. Hard work, but these men need someone to talk to. I'm keeping my distance this time - walking away more - and letting him work it out for himself.

Young T is back inside, and so is H – fuckin' pair of eejits! This time they are back for a long stretch, I think. They think they know it all! What the fuck do they know about life on the outside, when they've been in prison since they were teenagers? What life-skills can be learnt from fighting and bucking a screwed-up system? Madness, all of it.

T probably won't see the outside until he's past thirty; he was given every opportunity to help himself, but didn't take it. And H, too - what a fool. I'm hurt, but what can I do? There is nothing out there for them to cling to. What a life – I'm glad I'm me.

This is why my business plan for mentors on the outside is so important: if these guys had someone to lean on when they were out, they wouldn't be back, or, at least, they would have had the opportunity and guidance to possibly snap out of what they were doing. I'm not surprised, to be honest - just frustrated. Why do they do these petty things, and getting a longer stretch each time? Pair of dickheads.

At the moment it's just the jungle-drums, and I wouldn't want to base any of my opinions or decisions on rumour and hearsay - think I'll leave it a while, until I'm a bit more certain of the facts; I've spoken with T's Mum, but what else can I do? Apparently, T's going mad, raising hell at Maghaberry. He's in for a rough ride – a lot of people stuck their necks out for him, and he's shit on them from a great height. H is back on breach of licence.

Received another ninety-three percent in my previous TMA - my tutor feels as if I've turned a corner. Not true: if I'm honest, I've simply applied myself fully to this last TMA. Mr. Yeats helped me: as per usual, he keeps me on my toes, doesn't let me slack and questions everything I try to generalize; *'Don't change the subject - just answer the fuckin' question'* I recall, from the movie *'Braveheart'*.

Mr. Yeats has also been editing my bank-robber story; it's painful to see your work, thoughts and imaginings being dissected, and every word scrutinized and questioned. This is the first time I've done anything like this, and, I suppose, if I'm going to write more stuff, I'm going to have to get used to it.

Mr. Yeats is a great inspiration, though - he never really changes anything I say, just alters it in the finest of ways; he says it's a bit like taking a car in for a service: you've already looked after it and kept it running well - he's just going to fine-tune it to achieve maximum performance. Is this what happens if you have the courage to put your work out there?

I'm getting a bit of stick about my latest poem in *Inside Time*, and still no twenty-five quid; I'll keep going.

It's lashing it down outside; don't get me started about the Norn Iron summer-time – it didn't arrive this year.

11TH AUGUST 2011

Another *schiesse* day, as Hans would have said; miss him being around.

Sneezing my head off. The sneezing has managed to empty my mind - it's gone blank (not that there's much in there to wipe out). Listening to *'Joker and the Thief'*, by *Wolfmother*, and I've ordered *Alter Bridge*'s album *'Blackbird'*; wonder how long it's going to take - our tuck shop CD and DVD deliveries have become very hap-hazard recently. Mind you, like everything within these walls, they're winging-it most of the time.

Mr. Yeats has got our *'Postcards from...'* stories over to the print-shop - another little publication with my name in it.

13TH AUGUST 2011

Received the most encouraging letter from Professor Shadd Maruna, the director of the School of Criminology and Law at Queens University, Belfast (hope I got the titles correct). He has told me that 'we would welcome you on one of our masters courses when you complete your degree', and that he's interested in my business plan. What a turn up for the books - there was me, sitting here wondering where all this studying was going to lead me; now my mind has been made up for me, in a roundabout sort of way.

Drafted another letter, but feel as if I need to reign it in a bit: got too excited! Downloaded a lot of his work, and intend to give at a good going-over during the course of the weekend. Feel as if this is the start of something big – hopefully, I can take my studies, my experience and my knowledge of prisons to a whole new dimension; well, a new dimension for me, at any rate.

Here we go: 8.15am and the alarms are being checked.

Managed to collar two of the 'Criminal Justice Inspectorate for Northern Ireland' (CJINI) inspectors yesterday afternoon, for a brief chat, outside the wing. They were here following up on a report about vulnerable prisoners; couldn't help myself: had to tell them that we're all treated like vulnerable prisoners at night-time. They thanked me for my input and said our paths would probably cross again.

Everybody's going mad about being kept awake all night. The guy I was mentoring cut himself and was taken to the suicide cell, which means we get the banging and noise associated with staff coming on and off the landing, every fifteen minutes, to speak to him, even though he's in an observation cell with CCTV and an intercom.

17TH AUGUST 2011

Phoned my Dad last night and told him about my letter from Queens - he sounds like a proud father.

I believe my brother is doing a similar course at Jordanstown - who'd have believed it? He's got himself a new Porsche, too! Good luck to him. Maybe he'll pick me up from here when I'm getting out for a day or two - would certainly set a few tongues wagging; I'll tell everyone it's mine.

If only they knew! Told PI a little bit about my history, but he's not the type to go blabbing.

We were busy boys yesterday, us Listeners: we had a 'Cruse Bereavement Care' meeting in the morning and a Samaritans meeting in the afternoon. Didn't get my photo taken by the *Jaily News* again.

Don't know why we don't do our own prison magazine or radio in here - there's a lot of talent knocking about, plus, we've got our own print-shop.

I remember watching Brixton radio take its first faltering steps - it's now the *National Prison Radio*, beamed to prisons across the whole of England and Wales; all down to a governor taking a chance (the same guy who sorted the library out when I was at Brixton)! Think he's the head of *National Prison Radio* now.

19TH AUGUST 2011

Mum came up yesterday – a surprise visit, just the way I like it. It was over too soon, though; they're always late letting people in at visits – it was half-two before Mum arrived in the hall.

Need to get stuck into my final TMA for K101. Not enjoying it as much as DD208, but I have enjoyed learning about the Evelina Children's Hospital in London, where the architects formed a 'Children's Parliament', in partnership with patients and local schools to get their ideas for the hospital

Now, that is something I will hold on to for the future, as far as prisons go.

Brian is up in the morning – I think, to see George; hope I get to see him for five minutes - saves me the cost of a stamp.

20TH AUGUST 2011

Quarter past eight, and I haven't heard a peep from the circle yet.

Spoke too soon! Here we go: *ring-ring, beep-beep,* - fuckin' bells... *the bells!* Every fuckin' morning. *Aaggh!*

The usual guffaws of laughter from staff, then the sombre faces when we're let out: all business - all serious. C.B.s going too.

Think this is officer A's last day, or thereabouts - he's off to the 'Prisoner Development Unit' (P.D.U.), to look after the V.I.P. programme. It's a good show, and hopefully good things will come of it, but he needs to let other people - namely us - share the load, or it will just be another course in which prisoners are dictated to, instead of taking an active part. He'll be at the P.D.U; full-time, I think.

Spoke to the P.O. yesterday - he told me big changes are coming, and they can't come quick enough. It seems as if everyone is holding their breath, waiting for this magic wand to be waved. Wipe the slate clean and start again, is what I say: privatize the whole lot and use ex-cons as consultants!

24TH AUGUST 2011

Finding it hard to knuckle down to this last TMA - think the question has thrown me a bit. Listening to a bit of Slash - maybe he'll sort me out; need a bit of loud metal to get the day started.

Received a letter from Hans (will have to start calling him by his real name, now that he's out - won't mention it here, though, in case he sues me; I'm the only one in Norn Iron who knows it). He's back home, safe in the arms of his beautiful wife, and enjoying his freedom. Can't wait to hook up with him, on a sunny beach near the equator, when I get out - got a picture of the beach on my wall; *tick-tock.*

His letter was short, direct and to the point. I've arranged for my cousin to email him for me - too much hassle to use the post, and you can never be sure that it'll get there. Wonder if he's going to bother to initiate a website or blog about his prison experience, which we did discuss when he was here; wait and see.

12TH SEPTEMBER 2011

Its 5.00pm and I'm waiting to head over to the gym.

Spoke to Brian this morning, via video link. My JR is still pending - bloody judge is taking his merry time over it!

I've been trawling the 'United Nations' (UN) and WHO, and have discovered that between 1971 and 1975, as an extra-judicial procedure, the Northern Ireland authorities used 'sleep deprivation' to elicit confessions from prisoners.

The ombudsman still maintains that checks should happen between 22.00 and 23.00, and then again at 07.00, but need to create a compromise: the day-staff officers on Halward have now taken the responsibility of the 07.00 body check away from the night-staff, and there have been no problem.

We also discussed the Health and Safety implications of fifty-odd men using the same hair clippers, but I don't want to get involved in this one.

Think I'll get myself an Irish passport when I get out.

13TH SEPTEMBER 2011

It's 9.45 and we're on lock-down. Came back from Healthcare, and thought it was a bit quiet - everyone is behind their doors; didn't even ask why: don't care anymore. They could lock me up every day and I wouldn't mind, if I had a computer in my cell; that's all I do now: computer-room, Education, gym, and the Listeners - less is more.

Had to give some more blood and a urine sample at Healthcare – they are checking my liver… again. Every prison I've been in goes through the same process: I still have the same problems, four years on, yet I have never been treated for any of them.

The doctor did tell me that I was okay, and that the last batch of tests showed no abnormality.

Unlocked again and off to Education, to catch up on typing up this little lot; I've taken a week off studying to try and get it caught up to the present day - nearly there.

15TH SEPTEMBER 2011

Spoke with two guys from the CJINI *(Criminal Justice Inspection Northern Ireland)* yesterday afternoon at Education - three of us were asked if we would talk to the inspectors in relation to education at Magilligan. I must admit, they were very accommodating: Mr. McC ('Purple Rain'- the guy I spoke to, briefly, on his last visit - wrote a lot of stuff down, which is always a good sign, and the fact that he had four intelligent, well-spoken and well-informed prisoners to talk to made the whole process worthwhile, and productive for both parties.

I gave him my business plan and *'Prison Works'* prose, my letter of concern to the DG regarding O.U. studies, and another letter I'd sent to 'The Longford Trust', outlining my future intentions. We gave the governor in charge of Learning and Skills a right lambasting, and highlighted the flaws in the Northern Ireland system, when it comes to humanity, dignity and respect. The general opinion in the room was one of frustration - which was also the consensus across the board - when it came to learning possibilities in Northern Ireland's prisons.

Will our meeting help? I think it will. The system needs to listen to the people in it, if it's going to make any progress.

21ST SEPTEMBER 2011

8.30am

No sign of life yet.

Read an ombudsman report on Monday, about the dirty protest by Republican prisoners in Roe House at Maghaberry: it stated that prison officers are allowed to turn up for their respective shifts fifteen to twenty minutes late, and not be deemed 'late' for the shift. Now I see why we never get anything done on time.

Spoke to my father last night, and he tells me that the course my brother is doing is also a degree in criminology. Spooky or what? I knew he was doing something similar. Wonder if we can put our past differences to the side and form a company called *'Irwin Brothers'*. If only.

Oh, hold the fort: 8.45 and the alarms are being sounded and checked - all systems go. Not as long as usual - maybe they didn't have much else to chat about.

22ND SEPTEMBER 2011

Made a written request for new bedding and a new mattress on Saturday morning. The S.O. has not processed my request, but I have been given permission to have new bedding; he didn't know how long it would take for the mattress to arrive from outside contractors.

The current policy is that all bedding must be fire-retardant, and they will only allow a certain type of duvet. There was period of time when prisoners used to set fire to their bedding at Maghaberry, and then make a claim against the Northern Ireland Office for damages - the prisoners used to get a mate to set fire to their cell, the mate would get charged, and they would then split the difference when the money came through; four months' loss of Association and wages was nothing compared to a few grand. Understandably, the prison has to combat this behaviour: I was told that fire-engines used to sit in a layby at the motorway exit, near to the end of the lane leading to the prison - this enabled them to fly down the motorway to attend calls in the Lisburn areas, while remaining close enough to nip up to the prison if needed.

25th SEPTEMBER 2011

Well, there's another little goal achieved: I've typed up this little lot to date. From this day forth, I will attempt to set at least thirty minutes to an hour aside each week, to type.

8TH OCTOBER 2011

Taking a break from revision for an hour or so.

Been up since half-five to watch the rugby - Ireland got chinned by Wales. Looking forward to watching the qualifying for tomorrow's Japanese *Grand Prix*.

Finished Professor Maruna's book: *'Making Good'*. Found it very interesting, and have made my comments, or noted down some bits of interest – like: how on Earth do we change society's perception of convicts - do we move to Australia, or create another prison colony like it?

The criminal justice system is a weird and wonderful beast - am I doing the right thing by wanting to be part of it? Do I *want* to be part of it? All I *do* know I want to do is create more opportunities for people inside prison - the current situation is unacceptable to me.

Professor Shadd Maruna is here this Friday to see me; rather excited, and feel as if this is my chance to make an impression, and secure my future. I'll just be me - no airs or graces: best policy, I think. I feel as if this little part of my life is coming to an end, and a new beginning is in the offing. Expectations reduce joy, I know, but I feel as if my life is about to step up a gear, and I will have to put this experience - as it stands now - to bed. We'll see how my meeting goes; deep breaths, small steps…

Sitting here, trying to remember what happened last week, but my head is so filled with health and social care, and Professor Maruna's book, that I can't think of anything. Feel as if there's too much to learn and revise - found the level-2 so much easier.

Oh, aye: Mr. Yeats and I did another *'Postcards from…'* piece for the book, which should be printed within the next week or so. Mr. Yeats mentioned an idea, and I gave him my memories of it, tit-for-tat - it was a fantastic exchange; we wrote it in about an hour - pretty damn good, if you ask me.

I've jotted down some ideas for a book, but I'll have to put it on the back-burner, as I've got to get stuck into my psychology course the day after my exam (which is on the 17th) - no rest for this child. I have to get it into my head that an exam is not so much about the detail, but more to do with the concepts and ideas being discussed. I'm sure I'll pass, but, as my criminology tutor said: I've set a high benchmark. Won't think about it for the next few hours - will come back and do a wee bit more this afternoon.

Listening to a bit of *Muse* at the minute - played *'Alter Bridge'* to death, so I will give them a wee break, too.

11TH OCTOBER 2011

Just spoke to officer L - she tells me that she was talking to Speedo last Friday, at The Spring and Air-Brake, in Belfast. Good to hear my old friend is polite and well-spoken, and still a bit guarded when it comes to my name being mentioned.

Sitting up in the computer room, killing some time, as I wait to go to the Listeners' meeting later on. Was going to cancel, as I'm not really in the mood, but there's chocolate biscuits - not the normal fare from the tuck-shop (not that I buy biscuits anymore, but I do look forward to the fortnightly fix). It's also good to talk to people from the real world, as it brings a bit of social acceptability into one's life; even though the topic of suicide and self-harm is a serious one, we do have the odd laugh, which is good for the soul.

I've typed up all my notes and will spend the next few days reading over them – hopefully, it will be enough to get me through the exam on Monday.

13TH OCTOBER 2011

Busy day. I'm up in the computer room, having just finished typing up my revision notes - now I've got three days to digest them; should be enough time to think things through. I know I'll do enough to pass, unless I take a complete speed wobble.

Professor Maruna is up in the morning, and I think Mum is up on Sunday morning.

Spoke to the P.O. earlier about Listeners getting strip-searched, and he told me that all inmates who have freedom of movement will be targeted and that there was a lot of shit going on in the prison, and we weren't being singled out.

Do they even stop to consider the indignity involved when you are made to take your clothes off in front of a prison officer, particularly in the early hours of the morning, after listening to someone pour their heart out? On its own, strip-searching is one of the most demeaning experiences a body can go through, which adds insult to injury; if you get a nasty officer, you're definitely getting it done. They still search us (randomly) on the way into a visit, for the good order and running of the prison.

Speaking of not amused, I've been told two of my mates have been sent back from Foyleview.

14TH OCTOBER 2011

Well, there we go: met Professor Shadd Maruna this morning - what a lovely man! And, what a productive meeting; looks like my future has had a little bit more affirmation - it's up to me now, to keep the head down and get on with my work. I don't want to say too much about our meeting, as I feel it might belittle or trivialize the enormity of what really just happened: this well-voiced, well-connected and highly-regarded academic took the time to come and see *me*.

My probation officer came to see me this afternoon, as she had seen Professor Maruna in the office. She told me she was very proud of me, and that they were talking about me in the office - the professor and a couple of department heads. She wouldn't approach him, because she said she'd be too embarrassed - he's way above her league. This is why I don't want to say too much - as far as I'm concerned, I've just met a very nice, interesting human-being; no more, no less. Is this me being cocky, or above my station? No - not in the slightest; if you feel at ease when talking with someone, then you should feel exactly that: at ease.

Mr. Maruna has promised to come and see me again and get a few ideas moving - another opportunity. The thing I find most surprising is that there were no delays or cock-ups: the governor met him at the train station and delivered him to the prison; we met on the phase, as I was walking down - all cool and civil. I'm really pleased with the governor: he said he'd help me and he's come good.

I know this is only the beginning of the rest of my life. Life begins at forty - it did for me.

MINUTES OF 'SAFER CUSTODY FORUM'

Held on Thursday 19th January 2012 in the boardroom, H.M.P. Magilligan.

Listener Scheme

Senior 'A' gave his report on the Listener Scheme: he said that everything was mostly going okay, but there had been some issues with Listeners going to Sperrin to see any new committals. He said that on some occasions they have been refused entry to the landings. Senior 'B' said he would look into the issue.

Michael Irwin then discussed the issue of Listeners being present when a SPAR is opened on another prisoner - the Listeners feel that if they can speak to a prisoner before they are placed on SPAR, then they may be able to prevent the SPAR being opened. Senior 'C' stated that in some cases, such as self-harming, SPARs have to be opened. Senior 'D' stated that on SPAR booklets there is an information-sharing section, and that this section is important, and, therefore, if the prisoner does not want any information shared with anyone else, then this has to be adhered to. Senior 'B' then said that no information would be divulged to anyone if the prisoner does not want it to be, and a Listener can step in after the SPAR has been opened if the prisoner wants to talk to them. Senior 'C' said it may be useful to have the Listener waiting in the background so that they can be available at any time during the opening of the SPAR process to talk to the prisoner, but they cannot be allowed to influence the opening of a SPAR. Senior 'D' stated that Magilligan should try this out and report back to H.Q. with their findings, and if it is found to be successful then it can be written into the local policy.

Michael Irwin then gave a talk about an insomnia report he carried out, and how lack of sleep can lead to depression, which can then lead to suicide. He gave everyone at the meeting a copy of his findings. Bob stated that night checks are carried out by prison staff for the safety of the prisoners, and that these checks will remain in place.

This, of course, is not all that was said, and is a slightly more conservative account of events.

6TH MARCH 2012

Director General leaves the sinking ship - a politician asks: is the prison service in free-fall? I'll have to watch the news later – I don't normally.

Just back from Elaine's class, where I encountered 'Funeral Face' and his English cohort - he tried to take *post-it* stickers from my O.U. bag; 'What the fuck you need these for? You've got paper.' What an encounter - now I'm sitting in the computer room, seething; not going back down there again.

God grant me the serenity to accept the things I cannot change, courage to change the things I can and the wisdom to know the difference.

This place is really starting to get to me - roll on freedom. The more I look at some of these men and women the more I feel sick in my stomach - it's not the simple, sickly feeling of adrenalin: it's pure, unadulterated hatred.

Today I shall not judge....

My back is actually sore, due to the muscles tensed in my body - holding back the flood of violence seems to be getting harder. I'm keeping a diary again, purely in a self-preservation effort; *therapy of narrative* - something I'm learning more about in my level-3 psychology.

Just finished my first TMA, and I was able to quote some of Shadd's work. Mr. Yeates says it's the best I've done so far, and I think it was one of the easiest.

The best thing that can happen to you, is happening right now.

I've been ordered to lock my door when I leave the wing; this is the only door I have control over, and I choose not to lock it for that very reason: *because* I am in control of it - this has now been taken away from me. In three years now, I've never locked my cell-door when I've left the wing - I simply pull it to; the only time I've locked it is when I've been reading or locked-up early, looking for a bit of peace.

Have to see Brian from the community chaplaincy, and the life-coach people tomorrow. Okay - calm again; I'll go and do some more studying.

9TH MARCH 2012

It's 8.30, and I'm waiting to go to work. What a crazy week – the guy from the community chaplaincy hasn't shown up yet.

When I watched the news on Tuesday night, there was footage of Halward, and in it the officer opened and closed the metal door-flap; it must have been old footage, as we now have plastic ones, or perhaps it was at Maghaberry - these wings all look the same. Phoned my Dad and asked him if he'd seen the news - he sounded groggy and his words were slurred; my stomach turned - that childhood, gut-wrenching churn of disappointment that never leaves me, though it happens a lot less now. I asked him if he was back on the drink.

He got the hump, and said: 'Right, I'm sick of you! I wasn't going to tell you, but now I have to: I've just had a cancerous tumour removed from my throat, and I'm getting chemo, which makes me groggy. I didn't want to tell you, as you have your life to live in there, and I remember you telling me, when you were in Brixton, that if anything serious came up not to tell you, as there was nothing you can do about it from in there; you told me that anything serious only made you more frustrated, and prison was not the kind of place to run around with charged emotions.'

I was okay about it - in fact, I was more relieved that he wasn't on the sauce. Funny ole world, innit?

Mum called to see him on Saturday, and delivered a king-size duvet, pillows and some other stuff - he told me she stayed for a couple of hours, so my family is united again, if only from a temporary situation.

My brother has picked and ordered a bed for me; they're all doing their bit to help me. I feel... well, I'm not really sure how to feel. They all love me - I now know that - and it can't be easy for them. I suppose I feel humbled by this turn of events.

Got a letter from Mum and Gary last night - Mum was pleased about the visit with Dad, and explained how they 'acted as grown-ups, for a change'. Gary's got a new computer, and is busy trying to come to grips with installing software.

I've started my qualitative report for level-2 - it looks way too complicated; I'll keep going. Doing an hour or two at a time - before you know it, it'll be done, then I'll be free for a couple of months to revise, and do my level-3 assignments.

Shane Johnston was found dead in a toilet, on the Ballymena to Derry train - overdose. R.I.P. Shane.

Tony Anthony is here this afternoon, and I look forward to hearing his story again - I've already spoken with him at Rye Hill in 2008.

Just back from the Tony Anthony presentation, at the P.D.U.. I don't think anything has changed since the last time I spoke with him: his words are still emotive and reassuring. I watched a lot of the guys there, and they really are full of it. Maybe I am, too, but I think I'm sincere and respectful enough to listen, and if I feel moved enough to do something about it, then I will.

I actually prayed for the first time proper, in I-don't-know-how-long. The news from my father made me feel small, and yet again, my problems pale into insignificance. I prayed for him, not for me, but then I suppose if he's alright, then I'm alright.

I spoke to Tony before his presentation, and he's just given me a signed copy of his book. Spoke to Andrew, briefly - he tells me the guy from the community chaplaincy was here on Thursday, and that he's read two-thirds of my book.

It's my three-year anniversary today - three years back in Northern Ireland; one year of custody left (and I'm sitting here listening to two blokes speaking German).

Gavin is in tonight to finalize the last part of our short play-piece - we've got a little get-together on Monday night with the Derry *'Playhouse'* people. Can't stand one of the women involved: there's a difference between encouragement, and loving to hear your own voice. Was asked last night what goodies we'd like brought in - I told them that anything spicy would be nice; I then proceeded to tell them that pepper was banned in Norn Iron prisons - you should have seen the look on their faces.

Three years in Norn Iron - nearly five in total behind bars.

Five fuckin' years! Where does the time go?

14TH MARCH 2012

4.19pm

Feel like crying – needy… panicky. Want to lash out, want to scream, want to lie down, and don't know what to think - I think I'm having another one of my meltdowns: post-traumatic stress disorder? I feel in despair – just want to close my door and go to sleep.

My eyes are gritty and bloodshot, and I feel like shit. Haven't got a cold or anything - just feel like shit! Have a headache… *don't* have a headache; seeing stars. Feel like shit - think I'll have an early night.

Need to change my train of thought: not productive, feeling sorry for myself. Maybe I'm just tired.

I met a young lad today who's waiting to go to Foyleview and wants to do a university course at Coleraine, but he's frightened to complain in case he gets his home-leave cancelled. This is the sort of rumour that officers fuel: if you upset the apple-cart, the system will bite back - I suppose they're right, in a way, but if you *don't* complain, what chance does the next guy have? So, say nothing and keep the head down, and so it continues - I hear it all the time.

Officer B gave me back the final part of my manuscript - he said he thoroughly and genuinely enjoyed it. What a relief, to know that my words have made an impact. He also told me that it sounded as if I was at war with the system every single day. 'Do you really feel like that Michael?' he asked.

'*You* only have to work here a couple of days a week,' I said.

It's true: nobody can ever tell me they know what it feels like to be a prisoner, unless they've been one - it's fuckin' bonkers, and not in the way the movies portray; it's all crap - all smoke and mirrors and bullshit. The more I educate myself, the more I see through it. The more I read, the more I'm asked my opinion, and the more I want to say.

Maybe *that's* what's wrong with me: maybe I'm excited, but frightened about my future. Who knows? I sure as hell don't. I'll keep going, but what of tomorrow?

I've just finished another David Baldacci novel: *'The Camel Club Saga'*. Think I'll get into my shorts and close my door after dinner.

Gym in the morning.

There's the grub now.

We had our little showcase with the *Playhouse* people the other night. Nearly walked out twice, and nearly decked a guy for stealing my chair when I got up to help out - I asked him twice, nicely, then I ripped the chair from under him; the guy's an idiot with learning difficulties, but I still lay awake that night, wanting to tear him asunder.

Can't believe how often I still have to walk away from confrontation - maybe *that's* what's got me.

Maybe it's because I constantly have to deal with bad people - fucked up individuals, who have no sense or rationality (and that's not just the officers I'm talking about). Maybe it's because there's a guy who's a whore, whose very voice makes my skin crawl (I sussed him ages ago, but didn't have to see him too often – now I do). Maybe it's because I've watched a man's hair fall out over the past year, possibly because they took his child's photographs off him. Maybe it's because I make the prime-minister feel sick - and perhaps he is right - because I am a non-person. Maybe it's because one of the women was about to hand out metal forks, and I had to tell her it was best to get them back into her bag, pronto. Maybe it's because I had my first ever taste of banoffee pie, or maybe it's because all the goodies on the table reminded me of what it was like to be normal. Maybe it was being around normal people again. Maybe it's because I'm so close to the end. Maybe it's because I'm frightened.

23RD MARCH 2012
6.08pm

What a day… what a week; what a fuckin' place!

I spoke to my brother today on the phone for two minutes: good stuff; spoke to my Mum this afternoon - a surprise visit: good stuff; spoke to my Dad just now: good stuff.

Got a reply from the governor about attending a seminar before my first home-leave – declined. *Not* good stuff. Spoke to another two men, about the refusal for one to attend his wife and granddaughter's funeral, and subsequent charge on a resettlement day: *not* good stuff.

It's not easy being me. I'm so happy to have been able to hug and kiss my mother, I am so happy that I heard my brother's voice, and I'm so happy that my

Dad is on the mend. But I'm not so happy that my aunt fell down the stairs. I am chuffed that my brother has delivered and built my bed at Dad's place, and chuffed that my sister has already bought me a load of toiletries and stuff (she works in *Boots*) - these are the little things that I will remember for today. My Mum left me a couple of tops - I'll probably have to send two out in order to get two in.

Well, what can I say? Even just writing this has calmed me down - it's still all-too-easy to get caught up in this shit. I'll just be off to my cell and watch some telly.

I have listened to other men's tales today, also - they are in a worse position than me, and they are getting fucked about more than me, so my problems seem small in contrast.

I'll make a crack at the TMA tomorrow. It was funny talking to Mum about this psychology stuff today; turns out she did it too, when she was younger than me - maybe that's where I get it from.

Dad's booked for next Sunday, and this will be his last visit – *'Thank goodness!'* says he! It's hard for him, I know, but at least I'll soon be into single figures, month-wise – *tick-tock*.

1ST APRIL 2012
11.36am

Mmm.

Just back from a visit with Dad and cousin, waiting for lunch to arrive - think it's stew today. My *'Mmm'* isn't about the food, though: it's more do with feelings; I hope my face didn't give away my shock when I saw Dad - this chemo has wasted him. He looks like he's been shrunk, and his skin has outgrown his skeleton... or the other way round - not really sure. My heart is saddened, but at least he's still here. I promised myself I'd listen a bit more, and I heard him - everything seems to be broken, and he's blaming it on the chemo, but I think different. But, then, what do I know? My poor Dad - he looks so fragile, but his mind… Well, that's another story, for another day.

FRIDAY 13TH APRIL 2012

We didn't get unlocked until 10.30am; when I asked the officer the foolish question 'Why?', he informed me that there was no staff and he was the only one on duty (what a martyr).

I made my way down the stairs to have a chat with Pat in the servery, and on my way past one of the cells, I noticed the door was still locked and the guy (whose name is unpronounceable) was gently tapping the door to be let out. I said to the two officers:

'You forgot to let him out.'

'No, we didn't,' they replied. I just shrugged and thought nothing more of it.

I then discovered that the guy who wasn't unlocked had come straight from Maghaberry, where he had shared a cell with another guy who had a contagious disease. Apparently, there was a whole to-do: one of the officers on duty this morning has a pregnant wife at home and refused to work.

I'm now upstairs, in the computer room - didn't get to the gym this morning, and there's no staff on duty in the library to take my card; I've just had one of our 'care and appreciation society' members phone over - no joy.

I've decided to go on a mission with the treadmill: two hours every day, for the foreseeable future. I've been doing it for the past ten days; my muscles don't get sore - it's my feet that hurt the most: *rigor-mortis* setting in?

There's the grub in - lasagne today (it's actually quite good), then gym this afternoon to work it off. Maybe I'll just have a banana, and save the lasagne until tonight.

I'm enjoying this new Peter James novel: *'Dead Man's Grip'* - it revolves around Brighton, and it describes Lewes jail and Brighton nick, where I spent my first few days of incarceration; an endless flow of memories are resurfacing, five years later.

6.17pm

Just off the phone with Dad. My home-leaves have been confirmed for the 25th and 26th of June - can't wait! Don't think I'll have too much time to dwell on this, as I'll be busy revising, and starting the DD307 project.

Spoke to the governor on the way back from the gym. Think I'll go and read my book; got a bit of a sore head - too much aggro. The scales at the gym said 18.3-stone - I've forgone my lasagne and made do with a banana and two chip-baps, without butter.

10TH MAY 2012

I find it rather alarming to discover that the Prison Officers' Association in England and Wales has today ordered their staff to facilitate only a bare minimum of cover, and for the rest to 'walk out', taking industrial action. I'll have been in jail for five years, on the up-and-coming 19th June 2012, and it seems quite bizarre that I started writing on the day of a prison officers' strike, in August 2007; two different governments and five years down the line, it's back to square-one again.

17TH MAY 2012
JUDICIAL REVIEW: 'JUDGEMENT' BY JUDGE T.

No order has been decreed. I am informed by the governor that the last sentence of the ruling is what he will now adhere to:

CONCLUSION [30]:

`'I conclude that any interference is justified in accordance with Article 8 (2) of the Convention.'`

'Any interference is justified'.

20TH MAY 2012

10.05am

Had a bust up at visits yesterday - they seated me in the sex offenders' section, and Mum was asked to leave early.

'Why do I have to leave early?' she said. The young officer ignored her and walked away.

Next thing, the S.O. was over, giving it what-for: 'People in this section have to leave early for good order and discipline.'

'Why?' Mum asked.

'This area is for sex offenders,' he replied.

My mum said: 'Excuse me! My son is not a sex offender!'

The S.O. looked at me, and I looked at him; 'I ain't a sex offender, mate.'

Now he realizes he's made a mistake – more accurately, his officer has made a mistake.

But now it's serious - now it's personal, and now it must immediately become *my* fault. 'You didn't leave when you were told to leave,' he retorted.

This is the age-old win-win situation of the prison officer: if in the wrong, immediately attack the prisoner-try to get him to react, then have him up on a charge, for disobeying a direct order.

My Mum said: 'Why do I have to leave when all these other people are still sitting here?'

I just said: 'Mum, it's time to go. I love you; be careful going home.'

We left, but on the way out the S.O. told me that if I didn't leave when I was told to in the future, I would have my visits terminated. I never looked the guy in the eye - I couldn't: he'd angered my Mum, and my protectiveness towards my mother could have pushed me over the edge, so I'd have been here for a wee bit longer. I didn't stop shaking until around 9.00pm.

I told 'Starry Stars' and 'Visits Liaison', who just happened to be working on the wing.

26TH MAY 2012

11.31am

What a delightful morning - the sun is out and the temperature reached 26° yesterday. I've just been for a wee meander around the yard for half an hour - there's a lovely sea-breeze, and it's good to be alive.

It's been a funny ole week - busy studying and typing up exam questions, ready for the 11th of June. I've been practicing writing, and can get roughly a page-and-a-half of A4 completed in forty-five minutes. There's no problem writing – it's just *remembering* that will be a problem.

There was bit of a kerfuffle here on Thursday night. Young Mick got laid into by DQ: apparently, DQ said he was going up the stairs to *do* young Mick - he didn't. I was sitting in here, working away, and all I heard was shouting and cheering.

Hmm, I thought, *that sounds like a scrap*, as the alarm went off. It's been that long since I've seen a proper to-do, that as I sauntered over to my cell, totally non-plussed, I looked down the wing; I saw DQ's face all busted-up and covered in claret. *Couldn't have happened to a nicer chap,* I thought.

We were all locked up, of course, and later on, when we were allowed out to get hot water, I bumped into Davey in the servery; we both agreed that we didn't mind getting locked up on this occasion, as DQ deserved what he got.

28TH MAY 2012

9.50am

I think this world - the world I inhabit in here - has gone mad; *Too much sun?* I ask myself. The UK has been bathed in sunshine for the past four days, and this has led to a rather startling and remarkable discovery: if one gets sunburnt in here, one can be charged with 'being sunburnt'! Because, and I quote, it is 'self-inflicted'. This is only a verbal quote from a member of staff, but is it true? I spoke to a couple of other prisoners, and they said that they believed it was - in fact, there was one particular S.O. who was rather fond of handing out charges to sunburnt prisoners!

This leads me to the *'Reha-'* (I don't like using that word, as under the newly amended *'Rehabilitation of Offenders Act'*, if one serves over four years, one can never be truly re…). Anyway, I have read a significant amount of material on the *dos* and *don'ts* of prison rules, and this has indeed led me to consider that: yes, by all means, lap up the sun - enjoy the natural light of day, and not the artificial fluorescent kind, get some colour back in those cheeks… but, whatever you do, don't get *too* much of it, or you will indeed end up on a charge!

1ST JUNE 2012

2.24pm

Been a busy morning: down at the P.D.U., sorting out the rooms for the Listeners' do, on Wednesday. David Ford - our justice minister - is going to be there, along with some other important folk from the Irish prison system.

Robbie's going to read my stuff out - I'm too busy worrying about my exam to get involved with rehearsed speeches and responses. I will, however, be speaking to the press; oh dear - do they know what they have let themselves in for? Only joking. I'll have to be on my best behaviour, and not seen to be a belligerent, bad-tempered git who hates the system and all it stands for - this will have to be done after I get out! I look forward to getting my picture taken with them, and using it to my advantage in the future.

Just got my new glasses - two pairs: one for long distance and the other for reading. They really do work well, and are a dramatic improvement, but I suppose, like everything else, they're gonna take a bit of getting used to.

4TH JUNE 2012

11.58am

Just witnessed another scrap whilst on the treadmill - that's four fights I've seen in the past month, and prior there have only been three recorded fights on Halward in the past *three years*.

I've seen the drug abuse and attitude of prisoners on Halward take a steady rise over the past few months. The three fights I've witnessed have all been at the far end of the landing, amongst the young ex-Hydebank crowd. There is little or nothing for these young men to do, so it is inevitable that fights break out, especially when they're doubled up two to a single cell and living on top of each other, literally, and they're continually establishing their place in the pecking order.

2.28pm

Can't concentrate: this revision malarkey seems only to work for me in the mornings - come afternoon time, my brain is saturated and nothing seems to stick; or, perhaps, my episodic memory and attentional spotlight has been used so much, that the filtering process seems to block out all matters psychoanalytic and humanistic, including perception and attention. *Huh!?*

Going to go and have a chat with Pat.

6TH JUNE 2012

2.55pm

Just been down having a chat with S.O. - he's a very nice person, and we always end up having a good ole natter; it's good for me, sometimes, to listen to other people's perspectives. S.O. is one of these men who's been in the job for a life-time, and there is nothing that he hasn't seen, although one of the things we do agree on is that 'no person in authority can ever know what it's like to serve a prison sentence unless they've done it themselves'.

Of course, the likelihood of actually finding someone in authority, who has served a prison sentence, is rather remote (I hope to change that, should the system ever recognize me for the authoritarian that I've become!).

Looking forward to tomorrow's celebration of ten years of Listeners at H.M.P. Magilligan. I'm doing a Q-and-A with some of the press, so it should be interesting to see if I can keep my gob shut about the prison service and keep my answers short and precise, and pertaining to the *positivity* of what we do - for me, it's all about HOPE.

S.O. says: 'Christ is the answer'; if Christ is the answer, I say: why have so many got it wrong?

I'm not getting hung up on this emotive topic - there's a time and a place, and for me it's such a shame that good, intellectual and intelligent conversations seem to always end up with the believer waiting for his or her moment to slip in the 'Christ' bit. *Christ, here we go again,* is what I think. Why, oh why does it annoy me so?

As I said, I'm looking forward to this gathering. I was asked to write a little piece for the celebration, and good ole Robbie has stepped into the breach, so I'm glad that I don't have to read out my work - my nerves would be fractured by now if I did. I hope you enjoy my little prose - they seem to like my stuff at Listowell, and so I said I'd give it a go; here's what I wrote:

'What's to celebrate about death, suicide and self-harm?' you might ask. When do men ever talk about their emotions? I hear the women in the audience ask. Well, let me tell you: it happens a hell of a lot more often than you think; "Maybe a course in Listening might help".

'I keep telling people that prison saved my life, but I can assure you I will never recommend it! I'm currently studying the importance of learning from experience. People often ask me why I do what I do - to explain this, I have to tell you about my experience when at H.M.P. Rye Hill, in England: I'd recently been sentenced and moved from H.M.P. Brixton; the world fell apart and the walls closed in... I *fell apart.*

'I met a guy in a black T-shirt - an ex-marine, Hell's Angel and fully-fledged nut-case! He 'listened', and the thing that struck me the most was that he never told me what to do, or that it would be alright: 'You'll work it out,' he said, 'but while you're doing it, I'm in cell 52, across the way.' This man listened twice a day, seven days a week, for four months... until I worked it out.

'I finally 'got it' - I understood. And I put my name down to become a 'Listener' too. Three years and four prisons later I met Madge, and here I am; thank you, Madge.

'Many men speak to me, off-the-record - they tell me stuff that'd make your toes curl. We are all in this closed environment together, and my studies tell me how the human animal's survival instincts come about in the fight-or-flight perspective. Unfortunately, in prison there is nowhere to run - you have to deal with you*... deal with yourself.*

'The holistic approach to care involves listening, and reciprocal

respect. We, as Listeners, give people hope, by listening. Listening is an art, yet not everyone's cup of tea, but if Northern Ireland has taught me one thing, it is that we must listen to the other person - to the other side; let us, the so-called 'responsible' people, take time to listen to each other.

'I met a young man who was ready to throw the towel in. I listened, I cajoled, and I listened... and he worked it out. I saw him two weeks later, walking down the phase; 'Oi, big lad - cheers for that! By the way, everything is cool.' His shoulders went back, his chest puffed out, and he walked away with a spring in his step and a big, beaming smile - funnily enough, the exact same thing that happened to me. By listening, we help others work it out.

'Most of all, I felt pride - I wish we could all *feel this pride; if one could bottle it and sell it, I do believe we'd be onto a winner. So, let us celebrate hope - hope for the future, and for the Samaritans and Listeners who will follow us; hopefully, in ten years' time, we can come back to a room just like this, and celebrate the art of listening.*

'I could stand here, and yap, and moan...
I know I'm not alone.
But, then, I am *alone;*
Aren't we all, at some time, alone?
People often ask me why I do what I do;
Sure, if I hadn't become a Listener,
I wouldn't have met you.

'To answer my question, I go back to the start:
It was me who put me here, not some other fart.
Prison is mad - the system is mad;

It is what it is,

Yet sometimes I'm glad.

'People often ask me why I do this thing;

'I couldn't listen to him –

Do you know what he did?'

Today I shall not judge,

For non-judgment creates silence of the mind;

Have you ever sat in silence?

'I wear this black shirt, because of the hurt –

Self-inflicted *hurt, but hurt all the same.*

I'm proud of me - of my shirt,

My fellow Listeners: the Samaritans' own black shirt army,

Who listen... who hope -

Even to some who've simply run out of dope;

No dope, no hope!

'Seriously, though, I do what I do

Because someday it might be you.

It's personal... it's private –

It's between me and you.

To listen, sometimes at a price,

I know that I – we - help by being there

Sometimes, when one runs out of prayer.

'It's hard to describe this pride –

This rollercoaster ride:

We do our bit to make sure nobody's died.

My heart is what's left – though it was there at

the start.

Thank you for listening... for hearing my heart.

'Let's get real here: we're all human –

Prison is life and death for some –

But I hope we bring light into the darkest of rooms.

If I'm being real, prison saved my life –

So, thank you prison, for being there.

To my fellow Listeners, I say: 'here-here...

Here-here.''

I hope that sounds as good to those significant others, who are going to be there tomorrow, as it does to me.

Watched all of the live Queen's jubilee concert, at the front of Buckingham Palace. The stage was on the fountain, and half the crowd was stretched up The Mall, watching the show on big-screens staggered along its entirety. I've walked The Mall and driven up and down it loads of times, on the way to and from God-knows where.

The sound quality was pretty good for a live event, and there were no major hiccups or technical *faux-pas*, for such a major event. I thought the children's choir from Kenya was fantastic, and the little girl who sang on her own was remarkable - it was a real inspiration to see this young girl, of around ten, sing so flawlessly. The girl's fellow choir members all had beaming grins - the world would be a much better place if more of these smiles could be brought into our living-rooms. I know the simple life these young people have led, and it reinforces my belief that less is more - these children do not lead fancy lives, with fanciful clothes and luxurious items: they keep it simple and real; so what an adventure this was for them! And what a delight for me.

I remember the Ugandan choir that came into the prison, and Eddie having to leave, because one of the young girls reminded him too much of his daughter

- their impish eyes and beaming grins light up the darkest of rooms.

Where were you on the day of the Queen's diamond jubilee, Michael? Banged up, on a beautiful June evening, with the sun casting its glow across my cell, as the birds on the outside cast shadows of their wings up the walls, and across the ceiling.

Listening, choked with tears drying on my cheek, sent me back to another summer - the summer of 1974 (or was it 1976) at Noel and Peggy's grandparents', in Suffolk; not the English Suffolk, but the Norn Iron Suffolk, on the outskirts of Belfast, with machine-gun and rifle fire, and the shouts and whispers of cockney accents coming up from the yards and back gardens, like faceless figments of my imagination. They were there; you *knew* they were - you could hear them, but you'd hardly ever see them. We'd huddle close - me and my wee brother - then we'd be playing the next day, under lines of bullet-holes on gable walls, around the burnt-out cars and makeshift barricades, where spent rifle rounds were two a penny.

Time for the four o'clock head count, a shower and some grub, and then feet up, ready for *'Holby'* and *'Silks'*.

7TH JUNE 2012

6.41pm

Just back from H1, doing the committals with George. On the way out some English cunt in a white shirt says: 'I wish I'd a pair of scissors.' I take it this was for him to cut my long hair, so I said: 'At least mine'll grow back.' His two colleagues started laughing at him, so he got nasty and called me 'a big girl's blouse'.

8TH JUNE 2012

3.54pm

Just back from Education - Allison let me come over and get some revision material printed out; big exam, first thing Monday morning. I'm going to take a break for an hour, then do some reading of a NOMS document Jack got for me - I'll get stuck in over the next two days, and we'll just have to take it as it comes. I'm crapping myself slightly less at the moment, compared to last week.

I'm not as mad as I was last night - slept pretty well, once I'd calmed down. Spoke to the big fella about it this morning, and he laughed, as we both agreed how difficult it was becoming to continuously walk away.

I read somewhere, recently, about a guy feeling sorry for himself for getting an I.P.P. sentence (an indeterminate sentence where the prisoner only has a minimum sentence and can stay in prison for the rest of their lives akin to a life sentence), only to then find out that he'd stabbed a prison governor, which made him feel better.

Spoke to Jonty Taylor last night - he was out for a week and ended up back in on a breach of licence. I told him to turn round, and gave him a kick in the arse, as promised when he left here a few months back.

10TH JUNE 2012

8.43am

Sat up to watch the Canadian *Grand Prix* qualifying last night; it was over at half-eleven - way past my bed-time.

I didn't take any of my tablets yesterday - had to stop taking the omeprazole, as I'm due for the Royal on Wednesday. I also didn't take my mirtazapine, as I believe it suppresses my mental abilities - I felt really cloudy yesterday, and couldn't write down stuff I'd read five minutes earlier. I feel a lot more alert today, and will take a wee break every half an hour, for ten to twenty minutes, or so. I slept well, so I don't think there will be a problem for tomorrow - positive mental attitude, and all that malarkey.

Fuckin' alarm's just gone off - toaster again!

Ten minutes later, we're back in business. It was the fire alarm going off, because of a bit of smoke from the toaster.

Spoke to Mum yesterday on the phone, so all was good there; it's cool that the justice minister wrote back, and the ombudsman is investigating her complaint.

I'm out of time and out of interest with my revision - I know if I remember half of what I know, I'll get a 'PASS'. I'll have a good read of my notes before I go to sleep, and another when I get up in the morning – hopefully, that will be enough; if not, well: *c'est la vie.*

My esophageal reflux is now up to its old uncomfortable and painful tricks. I don't know how I survived on the outside, with the amount of crap I was putting into my body - I suppose it helped that I nearly always threw up what I had eaten or drank; I've only been without my tablets for a day and a bit, and my lunch has already ended up down the toilet! They've just brought the dinner in, and I'm blooming starving, but I know that whatever I eat will be repeating on me for the rest of the night.

I'll go have a shower and then have my dinner, watch the footie and try to stay awake for the *Grand Prix*. I'm very disappointed the BBC are not covering all the races - I think they stop covering them altogether next year - maybe I'll have Sky TV at my new hacienda in Seymour Hill.

11TH JUNE 2012
3.54pm

DSE212 module *'Mapping Psychology'* over and done with - done and dusted. It says at the start of this module that there is rather a lot of reading, and that it's a steep learning curve – boy, is that an understatement? I was correct in my predictions of question, and I had fully revised three specific answers - I was also correct in my prediction that I wouldn't do well in the short answers part of the essay. So, I've done poorly in one quarter of the essay, but much better in the other three quarters. I don't know how people come up with the answers they do within the time allocated. I only left out a couple of main points, and, from what I can remember, I covered the general gist of things.

My stomach acid and reflux is having a field-day, and I also haven't taken any of my anti-depressants, which really were making me dopey (*dopier*, more like). I'm now ready to get stuck into my 4000-word project, which has to be completed by the 4th July – so, what's that… three weeks?

Enjoyed the *Grand Prix* last night, and slept pretty well. Got up around six, had a shave, done me bits and read over the main points of the essays - I think it worked. Now going to read the big lad's judicial review, have some dins, put the feet up and watch the England vs. France game; the football's been pretty uneventful, and Ireland got well chinned last night.

Spoke to the governor earlier; he didn't realize that two people had moved to Alpha, and that I didn't get the next available bed - maybe I'll get down there at the weekend. As usual, there's no point trying to second-guess things. I've lent him a couple of statistics books - must remember to get them back off him before I leave this place.

12TH JUNE 2012
5.36pm

Meant to be going to hospital in the morning, and Gerard had his appointment cancelled today. I saw English Mick, in civvies, outside reception this morning, so he must've been on an escort. I hope they don't cancel me again tomorrow - there'll be hell to pay!

Had a piss test this morning, as I'm out on home-leave soon. Going to go and fill out Dad's card and stick it in the post - the only gift, and the best, that I can give him for Father's Day, is inclusion of the words:

'I'll see you in Dunmurry next week.'

17TH JUNE 2012

8.42am

Was out at the hospital on Wednesday - what an experience that was! Had to get a tube inserted through my nose and down into my stomach, and had to wear it back to the prison – freak-show, or what? Still, it worked, because every time I felt the slightest bit of acid, the pH levels dropped. It was a relief to pull it out the next morning, though: very uncomfortable night.

The big lad lost his appeal. No surprise, but you do hope. I'll see him tomorrow. In the same week, TC had his conviction quashed, four months after serving four years.

Got a letter from Shadd on Thursday, and haven't slept properly since, rehearsing speeches in my head for the seminar on Monday – I'll be at Queens University for two days of my home-leave! A totally unbelievable concept: prison in the morning, Queens for two days, and then back to prison; overwhelming, but in a good way.

Just got a letter from Gary - now grinning like a Cheshire cat; he's enjoying my poems and writing. Good stuff. It's a weird thought: Gary knows and understands me now, as friends should - glad he's in my life.

Must get transcribing finished, and gym later - haven't been all week

PART FOUR:

The Home Stretch

One year from release…

21ST JUNE 2012
2.39pm

I've been moved to Alpha, on Monday past - only getting my head round it now; been very busy… very unusual.

I've just been able to rest my elbows on the window-ledge in my cell/room at Alpha, and stare out the window - a big window… without bars; admittedly, I still have to stare through the wire-mesh fence surrounding the very small exercise yard (they only use the one on the other side).

I'm listening to three of my fellow cons on one side laugh and cackle, but it's a nice cackle - natural and not forced; obviously, from men who have formed alliances and friendships, and who feel comfortable in each-other's company. A far cry from the drug-fuelled, false laughter - born of fear and insecurity - of the other wings. Alpha is living up to all I believed it to be, good and bad.

''B'-wing head count!'

Just got my head out of the door in time. I could tell the officer was nervous: they have to walk down the wing to the end, and then walk back up again - I take it this is to facilitate making eye-contact with the object/prisoner.

Made a request to use the disabled loo - granted. The ole boy who's being using it (nobody else is allowed) believed it is his alone; I was told by another inmate that the ole boy was asking him what was wrong with me, that I needed to use the disabled loo - I told the fellow it was none of his business, but, as he'd asked nicely, I'd tell him, so I did. He told me that the ole boy had instructed him to leave two sheets of the toilet roll hanging loose, as this would enable him to find out if someone had been in the toilet, by his reckoning, to plant drugs; now, I may be wrong, but surely the toilet roll being tampered with would only prove that someone had blown their nose or taken a shit.

There is much to dislike, but so much to be grateful for. Life is cool, sitting here, listening to the birds cheeping; I'll probably want to blast them by the time I'm ready to go - noisy blighters! For now though, it's soothing. I'm excited; not expectant - just excited about Monday.

23RD JUNE 2012

9.27am

'The best laid plans of mice and men.'

I have been up from five o'clock for the past two mornings. I've managed to read some of the literature for my project during this quiet time, but, for the life of me, I can't seem to see how to start writing it up, never mind how to end it. I think it might well be impossible to simultaneously concentrate on study and contemplate getting out after this amount of time (5 years), but I just want to get stuck in and not think about it - I can't. I want to work, but I can't. I think it's really important for me to record what's going on at the minute, as it might help in the future.

Phoned my aunt last night - it's weird to say: 'I'll see you Monday'. This whole set-up is working out; I spoke to the governor yesterday, on Alpha, and could see the other officers cringing. Still, I have been called 'Michael' by two members of staff, and another, only this morning, said: 'What's your first name?' I told him happily and asked him his - he reciprocated; good stuff.

My tuck-shop money has been removed, as they give it to you when you leave. No member of staff has spoken to me about any of the procedures involved in leaving voluntarily - I have had to ask. I was told that *I* should have told *them*, the staff, that I was out on Monday, so they could then have 'phoned and told the administration people to hold back some of my money; 'Please tell us the next time; we'll let you off with it this time, as it is your first time going out.'

I wonder if it is in my contract, or prison job description, that I must advise staff of every procedure, even though I don't know that the procedure exists. This is one of the main facts of prison life: it is the prisoner's responsibility to ensure that a procedure is followed and obeyed, yet no member of staff has ever told the prisoner what it is. If it was done on induction, how the hell could you remember something that was said three or four years before the event?

I went into the office this morning to add my name and number to the gym list. Everyone writes their prison number - the whole sheet was just numbers; for me, it was so noticeable. The prisoners don't know how important it is for them *not* to do this! I was going to put down my *name and* number but, it would have stuck out like a sore thumb on the sheet. I'll wait until next week, and add my name first - this will be seen as a challenge by some, and they will spend every hour of every day trying to get one over on me.

That's another thing about Alpha: every single notice is worded with 'this will result in an 'adverse'', or 'this will result in your immediate de-selection from Alpha', or 'you will be removed from Alpha'. I'll give you an example: 'Any person who pours any liquid into a bin will be removed from Alpha', but there are no sinks or toilets in the cell.

Another cracker was Paul Beattie's story: just over a year ago he was removed from Alpha and charged with having a sachet of pepper - an unauthorized item, and a breach of security; it took him six months to get back to Alpha. When the Scottish parole board interviewed him about his parole and offender management course, they asked him about his adjudication, and they burst out laughing when he told them - at least they see it for the farce that it is.

Also, PI was promised a certain course by the NIPS when he transferred from Scotland to here, and he would only be granted parole if he carried out this course, but the NIPS *have* not and *can* not implement the course, so he cannot now get parole. Paul was also released under the 'Good Friday Agreement', and the Scottish system that he was convicted under recognized that this is his first and only offence, as all the rest were connected with his involvement in a paramilitary organization during the 'Troubles', but now that he's back here in Northern Ireland, they (the NIPS) keep referring to and bringing up his paramilitary past. There's more to this than meets the eye, but I've got way too much going on at the minute to work it all out.

I was given permission to use the study room up in Halward a while back - where I'm sitting now. Want to go for a stroll round the yard for ten minutes, to take a break, but I'm not allowed to as it's not my wing. I'm only allowed to move directly to and from study room. Just asked to speak to the S.O. to see if I can do this, but he's busy with a SPAR at the minute, so I'll have to wait. I'll just sit and stare at the screen here for a moment.

10.53am

I was sitting here, glasses off, staring out onto the landing, taking a break, and I thought about Monday - this is the first time I felt panic; the first time I thought: *Bollocks, I'm not doing it - I'm staying. It's too much; all of it is too much.*

3.28pm

Definitely getting butterflies now. Went for a quick walk round the yard – officer B gave me permission, but, as usual, I know there will be a whole steward's enquiry when security is eventually asked. The other guys are allowed out the front for a smoke break, etc., but it's the mixing with other inmates that's the problem - their issue is that if they do it for one, they'll have to do it for everyone. I'll tread carefully - I'm a 'D'-cat and a Listener, so *let's work it out, folks.*

I literally passed out at lunch-time. Going to lay off the coffee - think I'll need to watch the ole intake/output from now on; my spoonfuls have been getting bigger.

I'll watch the footy tonight - don't think there's much else on. It's the quarter-finals.

I've started to mark up Williams's transcript. It looks like a mountainous task, but I do hope I have the time and the energy, when I come back, to get it finished - don't have a choice, really. I suppose that's what the project is all about: we don't really have a choice - the self will have to wait until we have acquired what it takes to stand alone; even though it seems like we've always been standing alone, we haven't: we've been shaped continuously.

Off back down to Alpha. Good fun, this in-and-out at the weekend.

24TH JUNE 2012

9.37am

Is this the last day of my story? Who knows?

I'm not wound up about getting out tomorrow - I've resigned myself to the fact that I 'must' leave for two days. I listened to some music last night and had a wee scream into my pillow; I also watched *'Love Actually'*, and had wee cry over that, too - all I needed was a big tub of ice-cream... Maybe that officer was correct the other week, when he called me a 'big girl's blouse.'

I'm not frightened anymore - I've accepted it for what it is: it just *is*. Maybe I won't even have to speak tomorrow. I keep repeating the *Art of Living Foundation* stuff: *'Be 100% - the present moment is inevitable, and expectations reduce joy'*. So, I'm not expecting, just enjoying this moment for what it is, and not getting worked up about it. It is fuckin' weird, though.

Big DS was on duty in Alpha this morning, and he gave me a larger-than-life 'Hello, Michael.' This turned a few heads - this man is not renowned for his pleasantries, and there has been a dramatic difference in how he speaks to me over the past few months.

They had a little joke/dig about why I was going up to Halward. I replied: 'Study, study, study... you know that's all I do.'

One of my newly-acquainted hosts quipped: 'Knowledge can be a dangerous thing'.

'Oh, yes,' I replied, 'it certainly scares the bejesus out of some more than others.'

I had another interesting encounter yesterday, when I was in the office - there is a big poster on the wall from the M.O.J., asking for 'mentors'. I asked Ass if he could explain to me what that was about - he told me that it was to do with existing officers mentoring new officers, and fuck-all to do with prisoners. I laughed, thanked him and said 'Maybe they should get prisoners to mentor officers.' Maybe I'll suggest a prisoner consultation group for new recruits.

I cannot explain how much I want to be free of this institutional rationale - the men and women who work here are in so much... I can't think of a word befitting this scenario: they are as *broken* as we are, if not more.

RE-INTEGRATION MORNING

25TH JUNE 2012

9.55am

Sitting in the prison van, by the gate. Each and every process has to be repeated by officers who don't know what they are doing.

'This paperwork is in the wrong order,' one of them says, and disappears back into the office. Then, he comes back out, and starts the whole process all over again. We have to be driven the 25 yards through the gate.

They tried to stop me getting out, as I told them I was going to Queens to talk about crime - they told me I wasn't allowed to speak in public, and wouldn't be going anywhere. The governor told them to be quiet, and told me to enjoy my time at Queens, and to tell him about it when I got back

10.55am

Dear God, what a palaver getting out of prison is - they really don't make it easy! One of the guys said: 'It's a joke trying to get out of here.'

The officer driving the van turned round, and said to us all: 'In prison, *you* lot are the joke'; so much anger - so much hatred!

On the way to Coleraine I told the officer driving that I was busting for a pee - so he slowed down!

I finally got to Coleraine station - gone is the system now, and I'm having a pee.

That's when sheer panic set in - I had to take a deep breath or two.

Spoke to the guy at the ticket desk - he was very polite and helpful. He recognized me as being from the prison, by the travel warrant; I laughed and told him it was my first time. He said: 'Don't worry - you'll be alright.' *How kind,* I thought. He asked me if I wanted change for the phone and needed to phone anyone, as I'd missed the train to Belfast - more kindness.

Phoned my Dad. After I dialled the number, I punched in the # key and started to type in my PIN number – *oops*: forgot I wasn't using the prison phone. Dad and I had a laugh - it was great. Richard is picking me up later on, I think. I'm not going to try and control anything, but just let it happen.

I said to Dad: 'Bloody-hell - two gorgeous birds have just walked past me.' Then it hit me: a wave of realization of how much I miss female company. I joked and said I'd have to go and sit in the corner with my legs crossed. Dad said: 'You're lucky it's not sunny.'

Dad was miffed that there was a balls-up getting us out, but I told him I wouldn't have expected anything different from the NIPS. There were lads from Foyleview waiting in the holding cell since 8.30 - I didn't get off Alpha until 9.30.

So, I've taken up residence in a wee café round the corner from the station. Had to cross two roads - hard to deal with, especially with my two-week old glasses. I really am seeing the world in a different perspective.

I've just had a second cup of coffee - a top-up; don't know whether that was a good idea or not. Got a bottle of water, also - my throat and mouth keep drying up. I can't say that the whole process this morning was painless, but it wasn't as bad as I thought it would be. Mind you, I didn't exactly expect too much.

Can't dwell on this now - need to let it go; as my Dad just said on the phone: 'Enjoy your freedom, son.' As he said this, there was a train pulling into the station, and I said I might just jump onto it, and see where it took me - how cool would that be?

In the café, but not hungry - I'm frightened to order anything; my coffee cup was shaking the whole way down to the table, and the proprietor just called me 'Sir' ('Would you like another top-up, sir?'). Amazing! I'm the only person in here, so it's cool to have this adjusting time.

Going to have yet another pee, and head back round to the station. What a weird feeling.

11.42am

My bladder won't let up.

Just walked over the footbridge – wow; high up and not caged, with no wire or fences to block my cinemascope. It's cold but it's okay. I see the trains are all new.

I've just heard my first alarm bell since eight this morning: the sound of the level-crossing coming down - how cool is it not to have to drop everything and run back to my cell? If all these people on the platform only knew!

Or maybe they *do* know, and I'm sticking out like a sore thumb - I certainly feel that way!

I hope the train has a toilet! This is horrible: constantly going to the loo; I've lost count this morning - it's nearly every ten to fifteen minutes. Maybe it's just nerves (*d'ya think!?*).

On the train now – panicky. I think I can see the loo; do I leave my bag or bring it with? Going to relax - try to take my mind off the fact that I'm sweating like the proverbial oink. *Phew!*

This really is the weirdest thing I've ever done: just been for a pee on a moving train. Everything is automated - some woman told me to lock the door, and I told her I couldn't find the button, then I realized it was a machine talking to me; wish my peeing was automated.

The anxiety is coming and going in waves – from anger about this morning, to listening to mothers and children laughing, to a baby gurgling and making baby noises, to extreme jealousy of the woman sitting across the aisle from me, typing away on a tablet-type thing; I'm gently rocking, with pen and paper.

I had a very interesting interaction getting onto the train, when waiting for the passengers to alight. I let one lady step on in front of me, but then my desire to get a seat on my own took over my manners. This is really playing on my mind - how rude of me. I even left my bag under the supervision of a complete stranger when I went to the loo.

I want to stand up and shout: 'Look, I've just got out of jail - will you all just please give me a break?' This is mad - totally mad: too many sensations jumping all over the place.

The last trip to the loo was less dramatic; starting to spread them out a bit now.

At Cullybackey now – the perfume and the natural talk is lovely to smell and to listen to. I still feel guarded and self-conscious about being looked at (but maybe that's because I know I'm so good-looking!). Listening to a baby gurgling, and some sporadic laughter, further down the carriage - what a beautiful feeling; want to cry. It's so natural, yet all so *un*natural for me. It's cool and overcast outside, but everything is so green. Still don't feel like eating.

Good God, that girl was beautiful!

Ballymena – I'm getting there. But where is *'there'*? Where is home? My mind starts racing around past lives and loves.

One of the lads, this morning, said: 'Why the fuck do you want to go to Queens on your first day out - your first home-leave day?' He doesn't understand, nor could he; the other lads know me - this guy doesn't. They know what I'm about, and that what I'm trying to do will make their lives better in the future. That's the problem with a lot of these guys: they can't see further than the end of their noses.

Filling up now - is this what the next few days are going to be like: up and down like a yo-yo?

The train times and destinations are well displayed and announced - no panic about missing stops or figuring out where you are. I'm at Antrim now - not long (not long until what?). Can't get Queens out of my head. Mosley

West, next stop - never heard of it.

It's great to spread the legs out and stretch, too - feels really good, this. Reminds me of all the times I've been out and handcuffed – regret... regret... *regret* sweeps over me like a blanket; feel sad again.

Fuck it - forget all of this and just head back! Sensation overload - want to go back!

Well, not really, but the thought does keep cropping up. This is hard – something that can't be predicted. *'Be 100% the present moment'* is inevitable right now.

Listening to American accents on a Belfast train, after five years of imprisonment... give over! Watching a couple of pensioners in front of me, through the gap between the seats: she is trimming the hair on the top of his nose, with a wee pair of scissors. I'm smiling inwardly - love, care and affection after all those years. Or maybe it's annoyance - maybe the hair on his nose drives her mad! Why on Earth is she carrying a pair of scissors that size with her?! He sits placidly and doesn't bat an eyelid - life is simple between them; I think it's lovely: real. I suppose that's what life is all about: being natural - being real.

Looking at these two pensioners makes me sad, too, though: there were 'MURDER' posters up in the station - a male pensioner had been killed, and the police were appealing for information. Very sad, and it made me feel guilty because I'm a criminal. These people would not understand - they don't know me; they just hear the word 'prisoner' and I'm a *murderer*, *rapist*, *thief*, or all three.

Will I die lonely? Do I want a relationship when I get free? What next for me in the love department? Will I e-mail Fin? Don't know - not now, anyway.

I'm now resigned to the fact that I'm going to miss the seminar, and not going to get to say my piece; a missed opportunity, all down to the NIPS! *C'est la vie.*

There's the sound of the first mobile phone going off - not my phone, someone else's; been a while since I heard that. The TVs in prison make a noise like the old computers used to when logging on.

Tired now. Feel let down by the NIPS - I'm confused now: suppose I am grateful for them letting me out, but I'd have been released on a tag by now if I'd stayed in England, and all this would be behind me. But then, I wouldn't be home, and wouldn't have my Dad picking me up at the station in five minutes. A total conflict of interests: part of me wishes I'd stayed in England and been out by now, and the other part wants the comfort of my family.

Train is fairly full now, going at a high speed - strange sensation. I still feel really bad about getting on the train in front of that woman; she looks about the same age as me - black hair, with hints of grey; mature student-type, with an American accent (maybe this could be *the one*). I bet she's thinking: 'What a prick!' I'm sorry - I really am; I want to get up and tell her: feel the need to explain everything. Instead, I slump back in my chair and look out of the window - cowardly bastard! No I'm not - I'm just scared… scared of all this. I blank it out and breathe – big, deep breaths.

Yorkgate now - nearly there; the safety of Dad - the comfort of not being alone (on my own) and the relief of sharing. Panicking again: *breathe iiinn… breathe ooouuut…*

Oh, shit (in a good way) - there's Nelson's Nose! *Woo-hoo!* Belfast Lough to my left - now I am excited! To hell with the breathing exercises - need to pack this stuff away for a couple of days. See you all later.

MY FIRST HOME-LEAVE, AFTER FIVE YEARS OF IMPRISONMENT BY MICHAEL IRWIN

Walking onto the platform at Central Station was a big buzz, knowing my father was nearby. Walking out, I was thinking how much Central Station has changed, how it feels like an airport terminus - a bit like Heathrow, actually.

And there he was: sitting hunched-over, leaning on his walking-stick. Big hugs - not too hard: he felt so fragile and brittle, I was scared I'd break him; warm smiles and warm feelings, on a cold day. We walked to the car, chatting away, and he asked me about my morning; I said: 'Just forget about it - I'm not going to waste my time today on this negativity.'

He smiled and said: 'You know what? You're bloody well right, son.' This doesn't happen too often: my father agreeing with me.

I went to the hut to pay for the car parking, but found it was free. Before we moved off, he handed me my wallet (with forty quid in it), his phone and my passport - strange feeling, having all this responsibility.

Next I knew, we were outside Queens.

'I'll see you later,' he said. 'Good luck.'

I said: 'Love you, Dad, and thank you for everything.'

Walking through the entrance, down the path and into the iconic institution… wow, what a feeling! I followed the directions, but found the loo first. I then found the door and room I was meant to be in, went for another pee and threw some water round my face.

Big, deep breaths - this was now the culmination of all my efforts, all my dreams and all my hopes. What happened next may decide if this whole endeavour is going to serve any purpose at all for me - my future hangs in the balance; very intimidating.

Everyone was huddled around tables - eight or nine people, around eight or nine tables. I saw Shadd to my left, with his back to me, busy typing away on a laptop; I placed my hand on his shoulder and he turned round, jumped up and smiled warmly, shaking my hand; 'Welcome.'

We exchanged pleasantries, and, before going any further, I had to tell him how I feel about him, and what he has done for me – it felt important that I clear the air and get this off my chest; it was emotional, and he seemed a bit taken aback. We discussed the reasons why it took me so long to get here - after all, this seminar is about making the re-integration process easier, not only on the prisoner, but the family also.

There was a nice-looking girl sitting at an adjacent table; he introduced me to Claire, and told her who I am, and where I've come from - Claire was amazed, pleased and rather excited. 'Wow - this is going to be fun,' she said.

I didn't want to do my reading – I was petrified.

I sat at the front, listening and paying attention, as I sipped water; I was invited to comment after each table's presentation.

They were already nearly finished, and, all too soon, Shadd finished up what they were doing and introduced me…

It turned out better than expected - I got to say what I'd wanted and more; I held my own, and it felt fantastic.

Afterwards, I fled to the toilet, and when I came back most of the people had left, but a few held back to meet me. I now know who they are and what they do - I didn't at the time; I spoke my mind, freely, and they listened. Two have promised to come and visit me very soon.

One seemed genuinely angry at what I was telling him, and he said: 'Why do you think I have stayed behind to speak to you?' He then told me he was 'the person in charge of what is happening.'

I said: 'Oh, shit – so, I've come to the right place, then?'

It was great - we had a good head-to-head, and a few others joined in, while Shadd just sat there, grinning. This is what it's all about - I hope it leads somewhere. It better, because I ain't going anywhere.

I met Raymond and Pete, and we all headed to a café in Botanic. I'm not allowed on licenced premises, and I could see the others were a bit disappointed. I'll have to address this in the future - I don't drink and have no intention of doing so; drink made me ill. My Dad doesn't drink anymore, nor my brother, and now me - we three, united in abstinence. I have been offered booze and drugs in every prison I've stayed in, and already passed my own tests a long time ago. In the future, I want to be able to socialize with society, and the people I am working with, in an environment they feel comfortable in; others shouldn't have to bend, because of the restrictions placed on me.

This is part of the bigger picture for me - I feel that because I am compliant, it's good for the statistics to place me on these restrictions, but times have changed, and so have I: I'm already deemed 'safe' by the system, so why does it have to keep stating the 'risk', when there is none? You can't even go to a decent restaurant nowadays that doesn't have a licence. Maybe I'll open a non-licenced restaurant that does a serious steak or burger, specifically for prisoners on licence. Mmm… now, there's a thought!

We were chatting away and I was facing out of the window, when I spied my brother, walking across the road, in a side street. I jumped up and ran out the door, and I calmly called his name. He tensed and turned - it *was* him; oh, my God! We hugged and embraced in the middle of the road, and he came and joined our ensemble.

Eamon (a friend who made a movie) also turned up, and we shared stories, ideas and experiences. The next two hours were mind-blowing - I had to leave several times, as I became overwhelmed with emotion. My brother shared how he'd heard the news of my arrest, and how his first thought was that I was dead – it rocked me to the core, and I hate myself for what I've done. Still, that was then and this is now; nevertheless, it's humbling to know how much of an impact it had on everyone.

We all said our goodbyes and promised to keep in touch, then Richard and I drove up to Dad's. We stopped before we went in, and my brother showed me pictures of his boys - now young men… like the young men inside: just young men, nothing more. I've never met them, or spoken to them - it was nice that he shared them with me. The next photo he showed me was of the cut in my father's neck, after his cancerous lump was removed. It wasn't a wee lump or a wee scar - it fuckin' blew my head off! He nearly lost half his neck and his windpipe, for fuck's sake. The enormity of this, and then going to meet him in thirty seconds, doesn't do much for one's composure - we got in the door, and I was shown to the bedroom, where I jumped onto the bed, face down and spread-eagled, and I screamed into the duvet, for many different reasons. Then I jumped up and smiled; 'Had to do that.'

We sat and chatted - the three of us together again, after so long; not just prison time - a long, *long* time. Richard phoned for a pizza and went to collect it - I had three slices and a piece of garlic bread, before I couldn't eat anymore. My mate Gary phoned from London, and then Richard left.

I phoned Mum and we arranged to meet first thing in the morning, then cousin turned up to get me cybered-up, so I chatted to Dad for a while longer and then went online; I was frightened and a little unsure of the internet - then the emails started to come. I looked up the IRISS site and blogged about what I'd done today.

Got into bed around midnight and woke at 5.00am - no checks, no toilet trips… no nothing.

I've never felt as alive as I felt that morning, sitting and watch the sun coming up; as it did, it shone on the framed picture of Manhattan, which takes up most of the wall beside my desk - it looked like the sun was rising in Manhattan, too.

I heard my Dad getting up and we had a chat. Then I started to unpack, and looked through the brown bags I've sent out over the past few years - one held the contents of my suitcase. I lifted out a pair of jeans; the last time I wore those jeans, I was free, in Trinidad - I didn't think I'd ever get into them now, and I threw them on top of the pile, for rubbish.

Started to e-mail and *Google* stuff, surfing the net, and setting numbers on Dad's phone - I'll get my own the next time I'm out, My mind kept coming back to the jeans… *I wonder…*

Curiosity and vanity got the better of me, and I slipped them on, fully expecting them to not make it past my thighs. But, no: they were then round the waist! Yes – then shift the belly out of the way, and the button goes in nicely… pull the zip up, and Bob's your uncle! The euphoria I felt was pretty cool - I ran into the front room, dancing and laughing, to tell Dad, and he was laughing too.

He nipped down to Tesco and I slipped in to take a shower; not a good set-up - Dad's got loads of disabled stuff going on, and the bathroom is really tiny. Still, I got on with it and blanked the awkwardness out - at least I was now clean. Then I got back online and waited for Mum; I heard the door-buzzer go, but I stayed in my room.

Eventually, we met. Mum had a bag full of toiletries for me, and we sat in the room, chatting, as I got ready and finished off a bit of writing on the computer. Mum straightened the duvet and fluffed up the pillows; wow - mothers and their care, which comes so naturally. But it's so alien to me - so intrusive; *They're my pillows - leave them alone,* I thought, but I didn't say it. Dad headed off to get his feet done, and we were locked in. It's a strange concept: being locked in, in one's place of abode - Mum found it weird. For obvious reasons, I didn't bat an eyelid - perfectly natural behaviour, for me.

I put some aftershave on, and we got ready to head out into the world; Mum and Dad started trying to organize me. I flipped the lid, and said: 'Stop - stop trying to control me. This is really difficult – please, stop.' Then I stormed out of the room. I know they were only trying to help, but it's too much, seriously - way too much; now I was angry and I didn't want to be – and that just made me angrier. Now the hard part: we compartmentalized it and walked away.

'Where to?' said Mum.

We headed down by the Bible College, and I sat on the other side of the hedge from the motorway - the exact point I could see from the window of the prison van, as I passed in handcuffs, three years previously. Only, this time I was free.

This is what it is all about: remembering and regretting, but also knowing that it is only living in the moment that helps one say: 'no more "what-if"s'.

We drove round where I grew up as a child; I know it was hard for Mum, too, but we shared some nice memories: 'Do you remember when this hill was just a building site?' - stuff like that. Me and Mum will always be cool. We drove back up to Seymour Hill and looked at where I'm going to be living, then we headed to Lady Dixon's park.

It was great: the smells, the openness and the naturalness of life. We walked along, arm and arm, past the big house, which there were about sixty or seventy schoolchildren screaming and playing in front of. An elderly woman approached us and said: 'I'm really sorry: this is not a good day for a bit of peace and quiet.'

I said: 'Not at all - this is one of the most beautiful and natural sounds I've heard for a very long time.'

My Mum and the lady both paused and looked at me; I just beamed a big smile, and off we went. Mum was quiet for a while.

We went to Lisburn to eat and get passport photos for my provisional driving licence. I headed into *Happy Snaps*, where the girl took my pic, and Mum popped off into *Woodside's*.

The girl said: 'Would you like to see this before I process it?' She showed me the digital image on the back of the camera, and I grimaced.

'I know,' she said, 'it makes you look like a convict, doesn't it?' I wanted to tell her, but I couldn't.

Mum came in and looked at me, as I was trying to keep my composure; when we got out onto the street, I told Mum what the girl had said, and we cried with laughter, right in the middle of Bow Street, in Lisburn. People were looking at us funny, but I couldn't give a monkey's - this was the hardest I had laughed in years, and without the worry of it being used against me; another milestone.

We went to a restaurant, and I had a dirty-great big burger and chips - it was lovely. We had to wait ages for our food, but that was cool.

As soon as I was finished, I had to leave Mum sitting: I wanted to get my head round meeting probation. I left twenty quid, and Mum started to protest, but I held her hand and said: 'How nice do you think it will be for me, when I get back, to be able to tell people I bought my Mum lunch?'

I walked up Wallace Avenue, and was buzzed in to the probation office. The lady I was supposed to meet was off sick, and I met another guy - an American; very polite and kind. I was only there ten minutes – much easier than I thought, but such a waste of time and effort. Still, it was done now, and Mum arrived a couple of minutes later in the car.

I arranged to call in and see Brian (my solicitor) and Mike Moloney, in Belfast.

I wasn't sure of where I was going, so I popped into an office to ask directions - the woman behind the counter asked if I can wait for a minute. Embarrassed, I said: 'It's okay – you're busy. I'll head off.'

'No, no,' she said, 'I'll *Google* it now on the computer.' What a revelation - how helpful.

There was a wee cleaning lady, sitting with a cup of tea, and she said: 'I know - it's great, isn't it? Normally, I'd have been hanging out the window, pointing down the street - now you can just print out a map.' What got me the most was that these older people knew more about technology than I did.

I met Mike in his office and he gave me my prize-cheque from *Listowel*. We hugged, and it was great to be free of prison. He introduced me to his work colleague – Ruth, I think her name was… I can't remember.

The reason I can't remember is because my heart took a stutter! The woman was beautiful! My cup of tea completely - not just because she was beautiful, but because I felt she was nice also, with a lovely smile that made me feel warm inside. Ruth took our photo, then Mike came out to chat with Mum, who was patiently waiting in the car.

We didn't have time to see Brian, so we headed to *Starbucks* in Botanic, to meet with Shadd. We had another good discussion, and Mum joined in also. On reflection, I might have come across a bit terse, but it wasn't meant like that

- it was just that I needed to get things right in my head, between Shadd and I, and I didn't want to waste my time and his going over stuff we already knew - this is why I wanted Mum there.

It was good that she could see the obstacles in my way, although she did make a very significant point: I have a support network here; if I had stayed in England, I would have had none of this. This is a point I will always revisit - without them I can't do this. Simple.

Mum dropped me off at my aunt's house, around half-six, and I walked down the wee alley that I had trudged to and from primary school, with great memories, now really excited. We had an hour together - Dad, uncle, aunt and cousin. We had a good laugh, and I read out my poem - the first time I had ever read it out, yet it felt totally natural to me. Made them cringe a bit; I knew they were squirming, but it felt good for me. Then we ordered some Chinese, picked it up and headed home. In for 7.30pm - pain in the arse, but what are you going to do? Didn't eat much of that Chinese - it wasn't very nice, and pretty tasteless, actually.

My friend Davey came round, and we sat in my bedroom and nattered away. He gave me my belated Christmas present: a *Sweet Savage* CD, which I listened to later with my cordless headphones.

I had a chat with Dad, then went back online and answered some e-mails. I passed out around midnight, and woke again around five.

I lay on for about half an hour, as the bed is so comfortable, and I knew it would be another few weeks before I felt this comfortable again. Got up, had a banana and got online again. Started to type up some work, until I knew it was time to get ready to head back.

Looked at some photos in front of Dad - should have known better: got a bit tearful, but they were happy tears. He got upset because I was upset, and I roared at him: 'Don't you dare tell me how to feel - not now; not ever again!' I stormed out and came back about half an hour later.

I told him our relationship had to change, or it would be over; I've had enough of being told what to think, how to feel and having to be guarded all the time about my emotions. I pray that we will be okay, because if we're not, I will be gone from him forever - can't do it anymore; need my own life, but I'll do it, hopefully with him.

I don't think he realizes how close I am to walking away from him for good. The thought really hurts, but being hurt by him hurts more.

Having said that, I am lost without him, and he does more for me than anyone I know - he has borne the brunt of my anger and my frustration.

He just told me he was so pleased with me, because he knows, by my actions and my statements, that I have come such a long way.

Richard arrived and we three had a chat, then it was time to go.

It wasn't too bad - my brother and I had a good natter, and on the way back we stopped off at junction one for coffee, a bacon bap and apple tart.

I met an ex-officer in a garage, near the prison - he hugged me and shook my hand, and was so happy to see me outside of prison; it was actually one of the highlights of my time out.

I said goodbye to my brother, then a young lad came out of the NIACRO hut, and told me I had to go down to the other end - the gate wasn't working. I did so, and approached an officer, standing in the middle of the road.

'Michael Irwin: C7874 - returning from home-leave,' I said.

He didn't reply - just said into his radio: 'One home-leave approaching the pod.'

And, there we have it: back to being an object - a thing to be managed… a non-person.

27TH JUNE 2012

6.33pm

Completely knackered, journaling what happened on the outside. Will have to get some rest tonight and be finished chronicling my time out come tomorrow night, then I'm going to get stuck into my project.

Just filled in another home-leave form.

Maybe I'll wait. No, I won't - I'll just get on with it.

Time to head back down to Alpha; looking forward to chatting with Allison and Mrs. M.

10TH JULY 2012

5.51pm

Well, here I am, back in the land of make believe. Life has become a daily struggle - trying to keep my cool; my hatred and frustration, for many of the people who surround me, has overtaken my sense of self.

I've just finished a project about the self, and I now realize what an uphill struggle, and an assault on the senses, this whole prison experience has actually become. I think my main problem is that I've just been out - I was treated as a normal person for two days, by people who love me and people who don't know me; I had rational constructive conversation, without the constant parrying between myself and the men and women who wear the white shirts of authority, a few of whom are not very nice people.

They are not treating me badly, *per-se* - they simply exist to treat everyone badly. They should not be in this line of work - they do not want to be here, and they should just leave and let those who want to help get on with it. The constant waft of chewing-gum and alcohol is a big give-away; the purple heads are a sure sign that all is not well in these guys' worlds. I have eleven months to go – three-hundred and thirty-odd days: 48 weeks; if I'm lucky, tagging will be introduced in September, and I'll be out, like the proverbial rat up a drainpipe.

It's now time to get stuck into my next TMA .

11TH JULY 2012

5.32pm

The 11th night. Some of the lads have been planning a 12th day celebration fry-up for the past week - one of the Catholic prisoners has said he is offended by this, and now the same old shit starts all over again; loyalties are broken, and alliances and friendships are disbanded, because of a date in a fuckin' calendar. What a load of bollocks! The prods should be allowed their days and marches, just like any other culture and tradition - the Catholics should wind their necks in for just five minutes, and the powers that be should grow a pair of balls and say this is what's going to happen from now on: these marches, on both sides, will be allowed and respected by both sides - if you don't like it, fuck off and stay in your homes. I have seen so many different cultures, in so many different parts of the world - the other side still doesn't like it, but they let it be; it just is, and will always be.

FRIDAY 13TH JULY 2012

Home-leave has allowed me to experience interpersonal and inter-group sociality - reciprocal respect from people; I had forgotten what it is like. To come back in here, and be despised, is not only a daily battle of wits, but also of survival. I keep considering how disappointing this all is: I should be jumping from the rafters, but they won't let me - it hurts me, causes me pain and panic attacks, and fuels my depression, eroding my self-worth.

Yet, the most amazing thing is that I, Michael Irwin, have the tools and support of Listener training, my Listener colleagues, breathing exercises and hope for the future. If I have all of these coping mechanisms and strategies, and integrity to meet people half-way, yet I still feel like dying, then what chance for those who don't have what I have?

I hate this conflict; I want to be left alone.

There are posters all over this place which state: 'YOU ARE YOUR ENVIRONMENT'. The human animal's natural instinct to survive, and adapt in its own environment, is decided by how it negotiates conflict; this progression to Alpha is a hostile environment, which survives on misplaced authoritarian values, fear, intimidation and threat. Prison is an assault on rationality, and it creates frustration and duress.

I have to include officers in this, as they are here for longer than any of us - we will get out, whereas they are here for life. Too many prison officers die because of stress-related illnesses involved with maintaining the status quo that the system so readily yearns - alcohol abuse, and stomach/bowel cancers are some of the things we share as a population. I see way too many purple heads in this place; sometimes I think: *This guy is going to keel over, right now, right here in front of me.* Will I then be charged with murder?

What a horrible way to live, don't you think? I'll have only served six years, and it near got me on a couple of occasions.

14TH JULY 2012

6.00am

Well, I survived the 13th - this means that something will happen today or tomorrow. I can't say I'm pleased - I'm just existing at the moment; if I didn't have my books to take my mind off things, I'd be in trouble.

A thought has just dawned on me - maybe this is something to consider here in my research:

Smiling.

A natural act, yet one designed to cause effrontery in a closed institution (a closed institution where it is legal and lawful in the eyes of the law, to have *smiling* considered an *unnatural* act)!

I recall a story a prison officer told me: he worked with a charity in Uganda, helping kids, building schools… stuff like that. One of the children asked him what he did for a living, an eight- or ten-year old girl, full of innocence. When he told the girl he was a prison officer, her face scrunched up and her bottom lip pouted; she frowned, and said: 'But you are such a nice man - why do you beat people?'

So, what of stereotypes, group process and assumptions? Forty years on from Zimbardo, nothing has changed or been learnt from his experiment; well, I think there has been much learnt, but the problem is nobody wants to do anything about it. Crime is like war: an industry that thrives on social and economic downturns and conflict; the system constantly creates the system, then contradicts itself, for the sole purpose of creating that conflict – conflict that feeds off of moral social dilemmas, which are fuelled by a media supported and influenced by the system. It feeds the moral panic that buys the papers, which reach the homes of the electorate, who are, in turn, outraged at the crime which the system has itself created.

I did enjoy writing this little piece.

If the Great British union is expunged, economies will be stabilized and rebuilt - there will be no more of this infuriating institutional practice, whereby every British government since 1948 has followed the same lacklustre scenario: any advance made by the outgoing administration is automatically pronounced a disaster, and removed at the earliest opportunity, regardless of cost, practicality or logic. Without the benefit of a constitution, politicians bow and scrape to party disciplines steeped in nostalgia of what once was, often voting without understanding what they are voting for - following pointless manifestos which become obsolete, depending on current events. The prime-minister's use of almost unlimited power, alongside a plethora of home secretaries, has collectively diminished the concept of responsibility, to the point where government is no longer recognizable by the people it serves.

THOUGHTS AND CONTRIBUTION FOR MIKE MOLONEY, PRISON ARTS FOUNDATION:

> ''The devil smiles and laughs at me – says:
> *"You'll be back, just wait and see –*
> *you know I've heard all this before".*
> And I say: *"You can keep your high life and the hills,*
> *Your cocaine lies and whisky thrills -*
> *I don't need you anymore;*
> *This is not for me, this is not for me, this life is not for me...*
> *Anymore".'*
> *By Slash and Myles Kennedy;*
> *from the song* 'Not for Me', *off the album* 'Apocalyptic Love'.

'I have read Slash's autobiography, and I can relate to the addictions he had in his life. When this is combined with the 'Serenity Prayer' ('God grant me the serenity to accept the things I cannot change, courage to change the things I can, and the wisdom to know the difference'), *it makes for a good mantra in my head.*

'This is my fourth day of temporary freedom in five years and one month, and again I find myself in a room full of people who might be interested in what I have to say - a totally mind-blowing concept.

'I've recently completed my first ever research project: 'The Mature Student' - *a phenomenological approach to discovering "self" via education, and none of my present self-esteem would have been possible without the direct and indirect support of Mr. Yeates, Allison McCaughan, Mrs. M, the Education department at Magilligan, and not forgetting Mike Moloney. Mike's first recognition of me was a mouthed "well done", after a very nervous reading in Magilligan gym, in 2010.*

Oh, how I have grown since then.

'I have a satellite image of Cape Town, my old home, on my wall, in my suite at Magilligan. There's a little blip in Table Bay called Robben Island - I've been there a few times; indeed, my first ever experience of prison was having my photograph taken in Madiba*'s (Nelson Mandela) old cell. Maybe I should have paid a bit more attention at the time.*

'I sat in the dust, in the aptly named "chalk pit", and ran my fingers down the scrapes and tracks in the limestone walls used to pave the highways and roads of South Africa. As I knelt, I traced my name in the sand by my right knee; a gust of wind blew it away a few seconds later, my mark immediately obliterated. I immediately wondered how the hell these men could have acquired law degrees and education from a chalk pit on Robben Island, whilst armed guards, quite literally, hovered above their heads. This memory, combined with my recent thematic analysis of taped interviews by two tutors, and my own lived experience, has led me to the discovery of an overwhelming human desire to overcome adversity, through knowledge and education. This desire becomes part of the "self", and, eventually, a driving force behind one's very existence. I have always maintained that the Education department in each prison I have visited has been my sanctuary, my safe space - nowhere to hide, nowhere to run; just me and my pen and paper (or computer screen).

'My desire is that everyone should hear this, or at least be aware of it and, hopefully, share in it. I was barred from one prison's Education department, one out of six ain't bad; after all, not everyone has the same view of how education and knowledge is delivered.

'My contribution is simple: use *me and others like me. By constantly revisiting my own narrative, my cognitive "automatic processing" has removed so much negativity and fear, to be replaced with hope and awareness. You only have to look at* "The Clink" *at H.M.P. High Down, and Gordon Ramsay's* "Bad Boy Bakery"*, at H.M.P. Brixton, to see what can be achieved. This is only achievable by using us*

- the reformed, the converted, and the newly discovered self-believers.

'Without forward-thinking organizations such as the Prison Arts Foundation, *art, music, literature, education and hope will never reach these who need it most. Hope reduces crime and victims of crime, and creates purpose for a better future.*

'The music of Mr. Hudson and Mr. Kennedy inspires me to live - I get it: their message is clear: live and be yourself. Hope saves lives - we need to educate people that I, and others like me, are part of the solution, and not the perceived threat that so many significant others would have you believe.

'Thank you for listening.'

Dear Mr. Kennedy and Mr. Hudson

My name is Michael Irwin - C7874, forty-five years old. I currently reside at H.M.P. Magilligan, Northern Ireland - I have served five years and one month in prison, and will be free in eleven months. I had a long battle with coke and booze before my drug-trafficking conviction.

I liked G'n'R as a teenager; however, your collaboration on *'Back to Cali'* and *'Starlight'* blew me away - I then purchased *'Blackbird'* and *'AB III'*, then, two weeks ago, *'Apocalyptic Love'*. Your music and artistry transcends borders, cultures and diversity, and is something that moves me to tears of pure emotion every day. What you need to know is that you must never, *ever* stop what you are doing. Myles, your lyrics and vocals create hope - hope saves lives; *you* save lives. Slash, your music and guitar just make me crumble and scream with pleasure; it takes me to a place which is better than any drug I have ever taken. I hope you don't mind, but I have taken your lyric from *'Not For Me'* (enclosed) to emphasize how hope through art, music, literature and education can inspire the most desolate of souls.

I'm going to hook up with some old friends from *Sweet Savage* and *Thin Lizzy* at a concert in Belfast, on the 18th August 2012. I'm still in prison, but I get out a couple of days a month. I want to send a message of how cool it is for me to receive a bigger buzz from the art you provide now, in sobriety, than any drug and alcohol-fuelled past experience. The beauty of all this, of course, is that I will remember it clearly.

Thank you for hope. You might be interested in some of my award-winning poetry and life prose. I lived life a bit like a 'rock star' for ten years, in Cape Town and London, but it nearly killed me. Prison saved my life.

But you guys save my soul, every fuckin' day!

I arrived back on the wing at 18.55 - I always get back for 19.00.

The guy who'd tried to stop me going to Queens, said: 'What - you get fuckin' lost or something?'

I never replied, just said: 'B44, please,' handing him my card, in exchange for my key, as I tried to get away from him.

'Well?' he said.

I said: ''Well' what? I always get back by seven.'

He replied: 'No need to get fuckin' nasty - I was only askin'; all the others got back around ten minutes ago.' Now there is an issue: now he's mad; I get my key and flee.

This man didn't know where I was, and had no interest in finding out – he just knew the others were at a Christian fellowship meeting, and I wasn't. Why does this man assume that the manner in which he spoke to me will be seen by me to be anything other than confrontational?

SATURDAY 21ST JULY 2012

6.05am

Been up for a couple of hours now, reading - sorting my head out for Monday's one day release. Not as nervous as the last time, nor excited, for that matter; last time was massive - this time is diminished, because of the bureaucracy I have to wade through to actually get there.

22ND JULY 2012

6.55am

'Magnanimous': generous or forgiving towards a rival or enemy - origin in Latin *'magnus'*: *'great and animus soul'*. I never really understood its exact meaning. The line in *The Shawshank Redemption*: 'the prick actually managed to sound magnanimous' makes more sense now than ever before.

I stood in the dinner queue and watched these uniformed men go about their business - it turned my stomach. This is wrong - all wrong; the more I observe, the sicker I feel.

On a more positive note, I'm out in the morning, and then for good in eleven months - I can talk to people who will treat me and talk to me like a man, and a fellow member of the human race. Looking forward to that, but not the shit I have to go through to get it. It'll be nice to be at home again for a night, and then out again next week.

God, if I didn't have my music… didn't have my books… what life would I have? I can't say the thought of drugs or booze ever leaves me, but what has left me is the *desire*, the want, the need to take them - I know I'll only be sick afterwards, and I never want to be sick again. So, they have become obsolete - unconsidered.

Think I'll read for half an hour - Lemmy is winding me up; *'Dr. Dr. Alibi'*.

I wonder what further delights today will bring.

I've just thought of something: is this re-integration process designed to be such a monumental upheaval, that when a prisoner finally leaves it he is so traumatized by it, he will never question or mention it again?

Eleven months to go, five months to Christmas and two weeks of freedom.

Just remembered: no fruit, no coffee, no phone credit and no tuck-shop.

I put my name down for the gym list as 'C7874', as to write anything else will be considered a threat - a direct challenge to the authority of the *'A-team'*. BM also got a bit of verbal for trying to put his name down twice for Thursday, and him on remedial gym. He is one of these guys who laughs everything off, but deep down he's fuckin' livid. Why don't these big, tough guys stand up for themselves and say something? Maybe they are not so tough after all?

PRISON ARTS FOUNDATION RESETTLEMENT DAY

23RD JULY 2012

6.40am

Didn't sleep well - tossed and turned all night, though not because I'm excited about going to a seminar. I *am* excited, don't get me wrong, but it has been overshadowed by the enormity of this place - the negativity and constant watching of my every move is sapping my strength. Mind you, it was a hundred times worse at Rye Hill, and I'd only just been sentenced – then, as now, I got a rough ride, but at least this time I only have a few months to go.

It's another damp and cloudy morning - very sticky. There's sunshine on the way, but it won't reach here until Wednesday.

I'm not frightened about getting out this time - not nervous, hyped, or all over the shop; I did take my beta-blocker though, so this may be helping: this time I cannot wait to breathe. This time I'm going to let it all happen - let it wash all over me.

My neighbour is snoring away like a walrus, God bless him - I can't wear my plugs, though, in case they call for me. Going to go and run the iron over my jeans.

7.15am

That's me ready to rumble; getting excited now.

Eating an apple, but can't stop thinking about the unclean hands that handed it to me; I've rubbed this apple so hard, the skin has fallen off. Everything about this place gets me now.

Still pissing like a fountain - same last night; looks like I'll have to go. Have I reached the age where bits start falling off?

I keep thinking of the image of the guy leaving Brixton, with two clear, transparent plastic bags, with H.M.P. stamped on the sides, walking alongside his missus, pushing a pram down Jebb Avenue. Around the time of my conviction I remember thinking: *If I get set free, will I have to return to Northern Ireland with a big H.M.P. bag?* As it turns out, I did return, only with *ten* big H.M.P. bags; didn't half piss them off at Maghaberry! Maybe that day has followed me through the system in here - maybe that's why I've got the label *'whinger'*.

10.10am

Interview with governor, then out of jail. Asked if I could get a lift off a woman from probation, who was giving another guy a lift to Belfast; 'No chance,' was the reply.

10.45am

In a taxi with Liam - £60 to Belfast (£30 apiece - good stuff). It's wet and windy, and we're chatting away with the taxi driver. He's pretty cool; he's a bit guarded at first, but when we talk about our education, and the stuff we've achieved in prison, he really lightens up, and says: 'Well done, lads: it's great that you've used your time for some good.'

Big Ray was mad as hell at the gate. Again, we sat at the prison gate for ages, as they made three trips to the gate.

Going to sit back and enjoy the drive, not dwell on the bollocks of prison.

24TH JULY 2012
10.20am

Sitting on the train, eating a chocolate brownie.

Just had a fry-up, and popped into the ombudsman's office - the fry-up was mad: no sauce and no vinegar -just salt; forgot to put pepper on it - still pepperless.

What a crazy twenty-four hours - packed to capacity: *Yin-and-Yang*, *Yang-*

and-Yin, and *Yin-and-Yang* again, though nowhere near as emotional as the last time. Walking through Belfast with Mr. Yeates was an experience I'll always remember - I think he enjoyed it too.

The P.A.F. day was great: met John Crossan from Maghaberry, Austin (the governor of Maghaberry) and Nuala McKeever (beautiful girl; teaches drama, I believe). Nuala gave me a hug and a kiss on the cheek – wow! Now, that really was something!

This train is deserted - pretty cool.

Been online since 5.00am: emailed Fin and signed up to 'Facebook' - strange concept.

The police kindly called at the house at 8.30 last night, to breathalyze me in front of my father.

10.45am

Just passing the big blue fish, on the way out of Belfast, Samson and Goliath over to my right.

Thinking of Fin; pretty cool – nice memories. God, I hate the idea of going to live with these people again! Still, one more week and I'll be out again.

24TH JULY 2012

2.56pm

Hey, dudes! Back in the land of the living.

At home in Belfast, I spent the morning online, then got back here around 1.30pm, and headed straight up to Education, where I am now (to *no* broadband connection – *Yin-and-Yang*). Think I'll go and have wee lie down.

I had a nice chat with Al on the way in, and he told me that he delivered my letter to Mr. H Moore, who said he was 'very moved', and added: 'after all the crap I gave him'. My integrity and humanity is intact, despite what these men are trying to do to me.

I still can't get over Nuala's hug and peck on the cheek - she stood so close to me, it got my blood boiling. Also saw Fin's picture on 'Facebook' and signed up, as it was the only way to get in touch with her.

Very sleepy now. All the Foyleview guys were on their way back this morning, and everyone is tired. All in all, it was a good day out, and I spent some quality time in the company of the human race - the human animal, without the frown; that's what prison is to me now: a big bloomin' frown.

25TH JULY 2012

5.45am

Got the headphones on, and can't stop smiling - it's such a relief to be smiling again. I went to sleep at 9.15pm, and woke at 5.15am - no midnight pee, nothing; feel friggin' great.

Can't get a particular lady out of my head - hope my poem doesn't offend.

'THE ART OF HOPE' BY MICHAEL IRWIN

H.M.P. MAGILLIGAN

JULY 2012

Even her walk - there was something about her walk;
The way she carried herself - head tilted ever so slightly to the left,
A hint of shyness... vulnerability in that tilt. Or is it a lilt?
Girlie, but composed - hinting at innocence,
But also exuding confidence.

I caught myself staring, but not at the cliché of physical beauty -
More the cliché of mmm*; of ponder, I wonder.*
Then I look at the floor; Nah - don't be silly;
You've been in jail too long - too many years of paranoia,
Of seeing things that aren't there: figments of...

Lost concentration again... the lines of her neck...
I could imagine the softness;
The burning scent of a beautiful woman
Creates a roar in the core of man.

The intensity of her concentration, when I spoke;
The mischief in her eyes - the mischief in her smile:
Impish, yet provocative... only a trace, but there all the same.
I look away, momentarily trapped,
My brain trying to hold on to my words,
My stomach doing back-flips.

I've got the attention of the whole room;
Get drawn from the governor of Maghaberry, to this mischief - no

contest.

I listened - after all, that's what I do.

When this woman spoke she was offended -

I like offended; I like the cut of her jib.

I'll forget fear and try not to offend.

I spoke and said: "Hi" – her and her smile did not say: "Goodbye".

So much to contend with - me being me, she being she,

A potent, yet unnamed cocktail, of that I'm certain,

Then a hug and a kiss on the cheek,

Turned me to jelly... made my knees go...

Fight or flight? I choose flight,

But only temporarily; am I being coy?

Is it ploy? Is it hell? After five years it's only naturelle.

Dear God, Allah, Buddha... Jose Mourinho -

Whoever, I pray - don't let this woman go away!

Maybe I, too, pray for joy and pleasure - the reality of naturalness,

The simple complexity of human interaction,

Purpose and hope - what more can a body ask for?

I simply say: "WOW!"

Wow, for a multitude of emotions and feelings,

Born of a lilt and a neck.

I am smiling because I feel normal, and this excites me - these days out are allowing me to be normal again; I've been so *un*-normal for so long, not only in prison, but long before. I can't truthfully say that my previous life was a waste, or that I didn't enjoy what I was doing, but I couldn't be me today, if I hadn't done what I'd done before. I would have been nervous before, but not now.

Talking with Davey, his wife and his Mum, was so natural and so relaxing. I am starting to realize that this *me* - this current self - is pretty cool; I can see it in the faces of others. I've known these guys for a very long time, and they look happy.

I'm so proud of my friends, Davey and Ruth: they have three beautiful, well-spoken and intelligent children - what a beautiful legacy. All I've ever seen has been negative, but I now get this parenthood thing; I know it's hard work, but the peace and laughter in their house is infectious - it has certainly worked its magic on me.

Seeing the group of Foyleview prisoners at Great Victoria Street made it easier for me to come back; a shared camaraderie - we were all tired, yawning and smiling. I only said hello to them, as I was busy doing my own thing, as usual - I wanted to sit on my own and catch up with my thoughts and memories, but it was good to know that they were on the same train; I know most of these men, and, as we waited for the van driver to turn up at Coleraine, it made it easier. Definitely something to be considered in this process: the van wasn't there, and we patiently waited; when the officer turned up, the whole dynamic changed immediately: as a group of individuals, we instantly became a group under the control of an individual. The officer was fine, but the *system* oozes out of these men and women - they are superior in their beliefs and attitudes, when associating with us.

But, the difference now is that *we* have just experienced normality. *These* men spend more of their time with abnormality than *we* do, so, in that respect, how can they be expected to act and behave normally? One sees the odd glimpse of normality - the guy stopped at the garage for Lotto tickets, drove too fast, etc... 'normal' human behaviour – but, deep down, he wants shot of this responsibility, so that he can go and do something else - he said it himself.

I must tell the staff to tell I.P.C. to hold back some cash for my tuck-shop and fruit order. We have no responsibility in prison, but when things don't quite work out, it's always the prisoner's responsibility.

I did this on Wednesday or Thursday, and officer J even wrote it in the diary. I got my tuck-shop form on Friday afternoon, and when I got back from work I found £0.00 in my account - they haven't done it! I can't be bothered to tell anyone: it'll only be seen as personal criticism - a threat and attack on someone who hasn't done their job properly; ultimately, *I* will be the trouble-maker for pointing out that someone hasn't done their job properly. 'These things happen', 'Do you know how many requests I have to deal with?', 'Can't get it right all the time' and 'The computer says no' are all just some of the usual excuses for a constant set of balls-ups. Singly, they are not a problem, but when they start to combine with other minor irritants, a small problem becomes a big problem - this is not unique to Norn Iron, so why do they get so angry?

Its 7.00am: time for a bit of study. Still not allowed to use the study-room here, despite talking to Mrs. M on Tuesday - maybe they have bigger fish to fry. I think O.U. funding might have to stop, as the NIPS cannot supply the supervision and the technology to maintain the higher levels of study required; this does not fit in with the ethos of 'work' in prisons.

10.15am

Decided to clean and mop my floor, as there is nothing for me to do; tried to read, but there's too much noise - *AC/DC* is blasting from the mini-gym.

Ass has been really funny - the lads tell me there has been a remarkable shift in his attitude over the past few days.

I've been reliably informed that at Mr. H's funeral, it was mentioned that a prisoner had written to him – evidently this moved and touched Mr. H before he died, and his family also.

Mr. H: *R.I.P.*

You see how often I am starting to say this: 'R.I.P.'?

10.30am

I leave my door wedged open by the end of the bed, and head out into the yard for five minutes, whilst the floor dries.

Officer A calls me into the office: 'I will only give you a verbal warning this time - I know you are on an 'adverse'; I would normally give you an 'adverse', so I'm being lenient.'

A security S.O., hovering about, adds: 'He would, you know.' They think it's funny. Officer A starts to tell me about my 'contract'.

I say: 'I apologize: I did not purposely leave my door open to break the rules. Thank you for being so considerate, but many other prisoners do the same and do not seem to have an issue when waiting for their floors to dry.'

'I'll deal with them, too, if I see them.'

This is them demonstrating their lenience; I think I'll stay in my cell and watch the golf for the rest of the day - much safer.

1ST AUGUST 2012

Home-leave was great - went out on Monday. So glad Davey was able to pick me up. Can hardly keep my wee eyes open, but will have to wait for another hour until I can get to sleep. Still, home-leave is getting easier.

Had another blow-out with my Dad, but it was okay, because it cleared the air. He is proud of me, but he needs to treat me with kid gloves at the minute. He apologized, but it won't need to happen too much more often... I need to get my own place sorted out.

Spoke to so many old friends via 'Facebook' and e-mail - it was a real revelation.

I'm so fuckin' tired, I can't keep my eyes open. Going to go back to the wing; totally wrecked.

2ND AUGUST 2012

Our broadband is still down - two weeks now; the I.T.C. department, which is leaderless, forgot to pay the bill. It irks me, somewhat; that judge - Treacy - said the NIPS were in the best position to run the NIPS. Unfortunately, they are not.

Got my project results back: managed 73% - a lot more than expected. This is good news, so all I have to do now is get another TMA under my belt and pass the exam; need to forget about prison reform and work on my studies. Reckon they are going to stop prisoners from learning criminology and law soon: too many jailhouse lawyers, as it is.

Three years after the start of all this study adventure, I'm back to pen and paper, in cell, at the weekends - what progress?

3RD AUGUST 2012

7.05pm

Come back from the Christian Fellowship do with Gavin Peacock, and am ordered straight into the office, where S.O. and a P.O. are present - another officer comes in and closes the door behind him. No intimidation here, then? I'm asked to take a seat.

P.O. says: 'You have been making complaints to the Samaritans.'

I don't know if this is a question or a statement, so I just look at him, waiting for the next instalment.

Again: 'You have been making complaints to the Samaritans.'

I respond this time, and say: 'I had a discussion with the Samaritans about the Listeners, an issue that has now been resolved.'

'So, you are not making complaints, then?'

'No.'

'Fine - you can go.'

If I'd have said one word they didn't like, I'd have been on a SPAR - I'm 100% sure of it. At the minute I'm shaking like a leaf, but don't really know why I'm frightened - maybe I'm losing my marbles.

Perhaps these guys see me doing well, making a splash, and are determined to knock the stuffing out of me, because they can. Every transaction with belligerent staff makes me squirm, makes me boil, but also makes me stronger.

5TH AUGUST 2012

9.10am

'Hi Allison.

'I'm delighted to get this news - please pass on my warmest and hearty congratulations to Michael.

'Michael is an inspiration to prisoners everywhere - he shows that while the body is imprisoned, the life of the mind can be cultivated, so it soars beyond the walls, and, in doing so, goes beyond, also, the boundaries of "the man in the street", who doesn't know about the prison his mind may live in.

'I wish him all success.'

This was sent to me by one of my O.U. tutors, upon hearing the news that I had attended my first seminar at Queens University.

My current essay is: *'Social policies aimed at reducing prejudice and intergroup conflict would do well to take account of psychological research in this area'* - discuss this statement, making reference to relevant research in your answer!

This essay will discuss the impact of social policies aimed at reducing prejudice and intergroup conflict, by exploring the research of Zimbardo, Haslem and Reicher. These prison studies illuminate *'Social Identity Theory'* (SIT), the *'Contact Hypothesis'*, and how their aim was to explore identities formed between and by groups, and how they influenced and changed people's behaviour. Churchill stated that if we want to take a measure of society, we only have to look at our prisons; Dostoyevsky stated that prison mirrors society.

'CONTACT HYPOTHESIS'

P.146. Dixon states: *'Social psychology research can be evaluated in terms of its ability to inform social policies that promote positive change'*. Developing this theme, section 5 assesses the most influential framework for understanding how to reduce conflict, namely: the *'contact hypothesis'*. Adono's *'authoritarian personality'*, which depicted *'a type of person whose conscious respect for moral convention masks a repressed resentment towards all forms of traditional authority'* also argued that *'this unconscious anger tends to become irrationally displaced onto scapegoat groups, being expressed as a generalized hatred of anyone or anything different'*. Is this not similar to the idea of *'transference'* used by Freud in the psychoanalytic field?

Dogmatic by nature, authoritarians become the role - become the identity; therefore, as Rokeach (1960 - p.147) correctly points out: *'the dogmatic personality's similarly rooted prejudice is abnormal personality development'* and *'the problem of prejudice is construed as closely related to the problem of cognitive rigidity'*. I go back to my point about *'persecution complex'*: the complex would not have arisen, nor would the concept have arisen, if it were not for what Rokeach observes: *'Dogmatists suffer from deep-seated infallibility of thought and attitude: they tend to see the world in terms of black and white, good and bad, and they are unable to tolerate ambiguities, loose ends or uncertainties. Therefore, social psychological input, via research aimed at reducing prejudice and conflict, is, in itself, seen as a threat by the very authority it wishes to assist, and unless social psychological research is invited by the in-group of authority/policy-maker, then its point of view will not be welcomed, as it does not belong to the group.'*

There is an increasing recognition within the world of criminology that the phenomenological perspective of criminals, who have gone on to achieve Doctorates in this field, and who have lived in the institution of prison and experienced the justice system, are becoming an increasingly valued source of psychological research when considering the conflict and prejudice between criminal and justice system. When these criminologists' identities change from criminal to academic, they are able to relate to how the social policies already put in place by government have influenced and shaped their own identities, and are further able to explore how the rigidity of social policy creates the very problems it is attempting to resolve. Conflict and prejudice is unavoidable, in an increasingly diverse and accessible world - however, by taking a step back and learning about the culture of another, one can accept and influence the less knowledgeable and easily led of a society. A frightening development, for me, was the recent image of a Polish flag being burnt on the protestant bonfire, during the eleventh night celebrations in Belfast - the idea or notion of 'peace' in Northern Ireland, between Protestant and Catholic, has led to a void of love and hate: everyone needs someone or something to love, and therefore something to hate, or something to believe in; what is different, therefore, is to be feared - it is *wrong*. Protestant and Catholic are no longer the minorities, or socially repressed: they are united in a desire for peace - therefore, the ethnic minorities, such as eastern Europeans, Romanians and Polish, now fill the void of '*minority*'; something new, something adverse - something to be hated.

6TH AUGUST 2012

Oh, to be free of the smell of shit! The Alpha block really is spotlessly clean - apart from the holes in the roof - but the smell: YUK!

So, another Monday, another fresh start to the week, and another fresh set of dramas, no doubt. The governors are back, or, at least, are *meant* to be back.

I'm out of options of where to go in this place - Foyleview is looking good, but *not* looking good: the jungle-drums claim that ten men were sent back this side of the wall on Friday, for having some part in the sexual assault of a prisoner; allegedly ketamine was used, and the guy woke up with a sore clanger, saying he'd been assaulted. On the Wednesday beforehand, another dozen or so guys had been removed for *'partying'*.

They can remove all the guys they like, but, as long as there is no form of monitoring of nocturnal activities, noise and smuggling, then there will continue to be a problem. It's the same on here: a lot of the lads are at it, but they keep it discreet. Recently, I had to hold my breath when going to the loo - not for the smell of shit, which I mentioned earlier, but for the aromatic smell of some *really good* shit, emphasized by the giggling coming from a few rooms.

7TH AUGUST 2012

Just been told that I've failed my DSE212 level-2 exams by seven marks: 38%. Fuckin' crap, but what are you going to do? My head is swimming, my stomach is in knots and the self-doubt I'd managed to get rid of has come back ten-fold! This is another time when I have to dig extremely deep; this self-doubt will manifest itself into depression - I fuckin' know it.

This is truly heart-breaking - I keep thinking about my brother, and him saying all of this is way over my head. Apparently the re-sit is in October - the same time as my level-3 psychology DD307. I keep telling them I need all the time I can get - when I was revising I could not remember what I'd written half an hour after I'd written it; five minutes was enough actually; I know I was overlapping two when I did the exam. Or was I? Can't even remember at the minute.

I know what the problem is: these fuckin' anti-depressants. Just been chatting with Allison, and I've decided to throw my tablets out. Time to forget about home-leaves - about life and everything, and get stuck back into both psychology modules; need to get a fuckin' grip and sort it out.

My head is so fuckin' cloudy. What in the name of Christ am I doing this for?

Ho-hum - what a palaver!

17TH AUGUST 2012

8.19am

Just had a chat with S.O. BE, and it looks like I might be going to Foyleview in a couple of months, once I ride out my 'adverse'. It matters less to me as the days go by, but, if I'm honest, I'm still livid that these people can do as they please. Somebody recently commented: 'Well, you do have a tendency to put your foot down when you don't get your own way'. There may be some truth in this, but does it justify getting an 'adverse' for inappropriate behaviour? This, of course, brings us back to the age-old adage of 'one must never question authority'.

Still, I need to be careful. And, as I'm being honest, I think it's appropriate for me to let go, and concentrate on getting home in a good state of mind, rather than as an angry, bitter and twisted cynic. The sun is out, I've got my words in an academic report, and I've also been mentioned in *'Dispatches'* - not bad for my first day of semi-freedom.

31ST AUGUST 2012

9.26am

Lost the last ten days of this diary, as the disk packed up! Technology is not a concept that fits well with the ethos of prison, especially when you have D.U.P. peers challenging the legitimacy of giving prisoners the opportunity to reduce their deviant ways.

Wrote to my wee sister this morning - it was good to talk to her; I'll post her letter and birthday card to my Mum on Monday. It's nice to remember her beating heart on my chest, as a baby: nice memories - nice thoughts.

Jack got out today - left this morning. I'll hook up with him for coffee in a couple of weeks - *four* to be exact; so, for Jack it was not goodbye - more *adios*. It gladdens me to see his smile. The big fella will be next, then me – slowly, but surely, I'm getting there.

My days out are not even confirmed yet - they always wait until the last moment; is this an administration thing or a psychological thing? If it is just the way it is, then it must truly be psychological. You need to be told immediately if your request has been granted - not made to wait three weeks to find out of it is confirmed.

I'm not as nervous about getting out now - it's cool… ish; I was frightened before, but am becoming less so. It's still daunting and new, but it's also good to be free for a while - to be free of the greyness, the unpleasantness and the melancholy. It's not that I'm daydreaming - more to do with *hope*; everything revolves around hope and the lack of it in these places.

The sound of *learning*: listening to Allison quietly teaching primary-3 English to grown men… peace and sanctuary in education, and the tapping of rain. I decide to go and do a bit of work.

Shadd sent me in a book to do a review for Queens, but I'm not allowed the book by reception, as it's a hardback; I'm told I must cut the back off of it - something which is *against my religion*, as far as the written word is concerned. Defacing a book is like destroying art… well, not *'like'* - it *is*!

3RD SEPTEMBER 2012

9.42am

What you resist will persist - I must accept all that it is contrary to my own moral values. Other people are not the same as me, and as long as I foolishly believe that by showing respect to my fellow man – in here – there will be a reciprocal morality, I will struggle. Prison is not the place to go searching for morality - it is there in a few, but alas, not all. How can I rationalize with an alcoholic, who is drunk? I can't - never been able to. This place is full of selfishness, and I keep forgetting that just because my own values are in a better place, I shouldn't assume that others will follow suit.

I had a row with my neighbour. I did as he asked: banged the wall each time I heard his TV - I banged it five times yesterday, three times the day before and four times the day before that; this has been going on for weeks. I didn't want to keep banging the wall, as this can be misconstrued as threatening behaviour and bullying. My neighbour started shouting at me last night, saying the TV is not loud, so I went into his cell and said I would put a stop to it - I don't see why I should have to ask him several times a day to turn his TV down.

I went to sleep last night predicting that I would be in the office at some stage of the morning to defend myself, but the officers (fair play to them) sorted it out: they told us we would *both* be removed from Alpha if it wasn't sorted out. So, we both say it is sorted out, and that will be the end of it. Sorted out? Of course it is.

The problem with progression through the system is that we end up living in caravans with paper-thin walls.

The whole issue could be avoided if everyone was allowed headphones. Does it cost too much? I would personally buy everyone headphones, in an effort to keep the peace. It all boils down to money and accommodation, so temporary solutions in prison become permanent. Foyleview is worse, but hey, I'll give it a go; I've seen loads of guys come back from there because they can't handle it.

I gave my neighbour the lend of a set of headphones, but when he told everyone, a few gave him a bit of stick; he can't take the stick, so he threw them back in my face and called me 'litigious'; I decided to look it up:

litigious (adj.): *fond of disputes*, from L. *litigiosus: 'contentious, quarrelsome'*: from *litigium: 'dispute, strife'*; related to *litigare* (see *litigation*), meaning: *'fond of engaging in lawsuits'*; from 1620s - earlier in English than *litigate* or *litigation* (q.v.).

Received another letter from Shadd confirming dates, as there was bit of a mix-up. The guy is flat out - I don't know how he does it! Will ease up on the letter-writing and explain all when I get a chance to chat with him on the out.

Can't get my head on straight, yet - this whole endeavour/survival is becoming a daily ordeal; God, I need to be free of this place - it is a constant assault on the senses. The ability to dig deep is becoming intolerable - how many spades must I have gone through? I feel like using one of those spades to dig a few holes, like in the movie *'Goodfellas'* (*'Where d'you put the spades? Do you think I've never dug a hole before?'*).

Wrote a letter and birthday card to my wee sis - it's a shame how such a feeling of joy and happiness can be overwhelmed by the pettiness of prison life.

Looks like the I.T. guy has downloaded the driving-test theory DVD - think I'll spend a bit of time on that.

2.30pm

I think someone has been in my medical cupboard: I think there is stuff missing; I think my anti-depressants have gone, but I'm frightened to report it, as they will give me an 'adverse' for drug-dealing. I'll just have to keep my mouth shut, ride it out and wait for a couple of weeks until I've 'used' the tablets up - tablets that are not in my possession. I went to the nurse the other day, but, for the life of me, I cannot remember what I signed for. Mind you, I have lost all track of time and place - my only focus is on getting out.

Mr. Yeates is concerned about my exams, and I'm concerned about my exams; and there will be no point in any of it if I lose the plot and attack someone.

13TH SEPTEMBER 2012

Stayed with Mum on home-leave and wrote a wee letter when I got back:

Greetings Mutti,

Back in the land of the living.
No problems – I'm actually beaming like a Cheshire cat! Mum, I was full of dread this morning, but as I sat in the café at Gt. Victoria Street, with sausages and eggs and beans and tomatoes and... well, you get the idea, all of my woes seemed to disappear – it lifted off of me and felt physical. You did that! Being with you and feeling your warmth and your motherliness is something that now fills me with pleasure.

The trains were an absolute doddle, so there is no problem me getting a train to Bangor in the future; maybe the next time you'll be able to 'fit into' that coat, and we can nip down from the station and purchase it.

I enjoyed the silence in the car on the way back and also the silence of this morning, lying in your soft bed. The thought that my head lay where yours rests is also pretty cool. I left a couple of kisses on the pillow, so I hope you feel them.

Please tell my sis and niece it was great to see them again. If sis emails me or SMS's me her details, I can maybe get an hour away next time, or the time after that. My niece looks like a real button - bright, polite and intelligent - and I watched them interact, whilst pretending to be working on the laptop. Couldn't concentrate – it made me burst with pride; I'm so pleased for them both. They will always have each other and that is a great comfort. I know you know what I mean.

I thanked Ken and gave him a hug (twice!). I'm not pussyfooting about how I feel anymore. I have very few people in my life, and in one way or the other they/you have all helped me get to where I am today, even if it is only by supporting each other – supporting me. Anyway, I'm glad that he is there and he took the time to give us time, and move out of his own home. It was nice being a family, sitting round the table - one dying, one cooking, one young, one old and one glutton (a *content* glutton, though – taking it all in, sucking it up, and saving it for times like now, when I can share it what it was that, for me, was really going on: normal life for you, but not for me - could get used to it).

Thank you. Thank you for being my Mum, thank you for asking if I needed rolls, thank you for asking if I needed my omeprazole, thank you for asking, thank you for caring, thank you for you. I love you with all my *heart, and at the end of the day it's a pretty good heart (mind you, it may be a bit buggered after the amount of gluttony over the past 48 hours!).*

Try not to forget that I'm getting cantankerous, surrounded by cantankerousness, and am used to being selfish about what and who, why and how I spend my time. It's not easy being me, but it is getting better. I find it difficult to adjust, and even being around people is not easy. I lead a solitary life, and even though I'm surrounded by hairy-arsed eejits, I still like the quiet. I am so glad I don't want to be rushing around from pub to pub, girl to girl, and not knowing what end is up.

Mum, I'm going to go back to my pad and sleep, like a purring Cheshire cat, with a bloated tummy and feathers hangin' out of the whiskers – at least they're not 'Philip' feathers; not yet anyway!

Be safe, stay well, and thank you for sharing your time with me

Love

23RD SEPTEMBER 2012
10.30am

Woke at exactly 9.00am; had only one pee, around 5.00. Had a substantial breakfast: cornflakes, toast, banana and coffee. Now listening to the *Manic Street Preachers*, lying face down in my pillow, my head facing the door.

Completed my tuck-shop form. It seems funny to me that if my belly is full I don't particularly feel like ordering loads from the tuck - the stomach is constantly sending the brain happy signals.

Was going to go to the gym this afternoon, but can't be arsed - the *Grand Prix* is on, so I'll settle down and watch that. I've been lying around doing nothing for the past few days; I haven't done any revision, although I do have all that I need printed out - I'll take it home with me, along with a stack of other paperwork.

I'm not nervous or worried about going out anymore - looking forward to it actually. And looking forward to being interrogated by Shadd's Masters class! I can tell he's excited about my inclusion with his students; it should be insightful.

I still haven't been told officially if I'm going out again tomorrow or not, or if the dates have been confirmed.

HOME-LEAVE DAY SIX
24TH SEPTEMBER 2012

It's 7.20am - been farting around since 6.30.

Got *Queens of the Stone-Age* on again - seems to be my anthem of late; *'No-one Knows'* and *'You Come Back Another Day And Do No Wrong'*.

Trying to count up the days I've been out so far, but, for the life of me, I can't remember; think it's the zispin tablets I take - they do make one go slightly numb. Will have to knock them on the head in order to get some revision done.

It's still dark and lashing down. Got a new coat and a waterproof on my last outing, so we'll see how they bear up - it really is heavy, persistent rain.

Can't really decide if I'm happy about this or that, or one specific thing, or the other. Don't care for this place or the people in it - for now. My life has become so much easier since I took a step back; *'By becoming self-aware you gain ownership of reality; in becoming real, you become the master of both inner and outer life' - The Tao.*

There's WW getting called to go to court, to have his second conviction for rape squashed. He's still guilty of the first offence, and in the eyes of the law, that one still stands. He looked so baby-faced in yesterday's papers; I see this particular guy every day - in fact, several times a day - yet I would never have known he was in court this morning, had I not read the papers I don't normally read.

Not too worried about missing the train this morning - no pressure to be in Belfast for any specific time, and sure if I miss the train, I'll sit in the wee café round the corner, type this up and have a fry-up.

Time to go put my face on.

26TH SEPTEMBER 2012
10.17am

Slept from 7.30 last night to 7.30 this morning.

It was great to get out for the day; I thoroughly enjoyed seeing my Dad, and most of all hooking up with Shadd. I also had a great time at my aunt's - eating five steak sausages and homemade chips was the icing on the cake.

I've just had a heart to heart with Mr. Yeates. Feel a bit better, but it really is all getting a wee bit too much. I now seriously believe that this regime of the institution does keep people alive in the short-term, but in the long term, it kills us. I have known seven people in the past year who have died: four were prisoners, who died from drink/drugs and suicide; the thought of coming back to this place was too much to deal with.

I now genuinely believe that prison is a death-sentence for many - there are psychological factors at all levels of this incarceration; self-harm only scratches the surface of the trauma involved, to inflict such damage to one's body.

Only last night I received a letter from someone who tells me that her daughter has cancer, her other son is now self-harming and the older brother is tearing lumps out of himself in prison. How does this woman survive - how does she cope? I wanted to involve this lady in my future work, but I now know I have a minefield to wade through in order to get her on-board… or maybe I won't. Maybe she just needs to get it out there - speak plainly.

Her son has been in jail since he was twelve, and now he's tearing himself to pieces without actually killing himself, because he doesn't know how to live on the outside, or the inside. He doesn't know how to live because there is something wrong with him - this has been fixed by throwing him in this institution, because this is the only thing our society can provide for him. Is his younger brother going to turn out the same?

I cannot let go of this - my family want me to forget, and walk away, but I can't: Pauline Campbell and this lady make me want to fight. I have to remember why I am doing what I do - in fact, I just have: another *'kerching/eureka'* moment.

This is why I will pass my exams; this is why I will have a lie-in, then go hammer-and-tongs at my revision from the morning onwards, this is why I will do well, and this is why I will pass. I *have* to - for the sake of those who might have to get through this in the future, I must. This is not being bi-polar - it is just about me caring; about me saying we need something better than that which we provide now.

28TH SEPTEMBER 2012
5.53pm

Just now I'm sat in my cell, and then it starts: the pulsating *thump-thump-thump* of house/dance music in the rec-room - the lads going about their daily business, oblivious to my mental meltdown.

I don't want to be here - I truly fuckin' hate being here, and I want to lash out at everyone and everything; the only thing that stops me from doing this, ironically, is the thought of spending more time in here.

So, Martenson's theory that 'nothing works' is actually wrong: prison *does* work, at least for the *rational* mind, the system *does* work to the rational person, and long let it continue to reform the rational mind - the system survives as it is, because as soon as one leaves it, one wants to draw a line under it, close the door behind one and never look back. The only problem with that hypothesis is that when someone commits a crime, they are *not* thinking rationally.

1ST OCTOBER 2012

5.32pm

It's a new month, a new day and *I'm feelin' gooood.* Well, not too bad. Sort of got to grips with revision for my first exam on the 11th, but the second one is much more complicated.

The big lad is on hunger strike again: they took his digi-box off him yesterday. I mentioned Pauline and another prisoner's Mum (whose name I can't mention until she gives me permission), and this makes me continually realize that our problems are often petty and surmountable; I wonder if the big lad would think the same.

This afternoon, we sat in the wee Education room, working away on our projects. A young lad, who was doing his 'Education Assessment' at a table adjoining us, chirped: 'Fuckin'ell, this is like being back at school again.' We looked at the ceiling, as if to say: 'Here we go: this guy ain't ever going to shut up, and we'll get no work done.'

The guy asked a few questions about his own questions, and said he couldn't understand them; he was okay if he had it explained, but he was dyslexic. The big lad asked him if he had long to do, in order to determine whether it was worth his while pursuing any lines of help from the Education department.

What the young lad then said took my breath away: 'I've only got six months left. I found my family dead in a house fire and started smoking grass - I never went out, except to buy dope. So, I got caught buying it, and doing things to buy it, and now I'm inside. It's my first ever offence and I get time in jail. I'll not be going out to buy any dope anymore - at least I've learnt *that* much.' And then he laughs.

I wonder is this true; maybe it's worth digging deeper. Did a judge or solicitor not succeed in mitigating circumstances with this young man? Is it really true? If it is…

I don't really know what to think if it is. If they are sending this guy to jail, then there is something drastically wrong with our system. Or is that stating the obvious?

2ND OCTOBER 2012

5.45pm

Up in the suite, Mick has just made me a nice cup of coffee. Spoke at length with the big lad after I had my dinner. He's still not eating, but it seems there is a change in the offing – however, he is still refusing food and water until he gets things in writing, etc.

Oh, our book *'Postcards from … '* won first prize at the 'Koestler Trust'; I won second for a short-story and third for a poem. This is great news: to be part of the winners is an achievement in itself, even if nobody in authority recognizes this or supports it - if they do, they haven't said anything yet.

The Director General has left, the Head of Learning and Skills has left, and the 'Prison Arts Foundation' is looking for funding to stay functional.

5TH OCTOBER 2012

6.05pm

I've put my application in for Foyleview - hopefully this will be a move forward for me; *'the best laid plans of mice and men'*, and all that.

Was at Pamela's class this morning and it was great - good vibes; being creative - although I could tell that Pamela was a bit under the weather. I think we're all a bit under the weather at the minute - I know *I*'ve been feeling totally drained.

As from tomorrow, I'm reading and writing, and reading and writing, and that's all. I'll watch the *Grand Prix*, *'Strictly'* and *'X-Factor'* (my guilty pleasures), but I've abandoned *'Holby'* on Tuesday night - now started to watch *'Hidden'* instead; looks like a decent spy show.

Stayed up to watch the documentary about Jimmy Saville the other night; I always thought he looked like a slime-ball - now I know I was correct. It was the reaction of Esther Rantzen that got me: she was genuinely taken aback, and was horrified to know that she had in some way colluded with him in his activities! The news headlines today include that a five-year old girl has been abducted and is now feared dead in Wales, and here in Northern Ireland, a man is charged with murdering a baby. I hope he never sets foot in here. The whole business is sickening.

Earlier on I stood by the microwaves, heating up some soup, and I listened to the men I share my life with at present. I'm glad that the only thing I have in common with them is the label 'criminal' - apart from that: nothing; I despise the very air that some of them breathe, but I cannot, nor ever will, let myself dwell on the subject, as it will consume me. Sometimes I tremble when I stand too close to these men, or they stand too close to me in a queue, but I can assure you it's not from fear or anxiety: it's from something much, much worse - something I can never let go of.

9TH OCTOBER 2012

11.14am

Made a little bit of a *faux-pas*: got my exams mixed up; as a result, I have only two days - today and tomorrow - to revise for my level-3 exam. On the plus side, I have another week for my level-2 exam, next Wednesday - the re-sit. I've been up since 5.00am, but only really got to read over the bits in the chapter relating to one essay. It'll have to do - what's in my head may be enough, or, at the end of the day, it may not.

10TH OCTOBER 2012

Wow, what a productive day: off for a piss-test first thing this morning, and was able to extrapolate from the staff on duty that my home-leave dates 22nd-25th have been approved - that was, in fact, the reason for my piss-test. I just wonder how long it will be before a member of staff on Alpha tells me I'm going out.

Got my exam in the morning. Of course, it's not the one I've spent the last two weeks revising for! That particular level-2 exam is *next* week, and the level-3 one is in the morning. Oops! Still, I'm sure I'll do better at the re-sit.

15TH OCTOBER 2012

5.58pm

Slightly pooped. Busy reading and re-reading over my notes for the level-2 exam on Wednesday; I think – sorry, I *know* - I'll definitely nail it this time. I've applied myself more, and if I'm honest, I've actually only really now got to grips with it all, or at the very least, I know enough to pass.

Looking forward to getting out next week, but I will have no time to dwell, as I'm going to have to complete an essay by the time I get back. Think I'll write it by hand and type it up when I get back - this will give me a bit of practice for if and when I get to Foyleview.

It's amazing how one has to give up everything one has been working towards, in order to get open conditions. I sent a nice letter to the O.U. guy in Belfast asking about unlocking my website for use there, as I would never be able to use it again in prison. He sent Allison an email asking me to avoid a wasted trip to their office.

Going to head back down in a minute. Finding it hard to keep the eyes open - I think I've done as much as I can for now.

17TH OCTOBER 2012

5.34pm

Well, there we go: DSE212 over and done with. I know I've passed, because I answered so much more than last time. I'm now reading up on my level-3: *'Crime and criminal justice'* - this seems more appealing to me.

Sitting up in Halward, chatting with Mick - he's a good lad.

1ST NOVEMBER 2012

5.17pm

Managed to get my first TMA off for level-3 criminology - it looked good, and seemed easy to write; still, pride before a fall, and all that! I also completed my first ever book review.

I got turned down by 'Purple Rain' for another resettlement day, this time with the P.A.F. at Stormont. Well, when I say I've been refused, I mean Mike Moloney has been told 'yes' by the governor, but 'no' by Purple Rain - Mike told Mr. Yeates, and he told me; so, officially, I'm none the wiser.

Prison officer David Black was shot dead by dissident Republicans, on his way to work at Maghaberry prison, at 7.30 this morning.

Wow!

This is a tragic event for the man and his family, and throws a whole new dimension upon the prison service in Northern Ireland. Nobody deserves to die, and I condemn it and the people who did it.

But, I cannot get away from the fact that I have no *real* feeling towards the majority of people who work here - they are wrong in too many ways, and I seriously believe that this might be the first of many more. Dissidents may take responsibility, or be blamed, but there are many who are leaving here with hatred in their hearts towards these men and women.

This is a tough world, and Norn Iron is a tough place, but we have so much humanity to give; why should it all be swept under the carpet, because people in society refuse to recognize that what happens in here affects the world out there.

'Cheers' is back on TV - double episodes each night at seven, on ITV4. Enjoying it very much.

5TH NOVEMBER 2012

5.19pm

Taking a day off - this is just as well, as we're having another day off tomorrow; complete lock-down for the NIPS - the funeral of officer Black.

I'm not surprised, nor unsympathetic to this man and his family - there *should* be a day of remembrance - but I find it quite ironic that this poor officer's colleagues order prisoners to remove poppies, whilst they themselves are today wearing tie-pins depicting poppies; there are double-standards here, and contradictions all over the shop. I am a non-citizen, therefore I have no right to wear a poppy when I choose - I am only allowed to wear it as per governor's orders (5th November - 11th November); at least, on Alpha that's the score. It hurts me that this man's tragic death is now being used to justify and unjustify all sorts of shit in the political world.

The big fella has been removed from Alpha, and is now residing on H1 - good luck to him: he's going to need it on there. The blocks are fuckin' mad, and we tend to forget that we never want to go back there.

Looking forward to doing some reading in my cell tomorrow. I'll simply get up for the morning head-count and... well, I'm not going to second-guess what will happen tomorrow. It's no big deal, being locked on the wing, but worse if you're locked in the cell all day; luckily, this is something that Northern Ireland, or at least Magilligan, has moved away from, despite protestations of the older officers (ie. the majority). I can't be arsed with it any more, and patiently wait to get over the fuckin' wall.

There's now a multi-gym training session going on outside the study-room - all the young bucks, jostling for their position in the pecking order. I look over at Tommy Rocks, who looks back at me, then at the ceiling. Tommy's a boxer - an old hand, with a flattened nose and a battle-scarred face, indicative of the boxing fraternity. It's good that these young guys are using up their energy and letting it out (whatever it is that they are letting out); high jinks and high spirits: good stuff, this laughter - it's good to laugh.

8TH NOVEMBER 2012

MY BIO (or 'bibliography' - can't remember the right word for it; find out tomorrow at Pamela's class):

'Michael Irwin is an aspiring prison writer, with many poems and short stories published in *'Inside Time'*. Whilst writing his first book *'My Life Began at Forty'*, he decided to embark on a career in academia. He is currently studying for a Masters in Criminal Justice, and is beginning his PhD in Restorative Practices and Criminology in 2014. He grew up in Belfast during the 'Troubles', and spent most of his adult life in London and South Africa. He is winner of the *'Listowel Writers'* and *'Koestler'* Awards 2012.

Be careful what you wish for, and all that: now I have to go to Stormont!

Imagine how that sentence rolls off the tongue for me – it's a complete mind-fuck, but one I am very proud of. I was hoping to get a shirt and tie for the occasion, but that's been scuppered now.

I'm then out again on the 6th of December for a hospital appointment; taxis and trains, then trains and taxis on return - it's going to cost me a small fortune! I'll then write to Mr. Ford and tell him how easy it is for me to resettle and re-integrate to Belfast from here.

Nightmare on Elm Street, and all that, but sure, what's to worry about - I'll be out in seven months.

Seven months this Wednesday, actually. Four weeks to Christmas at home, and then six months more of this shit.

JC phoned the girl in charge of Foyleview applications - they have my application, but haven't done anything with it yet; here we go round the mulberry bush. Think I'll go and phone Dad, and let him know.

Last night my neighbour was pumping dance music, and singing, shouting and roaring. I thought he was talking to himself, but discovered that another prisoner was coming to his room with CDs, and urging the guy to play them. I heard my neighbour say: 'I don't really listen to this stuff now'.

The other prisoner said: 'Fuck him! Play it as loud as you like.'

My neighbour has problems and is not of sound mind - this other guy knows it, but is prodding him with this, because he knows the guy is searching for friendship, and will do anything for conversation; the visitor knows I like my peace and quiet, so he is going out of his way to disturb this.

I presume this is about me, and I don't want to do anything about it - I'll let it play out, and wait and see.

22ND NOVEMBER 2012

Well, stranger things have never happened! Was informed this morning, by Mr. Yeates, that I am allowed to go to the P.A.F. do at Stormont, on the 4th December – Purple Rain telephoned him, and told him to tell me to put in a 'resettlement day' request for that day. It turns out that PW is also taking the day off from teaching to drive Mr. Yeates, and they are picking me up at the gate, then delivering me back before six in the evening.

I know there has been so much negotiation behind the scenes in order for this to happen, and I am really grateful to all concerned. A day out with Mr. Yeates and PW will be cool, and it will take my mind off the fact that I now have to get up and make a speech at Stormont!

28TH NOVEMBER 2012

5.32pm

I'm seriously thinking of turning religious: I need something to believe in, something to have faith in.

It looks like I *won't* be going to Stormont now: the head of the Education department isn't allowing the teacher a day off to take me; too many restrictions in place to make it viable or reasonable. I don't want to go now - I've had enough.

Had to have a chat with the P.O. this morning, about my resignation from the Listeners - it is a good scheme and it is worthwhile, but the trouble is in the prison service: everything it touches turns to shit. Change will happen, but it won't happen the way people expect, because there are still too many rotten people left in charge.

29TH NOVEMBER 2012

2.42pm

Angel is in *Inside Time* and wins £25 for 'Star Letter of the Month'. Shithead! He doesn't do anything for ages and then gets rewarded with £25 - he'll definitely get published when he gets out.

My neighbour is driving me nuts with his music and singing and loud TV, but I have found myself frightened to say anything, in case it gives them reason to remove me – I'd prefer my last six months to be in some semblance of peace.

5.52pm

Spoke to officer B on the way up; he's always good for the soul. Called in to see the big fella, but he's got about four or five young lads in his cell. He is in the centre of the room, getting his hair cut - the centre of attraction, gathering his supporters round him; I know what he's at and it's cool: I hope that he gets the comfort he needs, wherever it may lie. Still, he's got less time than me to do, and really needs to wind it in a bit.

He told me he spoke to a guy about doing some community work outside - I'll get the guy's address, and send him a letter, and some visiting numbers; I'd love to be able to start getting involved in the Lisburn area. My future seems to be heading towards this area of endeavour, and I feel it is where I can do some good; watch this space, eh?

Going to have an early night - speaking to Brian in the morning.

30TH NOVEMBER 2012

5.38pm

Just walked past my old cell - 54 - on Halward; some other guy was sitting in the dark in there, watching the telly. A thousand memories flashed by in an instant - what a weird and wonderful life!

I hate where I am now, and I hate the thought of where I'm fighting to get to, but more than anything, I hate the thought of coming back here, to be woken up every few hours, with a torch being shone in my face. Once *'I'm a Celebrity...'* is over, I will put the earplugs in and read - this will block out the noise of the idiots shouting and fuckin' about on the wing, and my lunatic neighbour.

I did get a bit of exciting news this morning: I'm going to design a website for myself, about what I'm interested in: namely, assisting prisoners and families, and informing the general public of alternative perceptions of imprisonment, and the social values that are destroyed by this merry-go-round.

Apparently, the website will be up and running by March.

I'm also interested in helping anyone who can help people in here, and the *Playhouse* are interested in asking me to promote what they do.

Got a good letter from Pen - he does make me laugh.

Here's my speech for the P.A.F. do at Stormont:

'If you've ever seen the movie 'Apocalypse Now', *you might recall the scene where two of the characters - Chef and Captain Willard - get off the boat to go to collect mangoes, and are spooked by a tiger. Chef freaks out, and keeps screaming: 'Never get off the boat - never get off the boat!' For me, in 2007, prison was a bit like this; it wasn't totally apocalyptic, but it wasn't the best situation I'd ever found myself in. However, prison can be apocalyptic for some, and indeed many.*

'I used to say to myself, when I was writing: 'Never get off the page - always stay in the page, the safety of the diction and imagination therein.' The page was my safe space and, like the boat in the movie, education was the vessel that carried me along.

'The writer in residence I met in England helped me get started with my writing. Then, I returned to Northern Ireland and got involved with the P.A.F.. Without the P.A.F., I would not have met Mike, Mr. Yeates, Carlo, Shadd and all the other wonderful people who go above and beyond the remit of an education delivery system or curriculum.

'I was asked to explain to people what my experience of P.A.F. meant to other prisoners. I know what it means to me, and I used to find it hard to put it into words; now, after three years in the company of Mike Moloney and co., I am delivering speeches at Stormont and lectures at Queens. My phenomenological experience of writing has been teased, coaxed, cajoled, stroked, placated and extrapolated to such an extent that I am now able to write fully-fledged academic essays, research projects and book reviews.

'Oh, and there's the small issue of winning the Listowel *writers award for*

prison poetry, and the £500 in cash I've earned this past year, from various poems and short stories.

'So, how does my good fortune affect others? All I have to say is: 'Look at what I've done – you can do it too'. What they, these relevant others, see in me, gets soaked up with them - I have taught men to read and write, and this has done me the power of good. What I see is a physical and mental change in these men.

'We are all aware of the ripple effect of crime, but what about the ripple effect of reintegration, and the ripple effect of hope*? Hope spreads into the real world upon release - it makes communities safer and it reduces the likelihood of more victims. Confidence and hope spring from the pages, sometimes from the darkest of stories and imaginations.*

'What people like Mr. Yeates and Carlo do is much more than teaching: it's an art in itself. It's only when you've gone through the process yourself, do you realize what it is they have been doing all along; it *was always there - it's just that these guys know how to dig it out and use it.*

'Most forms of authoritative, curriculum-based education are the very thing that drove students away when they were youths; you can't do that again as an adult - a socially-challenged adult, to boot.

'Mike Moloney gave me hug on my first day of home-leave, when I popped into the office to pick up my cheque from Listowel. *He then popped out to see my Mum, who was waiting in the car; Mum got a hug, too. This is what the P.A.F. does: it* hugs *you; it gives you space - creates space in your mind to let the good times roll. It's not all airy-fairy or tree hugging: it's an unwritten contract of humanity, in an apocalyptic scenario, and it is more relevant in today's restorative-justice based political climate than ever before.*

'The writers, artists and musicians who belong to this family are art themselves - they demonstrate the art of humanity, *and without them, many of us would have stayed lost.*

'I used to think it was all about me - now I see the bigger family. How can anything be holistic if one doesn't jump in and get one's hands dirty? That's

what the P.A.F. does: it gets its hands dirty.

'Thank you for listening.'

3RD DECEMBER 2012

2.51pm

Well, would you Adam and Eve it? I'm off to Stormont tomorrow, and it looks like all is well in the organization of my transport/escort; Mike Moloney has had to dance a merry jig to get me there. Nothing is ever simple when it comes to Michael Irwin, but I am more than impressed, and grateful at the amount of people who are trying to help me.

I now have time to start cacking myself, as I now have to deliver - I've had to resort to my beta-blockers already; but it is excitement, not nerves.

My phone is charged - I hope I can take a few photos of me in and around the building. This is an historic moment for the guys and gals of the P.A.F., and I must not forget the brevity of the situation: the meeting is about getting funding for them to continue working and operating in Northern Ireland jails; I hope my contribution can make some difference - I must be doing something right, in order for them to go to such lengths to fit me in.

This morning, Allison asked me if I was able to continue my studies without internet access - this means that my Foyleview situation is obviously being revisited. All in all, I don't actually care anymore - I have the tools and the patience to ride out whatever these last six months throw at me.

What am I going to wear? If I'd have been allowed out today, I could have gone and got myself a shirt, tie and some decent trousers, and looked the part - now I'm gonna have to slum it. I don't want to look like a prisoner - a con, a convict: I want to remind these people that I am a human being, and not a number.

4TH DECEMBER 2012

5.15am

Having a cup of coffee, listening to *Elbow*. Got the desk-lamp on, and the shadows of the coffee cup are cast, elongated, across the top, left-hand corner of the page - the atmosphere, like the music, and like my mood, is peaceful and tranquil. This light creates softness, but, like a zoom lens, or attentional spotlight, it highlights everything in the immediate vicinity. The edges of the arc of light-art are blurred, as ghosts and ghouls and sprites dance around the periphery of my imagination; like my emotions, they gently blend in with the dark fuzziness of the room. The room is my world, my future, and my past; yet it remains misty - not with gloom, but rather a hesitant dusk, or a tentative dawn.

Under this light, so much is seen, normally unnoticed: the speckles of dust on the base of the lamp - clean, clear and vivid; the ink, in increments of millimetres, on my blue translucent ruler; the fibres in the grain of the recycled paper; the grain of the wooden desk-top, where tiny bubbles of the varnish protrude, where it hasn't properly set. How old is this table? How many have sat under this self-same arc of light, writing down their raw, innermost feelings, emotions and desires?

Being met at the gate by Mr. Yeates, at 9.00am. Mr. Y doesn't drive, so Mike has arranged for someone to pick me up. I am grateful, and humbled by this commitment, but I am also mad at the Purple Rain for dragging his heels, and making it so difficult, then making it sound as if *he* has given me everything I need.

I'd love to have been able to invite my Mum to this do, but it's set up to fail, so imagine how much disappointment it would have caused if I don't turn up - I'm afraid Mum will have to wait until next time.

How do I feel? Excited and awed at the thought of sitting here now, going to Stormont and then coming back, all in the space of six hours; I've taken my beta-blocker, in the hope that my heart doesn't jump out of my chest. Silently, I hope that my words will make a difference.

Directly in front of me, pinned to my noticeboard, not more than an arm's-length away (a legally designated area for displaying non-offensive material) is a card from *Inside Time* - it says: 'A voice for prisoners since 1990'. Think I'll hold on to that thought: *a voice for prisoners* - is that what I am? A voice? Will my voice be heard, will it be pleasing to the ear, or will it grind and make politicians sick?

Observing the diamonds of skin, on the base of the thumb and forefinger of my writing hand: they become more defined each time I write under this illuminating light, like the wrinkles of an old elephant hide, around the creases of its massive joints. It's an old-age wrinkle - I'm getting older, but my mind is getting younger. I've never been one to care about age, but these diamonds remind me of how complex we are as human animals - how precious and special we are, precariously residing on a bomb.

The news this morning carries stories of riots at Belfast City Hall, and roads blocked at May Street, at the bottom end of the Newtownards Road; I worry, for a second, about not getting there, or arriving late, but the memory of growing up during the 'Troubles' allows me to relax in the knowledge that we'll get there when we get there; if we're late, people will understand, because this is Norn Iron: we're used to this sort of thing! In the past, no matter how many bombs went off, if you could, you still made it to work. Mind you, if your work happened to be blown up, you welcomed the day off, because you knew you'd be busy the next day helping to clean up the mess.

'Throw those curtains wide - one day like this a year would see me right.' What a beautiful song, and how apt!

7.30am

Showered, scrubbed and ready to rock - pacing up and down the landing, quietly, so as not to disturb the others. All I hear in my head is *Stormont-Stormont-Stormont, overwhelming-overwhelming-overwhelming!* Thinking about the hundred things that could go wrong getting out of here.

Going to get dressed now. Can't wear my glasses: they make me feel dizzy. But I'll have to start wearing them full-time soon.

Deep breaths.

5.25pm

Oh, my goodness - what a day! Stormont went swimmingly - you should have heard the applause I got! Holy Moses! I'm going to sleep well tonight; I didn't even eat anything until after: two mini sausages and a couple of baby-wraps.

What a moving and invigorating experience: Mr. Ford, Mrs. McAllister, Mrs. McCabe, Mr. Masefield, Mrs. Masefield, Mr. Goodfellow, Mr. McNaught, and about ten or twenty others, all came up to see me and offer congratulations and support. God, it was really great chatting to Mr. and Mrs. Masefield - I honestly can't stop smiling; my Mum and Dad would have been so proud. I even got interviewed by BBC Radio Ulster, which will be aired tomorrow night at six-thirty.

6TH DECEMBER 2012

I wish you could see me smile, both outside and inside - Stormont on Tuesday, delivering my speech, then on the radio last night, talking about the benefits of education in prison.

The most remarkable thing of the whole process is that I have been refused and denied at every juncture for the past four weeks, by the powers that be in here. That was until the guy organizing the event phoned another guy at Prison Service HQ, who was also organizing the event, and told him that I was having problems getting out. The second guy knew me, and he phoned here on Monday afternoon, and told them to make it happen - it did. This guy also stood beside me, supported and protected me, and gave his permission for me to do the arts programme interview. I won't be getting into all the ins-and-outs of control and censorship, and all that: the point is that the Northern Ireland Prison Service helped me, and I feel as if I have passed some sort of test; they are under such scrutiny, that I cannot be getting up and spouting off about what *is* and what *isn't*.

After I'd delivered my speech, the Justice Minister, the Director General, the prisoner ombudsman, the old Director General and his wife, and the two guys from H.Q., all came up to me, shook my hand and said good things. The most important part for me was that each and every one of them said: 'I understand you had a bit of trouble getting here, Michael.'

I rolled my eyes, and said: 'Nightmare.'

They said: 'Okay: understood,' and left it at that.

I then had two hours of an endless line of people come and talk to me about my future, and the future of my fellow prisoners. I managed two cocktail sausages, then it was time to head back; the guy who organized the event had to bring me back himself.

I had such a laugh with retired DG and his wife, that people were looking at us funny; how or what, on Earth, could a serving prisoner and the old DG of the prison service have in common, and/or to laugh about? We were laughing about the way I used to do his head in about the heating. His wife told me that he had come home and told her about this man he had met in Magilligan, and how he thought I would end up being someone to listen to - this lovely woman, out of earshot of her husband, added: 'You proved him right today, Michael, and, believe me, that is not an easy thing to do. Well done, you.'

The Justice Minister told me that he enjoyed the short story about the guy who lived in South Africa and was now looking at a smaller version of Table Mountain - I told him that was me; he laughed so hard and told me now that he understood the message behind it.

This is the start; this is how it works: we talk, we share, we deliberate, we laugh and we talk… then we listen, and we talk some more. We don't rant and we don't attack (although, I must admit that there was one brief second, just before I started to speak, when I wanted to let the lunatic out; but I was a good boy) - I was calm, I was polite and, apparently, I was brilliant.

My friend and mentor, Mr. Maruna, told me he was one of the proudest men in the room, which had about two hundred people in it (a few of them had met me before at Queens, but in the end they became a bit of blur). Anyway, Shadd had to leave the room around 1.45pm and head over to another room to meet with NOMS: the English Ministry of Justice and the Northern Ireland Justice Department, but before he did, I told him about my troubles, Pen's troubles and Angel's troubles (guys, I gave him permission to use your names on your behalves).

He said: 'This is perfect; this is why your experiences are so important. I will definitely use them, now.' He also told me that he hadn't forgotten about you two guys, for that matter, but time and problems have been limiting his response times - he told me to tell you that a letter will be on its way to you as soon as he gets some other stuff cleared, and not to worry.

So, there you go - I was brilliant! I heard how I sounded on the radio and I am very proud of myself. It's my Dad's birthday today; I spoke to him first thing this morning, and he told me I carried myself very well, and that he, too, was proud of me. He's also frightened for me, but this is where we clash, and I had to leave it at that. I am surrounded by good people at these events; there will always be cynics, doubters and haters, but I have to admit, the amount of strangers who embraced me was overwhelming.

I had two minutes to myself, and as I sat looking down the avenue to Carson's statue, I said quietly: 'Hello, Mr. Carson. Do you think my family will be proud of me?' From a prison cell to the heart of government, and back to a prison cell - there has to be a story in that, somewhere.

So, now I've got to design my website and meet up with a whole bunch of people over Christmas and the coming months; I think they will have to come to the prison to speak with me, but, hey, only six more months to go.

I do not care about any of this anymore - not in here, anyway: in my mind I have already left here, and I am simply treading water, waiting for the off. The next chapter is looking up, and I am looking forward to spending some time at home at Christmas; I'll let the others worry, fight and argue about what I am and am not allowed to do. I recall at the very start of my sentence that I said to myself: people need to know about this and I'm going to make it happen - I feel as if I've achieved that already, and that this is only the start of a bright and beautiful future. It's amazing how much difference a day makes.

Thank you for your letters and kind words, which were sitting on my bed when I got back. I think of the lyrics from the Elbow song: *'Throw those curtains wide - one day like this a year will see me right'*, or the wee statement from the book of Tao: 'The best thing that can happen to you is happening right now'.

'Social death begins when the institution... loses its interest or concern for the individual as a human being and treats him as a body – that is, as if he were already dead.' (Schneidman, 1973).

10TH DECEMBER 2012

2.55pm

WW and Stevie were 'adversed' this morning. The fire alarm went off around 7.15, and Stevie headed down the landing to make a cup of tea, whilst WW went to go to the toilet, and Ass was there, ready to pounce. He's been gloating all day; I find it so hard to concentrate on my work, when it is all about social harm, power and control.

11TH DECEMBER 2012

Another fire alarm at around midnight. I'd just been to the loo, so that was a blessing. It wasn't raining, but it was bitterly cold - there will be some crying done if we get sent outside in the rain.

13TH DECEMBER 2012

Received my exam results on Monday, and, to tell you the truth, on top of my trip to Stormont, it's been a pretty remarkable week in the world of Michael Irwin. I'm still buzzing and, to be honest, I can't quite get my head round all of what's occurring.

My life in here is now fading into the irritation of a wasp or fly, and I can't wait to squish it – as a consequence they are grating on me more.

SA made a rather insightful observation earlier, when he said: 'I know the people you used to knock about with, so don't pretend to be all saintly and good, 'cos you ain't.'

He's correct, of course - the *lunatic* is still only millimetres from the surface, but isn't that true of all of us? Isn't it… or is that just me?

JS got scalded in the showers this morning, by wee F. There are fair digs going on in the wings, and the officers are telling prisoners which drugs they will and will not have on the landings – apparently, blues have lost favour over greens, etc.

JM is back at Maghaberry after a substantial fight; a subsequent search of his cell found phones, cannabis and blues. That's *all* the lifers come down from Maghaberry two years ago, that have now been in some sort of shit over drugs or misuse of medication.

20TH DECEMBER 2012

Oh no - how mad is this: sitting up in Education, and the new orderly is running around like a maniac, hoovering everything in sight.

Been for a piss test this morning, and had to see the governor to sign my home-leave warrant. The piss test wasn't all that, though: apparently, the line wasn't coming up (I think it's the same concept as a pregnancy test). The trouble is that lately there is nothing but fear and happiness in my heart, and I believe this may have had an adverse effect on my urine - not that I'm *taking* the urine! At the end of the day, I've been a miserable bugger for the past five-and-a-half years, and only recently have I started to perk up a bit – endorphins, I think they're called.

Anyway, the line eventually appeared, but there were definitely a few tense moments there; I thought my coffee had been spiked, or something - I wouldn't put anything past some of these guys in here. Roll on tomorrow.

I managed to get my TMA off - I now have four more essays and an exam, and I'm done in here; *twenty-six weeks* and I'm done in here. And, tomorrow morning I'm out of here again!

31ST DECEMBER 2012

Apologise for my absence - I've been sick, both physically and mentally: sick of this whole sorry affair; sick to death of the lies and the bullshit. Sick, sick, sick, I tell ya!

I can only reflect on Christmas at home - it seems like a lifetime away, but in truth it feels like only yesterday. The problem is, as soon as one gets back to prison, one has to block it all out and get back into prison mode.

7TH FEBRUARY 2013

11.06am

Well, here we go again with the computers. It's been over a week now, since I was on my website, and all I need is to read over some basic stuff, which will help me to get my head round what's needed.

Spoke to Dad yesterday, and the house is coming along nicely - it will be ready by the time I get out. I foolishly mentioned tagging and the D.U.P., and he asked: 'Sure, what good will getting out now do you? If it was me, I'd want to do time and leave, then have nothing more to do with it, knowing that the prison will have no more input in my life.'

I did have to remind him that I didn't *like* being here, that I'd had enough, and that he was not me. I know what he means, and though he's correct on a hundred different fronts, nobody can live this for you - you get caught up in the moment, and it swamps you.

I had a few thoughts about this reintegration business when I was sitting, waiting to leave the gym this morning, and thought that it might be a good idea to have some sort of forum for sharing experiences of it; everyone is different, and therefore each person will have a different idea of what 'reintegration' is. Some just go out and pick up where they left off: getting whacked and ending up in the same shit; some try to stay away from shit, but get roped back into it; some - like Dad suggested – just want to do their whole time, have nothing to do with temporary stuff, and then just be done with it; and then there are others, like me, who want to run before they can walk. My trouble is that I feel as if I've been born again - not in the religious sense, but definitely in my spiritual 'self', and I am excited and enthused about my future.

12TH FEBRUARY 2013

2.35pm

Still no computers working. I've listen to three different I.T. blokes blame the server, and each say that they are 'looking into it'.

I got a 60% mark for my last TMA, and I can tell my tutor is a bit disappointed. I wrote a nice note, explaining my fragile state of mind and my lacklustre approach to my work, but still, I'll have to get my finger out and get on with it, as time is marching on.

5.48pm

I'm sitting up on Halward, having just been speaking with officer L. I can hear the lads shouting: 'See you later, Celtic.'; my friend, Celtic P, has left the wing to go and live at Foyleview. I'll find out soon enough what it's really like over there. Spoke to him briefly before I came up the stairs - good luck to him.

It feels strange: I am the last remaining member of the original crowd that was on here three-and-a-half years ago, and I don't know how to feel. Celtic still has a couple of years to go, and this is a big milestone for him. We did the same job (servery), and worked together as mentors and co-facilitators on the 'Victim Impact Programme'.

Prison is a truly remarkable place - I feel as if something is lifting in me. Maybe it was getting out, and walking up the phase on my own, or maybe it was being here, yet remembering where I'd recently been. Maybe it was just talking to officer L.

Definitely work time tomorrow.

14TH FEBRUARY 2013

11.00am

Was over in the gym just now, on the old treadmill.

It's Valentine's Day, and there are loads of love songs being played; *'Hero'*, by Enrique Iglesias, was on, and I thought of Mandy in Cape Town.

Wow - what a nightmare that was! Totally bowled over, I was – totally. I know I've mentioned Mandy before, at the start of this venture, but I think it's good that I can now think of that time and that place in a totally different way; time is a healer, and a mender too - I smiled thinking about her, and didn't feel sad anymore. Mandy was all wrong for me, but every time I looked at her, or was in her presence, I was hit with some sort of chemical reaction that made my whole world ache, a bit like with Ellen, when I was younger. I think of Peter Sellers in *'The Pink Panther'*, when he was dressed as Toulouse Le Lautrec, singing: *'All the girls I loved'*.

I then realized that this is the last Valentine's Day I'll spend in jail. What will next year's bring? Will it bring me love? Will it bring me madness? Will I still be on my tod? I'm not really bothered any old way, but it might be nice to have a bit of *niceness* in my life; I certainly won't be chasing this elusive *'love'* - it'll just have to come and get me.

15TH FEBRUARY 2013

2.34pm

There we go - just sat down at the computer, in the wee room on Alpha, trying to get started with TMA 04. I'm not even going anywhere this afternoon, and it still takes half an hour to get off the landing and out on the wing.

I think I've been suffering from S.A.D., as there was a bit of sunshine today and the temperature has gone up a bit. It was nice to be eating breakfast in the daylight, for a change, and this seems to have lightened my mood slightly… only slightly, though.

I am in absolute agony… *sphincter* agony. Don't worry: I haven't been interfered with! But, whatever has been causing me trouble up there is now really painful; I'm waiting to go and collect some magic paracetamol.

Got some cream, paracetamol and some ibuprofen. All three are now starting to work, thank God, because I can't even sit down or lie face down on my bed for any length of time - so bloody uncomfortable and painful; it's not an itch 'way in there', as Billy Connolly once joked about, but more a dull, penetrating pain that only a small amount of pressure seems to relieve.

Spoke to AS on my way to and from Healthcare; haven't seen him for ages, then I see him twice in the space of fifteen minutes! He's a good sort, and I look forward to doing business with him in the future. He's finished his diploma in *'Restorative Practices'*, and tells me the only person who recognized this was the governor Alan Longwell, who wrote him a short letter (I can use Mr. Longwell's name, as it is public knowledge that he is the governor).

5.30pm

I'm up in Halward now - only came up here to get off the wing, for a bit of peace and quiet.

The big lad just popped in to say hello, handed me some legal stuff to read and headed off to do a few laps round the yard. I now look forward to sitting here for an hour, and doing nothing but chatting with you, Diary - if I don't, I might just sit here and do *nothing*; but I did bring my course material, so I should really do a bit of reading - there's nothing else going on.

Brendy Quinn arrives, and we sit and chat for an hour about psychology, being angry and *not* being angry – ie. controlling and rationalizing it. I see he's fighting for something better, and I hope my example sparks something in him - I already know my honesty is ringing some bells in him, and he's working things out. He looks so much healthier, and I'm really pleased for him - it gives me hope; it makes me think, and it makes me wonder. There is a lot to be said for this time - this waste thereof: it creates space to negotiate with oneself.

Borrowed *'21'* by *Adele*, and will probably give it a blast later on. Brendy's also lent me a zombie movie, with Woody Harrelson; I tried to say: 'No, I'm not into zombies', but he insisted. So, I'm going to head off now, watch some zombies and listen to *Adele* - what a fuckin' combination!

Walking down from Halward was really peaceful: nice and warm, no frost, no wind, no rain, a quarter-moon and a few clouds - looked up to see if I could see the meteor passing by; no chance: all I saw was the North Star, or was it a satellite? My imagination then took over, like in a disaster movie, because apparently a small meteor injured five-hundred people in the Ural mountains earlier today, and an even bigger one passed the earth by just 17,000 miles. Makes me think of how vulnerable we are - how perilous our life is: perched on a molten bomb, spinning round a bigger bomb, surrounded by millions of projectiles.

16TH FEBRUARY 2013

11.06am

Some individual members of staff put on a uniform and assume they are the be-all and end-all.

The institution of prison is based on a military model; if we want to have a 'holistic' approach to rehabilitation of criminals, then we need to strongly re-invent and re-invest in the official management structures in place.

Having watched *'Porridge - the Movie'* last night, I seriously wonder if some of these officials' get their ideas from TV. It still makes me laugh though.

It's been a lovely weekend, temperature- and weather-wise, and I look forward to heading out now for a breath of fresh air.

2.12pm

It's great to take time out, but the length of time I get to take it is becoming shorter.

The guys across from me are busting my balls, and starting to become hard work. One guy has had his TV on, full-blast, since one o'clock, but when head-count is called, and an officer is on the landing, it's turned down to a whisper. They're in and out of each-other's rooms every couple of minutes, and the doors are always banging; they walk with heavy feet, and every step is a bang - a boom in my space; my quiet space - my fuckin' peace of mind. I heard one guy say: 'I'm socializing – it's allowed,' and I suppose he's right: Still, I felt like socializing the fuck right out of him.

After speaking with Brendan last night, I feel those little anger pangs pinging in my belly again; I wonder how long I can hold out, but, deep down, I know that I will do nothing, and nothing will be done. So, I sit and argue with myself for an hour at a time, until I can take no more.

There's nowhere in this institution to hide, from oneself or others - there never has been; six years of annoyance! I suppose that's what prison is really, for some: an annoyance. It has been exactly this for me; it still is.

I just remembered one of the many *'near-misses'* that I had in prison. I got a bit panicky last night, as I realized that I have survived this whole venture without any physical injury or mental scarring, and then thought: *Holy fuck - I've just jinxed myself, and will have to turn major recluse in an effort to protect myself!* The ole paranoia creeping back in; it's always there – it just needs something to trigger it.

Spoke to Dad before lunch, and he tells me things are coming together nicely at my new home. He told me not to worry about a thing out there; like at the start of my sentence: there was nothing I could do then, and there is nothing I can do now. I got all excited: it will be done and it's great.

My family members are all doing their own little bit to help me - a very nice feeling, especially considering where I was at six years ago: this time six years ago, I was making all the wrong decisions and it was round about this time that I gave in to my doubts about making the trip abroad - the seed had been sown long ago, and I knew it was on the cards. What a contrast when compared to now.

What a future there could be looming in front of me - gotta get out of here first.

I'm going to practice my typing for half an hour before dinner.

17TH FEBRUARY 2013
5.58pm

Halward House; I think I'll come up here a couple of nights a week and write this – it is a lot more peaceful: no vibrating washing machines and thundering hooves.

It turns out there was a serious road accident near the prison, and a lot of the staff couldn't make it in. Later developments involved Mr. Yeates being escorted from the Education department, and I observed PW sitting over in the wee room at the library; the Head of Education came up to make sure we got our afternoon session. One of the lads told me that the car accident was mentioned on the news - three women were involved and one car was stuck up a tree; I asked if Allison would be in the next day, and the Head of Education told me no - forgive me for getting paranoid again. Why does one always think the worse?

I wrote a nice letter to Mrs. McCabe, wishing her luck for the future, and another letter to Shadd; I received one from him yesterday and, as per usual, he gives me hope. He tells me there is still a lot of red tape to get through, but we will do it together, and adds that I will be organizing 'some criminology' in September, and beyond.

This is how it works for me: I *doubt*, and then a sentence is produced which gives me so much hope and purpose, I cling to it with every vestige of strength that I have left; it gets my juices flowing. I have, as a direct result, decided to get stuck into my TMA 04 immediately after my independent essay - if I do it right I should have both finished in a couple of weeks, and this will leave me free to revise and concentrate on future projects, like my Masters, PhD and organizing university events.

19TH FEBRUARY 2013

4.40pm

Just back from the gym - got ten minutes before dinner, and my mind is racing again; as per usual, in a place where nothing ever happens, there is so much going on.

Our Education was cancelled this morning, and my mind is trying to process all the whys and wherefores of yesterday. Nobody knows or has said anything yet, which is hardly surprising, as I asked two officers that I know quite well if they knew anything about the rumours of Mr. Yeates being escorted off the premises. Mr. Y has worked here for ten years, and yet they both asked me who he was.

'Nope, can't picture him,' they said. Shows you how much cross-border communication and camaraderie goes on between prison and Education staff - it is quite contemptible that they have been here so much longer than me, and they don't even know one another.

23RD FEBRUARY 2013
10.46am

Oh, my God! *'You're Gorgeous'*, London, cider and Elisabeth.

This song, by *Babybird*, came out in the late nineties, and it was at this time that I met a girl called Elisabeth, from Uganda. Elisabeth worked in the local *Kentucky Fried Chicken*, and one night she turned up in my local with three friends, and proceeded to hug and kiss my friend Ollie; Ollie was, then, in his mid-sixties and an all-round character - he was like a second Dad to me, and I loved him dearly. Anyway, there was a squad of us there that night, and we all got ensconced around the big table near the fire; it was one of those nights: one of those happy nights, when you feel about ten-feet tall... when you slip into your favourite jeans and favourite shirt, and feel good - not good in the cocky sense, but good in the sense that makes you smile with comfort in your own skin.

I thought Elisabeth was stunning, and I kept stealing quick glances at her as the night progressed. Elisabeth was at the opposite end of the table to me, and by the end of the night I managed to speak to her at the bar. When the song playing now came on the juke-box, I just stared at her.

She leaned over and said: 'Mike, *you're* gorgeous'. You could have knocked me over with a feather, and my stomach flipped a few somersaults.

I can't remember how things progressed from there, but I do remember Ollie coming over and saying: 'I knew you two would hit it off.' Had that been his intention all along?

We ended up back at my place, and this was my first time with a true

African girl. Wow! There have been a few girls who have made my head spin, but this girl was something different. She giggled at my exasperation, and found it amusing that she made me tremble; this girl was in complete control of her sexuality, and of mine.

We hooked up a few times over the coming weeks. Then, one night she got very serious, and when I asked what was wrong, I got my first introduction to female African methodology and negotiation ('no' means 'yes', and *'yes'* means 'yes', but *both together* mean 'no', and at the same time *'yes'* - it's easy when you think about it!). With a very serious frown, and a pucker of her lips, Elisabeth said: 'Mike, do you want to have a relationship with me, or just want to fuck me?'

Me, being the cocky, arrogant arsehole that I was, said the latter. So, we did just that for a few months, and it was great. But, after one extremely vigorous evening, Elisabeth announced that she had met a man who wanted to have relationship with her, and that she would not be back.

'Good luck,' I said, in my arrogant arsehole way. It was only a week or so later, when Ollie and I were having a chat about Africa and women, that I realized I had missed the opportunity of possibly one of the most rewarding relationships I have ever had. By then it was too late, of course, but I now understood the simplicity of it all: it wasn't just about sex - sex was the easy part, the fun part.

Elisabeth told me that I was like a shining light, and when I laughed, everyone laughed with me; she told me that I was someone she would want to spend time with, and that she saw my inner warmth. I'd blown it by saying I only wanted to fuck her.

Maybe someday I'll feel like that again – maybe not. Whatever happens, I've still got these memories and experiences to hold on to, and if someone ever tells me I'm gorgeous, or asks me that question again, I will most definitely not be giving the same response.

Time for grub, and then to the rugby later. Got quite a bit done this morning - just have to put the notes into my own words and put them in some sort of coherent order.

28TH FEBRUARY 2013

Completed my application for the *'James MacQuitty Law Scholarship'* - I'll post it in the morning. Sent Bronwyn's letter off and another one to Shadd, then had a good chat with the big fella for an hour.

He's holding on, but I don't think it will be for much longer - he's juggling too many plates, and I feel as if something's going to snap: the continual self-destruct button. Hope he makes it, but I feel at a loss, as I'm all too aware that once you press that button, nothing will stop it - been there, done that.

MOTHER'S DAY
10TH MARCH 2013
4.29pm

Spoke to Mum this morning, and wrote a letter shortly after. My sis is with pregnantness, so things have changed in the world of Mum, Ken, sis and my niece.

Lady bumps and massive humps, while I like heffalumps;
Storks arrive, nappies are dry –
Sing you a lullaby 'bout flutterbies.
Fear and trepidation, joy and consternation -
Sure, what's the matter? A brand new beating heart
Makes a beeline for a destination.

19TH MARCH 2013

The big fella is on hunger strike and has had no food or water since Friday, and it has been relayed to me that one of our *'care and appreciation society'* went to speak to him as duty-governor. Apparently, he asked the big lad when he was due out (as if he didn't already know) and the big fella told him 'five or six weeks'.

The duty-governor replied: 'And you'll be dead by then.' Then, off he went on his merry way.

The war is raging inside him; it is swayed by good and evil, righteous and unrighteous – this is an Irish thing, or, in his case, a Northern Irish Ulster Scots thing. He was, like me, born to a certain ideology, but I was lucky: I escaped; he put himself forward, and is now paying the price.

I hope he makes it. I'll break my vows of heathenness and pray for him tonight; that's twice I'll have prayed for him now.

20TH MARCH 2013
9.24am

Over in the Education block.

Spoke to DW from Healthcare this morning. He called me Noel - my middle name; he always does and it's strange, because he's only known me for four years! I gave him a bit of abuse, but it was friendly, and we laughed. He had a letter for me about my gastroscopy, and I took five minutes to explain the situation. I am not going to attend Belfast hospital again now until I get out - this is *my* choice, but, again, it is forced by the ballix of the NIPS.

Spoke to an S.O. this morning about the big fella, and I offered, as a prisoner and a friend, to go and have a chat with him - this is not allowed, of course. I was going to write to his wife, but I really don't know what to do for the best. It's a very sad situation.

This is a callous place when it comes to hunger strikes - the governors have heard it all before, and are immune; 'He seems pretty determined,' are words that will stick with me for a long time, if he does pass.

Need to walk away from this one - he knows what he's doing and why he's doing it; trouble is, so do I.

4.30pm

Back on the wing, feel like shit: can't shake this chest cough and head cold.

The latest rumour is the big fella is down the block - the first stage of his disappearing act from public view. He was in the SPAR cell on Halward, but I suppose now that his condition has deteriorated, they need to monitor him more closely in the 'Care and Separation Unit' (CSU).

I don't think I'll be seeing him again, and that saddens me, but what can I do? I'm getting out soon, and want my life to be filled with hope and positivity.

This is how prison gets you: I might have been a selfish bastard *before* I came to prison, but I notice now, even more so, that death *annoys* me - it doesn't destroy me; life goes on, and it's what we do with it while we're alive, and we have opportunities, that really counts.

Had a nice chat with Christy earlier: we talked about the pros and cons of institutional life, and both came to the conclusion that they should bring back the death-penalty for all crime, and so get rid of crime forever.

I sit here typing, listening to an officer yelling out people's names, and it's driving me nuts!

Oh – a ten minute reprieve: I have to leave the room whilst *another* prisoner gets interviewed for Foyleview. I don't begrudge anybody; I suppose it's a bit like what's happening with the big fella: life goes on without you - I've been passed by, overlooked, denied – but, at the end of the day, everything just keeps trundling along on its merry way.

Just had dinner and been told that the big fella is not in the C.S.U., but one can never believe what one is told in prison.

What did happen, which I can't believe, is that two guys at the dinner table asked me what Easter was for, and was it a Catholic thing? I kid you not. I forget sometimes that not everyone has been blessed with the worldly knowledge that I have! - I told them it was to commemorate Moses and the parting of the Red Sea - at least that got a giggle. I could imagine them sitting with their grand-kids, and the kids asking: 'Granda, what's Easter for?' and them explaining it was about Moses; then the kids correcting them, and them sitting there, going: 'That bastard Mickey told us it was about Moses!' At least I'd be remembered, eh?

I'm going for a lie down: I feel like shit. It's a lovely evening, and the sun is out, so I'll just go and dream about freedom and judicial reviews.

21ST MARCH 2013
9.34am

Up in the Education centre, snow en-route, and there's a real bite to the wind. Reaching the final countdown, the final push - the final chapter of this endurance test - this extraordinary life experience. I wonder how it will pan out. The beauty about writing this is that I can always revisit, remember where I was, and take solace in the fact that if and when I'm feeling down or low in the future, nothing is ever worse than being in here. I suppose, in a way, I'm already preparing my own safety net - my own emotional cushion.

2.32pm

Slept like a log again at lunchtime, and woke up at twenty-to-two - shows how shit I feel.

Tick-tock - I hate this waiting ballix! Took another beta-blocker: my old heart is going *bumpty-bump* - a wee bit too much, lately.

I see KB just now; he's 'time-served' tomorrow, and he looks wide-eyed, crazy and alive - not that old, dead-beat, drudgery look of daily institutional life.

22ND MARCH 2013

8.32am

Listening to Keith being given his final orders by staff - I hear one say: 'Make sure that room's clean before you go anywhere'. The guy has had a spotless room for x amount of years; why on Earth would it need cleaning today - this morning - when they watched him do it yesterday. In other prisons the orderlies clean the rooms after someone has left, but not here; I suppose it's because there will be someone else in it by lunchtime.

Had a coffee with him this morning and he's still consumed by his appeal, which is in May - will have to keep an eye out for it.

He's also been given permission to return home by the *other* arbiters of community justice where he lives, and I'm not talking about police or probation; Northern Ireland is mad!

Never managed to read a book last night: Celtic came in and we had a chat.

Find it difficult sometimes to keep my non-judgmental head on, but it ain't easy when you know what people *did.* Horses for courses, eh? I suppose one has to get one's hands dirty to figure out how to fix things. He made a comment about mentoring for sex-offenders, and I thought to myself: *How on Earth will that work when it's all about trust, and a lot of those guys are in for* abusing *trust, particularly with children.* I don't know what to think - I try to block my mind off to the faces of the children, and the hurt they must feel when abused; it doesn't make me sick, but it does hurt.

And so my day starts, with another mish-mash of humane and inhumane thoughts, of rational and irrational behaviour, of shouting and slobbering, of bitching and moaning, and, permeating the whole sorry debacle, the sound of false laughter - forced *noisy* laughter; gets right on my fuckin' tits!

25TH MARCH 2013

4.30pm

I don't know who wrote the song *'What a Difference a Day Makes'*, but I've been singing it in my head all day.

I received my mark for my penultimate TMA this morning: 95%. To be honest, I didn't think it was all that.

This is my point exactly, about self-doubt: if I thought it was not up to much, and then I get a mark like this, I then automatically think that I don't know what I'm talking about, because I was wrong, and it was - does this make sense to you?

Nevertheless, it has added a spring to my bling, tautness to my inner smile, quiet surprise and a feeling of relief. As per usual, my mind is all over the shop with thoughts of freedom, and getting away from this ballix.

The Belfastish word *'ballix'* has started to creep into a lot of my thoughts and musings. It was my brother who wrote it in a letter ages ago, but only now have I started to realize its merit.

I'm going to go up to Halward later, brave the freezing cold and find out how the big fella is doing - I'll not ask to see him, though, as this will probably result in my not being allowed up there again; I don't really need to go there any more, anyway, but I want to be able to have the opportunity to say cheerio to some of the Halward staff in my last week. You see how all thoughts of going to Foyleview are now at the top of my agenda?

5.42pm

I'm up in Halward with wee Mick, and we're nattering away about the big fella, shit, life, computers and getting home. I spoke with the big lad, and all I can really say is he's *gone*! Unless he gets a written response from the Justice Department saying he can go home, then he *won't* be going home: he'll be going to his neighbours in the graveyard down the road. The emotional minefield doesn't get much worse than this.

The big fella ain't so fuckin' big anymore: he tells me he's down to 15-

stone. I called him a vain bastard, and said that his hunger strike had nothing to do with injustice: it was all about him trying to lose weight. We shook hands and had a hug - maybe it'll be the last I see of him; who can tell?

I then had to walk past the officer, who made me take my fleece off - I ignored him completely. It's weird: I know I rant and rave about being highly emotional, ready to blow a gasket, and often do, but at times like this, I feel absolutely nothing - no anger, no rage, no sadness; just ennui.

Allison isn't here tomorrow, so I've got another day on the wing. This I can handle, because it's friggin' Baltic outside! Binevenagh and the Donegal hills are steeped in a crispy milk-white and it looks idyllic - until you step outside, that is.

It reminded me of *'The Eiger Sanction'* on the way up, and the tears were rolling down my cheeks. Time to put the feet up, stick the ear-plugs in and read my Val McDermid book *'The Last Temptation'*.

27TH MARCH 2013

Why am I so tired? Want to lie down all the time. Went to the optician this morning and I'm getting bifocals in ten days' time.

Spoke to T. McK, and said that I had an invite to attend an O.U. presentation for my diploma - he got all stuttery and said it wasn't really anything to do with him; this person comes across as the sort of guy who means well, but at the end of the day wants no complications in his life.

A few of the guys on the landing have been up to their usual banging of doors, in and out of each other's cells.

I so desperately want someone to say something or make a move on me, so I can unleash all my anger, but I also desperately listen to my inner voice saying: 'Hang in there: two-and-a-half months to go.'

I take myself off for a walk round the yard - something I hardly ever do; I can't sit in my cell, with the walls closing in. I take another beta-blocker and try to breathe. I'm glad to get off the wing, to walk without the claustrophobia, and let my shoulders rise again.

I'm so very tired and I feel like crying - the waves of depression trip over me like the endless march of time, and it sucks the very life out me. I feel the way the big fella does all the time, but I will never resort to such tactics. The mental pain one experiences is almost physical.

The drugs must be starting to work as a calm has come over me. Amid the dread of going back to the wing, the dread of being in the company of others and the fear of losing my temper, the tablets work, and have been my saviour for years now - I've been in much worse conditions than this, and I still have to continually snap out of wallowing.

Melancholy and *ennui* riddle my psyche (I discovered the word 'ennui' in a book I'm reading, and upon discovering its definition, I stumbled upon a few others, like 'satiate' and 'surfeit'). I am full of prison - my cup overfloweth with the abundance of it, and the relentlessness of its ballix; I've got what is loosely termed and sneered at as 'gate fever', and I'm 'heavy whacking' (another term used to describe not coping well). There is no counselling or input from outside agencies, and I sincerely believe that there is nothing anyone could do about this anyway.

One of my neighbours came to see me before lock-up, and apologized for annoying me, and making a racket last night - I think he meant it.

The library wasn't too bad - a guy spoke to me out of that crowd, but I just ignored him; it was the usual strained politeness that I have come to rely on when I encounter these nasty, evil men. The beta-blockers have certainly helped me today, and I look forward to getting back to my cell and closing the door 'quietly' behind me.

I'd lasagne for lunch and a bag of chilli Doritos, so feel pretty stuffed at the minute - have decided to let the gym go. Besides, I simply cannot be around certain people for too long. We have to share our sessions with *'vulnerable prisoners'*, and, without being judgmental (as I don't know what they've done), I just look at some of these guys and think: *You just look like a wrong'un.* It's easy to forget that all of us are in here for a reason, and some of those reasons are pretty fuckin' horrific and sick - so this business of treating everyone with dignity and respect is a load of ballix!

29TH MARCH 2013

10.13am

Was sick last night - we got our Easter extras from the tuck-shop: chocolate éclairs, apple turnovers, chocolate cake, hot cross buns and soda bread. The trouble is we don't have fridges in our cell, so we need to eat it all within forty-eight hours of getting it (that's my excuse and I'm sticking to it)! One of my colleagues said he was wracked with guilt about eating half his chocolate cake in one go - I know how he feels.

I could be going to the gym in half an hour to work all of this off, but instead I'm sitting here looking forward to sausage and chips at lunch-time.

I'm taking my beta-blockers again, first thing in the morning. I need them: the anxiety attacks are coming thick and fast! Most people will assume it's because of the fear of getting out.

Still, the wing has been quiet at night, and I'm sleeping a bit better. I'm still waking around five-ish for the toilet, but instead of starting to read or write, I lie there, breathe and relax; I wake again around half-seven, so this is can only be a good thing. Not as irritable now. I've also taken to drinking my coffee and eating my bran flakes in my room, and then having a wee read of a novel.

Patiently waiting for some correspondence from the outside world, but there's not a lot coming in - I suppose my life has become such a tumultuous emotional minefield, that people might think it best to stay well clear for the time being; it's a funny ole game.

2.33pm

I'm walking down the phase, on my way back from Education, when I hear a tap on the window, and a finger beckons me to come - I think it's T. McK, the Head of Education, though I can't really see into the darkened room of the mobile hut. He appears at an elevated door at the back of the building, and my chest is at the level of his feet (just where it should be: it is Good Friday, after all - the only thing missing is the donkey and the palms. I am such an ass if I've got this all wrong, but I simply cannot drag myself out of this mire of servitude).

He tells me to read a letter from Queens, to see if it needs an urgent response, so I set down the two pints of milk and the folder I'm carrying, by his feet, and he hands me down the letter (then the sun caught my eye, and I could have sworn I saw a heavenly choir of cherubs, floating around his head!).

'What's it say?' he asks.

I say: 'Dunno yet - I'll tell you when I read it.'

I scan the first page, and the sentence that immediately jumps out reads: 'The University Admissions Review Panel was convened to consider your application for admission; further to this meeting, I am pleased to confirm that it will be possible to offer you a place, commencing in September 2013, subject to filling the following conditions…'

'Ach, Tom, isn't that just fantastic news?' I say; 'For me and for everyone who's helped me?'

This is the first time I've seen this man smile, and I thought it a pleasant change; 'That is great news, Michael!'

Maybe I can't see the wood for the trees, or perhaps my bitterness guides my every thought, but this environment of negativity and petty punitivity I writhe in every day won't let my mind climb out of the quagmire it's in - if the truth be told I'm well pleased, but I'm frightened to show it; remember what I said about certain people wanting to wipe the smile off of one's coupon?

I phone Dad when I get back to the wing and he sounds excited, then chirps: 'Where you going to get the money from?'

'Fucked if I know! I've applied for all the funding that's going, so there ain't much else I can do for now. I'm not robbin' any banks, as that kind of defeats the purpose.'

He laughed, and said: 'We'll sort it out somehow. I'll let everyone know.' He congratulated me and said: 'Well done'. For me, that's all I ever wanted from him: these words alone make me feel great inside.

I have now to put my faith and trust in other bodies - I've just realized that I've now signed up for another five-year sentence at a different institution, only this time it's by choice, and it fills me with optimism.

I then look at Ass as he does the headcount, go and bury my head in the pillow and scream like a lunatic.

30TH MARCH 2013

9.32am

Fell asleep around 9.30pm, woke up again at eleven and watched *'Person of Interest'*. Finally got out of bed at 8.30am and forced myself to have a shower, then toasted my last bit of soda-bread, and chopped up two boiled eggs, with a bit of salad cream to top it off - bloody marvellous. Tried to phone Mum to tell her my good news, but no sign of life there yesterday or this morning - I'll try again in a bit.

Sitting here now, contemplating getting stuck into some work, and all I hear is officer Ass yapping and moaning, effing and c'ing the NIPS. If he hates it and everyone in it so much, why the hell does he come to work each day? I'll tell you why: it's to bully and control and yap and moan - he obviously can't do this at home.

I watched a movie called *'Final Destination'*, about people cheating death, and 'Death' returning to get them - you knew they were going to die, and the directors of the movie created some elaborate final destinations; so, I too lay on top of my bed, staring at the ceiling, thinking about death, and ways to be creative with it.

No joy with Mum and no joy with *'The War on Drugs'* (my essay). Going to go and mop my cell and start another Val McDermid book. If the truth be told, I can't bear the sound of Ass's voice, so I will have to remove myself from the vicinity - I'll be back when he's not here.

EASTER SUNDAY
31ST MARCH 2013
9.20am

I just spoke to George about our transition and transfer from England to Northern Ireland. I let George talk, and he came up with more or less the same conclusions as I:

'I thought I was coming home - to my own kind - where I foolishly believed I would be treated firmly, but fairly, and not be called 'Paddy'.' The only truth in that statement is that we don't get called 'Paddy' anymore - 'cunt' is the new label, and utter contempt is the average treatment; I'm so glad I'm not a bad man (anymore).

Going to go back to my room now, and stay there for the rest of the day, only showing my face for food and toilet – self-inflicted lock-up, with the door not locked. After six years of imprisonment, I've managed to get myself living on the wing where the doors are not locked and one can walk about freely - yet, all I want to do is lock myself away, and avoid all contact with prisoners and staff.

2ND APRIL 2013
10.48am

Had to get out of my cell - was going a bit stir.

The constant foot-fall and door banging is driving me mad - I even noticed it on a TV programme last night: the floors were wooden, and the women could be heard clomping through the whole house; even the TV is invading my brain, with wooden floors. It might look nice, but it doesn't bloody-well sound it.

Goodness, aren't I such a sensitive soul?

Was recounting a bit of what I said to Allison this morning, and I hope things work out. We talked about how 'home-leave' has its benefits and drawbacks, depending on the individual; I've got two days of leave remaining, and will apply for them soon. I told her about the size of my back garden, and mentioned that I couldn't wait to feel the grass between my toes - it's not something I ever ran around doing, but it is something I look forward to.

I'm sitting here typing, now in my socks; I've had to put the desk fan on, as it's a bit close in here at the minute. The clocks have gone forward, the sun has come out and it feels like spring. I wonder: if I close my eyes for two minutes, will the gentle breeze of the fan, and the change in temperature, transport me to a different place..?

Nope, but it did let me get a bit of broken neck syndrome.

I'm forty-six the day after tomorrow, and this is another milestone in *'The Home Stretch'*: my last birthday in jail... my last Easter in jail... my last two-and-a-half months in jail. God, what a waste of time and money.

Mind you, it hasn't been a complete waste: I've got a serious future to look forward to now. Still, this does not outweigh the hopelessness of these places.

I'm unique in many ways, yet I'm surrounded by *un*-uniqueness - *everyone* here is unique, in their own dick-headed way.

Dickheads can be helped, but, if you simply throw a lot of dickheads together, with another bunch of dickheads in uniform, then the status quo will always be there.

My probation officer asked me what *I* thought should happen: I set a blank page on the desk; she didn't disagree. I like the idea of staff being educated to degree level in psychology, with a constant willingness to help if someone asks for it; you can only ever really help if someone wants it, but what you need to create is an environment in which this can be developed. The present situation is not working, nor ever has it - the proof of the pudding is in the eating.

3RD APRIL 2013

9.50am

Back in the computer room in Alpha - no Allison and no work. I think I'll go to the gym - need to spend a bit of time off this wing.

Managed to get up to Healthcare and get my omeprazole - I'd taken my last one this morning. The stress of abiding by the instructions given for medical issue over Easter was initially adhered to by me, but, alas, it didn't quite endure. I'm still being prescribed stuff I don't take anymore, and I had a chat with the guy about a future doctor and medication, so at least they got my new address on the system. This is a seemingly insignificant thing, but, psychologically, it reaffirms that I'm getting out soon. I need to build on that.

But, even though I keep thinking this in a positive way, my mind keeps jumping back to the negative of my still, currently, having to share oxygen with these bastards.

Just realized I can't got to the gym: took my beta-blocker this morning, and I know from past experience that means that when my heart rate rises from doing exercise, the tablet goes to work to slow it down, and I end up taking a whitey. So, no gym for me today.

'MASS BREAKOUT OF ONE' BY MICHAEL IRWIN

H.M.P. Magilligan

Forty six years ago today, I arrived in this world.
Intermittent flicker of a compound light
Illuminates a random snowflake, trying to escape.
Who is watching, who is guarding this mass breakout of one?
Intermittent thought - caught in the headlights;
Emotions, like the rabbit, get squashed by
The institutional eighteen-wheeler.
Sporadic flashes of optimism invade my daily drudgery;
Escape every day - freedom in my mind;
Beneath this intermittent flicker, intermittent thought.
As headlights fly by, in my mind's eye,
I slowly draw the blind.

4TH APRIL 2013

8.57am

I've got the image of 'Tucho' from *'The Good, The Bad and The Ugly'* in my head - the scene near the start, where he says: 'Ah, one bastard walks out and another bastard walks in'.

There's no officer Ass this morning - instead we've got 'Harry Kewell' (rhyming slang) - this man is Reginald Molehusband and Mr. McKay rolled into one; even his colleagues cast furtive glances at the ceiling, at his regimental, by-the-book approach to prisoner care. What they *don't* see is how he walks around slamming the door-flaps, or opening doors to let all the heat out; he always wears a jumper. Apparently, he was held hostage in The Maze by the prods, all those years ago - seems he still bears a grudge.

I'm not going to dwell on these rats today: it's my birthday; I'm going to phone my parents in a minute, in order for them to wish me a happy birthday. I'm not going to tell anyone in here, because I don't want to share it - this is *mine*. I'm now completely selfish, and need to get through this final little push to the end. I remember Dad saying: 'Not long 'til your birthday, and then the days will fly in.' In fact, I think I'll go and phone now.

Everyone's left the wing for work. No Allison again this morning.

3.24pm

There's nothing stranger than folk.

Spent forty-five minutes talking to Dad, which was great, then went to the loo. Poured some coffee, sugar and milk into a cup, and was about to put hot water into it, when I was called for a visit - it was Mum. What a surprise! What a result - just what the doctor ordered.

It's strange, but I didn't realize how much I'd missed her until I was actually in her company. We'd a good old natter, and Mum met George's Mum and Dad, too. I needed it, more than I'll ever let on; mind you, I'm not ashamed to let on: I need my Mum - what we've got is nice. There were no dramas, and the room was quite empty; all is well with the world.

Mum told me she'd written two letters, and when I got back to the wing I received one of them - there was a nice poem inside, from my niece and Grace, called *'Hope'*. I wrote my own version; maybe I'll write a new version each year, and find out how much one's view of hope changes over time - what matters now doesn't matter tomorrow, because we've already done it

'HOPE – WARTS 'N' ALL' BY MICHAEL IRWIN

Without it we are nothing - when did it arrive?

Where did it come from? What is it, this 'Hope'*?*

It's tangible, it's sometimes a mirage -

A figment of one's furtive imagination;

A contradiction of time and place, of cliché:

In all, hope springs eternal.

It's never there, but always there: a paradox of the self -

Without the self, there is nothing.

I'm glad I found myself - my hope:

Hope is a creation, hard to pin down -

At least, when we find it, we lose the frown.

I'm only sitting here writing because I can't be arsed sitting in my cell. Think I'll take a wander up to Halward later, and go through my files, ready for the clear out.

5TH APRIL 2013

8.40am

Do I feel any different, now that I'm forty-six? Well, yes I do, actually - I think it's to do with closure, and milestone events like birthdays put things in perspective.

Spoke to officer J last night on Halward, and she said: 'I met your mum - Grace – earlier, at visits.' I thought this was quite weird, as J was the officer who phoned Ken to make sure Mum was okay, the day things went wrong - the last time Mum was here. Weird that the person who showed kindness then was the person to greet her upon her return.

I've written a couple of letters to Pen in Brixton, and Debbie over here - it's good that they keep in touch, and I'm always looking forward to meeting up with people out of here, and away from this place. My time here is drawing to a close: its now ten weeks to D-day!

Ten fuckin' weeks! Two-point-two months. Fantastic stuff!

I sat in my cell in the early hours yesterday, thinking about how I felt, and where I was this time six years ago - all I can really remember is *maggots*: there had been a couple of rubbish bags sitting in the kitchen for a few days, in my house in South Africa - I kept forgetting to put them out. What happens then is maggots - I woke up and they were all over the floor! Bronwyn was there, and helped me to sweep them up. I could hardly breathe with panic and anxiety - coming down from the coke and the booze, and everything else; *yessus*, I was sick! It makes me feel sick now, thinking about it, but I am grateful that, in my heart, I know I will never feel like that again. What a disaster!

Yet, ironically, if I hadn't been such a mess, and so in the *kaka*, I wouldn't have done what I did, ended up here, and be in the position I'm in now… which is? On the verge of having purposeful life upon release.

So, my life has come full-circle, and I look forward to revisiting this time one day, and seeing where I ended up.

I just spoke to Peachie, who's back after his last two days at home, before he gets out in four weeks. He's not a happy chap - the pain is etched all over his face, and he looks older than he did two days ago; he left here all smiles, and full of the joys of spring, but not now, I'm afraid. This is not unique, of course, and the joys of getting out for a couple of days far outweigh the hardship of coming back. The very fact that you come back, and don't even consider *not* doing so, allows one to mentally and subconsciously prepare for the hardship this entails.

Prison is not all bread and water, but it is soul-destroying. When you're at home and back in society, there is always some sense of polite respect in any social interaction and negotiation - this is because nobody knows who you are: you are just another citizen, like anyone else. But not so when you come back to prison - *politeness*, *respect* and *humanity* in prison mean not getting the crap beaten out of you anymore by officers and even that still happens.

8TH APRIL 2013

10.18am

Back at work in the Education centre. Well, when I say 'work', I mean I've been busy finding out via *Wikipedia* what an upper second-class honours degree entails - I think it's above 60, but in how many modules? Time to go exploring again.

My story: *'The Great U.K. Con'*, was published in *Inside Time*, at last - they finally got it; no cash prizes this time, though. Not a problem - I'll send a few more in this month, and maybe write a parting letter. I've enjoyed the prison newspaper over the years: it's been a great source of fun, wonder and bemusement; *'Ben's Blog'* always made me laugh out loud, but now I can just email him when I'm at home.

Spoke to Allison (probation) in passing this morning; she's had a word with the deputy-head of probation, and they will come see me, together, when next in the prison. I don't think it will be a problem, and I'm assured it shouldn't be, but like everything else connected with prison, we'll just have to wait and see…

16TH APRIL 2013
11.14am

God, I'm so tired - *permanently* tired; woke up at 4.00am this morning. Mind you, a lot of guys woke up around this time - must have been the wind: it's howling a merry gale at the moment!

I'm waiting to get the strength and the focus to write my last TMA, but I don't think it's going to come - I think I'll just start writing in the afternoon.

16TH APRIL 2013
5.47pm

Up in Halward, doing a bit of revision - it's nice and peaceful.

I've enjoyed having a chat with officer B - we were reminiscing about the old days, and how good this wing used to be for staff and prisoners, when 'The A Team' ran the show; they vetted everyone, and did a lot behind the scenes to make it work. It's all been blown out of the water now, because of the temporary suspension of selection criteria for house-blocks, and the temporary doubling-up, which has now become permanent.

I'm so tired, and I find it hard to think, or get the energy to do anything at all. I really *must* do this essay, and then I can sit back and revise for the next six weeks, but as I said before, I'm waiting for motivation that isn't going to come - there's no point trying to convince myself otherwise.

Wrote a letter to Shadd and Carlo this morning, and I look forward to seeing them as an ex-prisoner!

It's great to sit here with my eyes closed, forget and be quiet. I cannot wait to be quiet - to sit on my own, in *my* house, and just be *quiet*. It's like a cat-nap: you only need a wee bit of it to empty the mind and get rid of the clutter.

18TH APRIL 2013

2.51pm

Made it to the hospital this morning. Got sea-sick on the way back, and crashed as soon as I got back to my cell.

The outcome is that what I was told the last time, about the ole plumbing, was not correct - this time, I was told I had to go for a very invasive test, which involves sticking stuff up my penis and arse at the same time, and pumping me up; it takes about an hour, and is extremely painful. I do admire their honesty! I thought it might be best if I had my treatment in Belfast, as I'm out in couple of months, but I was told there is a one-year waiting list at the City Hospital. The most alarming bit of news, though, was that no surgeon will operate on me at my age, because the procedure means I'll be dry-ejaculating for the rest of my life! Now, there's something I didn't know: the last guy told me it would be a simple little procedure, involving a little cut, and all would be well - it makes me wonder why he's not working there anymore! This guy was actually very abrupt, but I presume it's because they are busy.

I was picked up at Alpha and placed in handcuffs. On a positive note, though, the fact that I sat in handcuffs again, so close to the end of my sentence, and after having been out on my own for twenty-odd days, reminds me that I never want to be in this situation again. I took in the smells of the van, the claustrophobia, the jolting of the back over bumps, the rattling of the chain on the door, the door banging, the beeps of the door alarms, the overwhelming heat of the cell-fan at one's feet (you have to keep moving your feet, 'cos they get burnt!), the freezing cold when it's off, being cuffed to another officer, climbing down from the van, the heads turned, mine bowed and off we go; *'dead man walking'.*

LAST TWO DAYS OF STATE SANCTIONED RE-INTEGRATION
21ST MAY 2013
5.00am

'Bohemian Rhapsody' playing on my headphones - how poignant! *'Jus' gotta get out, jus' gotta get right out of he-re... nothing really matters... to meee.'* How true, Fred.

This forced integration drives me mad. Cannot spend more than ten minutes with my fellow inmates - so happy to be locked up at 4.10pm yesterday, and thank God for the headphones! Change of tempo now: got Slash and *'Halo'* pumping away - reminds me of Christmas. Going to enjoy today and tomorrow - soak it up, breathe a lot and try not to become excitable.

Chris from reception told me he found a bag full of paperwork belonging to me – don't know how I'm going to manage to get that little lot home.

There's a wood-pigeon nearby, cooing away in the background. It's getting light, but not quite - close my eyes, and I'm back in London, South Africa, Belfast, Lisburn or Dunmurry; everywhere I've lived there's been a wood-pigeon cooing at this time of the morning. A strange concept for me: I didn't know wood-pigeons were so well travelled.

7.10am

That's me showered, shaved and sorted; haven't got the headphones on: it'll ruin the hair! Instead, I've turned them up full-tilt, so I can listen away over the whirl of the fan, gently blowing cool air over my ever-overheating body. There's a blackbird/crow sat watching me, from his perch on top of the fence, as I lie on my cot, eating an apple and writing this.

Popped a beta-blocker, pre-empting later anxiety. The London traffic update is on, and I'm transported to different times and different places. How do I feel? Warm, numb and relaxed. And *clean* - yep, 'clean' is a good word. Though I keep worrying about fees, funding and Dad. Was watching a programme about Ohio slaves last night, and there are way too many similarities to compare: the state-sponsored crushing of identity - is this not what prison is?

FOYLEVIEW
25TH MAY 2013
7.00am

Oh, my God! What a turn up for the books, and what an unbelievable chain of events!

I'll get this out of the way first: the accommodation lives up to its reputation. I'm in suite 13-10 - they call it *'The Bronx'* over here. I've already had a run-in with one of my neighbours about his music - he basically told me to fuck off and mind my own business. This fella's the guy who had a fight with my mate George; he'll need some watching and some delicate handling, as I've only got three weeks left - if I'd longer I'd just fuckin' plant him and be done with it.

So, to the chain of events which led to my being in Foyleview (I'll probably repeat this several times today):

On my way out to home-leave on Tuesday, I met and spoke to the new residential governor: 'Genetically Modified'. He told me that he could probably get me to Foyleview when I got back from my leave - to be honest, I dismissed it as soon as it was said, because I have absolutely no faith or interest in anything these NIPS representatives have to say.

Upon my return:

The yard was busy, as it was a lovely, sunny day, but I managed to grab the last free bench - ten minutes later, the governor appeared, walked across the yard and joined me and JS.

Now, in all my time there, on any wing, no member of staff has *ever* walked across the yard while we're in it - one normally gets hollered at from the doorway, or another prisoner is sent to get one; it was amazing - you could have heard a pin drop.

'Do you want to go now?' he asked.

'Okay, let's go,' I replied. and off we went.

He came down to the cell with me, and even helped me to pack, as I had a couple of phone calls to make. The governor did make me laugh, saying: 'Michael, no offence, like, but the sun is out, the pub is open and it's Friday afternoon - you get my drift?' In other words: 'hurry the fuck up!'

Must mention here that the look on prisoners and prison staff faces was something to behold - this interaction will do wonders for morale. The man has restored a bit of my confidence in management; to be honest, the more I think about it, the more I realize how massive this all is.

I got five minutes to say my goodbyes, before Starry Stars appeared, and whisked me off to Foyleview in the van. On the way, we stopped and picked up another officer, and he gave me a quick spiel on the *dos* and *don'ts* in the *'Land Of Narnia'*. He told me not to worry about anything, as it was Foyleview's turn for lock down, and I would get a full induction and sign the contract in the morning – fuckin' contract, indeed?

I've now got twenty five-days left to serve, and by getting here, I've achieved much greatness. This is all down to the new governor and his approach, which obviously comes from the new DG.

26TH MAY 2013

7.50am

It's fuckin' cold - the heating is off and has been since yesterday; sitting here, fully clothed with my coat on, drinking a piping hot cup of coffee.

My lovely neighbour has just woken up, snorting - his habitual snort; sounds like an old man, but he's not. I don't think he'll ever reach old age the way he gets on. Spoke to an old bloke who was complaining about the noise that continued until 11.30pm last night – it's meant to stop at 10.30-ish, but nobody really gives a fuck, and if you say anything you become a leper. Met up with lots of old faces, and lots of old pains in the fuckin' arse! *Yin* and *Yang* again.

Spent the day with Celtic in his cell yesterday, catching up on gossip and life in general. He's in one of the newer Portacabins - proper bed, chair, wardrobe, etc.; it's cool, nice and homely, but has the same paper-thin walls - still feckin' noisy! I suppose that's just men living together - my idea of respect is not the same as others'.

God, it's still deathly quiet at this time of morning – this might have something to do with the fact that it's a Saturday, and most of the guys are out on town visits or home-leaves. Of course, this means that an inevitable percentage bring drugs back – can't tell who's doing what, as I try to ignore it, but there's a lot of it going on. All one really has to do is observe whose cell is the busiest after a leave, and... well, you can figure it out yourself.

The 'zero-policy' is not very 'zero', and not very easy to enforce either (bar giving everyone a laxative on the way back in, and watching them vacate for the next twenty-four hours. I find it sad, but at the end of the day, what am I going to do about it? Nothing.

It does reinforce how Foyleview got christened 'Narnia': the land of make-believe - quite shocking, actually.

Got to remember I'm still a prisoner, not free yet and, like *'The Pirates of the Caribbean'*, I must honour the code; *Ooh-Aarrrghh! Hoo-rah!*

Who gives a fuck? Nobody, in my eyes.

So, how do I feel today? Well slept, relaxed, comfortably numb and getting warmer, even though the heating is still not on. In a bit of a daze actually – 'comfortably numb' is a good way of putting it.

4.05pm

Well, there's another day of semi-freedom over and done with. Popped into the office at 9.00am to get the key for the classroom, and bumped into S.O. BE - next thing I know it's eleven o'clock. Had a good wee chat – he's a good bloke, and it doesn't seem to matter what we say to each other now, as we are both near the end, ready to walk out the gate. Out of respect for him, I won't repeat what we talked about - the laughter tells its own story. Maybe he did or didn't say: 'The sweet taste of victory tastes and smells good.'

27TH MAY 2013

Pretty restless night: rain, wind, neighbours, TVs on until 2.00am and snoring from both sides – feckin' nightmare. Imagine having to endure this for years.

Can't really complain, as I was up and down to the toilet all night – I'm using a measuring jug, as it saves my door squeaking; I'll probably get charged and thrown out for using this jug as a piss pot.

Got a pain in my neck, and in the old lumber region. Know what it is: stress, and different sitting positions. Sitting on Celtic's bed is uncomfortable, as it's so soft (as in *bad* soft) - one sinks into it and struggles to get comfortable, unless lying down. The trouble is if you lie down you inevitably want to go to sleep. Plus, add to this the fact that I have now foregone the relative comfort of having two mattresses for the past few years, and am now back to an original soiled, thin job.

28TH MAY 2013

12.40pm

Good golly, Miss Molly! What a morning.

My new job is 'Compound Litter Picker'!

'Purple Rain' asked me what my skills are, in order to find me a suitable job that suits my resettlement needs in the short couple of weeks I have left. I started with the fact that I'm a printer by trade (Foyleview has a print shop), and rhyme off a list of academic and mentoring skills, all the while knowing fine rightly that this conversation is completely irrelevant. I asked if I could brush up on the technology used in the print shop, as I will be looking for a job as a printer on the out, to fund my studies and enhance my job prospects.

He laughed: 'Laundry or litter-picking is all that is available.'

I replied: 'Oh, litter-picking, please - on a lovely sunny day like this it'll be great.'

He replied, with ferocity: 'Aye, but it won't always be sunny. Now get out!'

I met a fellow AC/DC fan, in charge of the works-department at Foyleview, and I told him what Purple Rain said about my new duties as 'Compound Litter Picker'; I wasn't allowed to walk there, there or there, I explained, pointing to different areas of wide open space.

He put his arm round my shoulders and said: 'Fuck that fat bastard! You work for me now and you do as I say - if anything comes of it I will tell him you have only done what I've told you to do. And, if you ever repeat that I'll deny it.' This conversation obviously did not happen and is a pure figment of my imagination, as has been the last 200,000-odd words.

AC/DC then, himself, told me where I could and couldn't go - he pointed to the main gate and said: 'See that big gate over there?'

'Yes,' I said.

'Don't go out there.'

I laughed.

'At least not for a few weeks yet,' he added. He spun me round and, pointing to the inner gate, which is part of the prison wall, and the main access to the main part of the jail, said: 'See that gate?'

'Yes.'

'Don't go in there.'

I laughed again; 'Are you are telling me I'm not allowed *into* the jail?'

He looked at me; 'Funny, eh?'

I put my arm round him; 'That's the nicest thing anyone has said to me for years.'

Imagine being ordered, after six years, not to go into the place that has held you.

So, I picked up my 'Helping Hand' litter-picker, and a black, plastic bag, and headed off to explore my new surroundings in this part of the prison. I walked round picking up bits of paper, and about an hour later a guy picks me up in the little buggy, I'm given my new security card and I go into the prison, swiping in and out in the process.

It really is cool, walking round the prison, swiping my card and scanning myself in and out without having to deal with twenty apes - maybe I'll get to do it again one day when there's a new prison built, only this time I'll be back in a suit.

I chatted with S.O. BE on the way back in, and he put my name in the book for the exam on the 12th June, saying: 'In case someone else tries to veto it'. I then get my lunch: the loveliest portion of freshly fried chips I've had for a very long time - Saturdays chips were good, but these were momentous!

So, now there's me sitting on my tod again. My wee cheeks are warm and I'm of that *out-in-the-fresh-air-all-day* feeling - that warm buzz that only summertime brings. I'll sleep well if I get the chance; tomorrow's another day - probably an eventful one in my crazy life. Sitting here daydreaming, my eyes are so blurred, I can hardly see the words I'm writing. Listening to the patter of men in prison; I've got to know all these men over the years - there are only a few faces I've never seen before.

29TH MAY 2013

The sun is peaking its head over the fence of the dog-pound, which is next to this hut - heard all the residents barking as soon as I took my ear-plugs out. Mind you, it was only for a couple of minutes, and now it's deathly quiet again.

It's ten-past-seven and I've just heard the first prisoner rise and go to the toilet - that's two hours I've been awake, and nobody else has surfaced; think chemicals might have something to do with this. They're already planning 'party-time' for Saturday night. I've been told stories about what it used to be like in Foyleview - the Cunningham building (another pre-fab where we collect our dinner) used to be a nightclub! The adjoining room has a full-size snooker table, a couple of pool tables, and a mini-gym.

Bloomin'eck! A prison van has just pulled up and all the dogs have kicked off; holy shit - what a fuckin' racket! Why do they have the dog-pound next to a residential unit, when there's so much fuckin' space? Walked round this complex yesterday and there are loads of empty buildings and even more open space; there's a whole block called the 'Governor's Suite', which is derelict. I kid you not, it looks like one of those cold-war *Stasi*-type buildings, where all sorts of illegal and mysterious stuff used to be carried out; it's actually tucked away out of the road, right at the back of the complex, beside the army camp - very sinister indeed! I don't want to actually think about it much.

Dogs have gone quiet again - must be feeding time... no - one fucker's still at it; there's always one yappy bastard, eh?

7.35am

Somebody up now.

One thing that did blow my mind yesterday was walking into the staff locker room for a pee (I pee a lot, so have to go pretty sharpish) - nobody saw me, and there was nobody in it. Didn't linger, but it reminded me of my locker-room at my golf club in Cape Town; *wow*, what a world apart that is now! Shit - the more I think about it, the more the enormity of all this kicks in: I've come a long way and been through a lot.

Sitting here, visualizing, smelling and tasting the cocaine and the hunters, dry-gushing round my E.N.T., stimulating the endorphins and luring me into a false sense of security; *yessus*, I was a fuckin' train wreck! How good is it to sit here now, not a wreck – in sobriety with most of my marbles still intact, surrounded by fuckin' lunatics, with exactly three weeks to go until I'm back in the real world again.

12.20-ish

What a morning - walked around the complex again, and chatted to a few peeps. Then, went down to the workshop to brush up, pick up off-cuts, clean an office bin and make a bit of space, by shifting some lengths of roofing and wood.

I'm sunburnt - can feel my face tighten. It's a beautiful day, and a lot of the guys are beach-whaling by the fish-pond; I sat there this morning, before work, all alone - it was great.

Just remembered: I heard this kid screaming in his sleep the other night. I'll cut him a bit of slack – he's going to end up a statistic on someone's list someday. Some of these guys are just unreachable - well, for *me* they are: they don't see me as one of them.

30TH MAY 2013

6.45am

It really is a glorious morning already. Had something profound to write at about nine last night, and promised myself I'd remember in the morning. This morning, I couldn't be arsed to get up out of my cot, and now I can't remember! Welcome to my world at the minute; wonder if another cup of coffee will do the trick.

How do I feel today? Not sure yet. Physically, I have muscles voicing their protest at being woken a bit sunburnt, but I'm not complaining. I've been doing some walking over the past two days, but I know it is all a novelty - it will wear off.

The news is on the telly, but the sound is off - the images show the Woolwich incident. Feel so detached from the world, and the events in it; just read yesterday's paper, and the picture of the baby in China, who'd been flushed down the loo, actually stirred more emotion in me than the Woolwich incident. Is that normal? Has prison turned me into a heartless bastard? Mind you, I used to be pretty non-plussed about certain events *before* I came to jail - maybe sobriety just makes me more aware of it.

The radiator is cracking away as the heating comes on; it was off all day yesterday and then all night.

Spoke to Tom from the community chaplaincy for five minutes, and he promised to e-mail me; he seemed very interested in what I had to say. I also spoke to TB, and we had a giggle; he's a cynic, and all about the negative, and the flip-side of life. He says he's on the same page as me, but I'm not sure; I don't suppose we ever have been.

Just watching a wee bird move about inside the yellow hedge outside the window - one might never have known that it was a bird inside the bush, if one had not seen it go in.

It was a mad morning, and this pen has just run out.

5.15pm

You see, there are things that happen in life for a reason? I arrived in 'Narnia' on Friday and spotted something interesting in the kitchen. The previous evening I was told that the tuck-shop would be on Thursday, and one of the officers came down with the menu sheet for me – I ordered a ham salad for tonight, and Saturday morning I ordered cheese and mayonnaise. After work today, I can't get into the classroom, because there is a RC service, so I go have a shower and, just before tuck-shop is collected, I go make myself some dinner; have now just enjoyed two toasties – cheese, ham and tomato - made on a *George Foreman* grill; big dollop of mayonnaise on the side, can of Coke, and Robert is the proverbial uncle. Was trying to remember the last time I had proper toasties: all I can recall is eating them with Colleen, in Jo'Burg, way back in 2001 - it was fun, and we made ourselves sick.

Each and every time I try to revise, my mind goes to a different place; each time I leave this page, I become exhausted and want to lie down. Everyone (well, not *everyone* - *most* of the rats) have gone to the gym, and it's now very quiet; all I can hear is the wind blowing through the open windows and rattling the blinds. Tiredness overwhelms me - tired all the time now, more so than ever before.

Managed to come to the conclusion that I'm not going to get any peace whilst I remain in prison: I'm not a prison-type person – I'm not made that way; never actually thought I'd make it, but I have.

Or have I? Can I make it to the gate? Will I get there without killing someone and/or myself? Every day - every *single* day - I stop myself from doing just that; suicide is my constant companion, but only after I kill about twenty others first! *Tick-tock, tick-tock...*

Still can't remember what it was that I promised myself I would remember last night. See y'all later – I'm done for now.

31ST MAY 2013

7.55am

Told you I was tired!

The dogs are off again - looks like a regular occurrence. We had officers waking us up on the landings for four years, and now we have officers feeding *dogs* who wake us up. Still can't remember what I was meant to remember the other night.

Gotta put me work boots on, in case I forget. Not going to order any tuck-shop: got enough bare necessities to do me.

12.15pm

Phew! Another busy morning. It was raining, so I got the job of cleaning 'AC/DC''s office - the place is a woodwork shop, so everything is covered in saw-dust. We had a wee chat, and I promised not to mention him in this story; so this is me *not* mentioning how this kind and decent man treats me like a member of the human race.

I'm loving looking at this hedge, about ten feet in front of me. It's deathly quiet, nobody about, and cloudy, windy and damp - all I can hear is the hiss of the radiator, and the thudding of someone running on the treadmill.

1ST JUNE 2013

7.00am

'Bee-bop-a-loola' - seem to recall some guy in a suit analyzing these rock-n-roll lyrics, back in the fifties or sixties; 'This is the diatribe our youth of today are listening to.' This morning I feel a bit like rock-n-roll: *all revved up and no place to go.* And, even though I'm certainly no youth, I have a sense that nobody understands me, my story, my charm and my sense of morality. Still, the lyrics of *'Tutti-Frutti'* may have been incomprehensible to a certain generation, but then, as now, music was the voice of change in a developing world – and, *my Mum* understands me, so this makes it okay. Can't wait to phone her later.

I keep going on about being reborn, and this, for me, is exactly what goes on each and every day now: every twenty-four hours is a lifetime. It starts with this, the writing, of thoughts, emotions, feelings, regret, reminiscence and hope, sprinkled with despair, hatred, anger, frustration, and a wee touch of suicide thrown in for good measure.

The weather in Northern Ireland is compared to four seasons in one day - can it be possible that a lifetime is thrown in there, too?

The working week ended with me being summoned to the office for yet another ticking off. This is how close one comes to doing a life sentence every single fuckin' day. Thank God I was outside, and the breeze carried away my incoherent rambling and threats.

I've been walking on grass all week, picking up litter - penance for my success. For one brief moment yesterday, I was filled with the urge to throw it all away - to give in, to end it all, to curl up and die, but something in me smiled; don't know what that was, but it was real. It needs investigating - needs to be bottled and sold.

A friend of mine, about a year ago, told me to consider writing about the reintegration process. It - the process - is fraught with danger, hurdles and challenges, but there are also many inner smiles. This is only one day of the many I've recorded – I'll come back to it later, and tell you how my weekend went.

I hear another lyric kick in on my internal juke-box: *'I want to rise today and change this world...'*

5TH JUNE 2013

6.45am

We were woken by the fire-alarm half an hour ago - false alarm, as always.

The guy next door to me is doing his daily ritual (actually, it's not just in the morning he does it – it's all fuckin' day!): sniffing, snorting, hacking and coughing. His snorts cause my stomach to vibrate - I can actually feel the *table* vibrate - and this disgusting noise creeps up my arms and exploits my brain; I range from annoyance, disgust and resentment at being here, to having to listen to this shit and rottenness. I've had to put the headphones on again: *'Under the*

Boardwalk' is playing - how fuckin' apt. I know who I'd like to put under the fuckin' boardwalk!

What a glorious morning, already warm, and I can't wait to get outside again, bathed in sunscreen and take a wander around the jail.

Coming back from last home-leave was pretty cool - had coffee with the with a childhood friend, and she asked me lots of questions; rapid-fire, as girls seem to do. I asked her to slow down.

She cut me short, and said: 'Ach, stop. I haven't seen you for years - wise up.' It made me think - it made me thankful that someone was interested enough to ask.

Marie-Louise Muir, MG and T. McK turned up at my door around 2.00pm, and I was asked to give a tour of my block, and a short interview in my cell; *welcome to Terrapin-13, or 'The Bronx', as it is referred to here.* We all got firmly ensconced in my cell (well, not all: the rest of the ensemble are stranded in the corridor), Marie-Louise sat on the plastic chair, I sat on the bed and Connor, the sound guy, stood in front of me with a microphone. I was asked if I could read something - I told him the only thing I had left in here was my book.

Mary-Louise's eyes lit up, and she sat bolt upright in the chair; 'You've written a book? What's it called?'

'*'My Life Began at Forty'*,' said I.

'Why that title, and what's it about?'

I explained: 'My life started when I came to prison - I was forty. It's about my time in prison - all six years of it - and it'll end in two weeks' time, when I walk out the gate.'

There was a long pause - I don't know why - and I was then asked to read something.

I picked up the loose pile of 600-odd sheets, and the page that popped out was my first ever poem. I thought I was doing okay, until I started to read it: oh, my God - I read out loud, and nearly choked a couple of times. This was enormous - even bigger than me: here was I, sitting in my cell, at the end of my sentence, reading a poem I wrote at the very start.

This recording is going to be broadcast in September. My goal at the start of all of this was to get it out there - my feelings and experiences - and here I was, doing just that!

Can't remember all that went on - I got confused a few times, but I know I made an impression. Then, we all went round to Celtic's, and it was his turn. I stood outside, talking to MG, but we were told to go away as we could be heard inside Celtic's room. So, I had a good chat with MG by the fish-pond, and I left them all, feeling a bit more optimistic than before.

6TH JUNE 2013

6.15pm

There are times in one's life when things happen, that are just too freaky for mere words – more, incredulous disbelief. I'm sitting around in Celtic's cell, talking about the price of oil, getting out, legislation on tagging, home-detention curfew, and how it works for those in England and Wales, when there was a rap on the door – T. McK was there, accompanied by three people in suits: two men and a woman.

T. McK introduced us to the suits, and I asked the man (called 'P') what department they were with - P replied: 'We're with the public accounts committee.'

I told him about my trip to Stormont, we spoke about the tragic death of Mike Moloney, and I mentioned that if it wasn't for these guys - the Education department - I wouldn't have made it. P knew I was going to Queens; he told me his daughter was doing criminology, and in her second year.

When they were leaving, I asked the man his full name, and if I can contact him when I get out – I nearly had a heart-attack when he replied: 'I'm 'PG'.'

I jumped up off the bed with surprising speed and agility, shook his hand and said: 'Oh, now I know who you are, you and I have a lot to talk about, if you'll allow me.'

'Look forward to it,' he said.

When they'd said their goodbyes, Celtic said: 'Who's he, then?'

'He's the chair of the Justice Committee.'

We sat quiet for a while, and discussed the fact that no one will believe us if we told them what just happened.

This is another big deal - there seems to be lots of MLAS's plodding about in here at present, and I'm bumping into quite a few of them. I hope he engages with me.

7TH JUNE 2013

5.30am

Another glorious day (weather-wise) beckons. We had another fire-alarm at 10.30 last night, and it became pretty obvious that there is nobody here at night. A van with an S.O. and two other staff appeared, a few minutes after we assembled outside, and when they arrived, they proceeded to unlock the reception building, where they spent another five minutes trying to turn off the alarm.

Still can't believe how lucky I was to talk to PG last night - I'll have to look up the public accounts committee to find out more, and who the other two people were, before diving in. Then I'll go finish up the tea-towels for the training staff and pick up the litter in the staff car-park.

All this, combined with my imminent release, means I simply cannot find the energy, or focus, or whatever you like to call it, to revise/study for the final exam of my degree - I'm beat… done, and I've already resigned myself for a re-sit. I sat here last night with the headphones on, listening to *Magic FM*, either staring at the wall or dozing - I am in a complete stage of lock-down/melt-down, as soon as I close that door; with the TVs on either side, music, shouting, snorting and slamming doors (sometimes on purpose), I cannot afford to remove myself from this trance-like state of suspended animation, or I will flip the proverbial lid. Foyleview was a bad move as far as study is concerned.

5.40pm

Sitting with Celtic there, looking out over the Foyle to the hills of Donegal - lovely. I had to leave the classroom because the Christians were coming! So, I go and sit with Celtic and a few of the lads, in a quiet corner of the compound, at the back of number seventeen, take my trainers and socks off, and sit in the shade, with my back on the fence. I squeeze my feet into the soft, mossy grass - aaahhhh! Now, there's something I've been wanting to do for five years. It was unexpected, unplanned and bloody lovely in its simplicity. Somebody asked me a question, and it got a bit of a giggle, because I was completely lost in the sensation of the grass between my toes.

I'm not out yet, and I'm walking around on my own, burnt to a crisp, and sitting in my bare feet, lapping up a summer's evening, on the banks of the Foyle.

8TH JUNE 2013

8.25am

Another glorious day beckons, and I have to admit the weather is making this final stint a tad easier. To be honest, I try to be so detached from everything, I don't think it would matter if it was blowing a blizzard - I'd still feel the numbness and nothingness of detachment.

This does not bode well for revision and my impending exam.

Again, being honest, I'm so detached I don't even want to go to Queens, study or do any of it - just want the world to stop, and restart on Wednesday week.

Sitting here, staring at the back of my Kenco coffee refill packet, and I see the address is in Uxbridge Business Park. I remember it being built - I lived beside it - and I recall sitting in Stockley Park on a morning just like this (1996-ish), wondering what I was going to do with my life. I was so nervous and excitable in those days.

9TH JUNE 2013

7.35am

Oh, my God! I've just realized that if I get out next weekend, I only have five more days and one night in custody!

Also, 'oh my God' to this weather: it's already another glorious looking day - I think the forecast says it's going to rain around Tuesday; rain or shine, it doesn't matter to me.

Managed to get a bit of revision done, but, to be honest, I've given up: there is no peace here - just music; have to wear my headphones all the time when I'm in my cell, just to block out the TVs and hi-fis on either side of me. I cannot, for the life of me, understand how people put up with this.

There was talk of mad parties last weekend - maybe the management got wind of it, as they warned everyone not to meet people in the kitchen at all hours of the night, or take too long making a cup of tea. Heard some sort of commotion, but it was probably the guy next door, snorting - he's in his early twenties, yet sounds like a fifty-year old man!

Still, not long now, eh?

The dogs have started barking again, right on cue; it's a funny old ten minutes. Someone else up now.

Forgot to see what's for breakfast… sausages – oh, yummy! Maybe I'll save them for lunch-time.

Mandela is in hospital again - think it's time they let the old boy go. Saw an image of him, the last time he was in hospital, and he looked like a puppet, being wheeled out to reassure the nation that he was still alive - it looked awkward and horrible; I might be wrong, but I felt as if he didn't want to be there. My heart goes out to him.

I look at the images now (8.11am, 9th June 2013) on the BBC news, live from Johannesburg, and the guy is holding up the local newspaper - the headline reads: ''IT'S TIME TO LET HIM GO'.' So, maybe I'm not wrong.

It's really weird: the skies in Jo'burg are as crystal-clear as here, but I know from experience the temperature in the air will be freezing; don't let those skies fool you - it's fuckin' Baltic.

Moved to South Africa in May 2001 (I think - not entirely sure of the year, but it was definitely May); I had to buy an electric blanket. Making love to Colleen was a tentative experience, as I already had several bruised ribs, plus, if the cold air got in under the duvet, my beautiful goddess would moan, and certainly not in pleasure! I recall sitting by the fish-pond in the front garden, like now, listening to the dogs yapping as a black person walked past the gate; sometimes this person would hesitate, and hold his/her hands out, begging for something... anything: *'Bass?'* I'd been forewarned not to give, as they would keep coming back, but I held my finger up to my lips in a conspirator's silence, and I'd pass a couple of cigarettes through the gate; then I'd wink and point to the house, running my hand across my throat. That black human-being's eyes would light up in understanding: I was breaking a code. The hopelessness in those faces still haunts me, but their eyes and smile still warms me. A bit like the wee girl who sang Beyonce on *'BGT'* last night: so serious, so much the act of a Diva, yet her smile lights up the room.

Now, I sit at our fish-pond, with the goldfish and the koi-carp, and my mind continually flits between here and now, and there and then... from imprisonment to golf courses in S.A., wine, women, song and the odd orange thong. But, what I remember most is the sense of freedom, and an opportunity to turn my life around - to reinvent myself. It's funny, I know, but twelve years later, I'm doing exactly the same - similar thoughts but with a different agenda. Don't think I'll balls this one up - how many more lives have I got?

Okay – it's now 9.40 and I've surrounded myself with answers, TMAs and previous exam papers. Managed to get into the classroom before the Christians come - they should be here around ten-ish; this gives me a chance to read over the summaries of book 2, chapter 7, and get them floating around in my head.

I'm panicking about not getting my sausages.

I'm trying to follow a pattern here, of reading from my own notes on the computer for ten minutes, then writing in here for ten minutes, but all I really want is to put the headphones on and sleep. As soon as these guys get up, I'll put on the music and sit outside this window – I'll get nothing more done. Think I'll go back on the screen and read over some of my writing, which I can maybe use for a blog.

10TH JUNE 2013

7.00am

I'm in the middle of one of those anxiety attacks I talk about - tried to doze, but felt sick, my heart racing; I want to run, to cry, to lay down and die. I smile at the thought of that - know it's not real, but I'm dizzy, cloudy and disheartened. Don't want to face the day - want to smash, want to lash out, but can't give in. Deep breaths, a bit of toasted bread and sips of water… more deep breaths; wish I could breathe as deeply as the guy snoring beside me, because he's causing the water in my bottle to ripple, like in the scene from *'Jurassic Park'*. Feel sick; even being outside I'm trapped, trapped and trapped - nowhere to run and nowhere to hide!

This is how it gets you: you let your guard down for five minutes and *BAM!* – it's on you! Smothering you, stifling you, and ripping your logic and rationality to shreds.

Maybe I made my coffee too strong. The back of the bran-flakes packet says: 'Like you, we believe every child deserves a nutritious breakfast to fuel their imagination'.

In… out… slowly breathe in… and slowly breathe out…

'*Sooooo Hummmmm…*' - the comforting memory of Sri Sri Ravi Shanker, from way back God-knows when. Oh, God, please set me free from this madness.

I'm going to throw my stuff in a bag, ready for the block! I ain't even done nothing, and I'm going to put myself in the block - how fucked up is that? Gate fever? You bet your bloody life it is!

7.40am

I'm sort of smiling again.

The old boy who looks after the kitchen moans that 'There is a rail on the wall for towels, and these fuckin' bastards don't even see it!' I rinse my cup and use two paper towels to dry it, to avoid upsetting the poor man any further; you see: there is always someone worse off than you. This actually makes me smile.

Another cloudless day, but it sounds a bit windy, so still probably a bit of a chill coming off the sea.

5.00pm

A pretty depressing day - any highlights enshrined with fatigue and mental shutdown. My head is down and my shoulders are slumped; I have slipped back into servitude mode, and find myself being overly nice – worried, in case something happens in the next four days to stop me getting out at the weekend. That's all I want now: the weekend, then back for one night next Tuesday.

AC/DC is a very nice man, and he has decided to give me the day off, to do some studying.

So, tomorrow will have to be my D-day - my penultimate day… my *enthusiasm* day.

I'm sitting here sweltering and stinking, and my eyes are half-shut from sunburn, and tiredness of being outside in the wind all day.

Shit, I really was messed up this morning, and passed out as soon as I put the headphones on at lunch-time. Feel the same way now - going to close my eyes for ten minutes and hope the cameras don't record me; I'm so fuckin' paranoid. A wee cat nap usually does the trick.

I'm going to sit in my room all day tomorrow and read - try and get this lot to stick. I might actually get on my knees and pray later on - maybe I'll do it now:

'God grant me the serenity to accept the things I cannot change, courage to change the things I can, and the wisdom to know the difference.'

11TH JUNE 2013

8.13am

'For a new lease of life, throw caution to the wind and let the breeze catch your hair. It is time to relax and let others find their own way. Let your cares vanish on the wind and listen to the voice within. In all things, give up trying so hard - you can barely please yourself at the moment, never mind anyone else.' My horoscope for yesterday.

Yesterday was a bad day, and I'm glad it's over - maybe I'll let loose after tomorrow: I think I've got the day off to revise in my room. AC/DC joked that Purple Rain will probably watch the cameras to see how many times I use the toilet; sadly, these quips are not made from fresh air.

It's wet and the dark, grey sky is low - makes the world smaller, and puts the mind back in its box, where it belongs. When blue skies open up, the universe creates too much space, enabling the mind to wander.

Roll on tomorrow afternoon, so I can blank out the exam, get out and prepare for the next chapter in my life. As per usual, others have faith in me, and I don't.

Read Nuala's column in the *Belfast Telegraph* again just now, about the loss of Mike Moloney (her partner) - went to sleep thinking about her, and woke up thinking about her, but not in *that* sort of way. God, my heart really does go out to her - wish I could give her a hug, hold her hand and make it better. Of course, I can't: one will never be able to make better what Nuala is going through - only time will keep adding sticking plasters to the cut that runs so deep. It will hurt and it will mend, but it will also split, burst and seep when one least expects it. Nuala writes nicely. I've hardly ever read *'The Telly'* or her column - just a quick flick through; maybe I should pay a bit more attention.

Must go and get ready.

9.45am

I've stuck my two essays and a few quotes on my walls - I will spent the rest of the day and night looking at these. The essay is in front of me is called *'The War on Drugs'* - I got 97% for that one; the essay behind me is *'Globalization and Human Rights - TMA04'* - 95% for that one. I've got a few previous exam papers and quotes, pasted on the wall in front of where I lie, with my headphones on.

I'll have to put my headphones on again at lunchtime and the evening, as it's raining, and the lads on either side of me and all around me will be pumping away at the TV and music - it was half-eleven before they stopped last night.

10.30am

Now, this is great – I've positioned my cot along the centre of the room. This allows me to assume the identity of a Roman god - all I need now are a few dusky maidens, peeling and feeding me grapes (maybe next weekend, eh?).

This positioning allows me to lie on one side and read one wall, then when the hip gets sore, turn and read the other wall; when I lie face down, I have the quotes in front of me. The psychology of this is that I can flash sentences in my mind's eye, which will hopefully prompt me. I've just thought of four points that jump out of the course at me, and I can use as templates for each essay - if I can elaborate on these, I think I'll be safe. If not..?

Going to listen to some Slash and *Chickenfoot* for a bit. God, it's so quiet: all I can hear is the tiny beat of music coming from Rick's cell, the odd gust of wind and the sporadic sound of van tyres on loose stones out the back. It will not last long - I know it.

10.45am

See! The plumbers are now in, fixing the kitchen hot tap, that stopped working this morning. Slash is now keeping me company, and I've had to put my fleece on, as it's chuffin' Baltic.

This is mad! I keep getting little rushes of panic each time I try to remember something. What's even madder is that I keep fantasizing about being with a woman… *any* woman; what's weird is that I've never really given this a lot of thought over the years - strange how it feels, popping up now (literally). The last time I felt anything like this was Catford police station in 2007; of course, there has been masturbation but that's uncontrollable and gone in sixty seconds - a natural occurrence for me (can't say the same for others: I can hear them pounding away for hours).

4.30pm

Managed to get a bit of revision done - hopefully it will be enough. I really don't care at the minute: I've had enough. I'll take a deep breath in the morning, and read over my walls.

To be honest, I'm quite dizzy and could sleep forever - keep nodding off for five minutes (or is it more like half an hour?). My NIACRO support person just left and gave me a few details of appointments, etc. – I'll process it some other time, but not at the minute.

Sitting here, typing away, as P teaches his class of three or four – it's weird that four years down the line I'm listening to his dulcet tones teaching C.L.A.I.T.. I'm well beyond C.L.A.I.T. myself now, but the irony is not lost on me. I'm nowadays able to whizz around Microsoft Word because of some of the stuff he taught me – thanks, P!

'Starry Stars' bade me 'goodbye and good luck' yesterday afternoon - it was a surreal moment. As he was walking away, I called to him: 'Thank you! Thank you for everything - thank you for helping me.' We both started singing *'Starry Starry Stars'*, and parted laughing. I have to admit, though, I had a dirty, great fuckin' lump in my throat. Hope I get to see a few others before I leave - it will be a crying shame if I don't. They know where I am, so they can pop over and see me on their way in or out.

Think I'll sit here until P leaves, then at half-six head round and make some tomato soup and ham sandwiches - sounds like a plan.

NIACRO person warned me that life will be slow once I'm free, simply because I've been so busy in here. I don't know about that – it'll be what I make of it, I suppose. My Granda Watson always had a regime - I think I'll do the same (but not immediately, eh?).

I've just heard a helicopter hovering around, in and out of the army camp next door - brings back strange memories!

DAY OF FINAL EXAM
12TH JUNE 2013
5.30am

God, it's freezing. Had to bang my wall last night, as my neighbour's TV was blaring - I think he actually turned it *up* after 10.30. I was sleeping, and woke shortly after eleven - reinserted my ear-plugs, but to no avail. Think I'm close to a nervous breakdown: the rage, sweats and depression consume me. He did turn it down, but I lay tossing and turning until the early hours.

It's strange that I've had this date for my final exam in the old napper for a long time, and now that it's here, I don't care: I'm just going to turn up, write what I can remember and leave. I've ninety minutes for each question, so I should manage something - whether it'll be enough remains to be seen.

I've had a coffee, opened the blinds and blown my nose several times - got a head cold 'cos there's no heat. Going to try and sleep for another hour – can't keep my eyes open. I'm not nervous or panicking yet - I simply don't care: caution to the wind, positive mental attitude and all that ballix.

7.15am

Wow! Why do we do this to ourselves? Did sleep again, but my brain has now developed a heartbeat all of its own! It could be worse: I could be living next to P. McH - his walkie-talkie is extremely loud, and I can hear it even when I close my door, even though I'm at the exact opposite end of the landing; poor old M: his head must be fried. M and I discussed banning TVs and hi-fis from prison, or at least providing headphones for everyone; oh, I've suggested this many times, but nobody seems to listen.

Going to take these essays down now, brush my teeth, make a cup of coffee and just sit and breathe… a lot.

7.55am

Shit! You should hear the voices going off in my head: the arguments - the language is fuckin' atrocious; give me the dentist's any day. All I can think about is James Frey's description of the dentist's chair in *'A Million Little Pieces'*: painfully excruciating to read, as you live every horrifying detail, but worth it afterwards, because you *get it*.

Know the next three hours will whizz by and I won't remember a single thing I've written. Each exam has been the same and one never gets any feedback – it's either a *'yes'* or *'no'*. The important thing to remember is to listen to my own advice: this is not the end of the world and I refuse to write what I think others want to hear - I can only write what I can remember.

The dogs are barking away and people on the landing are starting to surface, going about their business, oblivious to Mickey Irwin's world of madness.

I recall previously going into my level-3 psychology exam with total dejection, having done no revision at all, as I'd mixed the dates up, and totally resigned myself for a re-sit. My last answer wasn't even a page long, and yet still I got 69%; so I live in hope, because that's all I have - my mind won't allow me anything else. God, I hate this fuckin' place.

Rick just wished me 'good luck' - first positive I've heard all day!

1.30pm

Back in cell - one degree with 'honours' finished, I hope. Managed to write for most of the time, and I think I said what I wanted.

Now I'm just going to blank the world out and write here. I'm back in my room, as they've just done a search of the block with dogs - it looks like a few cells, the kitchen and the toilets were targeted; my sun lotion and ear-plugs are still here though, so I'm fine for now: nothing looks to have been disturbed, so I'm alright, Jack (unless they used it as a ruse to plant something in my cell, come back tomorrow and stitch me up!).

So, how do I feel? Tired… relieved… proud..? Yeah: *proud* is good.

Fuck-face next door is in, and his music has just been turned on. It doesn't really matter anymore – I'll take myself off for a walk in a minute.

5.55pm

There are four corners to this classroom; I am allowed to use one computer and it's in the corner where all the boys have decided to congregate outside, as it's very nice and sunny. Came round here to get a bit of peace, but no luck. This is also the classroom I'd have preferred to sit my exam in this morning, so perhaps for the best.

AM has just informed me that probation will be here on Friday morning at 9.30, but warned me not to rush in, making demands; doesn't she read my horoscope? Just sit back and let it happen.

Apparently the other A is off - over in England - as her daughter has just had twins. I'm so pleased for her - not only because she has had a few weeks off, but because these babies will bring a bit of peace and love into her life - something *this* place is totally devoid of.

There's been a couple of helicopters flying round here all day, landing and taking off from the army camp next door - it looks like they're practicing.

Was going to take a bit of time and post-mortem my exam, but there's no point: it's either good enough or it isn't. You know what: fuck this – I'm going to get the shorts on and lie down; I'm burnt and beat!

Nothing on the system about home-leave, so I don't know yet - need to ask again tomorrow. This is why, sometimes, you should never ask until the last minute: there's now two days' worth of wonder, but better than if it had already been granted, and I then had to spend two days waiting to see if they were going to take it off me. Dad says there's plenty for me to do, and it would be nice to be at home for Father's Day - maybe my bro has something pencilled in, also. It would be really nice to get the fuck out of here, and in a perverse way, I look forward to coming back: one more night and then the ritual of being *'time served'*.

Shit: 'time served' sure sounds good!

Got the headphones on, listening to *Chickenfoot*, and the sun is splitting the skies again. I'm toasted, and got my blinds up for a change, enjoying the summer's evening; still locked up - still a prisoner - but nearly there.

Had a couple of quiet moments to myself whilst out on my litter-picking duties. There's this lean-to shed-thing at the back of one of the old, abandoned Nissen huts, and I took a little look-see. God, it was spooky: unreal - it looked like a cell from the old army barracks; maybe it was a cell for soldiers. It chilled me.

I then went and plonked myself right at the base of one of the very high, spherical, globe-type cameras - wondered if the base of it is a blind-spot. Sat there for twenty minutes, getting a tan, watching the helicopters and enjoying the scenery, whilst observing the four people who were around, going about their business - very tranquil. I then wandered around to the back of the compound, beside the aviary, and joined Celtic on a bench for another twenty minutes.

Don't care about any of this anymore, if I'm honest - my exam is done and so am I.

13TH JUNE 2013
5.00am

Fell asleep at 10.30pm and woke at 4.30am; I've already had a coffee and a bit of toast. I met Jack in the kitchen - another early riser.

Jesus fuckin' Christ - you should hear the guys on either side of me, snorting, snoring and farting. I've put my ear-plugs back in - I so enjoy the sound of silence.

Oops: 8.30 - slept in. I think, in the past six years, I've overslept only on a handful of occasions - shows you how *relaxed* I am!

Off to see if I'm getting out at the weekend - either way, I have a maximum of five days to spend in jail. Five fuckin' days! Wow!

Celtic's doing the servery, so I got two extra sausage rolls - purring like a kitten. Got the headphones on again to block out my neighbours' grunts, snorts and music.

Was just recalling when I sat the base of the security camera, taking a wee rest: the grass was crawling with little winged beetles - I mean *crawling*! It's like the Earth was moving. I'll have to *Google* them at the weekend.

Waiting for my washing to finish - got one T-shirt, one Chelsea top, one pair of joggers, shorts and a handful of socks.

Going to try and kick the beta-blockers: don't need them anymore.

4.40pm

Sitting at the picnic table, looking at Benevenagh, as a helicopter buzzes the area. The aviary is behind me, and the quiet chirps of the budgies, and gentle flutter of their wings, soothes me. Waiting for the Christians to leave the classroom again.

The thumping of heavy calibre gunfire drowns out the sound of the budgies. There's a man in uniform hovering around, and I try to avoid him - trying to avoid *everyone* at the minute. My time-bomb seems to have stopped ticking, and I like it that way.

Oh, there's the Christians leaving.

No - false alarm. They do move about a bit, the ole Christians - never a dull moment.

Can make out the soldiers in the helicopter as they buzz by.

Just got told that I'm out for the weekend! *Woooooohoooooo!!!!*

14TH JUNE 2013

5.15am

Been lying here, half-awake, since 4.00am - got up, made a cup of coffee and read the paper; I'll probably go back to sleep in a minute.

I'm so pleased to be getting out at the weekend, but after talking to a lot of the lads, I can see how right I was about Foyleview: nobody is really benefitting in the long-term - nobody is being taught, and nobody is getting great qualifications. Some are getting new skills - making garden furniture - but most guys seem to apply existing skills to fit jobs that only need doing round the jail, and Trades could actually be done away with; in fact, two competing workshops, whose jobs overlap. Foyleview is an institutional trade off - nothing to do with rehabilitation or education: town visits and home-leaves are simply a payoff from the system, which are cheaper.

7.30am

Just had my last ever shower in prison, with lukewarm water, in a freezing cold public toilet, listening to other men vacating their bowels - sometimes it's great to have a summer head-cold. Must admit, though: this shave feels great on so many different levels - another ritual complete; I'll have a shave at Dad's, of course, but will not need one when I leave next Wednesday.

Meeting 'R' from the probation board in an hour or two - I hope we connect: I'd love to have their support. As usual, I'll just be truthful and say what's on my mind, while making a conscious effort to stay away from my bitter resentment of this place.

It's not only the toilets that are freezing: the whole chuffing place is! I'm going to take my shoes off and get back under the duvet, fully clothed, in the middle of June - go figure.

1.00pm

Heavens to Murgatroyd, even - what a morning! Just got soaked coming back from the main jail!

Spoke to R - very nice indeed. We had good chat, and I now have my mind set at ease.

Spoke to a guy call T. McC - a lifer - by the fish-pond; he, too, studied criminology.

15TH JUNE 2013

5.00am

Reinventing assumptions, but who am I to assume? I'm fully clothed, under the duvet, loaded with hot coffee, plugged into *Led Zep*'s *'Mothership'*, and loving the battering wind and rain lashing off my window. Still in prison, but I'm heading out around nine to get processed for a few days at home. Then back Tuesday, for one night, and 'time served' on Wednesday.

Some might assume that I'm jumping all over the shop, like a cat on the proverbial hot tin roof. On the other hand, one might also assume that the crap weather has put a dampener on my day, and no doubt I will have this brought to my attention on several occasions before I get onto the train.

But nothing could be further from the truth: the weather has never dictated my mood in prison - my perception of it is like most things of the outside world: complete indifference and detachment; the physical storms of Mother Nature cannot compare to the inner battles and raging tempests that go on in the mind of yours-truly.

I've had a couple of tetchy conversations with family recently about prison, and me being in it. My problem is that I have assumed that they accepted it, as I have, as part of my life, and that it is something they will willingly and openly discuss. It's only now, when I stop to think about it, do I see in their eyes the politeness of love, tolerance and patience, accompanied with flashes of anger which betray their true feelings. This prison sentence has been my life, and I assumed, because they support me, that my family members will want to share it with me. The last home-leave has put the kibosh on that little notion.

It all started over garden furniture: each and every time I have been at my new home, the garden has been mentioned – it's pretty bare at the minute, but has the potential to be something special; it needs constant maintenance, and my brother has supplied me with a petrol mower. On my day at home, Dad was sifting through the *Argos* catalogue, looking at garden furniture. This planted a seed of assumption in my head…

Recently, back in 'Narnia', I was sitting at one of the newly-made picnic tables outside the workshop, lapping up the sun and resting my legs, after a very concerted hour of litter-picking. As the mind is prone to wander, I imagined myself in my new *'free Narnia'*, with the smell of burgers on the *braii* (South African for barbecue), the sound of beer bottles chinking, and the laughter of friends and family. I enquired as to the cost of the furniture the lads at Magilligan made, and who it was for, and was told it is for prisoners, prison staff or anyone who works in the prison; the cost is for the materials - there is no labour charge, as all of us work for a flat £19 per week (after £1 deducted for TV rental).

My assumption was that my family members might like to know that they could get something on the cheap, which wasn't hooky or stolen. Oh, boy - did I ever get that wrong?

'I don't want anything from that place,' and 'As soon as you come home, I want to forget all about prison,' were two comments from two different people - the intensity with which they were delivered had me reeling.

I found myself in the unchartered waters of indignation, and, I kid you not (it was on the tip of my tongue), I caught myself about to defend the prison and the prison service! I'd taken this slight on the work that the lads, staff and the system do personally - I had become one of *'them'*.

Had a long, hard think about this, and have come to the conclusion that I will have to keep my gob shut about all this and move on from it, as far as family is concerned. I don't want to alienate myself and push my friends and family away now, so I've decided never to mention prison in front of them again.

Of course, this now throws a completely different slant on the re-integration dynamic. I found myself thinking: *Who can I talk to? I'm all alone in all of this.* Thank God I've got a blog now, and am able to use it as a form of cathartic.

I will also have to reinvent my thought process and assumption dynamic: I've *really* fucked up, and have seriously damaged my loved ones in the process. We (prisoners) always say we regret what we've done, but we still lead a selfish existence, and, indeed, are forced to continue to upon release.

I'm starting to hear about other men's experiences of families, and how break-ups are commonplace, because the assumption was/is that we pick up where we left off - it seems this is another 'Narnia' fantasy. The message is simple: 'get over yourself, forget it and get on with it'; the trouble with that little lot is that one *can't*. I spoke to a lifer yesterday, who's done sixteen years and is on the cusp of release – I could see the pain in his eyes when he relived the moment of committing murder. It's a strange feeling, sharing such an intense and horrific moment. Though he never actually told me what he did, I know the distant look in his eyes; someone else informed me later on. This whole business is a cauldron of feelings, emotions, perceptions and of wrong assumptions.

17TH JUNE 2013
4.15pm

There seems to be a problem with my next-door neighbour: apparently this guy, who Purple Rain calls a 'model prisoner', has been fighting on his home-leave, all weekend. He seems to have brought the best of his exemplary manners and attitude towards others back home with him - he just whacked me with the fridge door as he opened it, and said: 'Watch yourself.'

I said: 'For fuck's sake,' and left the kitchen pissed off – now, apparently,

I'm going to get a punch in the mouth for my efforts. As I left, walking away and trying keep my composure, he got louder, and the threat was repeated, over and over. I simply cannot explain how much it takes not to let rip.

Flipped out earlier when probation came to see me, and nearly chucked myself into the C.S.U. for the night; had a full-blown panic attack and nervous breakdown. My probation officer looked quite shocked at the transformation, and my complete lack of control over it: I literally changed shape, and my eyes changed colour, right in front of this person.

Had a couple more minor flare-up incidents, even when I went round to see Celtic. At lock-up, one of the increasing number of button-pushers chirps up and says: 'I hear you're getting the bumps later.' Another threat, said with a smile. I tell him to 'fuck off!' I then laugh, look him right in the eyes and say: 'FUCK OFF!' I think he got the message.

My door is now locked from the inside, and I'm sitting here, propped up, with the headphones on, listening to *Led Zep*. Can't hear a thing, except between tracks - decide I'll go back to *Magic FM* in a moment, so I'll hear *nothing* from outside.

18TH JUNE 2013

Well, here we go: my last night in custody. I got back safe from today's home-leave, and enjoyed the journey with T - a nice man (too good for this place). Enjoyed listening to him tell stories about his dogs, and he even showed me a picture of the tractor he restored. He's not well-read or educated, and has difficulty reading and writing, but is a master of many trades. We swapped numbers – I'd like to see him again one day.

The staff on duty at reception I knew, so all was well: it'll be a simple process in the morning; they left my laptop plugged in for me. On my way out I met officer TB, and we had a laugh; he told me to do something, and I couldn't resist:

'You don't ever tell me what to do again!' I said.

He quickly retorted: 'We don't have to let you out until twelve, you know!'

'There goes a happy man,' is one of the remarks which greets me, back in Narnia.

I *am* happy - I really am.

One young lad said: 'Well, Michael – you've done your whack!'

I roared with laughter - this was the first time I'd heard this. He's a serious young man, so the way he said it made it all the more profound.

'Sunshine on a rainy day', by Zoe, is now playing in my head. I went to my work and sat on one of the newly-made garden chairs; I loved it when the officers walked past and saw me sitting there, doing nothing - it will drive some of them completely mad. Fuckin' awesome!

'TIME SERVED'

19TH JUNE 2013

5.00am

Slept well, but still tired - think it's going to be a long day.

There's an image on the TV of Taliban fighters, with R.P.G.s and machine-guns, sitting on a snowy mountain top - their arses must be freezing! *Mine* isn't: I'm snug as the proverbial bug.

There is no urgency, no mad panic, no great excitement and no anti-climax – it's a day like any other:

The sun will rise, the sun will set;
Haven't made home - not quite, not yet.
There's still, there's peace,
There's love in my heart - the day of my release.
Advice from friends... strangers... new friends...
One on the out, who doesn't like Rangers:

Give yourself a hug, give yourself a break –

I will: I'm no mug – I'm done blaming myself for this horrible state;

What to follow in my wake?

I wonder, is it a big wake, or have I just muddied the waters?

There's clean air ahead - I live in hope.

6.00am

Listening to *'Ramble on'*, as promised – thanks, *Led Zep*; *'The time has come to be gone!'*

Wow, now I'm fuckin' buzzin': *Woo-fuckin'-hoo! Yes, yes, yes!!!*

There we fuckin' go: my emotions implode and explode, and the crying starts - tears of relief, anger, sorrow, relief and letting it go… letting it *all* fuckin' go! *Aahhh!* I'm thinking: *this is better than any cocktail of coke and booze and sex I've ever taken* – it's actually quasi-sexual. A weird feeling: the loins stir whilst losing and regaining the plot! Phew - that was good.

I've a funny feeling there will be plenty of exclamation marks during the course of the day.

The sun is trying to break through high clouds.

Just performed another little ritual by binning my toiletries, especially my razor; the razor is symbolic: even though it is an expensive item, one doesn't want to stand in front of the mirror every day at home and be reminded of here - memories are good, and will be plentiful over the coming years, but one doesn't need to shove it down one's throat, now, does one? Everything that I relied on in here has been binned. I'm keeping my Tupperware and work-boots though - fuck it!

7.00am

Slash and Myles are on *Kerrang* radio - *'So, keep your cloud and gloom and darkness off my parade today'*; sure, where else would you get them?

Well, that's me packed: ready for the off. Nothing matters.

Going to take the headphones off now and place them on top of the pillows.

Heading over to reception in about an hour. I'm cool, and not nearly as excited as I was this time last year. I think being out at the weekend was a good idea.

The promise of peace, no longer wishing to be dead,
Lying in my bed, 'Ramble on' *playing in my head,*
My heart no longer filled with lead,
The day of my release –
My promise to myself: 'Give my head peace.'

One officer said to me: 'Oh, you're back to being your own man.'

Arrogant fuck! I've always been my own man, just not in front of you, officer! (You'll have noticed I don't like using the term 'screw', a name derived from the turning of the screw on the treadmills of Victorian jails, and have refrained throughout my little tale.)

Life in prison is a continually implied threat, and it's worked for me on many different levels; I've said before: 'I'll die before I set foot in one of these places again as a captive - suicide would be my only option.' The fear will always hang over me – prison has done its job well.

My whole biological make up and functioning changed for the better, each and every time I left here over the past year - *each* and *every* time.

'My own man'! What a sorry, *sorry* man.

Still, time to move on, sing my song and paddle my wave. You'll see as my mood lightens that the heart sings, and fills me with poetry and love.

In a coffee shop on one my home-leaves, my beautiful friend A once asked me: 'What have you missed the most?'

'Love,' I said.

I can and will find it again - as soon as I leave here, in a couple hours. I will find the real man I have become.

I've got two A4 pages left in this, my one and only writing pad; which is quite ironic, as this is the end of *'My Life Began at Forty'*.

I'm going to say goodbye now - going to take down my *Inside Time* wall banner, with the words 'Sweet Home Alabama' scrawled over today's date; I've been aimlessly staring at these words for six months now, and more intensely in the past few weeks. I'll keep it in a shoe box somewhere, and maybe look at it from time to time, just to remind me of this moment.

I've turned off *Kerrang*, unplugged the headphones from the TV and put them in my bag. Now just going to sit here and breathe, in my final hour on the wing, in my cell.

Hope you enjoyed my tale.

In reality, it's only just begun.

Good luck, stay safe, be well.

I'll leave the final thought of 'PRISONER MICHAEL NOEL IRWIN - C7874' to Friedrich Nietzsche: 'Behind every thought and feeling, my dear brother, stands a mighty commander - he is called: *'Self'*...'

7.40am

The sun is out.

Can't breathe... *can* breathe - it comes, it goes... going to have to keep my game-face on. Jesus, this is a lovely feeling.

God grant me the serenity to accept the things I cannot change, courage to change the things I can, and the wisdom to know the difference.

The trouble with breathing is that it fills the blood with oxygen and heightens the senses!

Nearly there...

Afterword

This is a book of hope. Hope and achievement, against a backdrop of hopelessness and *under*achievement. It is about one extraordinary man's metamorphosis from a common arch-criminal to a student, and then a master of criminological studies.

Because it is a book of hope, it is not the 'other' type of prison book, the ones which focus on all the 'bad' in prison; the violence, the lack of will to grow seen in most prisoners, and, in Michael's own words, the 'bullying, slabbering, bitching and… two-faced fucks… a continuous threat of being put back over the wall by the officers - the fear is drummed into you from the very first day… what wasn't fear previously , now becomes it.'

Because this is not 'that' prison book, these scenes - which *were* present - have been played down, or cut altogether. This is not to say that this edited journal paints any rosy picture of prison life – Michael was engaged in many complaints and conflicts with 'the system', as well as other inmates, almost continuously throughout his prison sentence. But the battles are negative – they are distracting, and they are not what 'My Life Began at Forty' is about.

Michael is not running scared - he was the first to admit to his many battles with the prison service over his six years in prison, which he hopes to put together for his next publication – maybe *that* book will be 'that' prison book.

This book is a book of hope.

In April 2012 Michael took the prison service to court for a judicial review of the night-checks he makes mention of throughout his journal. He lost.

But, in true Michael Irwin style, this setback was just the beginning: following the defeat, he vowed, as he had done from day one, to strengthen his resolve to apply his academic gatherings to fighting for the rights of prisoners; but, more importantly, to champion the importance of an alternative to the criminal justice status quo. He extensively promotes – on the outside, just as he did on the inside - the importance of education, opportunities and rehabilitation as actual occurrences, rather than mere superficial political discourse. Michael knows, as most educated people know, that more opportunities – more motivation – create less criminals; less criminals create less victims.

Before and even on the very day he was sentenced to twelve years, Michael vowed that he would use his time in prison to create a better future – not just for himself, but for his fellow convicts. The vow became a promise, and it is one he has pursued passionately to the point where it has become not just a cause, but a calling. Michael is, quite simply, one of the most inspirational men one is ever likely to meet, with a motivation that, at times, beggars belief.

Michael's last entry into this journal includes the words 'it's only just begun' - he wasn't kidding. The Psychological Studies and Criminology degree he gained in prison was the start of a journey which has done nothing but snowball, in scope and momentum. While still incarcerated, he was delivering talks at Queens University in Belfast about the detrimental, contrary effects of the system on criminality, then speeches at Stormont; all the time knowing that he would be returning to the spirit-vacuum of his prison cell immediately afterwards. He knew, as the students, professors and politicians knew, that in him they had found a truly valuable case study: a prisoner with insight into criminality, the education to know how to change it, a cause, and the will. Since his release, the media have got to know this too.

On 3rd July 2013, just twelve days after his release from prison, Michael attended the *British Society of Criminology*'s conference in Wolverhampton, with his friend, Dr. Toni Wood, literally holding his hand throughout. There he met many of the academics he'd only previously read about in the pages of his Open University study books. And *they* knew *him*. He left a lasting mark and made many friends in the world of academia. Three weeks after that, he attended *The Irish Penal Reform Conference* in Dublin.

This dedication to his work did not abate, but instead intensified, and his roadshow did not slow down throughout 2014. In June of that year Michael was asked to be one of the assistants at the *European Restorative Justice Conference* in Belfast (there he met one of his old governors from prison and they proceeded to get very drunk together – the fact that a still serving governor and a former prison could laugh, drink and be merry like old friends was an intriguing talking point amongst many of the conference delegates).

On 8th July 2014 Michael attended the *British Society of Criminology's* conference in Liverpool, where he says he met old friends and made many more new ones, and on 3rd September 2014 he attended the 42nd annual conference of the *European Group for the Study of Deviance and Social Control* in Liverpool, where he presented his first conference paper, and, alongside his friend Toni Wood, sat on the 'Panel of British Convict Criminology'. On 16th September 2014 he delivered a talk to the *Prison Education Trust* at Oxford University.

On 27th November 2014, with Dr. Ruari McBride, Michael himself hosted an international online conference gathering of criminologists and ex-prisoners; despite the fact that it was Thanksgiving, the American delegation gave up their time with family to participate in the conference - testament to the regard in which Michael was now being held. Michael has said he was 'humbled' by the turn-out.

It was around this time that he graduated again, this time from Queens University, with a masters' degree in criminology.

Since this time Michael has delivered several guest lectures, appeared on local radio, and more recently on national television with the BBC, discussing the topics of death in custody, and suicide, self-harm and mental health in prisons.

But despite the character and determination of Michael's ambition, leaving prison after such a long time is, at the very least, a culture shock. Upon his release, and following his return from the first conference in Wolverhampton, Michael was in a very low and fragile state of mind, and finding it tough to cope with life on the outside. He cites the fact that he was fortunate enough to meet up again with his friends at the *Art of Living Foundation* as the stroke of circumstance which saved his life at this time. He was able to re-engage with the breathing and meditation classes he attended in prison back in 2008, without which Michael firmly believes he would not be here today.

In March 2014 Michael flew to London to record a video for their *Prison SMART* programme, and was delighted to once again meet up with Adelita, the lady who taught him *Sudashran Kriya* and the art of breathing, all those years earlier. It was an emotional meeting for Michael and Adelita - the warmth and compassion came flooding back as they sat and swapped stories about life, hope and future dreams.

With this help, something changed for the positive in Michael this year – his low mood ebbed as the conferences gathered momentum; to have people laughing with him, congratulating him and applauding his words; to be laughing and chatting with Professor Steve Tombs about matters other than work; to see Phil (his masters supervisor at Queens) beaming with delight during his panel presentation; to laugh amongst the seriousness...

On 20th October 2014 Michael went back to H.M.P. Magilligan to visit one of his friends – Michael reveals that this was 'a truly harrowing experience'. Yet, ironically, it was in prison, in June 2016 - whilst delivering a talk to prisoners and staff at H.M.P. Thameside on *Prison SMART*, that Michael actually met Sri Sri Ravi Shankar, the founder of the *Art of Living Foundation*. At the event Sri Sri invited Michael to start the process of becoming a *Prison SMART* teacher, and to appear with him on stage to share his story at the Royal Albert Hall.

In May 2014 Michael attended his Open University graduation at The Waterfront Hall with his mother – unfortunately, his father was unable to attend, as he was in intensive care at Dundonald hospital. Following the ceremony, Michael took his father's place on a pre-booked holiday to Greece.

The holiday was not an enjoyable one, but a horrible time full of mixed emotions: wondering if his father would still be alive when he got back overcame the joy of feeling sand beneath his toes, swimming in the sea and enjoying his first pint in seven years. During this time, he fought, hard, the temptation to slide back down the slippery slope to booze, drugs and addiction.

Michael Irwin won the *2012 Listowell Writers' Competition for Poetry (Prisons)*, and came second for his short story. He has written approximately fifty poems, which he intends to publish, has a short story published called 'The Day I Made Good', and hopes to publish several more.

Michael is an active member of the following bodies:

- *The European Group for the study of Deviance and Social Control*
- *The British Society of Criminology*
- *The Howard league for Penal Reform*
- *The Irish Penal Reform Trust*
- *The Northern Ireland Prison Arts Foundation*
- *British Convict Criminology*
- *The Art of Living Foundation - Northern Ireland*

Author’s Acknowledgements

This book is dedicated to my father, because without him none of it would have been possible, and for my mother, whose unconditional love knows no bounds.

For my brother, who stuck by me and helped me meet Maslow's basic needs of hierarchy, and my aunt, uncle and cousins. For my friends, Gary Mitchell and Davey Wilson, who came to visit meet, and the rest, who were waiting for me when I got out, and had to listen to my ramblings - you all mean the world to me in your own individual way. For Gary Docherty and Ellen Scott, who helped me type up the end of this book, because for me it was just too much at the time.

In academia, I dedicate to the one and only, my friend and mentor, Professor Shadd Maruna, who took the time (and the patience) to reply to my letters, meet me and guide me to university and beyond. For my dear, beautiful friend Dr. Toni Wood, who, like Shadd, wrote to me and guided me, but most of all, held my hand. For Professor Phil Scraton, who, almost single-handed, taught my Masters degree. For all the O.U. tutors and teachers in prison, who kept pushing me, and most especially to Allison McCaughan at H.M.P. Magilligan. For all the Writers in Residence, who tapped into my creativity and let me run: Mark Norfolk, Carlo Gebler and the most amazing Mr. John Brown. And for the late, great Mike Moloney - R.I.P. my friend! For my my dear friend Paul Irvine who listened to me in and after prison'.

For Sri Sri Ravi Shankar and all the folk at *Prison SMART* and *Art of Living*, for showing me how to find my inner peace - my first teacher Adelita Bloom, Dr. Katrien Hertog, Gaurav Guar, Nitin Kakde and my most special friends Sooksham and Tanusha Dhiman; big love to the rest of my *Art of Living* family.

And, of course, to my editor Matt Vidler and publisher Russell Spencer at L.R. Price Publications who has done the most amazing job.

Thank you all, with love and the biggest of hugs, Michael Irwin.

Publisher's Acknowledgements

The publisher would like to pay a special tribute to its senior editor Matt Vilder who has passion, dedicated and commitment, without which this book would have never been published.

The publisher would also like to thank Leonard West, Susan Woodard and Kate Harris for their support and assistance.

The publisher would also like to thank www.canva.com for their assistance in the cover design and also Hastac (www.hastac.org) for the use of their image which we adapted for our cover. (*Used under creative commons licence, original site: https://www.hastac.org/blogs/fionafi123/2017/01/18/thoughts-american-prison-writing-archive*).

The publisher and author would like to thank the following people for their good will, support and contribution in making this book a reality: James Mehigan, Katrina, Katrien Hertog, Andy Diaper, Ruth McFarlane, Christopher Uggen, Bill Davies, Melissa Pepper, Gary Irwin, Keir Irwin-Rogers, Steve Hall, Adam Matthews, Paula Skidmore, Helen Jones, Gillian Mcnaull, David Whyte, Jessica Bird, Steve Tombs, Jane O'Loughlin, Brian G, Debbie Faulkner, Paul Gray, Les, Sooksham Dhiman, Kathy Biggar, Janie L Greville, Matt McAvoy, Ingeborg R. Hahn, Pamela Brown, Susan Woodard, Britte van Tiem, Angela Doran, Ellen Scott, Graham Malley, Fiona Flynn, Richard Irwin.

The publisher and author would also like to thank all those people who supported, contributed and gave their good will to this book anonymously.

About the Publisher

L.R. Price Publications is dedicated to publishing books by unknown authors.

We use a mixture of both traditional and modern publishing options to bring our authors' words to the wider world.

We print, publish, distribute and market books in a variety of formats including paper and hard back, electronic books e-books, digital audio books and online.

If you are, an author interested in getting your book published; or a book retailer interested in selling our books, please contact us.

www.lrpricepublications.com

L.R. Price Publications Ltd,

27 Old Gloucester Street,

London, WC1N 3AX.

(0208) 1449188

publishing@lrprice.com

CPSIA information can be obtained
at www.ICGtesting.com
Printed in the USA
LVOW07s1847260917
550135LV00015B/1323/P

9 780992 903763